Church of England Record Society
Volume 30

THE EARLY JOURNALS OF HENSLEY HENSON: BIRKENHEAD AND ALL SOULS 1885–1887

THE EARLY JOURNALS
OF HENSLEY HENSON:
BIRKENHEAD AND ALL SOULS
1885–1887

EDITED BY
Julia Stapleton and Frank Field

BOYDELL PUBLISHING SERVICES
CHURCH OF ENGLAND RECORD SOCIETY

© Julia Stapleton and Frank Field 2025

All Rights Reserved. Except as permitted under current legislation no part of this work may be photocopied, stored in a retrieval system, published, performed in public, adapted, broadcast, transmitted, recorded or reproduced in any form or by any means, without the prior permission of the copyright owner

First published 2025

A Church of England Record Society publication
supported by Boydell Publishing Services
an imprint of Boydell & Brewer Ltd
PO Box 9, Woodbridge, Suffolk IP12 3DF, UK
and of Boydell & Brewer Inc.
668 Mt Hope Avenue, Rochester, NY 14620–2731, USA
website: www.boydellandbrewer.com

Boydell & Brewer's Authorised Representative for product safety in the EU is Easy Access System Europe – Mustamäe tee 50, 10621 Tallinn, Estonia, *gpsr.requests@easproject.com*

ISBN 978-1-83765-306-5

ISSN 1351-3087

Series information is printed at the back of this volume

A CIP catalogue record for this book is available from the British Library

The publisher has no responsibility for the continued existence or accuracy of URLs for external or third-party internet websites referred to in this book, and does not guarantee that any content on such websites is, or will remain, accurate or appropriate

Printed and bound in Great Britain by
TJ Books, Padstow, Cornwall

Contents

Preface and acknowledgments	vi
Introduction	viii
Editorial policies	xxx
Annotation guidance	xxxi
Table of sources and abbreviations	xxxii
List of illustrations	xxxiv

THE JOURNALS

Volume 1, 12 May – 20 July 1885	3
Volume 2, 20 July (cont.) – 31 August 1885	45
Volume 3, 1 September – 12 December 1885	81
Volume 4, 4 May 1886 – 11 July 1887	129
Select bibliography	237
Index of names and subjects	239

Preface and acknowledgments

This edition commenced with Frank Field's Hensley Henson lecture in Durham in the spring of 2017, followed by a visit to the cathedral archives to consult Henson's early journals. Both as the long-standing MP for Birkenhead and as an active member of the Church of England, he was struck by their insight into the social, economic and religious conditions of the town during the trade depression of the mid-1880s, and the permanent mark this had left on its young visitor. While critical of Henson's response to his early encounters with poverty and the poor, Frank, Lord Field of Birkenhead, as he became in 2020, admired his independence of mind, forcefulness in controversy and ability as a speaker, already in evidence in these volumes. He engaged closely with Henson's description of and interaction with the persons and places mentioned in the Birkenhead journals. He was equally attentive to the account in volume 4 of his activities at Oxford following his return from the north-west, and of his presence in the East End of London at the time Charles Booth (1840–1916) commenced his landmark survey. As well as undertaking local research for the edition in libraries in the Wirral and in Liverpool and providing key references, he wrote an early version of the Introduction and made valuable comments on later drafts. Sadly, he did not live to see the work published, but he was involved in its preparation at every stage.

Julia Stapleton has worked on a wider project which has brought into digital publication the journals covering the years from 1900 to 1939, when Henson became a leading figure in the church and in British public life more widely. However, the first four volumes of the Journal merit separate publication as a record of the experiences that shaped his conception of the importance of the Established church to the spiritual welfare of the poor and to the wider nation. It was to become a defining feature of his public voice for the next four decades, and of his case for a national but disestablished church after the prayer book rejection of 1927–8, as the digital edition makes clear.

The aim of both editions is to enhance understanding of the church and its changing relationship to the state and the nation during the late nineteenth and early twentieth centuries. The Journal's lively account of events and trenchant observations on personalities and places are central to its interest in this respect. Maintained almost uninterruptedly over a period of sixty-two years between 1885 and 1947, it comprises 100 volumes, with a total word length of approximately four million words. The word length of the four volumes here is around 81,000.

Among other illustrations, the edition includes three sample pages from volume 1. These will give the reader an impression of the physical appearance of the earliest volumes of the Journal.

There are no surviving photographs of Henson during his Birkenhead period and its immediate aftermath; however, we include an earlier likeness from the group photograph of the Stubbs Seminar founded by Henson as a Society while still an undergraduate in 1884.

We would like to thank the Dean and Chapter of Durham Cathedral as owner of the copyright in Henson's writings for permission to publish the first four volumes of his Journal. We are also grateful to Durham Cathedral Library for making the journals available for transcription, and to the library volunteers who completed a first draft of the text. We thank the librarian of All Souls College, Oxford, Gaye Morgan, for her help in providing access to Henson's correspondence with the warden, William Anson, and to the fellows of the college for permission to make references to the material. We are much indebted to Sheridan Gilley and Philip Williamson for their detailed comments on earlier drafts of the Introduction; these helped to bring the themes of the journals and their wider significance into sharper focus. For his assistance with translations of Henson's quotations from Jean-Baptiste Massillon we are grateful to Martin Crowley. We are especially indebted to Gareth Atkins for his meticulous editorial work on the entire manuscript, and for his expertise in enhancing the editorial apparatus.

Introduction

Herbert Hensley Henson (1863–1947) was described by Owen Chadwick as 'the most celebrated Anglican mind of the twentieth century'.[1] He was a renowned preacher and public speaker, a prolific writer, and in his readiness to challenge beliefs and opinions that enjoyed wide acceptance, a sharp controversialist. His trenchant insight, relentless logic and acerbic judgment added depth and vigour to debates on numerous issues relating to both the church and public life. These included marriage and divorce, unemployment, temperance, anti-Semitism and the policy of appeasement, as well as religious and ecclesiastical issues ranging from religious education, theological Modernism, prayer book reform, church self-government, the Sabbath and the division of bishoprics, to disestablishment. He had a strong aversion to 'canting' and was wary of movements driven by 'enthusiasm' and 'fanaticism', for example faith healing, prohibition and militant trade unionism, or the European dictatorships of the 1930s, of which he became a leading critic. Yet while the overall mark of his mind was one of scepticism, he was driven by a deep loyalty to the English nation and to the church as its principal organ of spiritual expression.

The journals published here well precede the starting point in 1900 of the online edition of the journals covering the four decades of Henson's career in the church, when he was at the forefront of major events in national life.[2] They have been selected for publication in a separate edition for the insight they provide into the formative experiences in Birkenhead and at All Souls College, Oxford, which shaped his churchmanship for the rest of his life. Following a transformative education in the School of Modern History at Oxford, he was elected to a prize fellowship at All Souls in November 1884. Six months later, on 23 April 1885 (2: **30**),[3] he travelled to the shipbuilding town in the north-west to take up a temporary position as tutor to the uninspiring son of a leading shipping magnate in Liverpool. It was there that he commenced his Journal.

The first two volumes abound in impressions of a town dominated by the docks but suffering heavily under the impact of the depression of the mid-1880s; as such, they represent a significant contribution to the documentary history of poverty and unemployment in industrial Britain and the responses they elicited, and a rare example of such testimony outside of London, where Charles Booth's *Life and labour of the people in London* looms large alongside the work of other concerned commentators.[4] As a recent Oxford graduate with a connexion to the local parish church, Holy Trinity in Price Street near his lodgings, Henson moved in both the poorest and wealthiest circles of Birkenhead and Liverpool society. It becomes clear in the journals that a childhood spent exclusively in the south of England – in his words in 'beautiful and

---

[1] Owen Chadwick, 'The idea of a national church: Gladstone and Henson', in *Aspects de L'Anglicanisme*, ed. Marcel Simon *et al.* (Paris, 1974), pp. 183–205, at p. 193.
[2] Henson Journals Online.
[3] Volume 2, page 30: this form is used henceforth to indicate further references in the Introduction to the journals included in the edition.
[4] For other examples in the 1880s but wholly within a London context, see Seth Koven, *Slumming: sexual and social politics in Victorian London* (Princeton, 2004).

healthy surroundings'[5] – ill-prepared him for the squalor and overcrowding of the Merseyside towns, and the snobbery of the provincial *élite*. The narrow influences of his evangelical home also coloured his experience of a town beset by religious divisions and what he considered to be heretical forms of worship. As will be seen in this Introduction, he reacted strongly to the sects that had prospered by the Church of England's weakness in the face of shifting and impoverished populations such as that in Birkenhead, the majority of which was unchurched. He returned to All Souls determined to strengthen the church's authority as *the* national church, its unifying and uplifting influence available to all, regardless of circumstances. This meant defending the church–state Establishment against its numerous critics, both within the radical movement in Britain and in the church itself, as a bulwark against religious inequality (4: **155**). To this end, he established and became secretary of the Oxford Laymen's League for the Defence of the National Church in May 1886, an organization that sought 'the union of the religious laity throughout the country without reference to sects or parties'.[6] He took his work for the League to the East End of London, defending the church in lectures to often wary audiences of working men, and to rural areas beyond, as documented in volume 4. While he was made chaplain of the organization following his ordination to the diaconate in June 1887 (4: **365**), it does not seem to have survived for much longer without his direction; but it provided the basis of his reputation as one of the most ardent supporters of Establishment during the next forty years.

His career thereafter is familiar from his three-volume autobiography, *Retrospect of an unimportant life* (1942, 1943, 1950) and entries in the *Dictionary of national biography* and the *Oxford dictionary of national biography*, as well as the main biography by Owen Chadwick.[7] Following his first living at Barking shortly after his ordination in 1888, Henson became the chaplain of the hospital of St Thomas and St Mary in Ilford; this was a position in the private gift of the prime minister, Lord Salisbury (1830–1903), with whose youngest son, William ('Fish') Cecil (1863–1936), he had been ordained at Cuddesdon in 1887.[8] Salisbury then exercised prime ministerial patronage in 1900 in nominating Henson to the vacant canonry of Westminster and rectorship of St Margaret's, the 'House of Commons Church'. He became dean of Durham in 1913, bishop of Hereford in 1918 and returned to Durham as bishop two years later, a position he held until his retirement in 1939.

Henson is remembered chiefly for defending a conception of the church free from denominational bias, and one that was characterized by a wide latitude for freedom of discussion and belief in interpreting the creeds. This was against concerted opposition on both accounts during his lifetime.[9] His opposition to the confusion of Christian ethics with 'social ethics' and political advocacy – particularly of a socialist nature – has also since found resonance.[10]

---

[5] Henson, *Retrospect*, I, 3.
[6] Henson, letter to the editor, *Times*, 13 Aug. 1886, 6.
[7] Alwyn Winton [A. T. P. Williams], 'Henson, Herbert Hensley, 1863–1947', *Dictionary of national biography, 1941–50* (1959); Matthew Grimley, 'Henson, Herbert Hensley', *ODNB*; Owen Chadwick, *Hensley Henson: a study in the friction between church and state* (Oxford 1983); and see also John S. Peart-Binns, *Herbert Hensley Henson: a biography* (Cambridge, 2013).
[8] For Henson's connection with the Cecil family, see 'The Cecils', Henson Journals Online.
[9] Both concerns were central to the crisis in the church that followed his appointment as bishop of Hereford: see Philip Williamson, 'Hensley Henson and the appointment of bishops: state, church and nation in England, 1917–1920 and beyond', *Journal of Ecclesiastical History*, 74 (2023), 325–48.
[10] Edward Norman, *Church and society in England 1770–1970* (Oxford, 1976), p. 11.

But perhaps his most enduring legacy is his Journal, one of the most extensive and detailed of the late nineteenth and early twentieth centuries. Running to 100 volumes across sixty-two years, it is a masterpiece of opinion and commentary on the great events and leading figures of the day, as well as the changing fortunes of the church in the diverse settings in which he held clerical office. It is one of several outstanding journals of this period, being comparable in scale, interest and literary quality to that of the schoolmaster, college head and writer of 'Land of Hope and Glory' A. C. Benson (1862–1925), for instance.[11] It discloses not only Henson's extensive networks in church and state as his career advanced, but also the richness of his intellectual interests. It also reveals a complex personality, plagued by self-doubt, the temptations of unbelief, self-recrimination and an abject sense of failure. These tendencies are already present in the first four volumes of the Journal reproduced in this edition; mostly written in the perfectly formed hand that became familiar to his correspondents, the early journals also include sketches of men's profiles – their identity often unclear – and strange, often bird-like creatures, a clear indication of his restless and searching mind.

Before turning to the early volumes, it is necessary to note the unusual family background from which Henson emerged as a leading clergyman and prelate. The Introduction then considers the origins of the Journal during his sojourn in Birkenhead from early May until early October 1885. Next, it focuses on the social and economic conditions that existed when he arrived there, together with the religious composition of the inhabitants and the churches, chapels and missions that were established to meet their needs. His response to these, and to other features of the town will feature prominently here. This is followed by a discussion of some of the wider themes of the first four volumes: his interest in General Gordon and in the causes of and solutions to poverty and unemployment. Both were central to his Birkenhead experience and, as will be seen, were pursued further in London's East End following his return to All Souls, as he contemplated ordination. The final section shows that in these and in other ways, Birkenhead provided the material for much critical reflexion on the *rôle* of religion and the changing authority of the church in industrial Britain, marking a crucial stage in his intellectual and spiritual development.

Henson's background

Throughout his life, his early years, spent mostly in Broadstairs, Kent, remained painful to recall. What little account he left – principally in the *Retrospect* – centres upon a childhood overshadowed by the death of his mother when he was six. The vivacious Martha Fear (1830–70) was the second wife of Thomas Henson (1812–96) and mother of all eight of his children, and her loss intensified her widowed husband's already rigid evangelicalism. Retired from the small business he had established in London and having distanced himself from his roots in the Church of England under the influence of the famous Baptist preacher, Baptist Noel (1798–1873), Thomas Henson's only connexion outside his now shattered family was with a local following of the Plymouth Brethren, an extreme protestant sect.[12] Henson held the organization

---

[11] See *The Benson Diary*, Volume I, 1885–1906; Volume 2, 1907–1925, ed. E. Duffy and R. Hyman (London, 2025).

[12] For Noel, see Philip D. Hill, *A rebel saint: Baptist Wriothesley Noel, 1798–1873* (Cambridge, 2022).

responsible for the hardening of his father's religious convictions and its adverse effects on the home. This was despite Thomas Henson's continuing membership of the Church of England and openness to other nonconformist churches, including the Congregationalist church, to whose minister at Broadstairs he sent Henson and his elder brother to live following the death of his wife.[13]

Although part of a large family, Henson quickly established the pattern of his life as what might be termed an 'aloner': he never learned to play games,[14] either with friends or siblings, and his account of walking by himself to explore the surrounding countryside around Broadstairs suggests the action of a young person who had become used to his own company, and, indeed, one who thrived on it. It was during one of these walks that Henson discovered St Augustine's Roman catholic church in Ramsgate, built and paid for by Augustus Pugin on land neighbouring his home and styled as early English. As a mission rather than a parish church, it was part of a fully fledged Benedictine abbey of the Cassinese Congregation, with some fifteen monks, an abbot, four daily masses between Easter and September and daily confession offered in English, German, French and Italian.[15] Here, he would have found himself in another world, witnessing a celebration that combined colour, ritual, singing and much incense. Once a neighbour – having observed his presence there – had informed his father, he resolved not to attend St Augustine's again.[16] But the abbey church, probably, is the root of Henson being seen, and wishing to be seen, as strongly high church in his sympathies.

As an 'aloner', Henson read avidly among his father's extensive library of theological works and made friends among the books; these included Milton's *Paradise lost*, the one work of poetry in the collection which he later read to his household each Christmas. The arrival of a stepmother three years after the death of his mother relieved some of the weight of the spiritual atmosphere of his home, to which he and his brother now returned; Emma Theodora Parker (née Münchenberg) (1841–1924), affectionately referred to as 'mater' and later 'Carissima' by Henson, was a widow from Germany whose first husband had been English. She widened Henson's reading with the novels of Walter Scott and introduced him to historical works such as Thucydides, Plutarch and Livy using editions from her late husband's library.[17] Against his father's wishes, she also supported his insistence on baptism – a requirement for Confirmation – following his attendance as a fifteen-year-old at a missionary meeting in Ramsgate near to where the family were staying on holiday. There, a lay preacher – a seaman named Captain Field – had urged his audience to seek Confirmation at the parish church of Broadstairs following an appeal for candidates to come forward. Henson recalled that while he was not 'converted', he was 'greatly moved' by the address. Following his stepmother's intervention, his baptism, along with that of his two younger siblings, took place shortly afterwards at Minster-in-Thanet. With much satisfaction he commenced his preparation

---

[13] Chadwick, *Hensley Henson*, p. 3; Henson, *Retrospect*, III, 355. The close parallels between Henson's experience of a childhood coloured by the influence of the Plymouth Brethren and that of his near contemporary, the writer and critic, Edmund Gosse, are striking: see Edmund Gosse's autobiography, *Father and son: a study of two temperaments* (London, 1907).
[14] Journal, 28 Aug. 1932.
[15] *Catholic directory* (London, 1873), p. 220.
[16] Chadwick, *Hensley Henson*, p. 11; Peart-Binns, *Herbert Hensley Henson: a biography*, p. 19. I have been unable to trace the original source here.
[17] Henson, *Retrospect*, I, 3; Journal, 15 Mar. 1932.

for Confirmation with the high church rector of Broadstairs in private, informal sessions; it was completed at Ramsgate, in the vicinity of which his family had now moved to take advantage of the evangelical ministry at the parish church. While the religious needs of his father were now met, Henson was unimpressed either by the remaining Confirmation classes he attended there or the service itself.[18]

Recognizing his intellectual promise, his stepmother also overcame Thomas Henson's resistance to sending Henson and his youngest sibling, Gilbert (1866–1947) – or 'Gid' – to the local school in Broadstairs. He was then fourteen years old and did not stay long, although long enough to acquire the smattering of Latin and Greek that provided a foundation for the entrance examination to the University of Oxford later. Again, his stepmother's support was crucial.[19] The limited means of his family owing to his father's financial mismanagement in retirement meant that Henson lived in penury away from the mainstream of undergraduate life as a non-collegiate or 'unattached' student.[20] In the *Retrospect*, he failed to mention other students who would have shared his Cowley address. However, he formed a close bond with Thomas Denham (1856–1939), who is mentioned several times in the journals included in this edition. A contemporary in the Modern History School, Denham was among the non-collegiate students who 'migrated' to a college, in his case Queen's, after two years. Henson disapproved of the practice, probably because it exacerbated the sense of stigma of those left behind (4: **34**); but this does not seem to have affected his 'intimacy' with Denham.[21] The son of a general dealer in Islington, Denham went on to become an educationist in India, maintaining contact with his old friend for several decades after he left Oxford.[22]

The prize fellowship that Henson won at All Souls College following his first-class degree in Modern History in 1884 also resulted in long-standing friendships. These included the warden, William Anson (1843–1914), a leading constitutional theorist, who also provided much-needed financial and moral support as Henson established himself in the church;[23] A. V. Dicey (1835–1922), Vinerian professor of English law; and the historian Charles Oman (1860–1946). Together, they shaped the legal cast of his mind and deepened its historical foundations, as well as enhancing his Liberal Unionist sympathies, particularly as the Liberal party became a focus for Radicalism under the influence of Joseph Chamberlain (1836–1914).[24] He also formed a valuable friendship with Henry [Harry] Reichel, later Sir Henry Reichel (1856–1931), the son of Charles Reichel (1816–94), bishop of Meath (4: **170–1**). Invited to stay at Dundrum Castle, the bishop's home, shortly after his ordination, he was introduced to a formidable ecclesiastical controversialist, one who was then absorbed in the reorganization of the Irish Church following disestablishment and

---

[18] Henson, *Retrospect*, III, 356–7.
[19] *Ibid.*, I, 4. Durham Cathedral Library holds his heavily annotated copy of Charles Duke Yonge's edition of Virgil, *Bucolica, Georgica, et Aeneis* (1862), dated January 1881; he matriculated in October of that year.
[20] Henson, *Retrospect*, I, 1.
[21] Journal, 31 Dec. 1923.
[22] *Ibid.*, 10, 17 May 1908.
[23] Of the many letters from Henson in the papers of William Anson at All Souls College where this is apparent, see especially his recognition of the debt in the letter dated 8 Aug. 1892.
[24] For the legal, historical and Liberal Unionist tenor of All Souls College, particularly against the perceived threat of democracy to constitutional stability in the late nineteenth century, see Richard Davenport-Hines, 'The trimming of Herbert Hensley Henson', in *Conservative thinkers from All Souls College Oxford* (Woodbridge, 2022), pp. 84–7, 98.

prayer book revision. While impressed by his visitor's aptitude for vigorous and sustained argument, Charles Reichel recommended protestant theologians such as August Neander (1789–1850) as an antidote to his Roman catholic sympathies. Henson later acknowledged his influence when approaching prayer book revision himself in the Church of England, and in including Neander in his list of recommended 'big books' for a young friend interested in taking Holy Orders in the 1930s.[25]

In keeping with widely held views at All Souls concerning their subordinate *rôle* in society,[26] he showed little interest in women before his marriage in 1902; apart from his sisters, to whom he was devoted (1: **77**, n. 46), he disliked their company and conversation, as the volumes here well testify, although there were exceptions later on.[27] The early journals also make clear his physical attraction to younger men, especially Emil Haag, son of the German artist Carl Haag (1820–1915), who had entered Oxford Military College at Cowley in 1887 (4: **289, 321**).

However, in general, he was careful to keep his distance from others, remaining free of the debts that close friendship brings. His indebtedness to Anson and Dicey was not of the kind that required any repayment. His ability to survive without close companionship enabled him to develop a rare and impressive independence. It contributed to the angularity and personal force that carried him far in the church, his obscure family origins notwithstanding. Eschewing popularity from the outset, his prolific writings, sermons and speeches were driven by the powerful working of his mind, their persuasiveness enhanced rather than diminished by their impersonal nature.[28] To the young Henson, intellect was the missing dimension of the moral revival of the clergy in the nineteenth century (4: **273–4**). Engaging closely with uneducated audiences in the East End of London in 1886 to 1887, as documented in volume 4 below, he quickly became aware that without sound and informed thinking on religious and social matters, and a willingness to answer its secularist critics, the church was doomed to irrelevance (4: **228–9**).

The origins of the Journal

The first four volumes of Henson's Journal commence in Birkenhead in May 1885, and conclude at All Souls College in July 1887, shortly after his ordination to the deaconate. The entries are mostly continuous, except for an unexplained break between 13 December 1885 and May 1886, and only sporadic entries for August to October 1886, and for February to May 1887, which included a visit to Rome. There is no suggestion that he had either kept or contemplated keeping a journal earlier. What was it about his Birkenhead experience that provided the incentive? To answer this question, it is first necessary to consider the reasons for his presence in the town.

Anxious to earn money to help support his father, stepmother and two sisters

---

[25] Henson, 'School and Oxford', in *Sir Harry Reichel, 1856–1931: a memorial volume*, ed. J. E. Lloyd (University of Wales Press Board, Cardiff, 1934), pp. 67–71; Lambeth Palace Library, Morrison MSS 3992, fo. 30, Henson to Andrew Leslie Morrison, 20 May 1934.

[26] Davenport-Hines, 'The trimming of Herbert Hensley Henson', p. 87.

[27] For example, the social campaigner Violet Markham (1872–1959), and the teacher of Italian Linetta de Castelvecchio (1880–1975), who became the first female professor at the University of Birmingham in 1922.

[28] See the report on his speech at Westminster Chapel, 7 Mar. 1926 in *Christian World*, 11 Mar. 1926, 11.

still at home, and with Anson's encouragement, he had taken up a six-month post as tutor and companion to Acheson Lyle Rathbone (Lyle) (1868–1923), the son of the merchant, philanthropist and Liberal MP, William Rathbone VI (1819–1902). Like his ancestors, William Rathbone had quickly established himself as a city father, living at Greenbank in some style in the Mossley Hill area of Liverpool. The grounds were so extensive that when the house and grounds were given to the University of Liverpool they provided the space to develop four halls of residence.

Lyle was the third child of Rathbone's second marriage to Emily Acheson Lyle. Although he followed the family tradition of public service later in life by becoming a city councillor, it was his sister, the MP Eleanor Rathbone (1872–1946), who saw herself as the natural successor to her father. She was regarded so by at least one of her half-sisters, Elizabeth Lucretia Rathbone, known as Elsie (1851–1920). The wealthiest of William Rathbone VI's eleven children, having conserved her share of the family fortune better than her siblings, Elsie left most of her estate to Eleanor unconditionally, unlike her bequests to her male siblings. Eleanor's biographer, Susan Pedersen, writes that when in 1917 Elsie made her will, she showed that she shared her father's view that 'the family wealth was a trust, to be used for the good of others', and had also come to share his disillusion with his sons.[29] Although not an MP until 1929, Eleanor had by 1917 established herself as a social worker, a leading social investigator and a campaigner for family allowances provided by the state, as well as becoming the first woman to sit on Liverpool city council, a position she held from 1909 to 1935.

Aged seventeen when he encountered Henson, Lyle had been dispatched to Birkenhead to earn his living as an apprentice in Laird's shipyard. Aware of Lyle's shortcomings, both moral and intellectual, William Rathbone had sought an elevating influence for his son. He had maintained close links with Oxford following the success with Lyle of Sidney Ball (1857–1918), fellow and lecturer in philosophy at St John's College, who had served as his tutor for several months in 1882. Eleanor Rathbone recalled, '[f]or years afterwards my father consulted Mr. Ball every time he needed a promising young man for any public or private purpose, and however busy with the work of term-time, Mr. Ball always threw himself into the search with his usual freshness and energy'.[30] Henson's Journal makes clear that he was answerable both to Ball and to Robert Raper (1842–1915), founder of what became the Oxford University Careers Service (3: **106**), whom Ball would have consulted over the appointment. Raper would have known Henson through his close friendship with William Anson, in whose company Henson later claimed to have met Raper frequently.[31]

Unlike Ball, who seems to have got on well with Lyle, Henson took an acute dislike to his charge, and was particularly exasperated by his lack of self-discipline (3: **87**). Sharing lodgings with him at 41, Hamilton Square in Birkenhead, he made little allowance for Lyle's fatigue at the end of his working day and despised his preference for entertainment rather than education as an outlet for his remaining energy. His ill-feeling towards Lyle seems to have been reciprocated (1: **42, 86**; 2: **42**). After scarcely a month, he wrote to Anson that he was considering abandoning his tutorship such were his difficulties in getting Lyle to work sufficiently to satisfy his

---

[29] Pedersen, *Eleanor Rathbone*, pp. 155–6; and see family tree at p. xv.
[30] Oona Edward Ball, *Sidney Ball: memories & impressions of 'an ideal don'* (Oxford, 1923), p. 37.
[31] Journal, 9 Aug. 1915.

conscience in maintaining the position.[32] However, strengthened by Anson's advice to persevere, and mindful that failure to complete the task would be a heavy blow to his standing in Oxford, and more generally to his self-confidence, he pressed on.[33] He continued with the introductory course in history he had devised (1: **31–3**), sensing the need to assert his position despite Ball's advice against seeking regular work from Lyle (1: **86**). A severe lesson in the evils of cynicism had some effect in reconciling Lyle to his presence (2: **92**); nevertheless, he continued to count the weeks until his departure (1: **77**; 2: **79**; 3: **97**).

Volume 1 of the Journal had initially served as a notebook for crossword puzzles: the first page is torn out leaving the word 'Crossword' clearly visible at the top. However, almost three weeks after his arrival, he turned to journal-keeping as a means of relieving the strain of his responsibility for Lyle.[34] As well as wrestling with his spiritual difficulties, he used the Journal to record his impressions of Birkenhead and of Liverpool, where he frequented the Athenaeum and the Picton Reading Room, and visited the art gallery and assorted menageries, commencing a life-long enthusiasm for visiting zoos. The rise in cholera cases across the world and unemployment locally are also well documented in the Journal. The Journal also served as a record of his reading, much of it theological, as it seems that he was already contemplating a further undergraduate degree in the School of Theology while in Birkenhead (2: **94**; 3: **156**; 4: **166**). Once back in All Souls, however, the gentle pressure of other fellows against taking this course of action prevailed.[35]

Birkenhead

To what kind of town did Henson arrive in the spring of 1885? Had he arrived earlier in the century, he would have entered a hamlet with a population of a little over 100.[36] Instead, he was part of a bustling town of over 100,000.[37] Since 1882, Birkenhead had been included in the registrar-general's expanded list of the twenty-eight 'great towns of England', and was among the most densely populated.[38] At that time, the irony of Disraeli's (1804–81) reference to the town as a modern Damascus, in constant process of change and renewal, in his novel *Tancred* (1847) would not have been obvious.[39] However, the crushing of its economic strength by global economic forces in the mid-1880s seemed to vindicate Disraeli's scepticism of the 'disciples of Progress'.

Henson almost certainly made his way from Oxford by train to Woodside railway terminus. As he came out of the mock Norman station building, he would have faced across the river Mersey the city of Liverpool which vied with Glasgow as the

---

[32] All Souls Coll., Oxford, Anson MSS, Henson to Anson, 5 June 1885.
[33] *Ibid.*, Henson to Anson, 13 June 1885; and 1: **74**; 3: **105** below.
[34] The interval is calculated using information provided in 2: **30, 46, 89**, and 3: **34, 97**.
[35] Chadwick, *Hensley Henson*, pp. 32–3; and 4: **85**.
[36] The population in 1810 – the first such record – was 106: Philip Sulley, *History of ancient and modern Birkenhead* (Liverpool, 1907), p. 48.
[37] GB Historical GIS / University of Portsmouth, Birkenhead PLU/RegD through time | Population Statistics | Total Population, *A vision of Britain through time*; www.visionofbritain.org.uk/unit/10154820/cube/TOT_POP, accessed 5 Jan. 2023.
[38] Francis Vacher, *Report on the sanitary condition of the borough of Birkenhead, for the year 1882* (Birkenhead, 1883), pp. 6–7. Vacher was the medical officer of health for the town.
[39] Benjamin Disraeli, *Tancred: or the new crusade* (1847; London, 1871), p. 379; cited in N. Pevsner and Edward Hubbard, *The buildings of England: Cheshire* (Harmondsworth, 1971), p. 75.

second city of the empire. He had only a short walk up the riverbank and into his lodgings in Hamilton Square. The lie of the land was inspired primarily by William Laird (1780–1841), a Scot. In 1824, he spotted the advantages of basing his boiler works, and what was soon to become the great Laird shipyard, on Wallasey pool at the top of the Wirral peninsula, then covered with birch trees. Lairds soon became one of the two largest employers on the Cheshire side of the Mersey. But he was not ambitious on his own behalf only. Like so many fellow entrepreneurs of this time, he possessed a vision for the new town he was visibly creating. The extent of Laird's ambition for 'his' town is never better recognized than when he employed James Gillespie Graham, an Edinburgh architect, to design the layout of Hamilton Square and the surrounding area in a classical style. Despite some impoverishment subsequently, all of Hamilton Square, apart from the town hall which was built later, had the equivalent of what was a grade one listing and remain collectively one of the most intensely developed group of grade one buildings anywhere in the country. Nikolaus Pevsner thought the rectangular street plan of Birkenhead one of the most ambitious instances of nineteenth-century town planning anywhere in Britain.[40] Henson lived in the Square alongside a number of prosperous middle-and upper-middle-class neighbours, although this spectacular collection of architecture was all too quickly surrounded by slums, not many decades old.

Laird was soon joined by other substantial entrepreneurs in developing Birkenhead, for example, Thomas Brassey (1805–70), the leading railway builder. The economic development of the town was also assisted by an increase in legislative activity following the extension of the franchise in 1832.[41] In 1844, the Birkenhead Docks Act was passed and within three years the first new docks in the town, Morpeth and Egerton, were opened. Determined to assert its supremacy over its rival on the other bank of the Mersey, the Birkenhead Docks were taken over by the Liverpool Corporation in 1855 and transferred to a newly formed Mersey Docks and Harbour Board in 1857 (1: **64**).

The dock development in Birkenhead led quickly to the other industrial activities of most port towns: for example, flour milling and grain and cattle importation. The routes for the latter were quickly established from North America and Northern Ireland, and the development of this trade subsequently gave rise to tanning, glue, suet, gelatine and associated manufacturing. Some of the best passages in the early journals are Henson's impressions of the dock scene, both when it was very busy and in periods of surprisingly total calm.

The shipbuilding and ship repair industry in Birkenhead quickly acquired supply firms: the manufacturing of ships' propellers, pulley blocks to stabilize the ships which were being built, the setting up of machine woodwork and rigging shops and marine engineering of all kinds. For over four decades – 1833 to 1879, after which it was incorporated as a borough – the town was in the hands of improvement commissioners, a body established by parliament in response to a local petition to enhance the living and working environment.[42] The development of major shipbuilding, docks and allied supply services was paralleled by a town centre, shops,

---

[40] *Ibid.*, p. 76.
[41] This activity reflected the continued salience of the pre-reform conception of 'interests' rather than individuals and classes as the focus of parliamentary representation after 1832, with the interests of newly represented places central. See Miles Taylor, 'Parliamentary representation in modern Britain: past, present, and future', *Historical Journal*, 65 (2022), 1145–73, at 1155–8.
[42] Sulley, *History of ancient and modern Birkenhead*, p. 96.

public libraries, railways, various churches and chapels, schools, wide gas-lit streets and a public park developed by Joseph Paxton (1803–65), soon to be followed in its layout by the Central Park in New York. Tramways were running in the 1860s and were the first such convenience to be established in Europe, while gas, water supplies and sewage systems were being developed before 1860.[43]

Like many of the new industrial towns, Birkenhead was dependent largely on a single employer. When the yard prospered, so did the town. A shipbuilding recession, with its unemployment, ricocheted through the supply chains linked to the yard and then, leaving many workmen without wage packets, into the wider local economy. In 1885, it was suffering badly from unemployment. The national unemployment data for the period of 1875 to 1885 show that the percentage unemployed almost quadrupled, with engineering, metal and shipbuilding particularly hard hit, up from 3.5 to 12.9 per cent.[44] The economic downturn that provided the backdrop to Henson's experience of Birkenhead played an instrumental *rôle* both in strengthening his Anglican commitment and in shaping his social and political thought.

Religion, church and sect

Perhaps an indication that he was seriously contemplating a clerical career when he arrived in the town, Henson's immediate impressions were of a church that belied its national status. A substantial programme of church building had taken place around the middle decades of the nineteenth century: by 1866 and the foundation of St Peter's, five churches had been built to supplement the mother church of St Mary's, constructed in 1819, although none of them a credit to ecclesiastical architecture, least of all Holy Trinity.[45] However, while flourishing centres of worship with mission churches, church schools and even a heavily subscribed nursery attached in one case,[46] other denominations were strong competitors for religious influence. As noted at the start of the Journal, a large proportion of the inhabitants were Irish Catholics, with whom the church had nothing to do. Tensions existed between these Irish immigrants and parts of the protestant population, some of whom joined the anti-catholic Orange order. Two decades earlier, Holy Trinity had been at the centre of fierce Orange–Irish sectarian rioting stoked by the first rector of the church, Joseph Baylee (1807–83), an evangelical zealot, in defence of the Italian nationalist leader Garibaldi against Irish catholic assertions of papal supremacy in Rome; he was already unpopular among Catholics through his proselytizing efforts among the Irish dock labourers.[47]

The Roman catholics in Birkenhead were served by three large Roman catholic churches, two of which were of distinguished architectural and interior design and had attracted devoted priests; however, Henson does not mention any of them.

Another influx of population had come from Wales, often unable to speak English, and mostly bred in traditions of dissent. Three Welsh chapels – Baptist, Presbyterian and Congregational – catered to their religious needs, although Welsh services had

---

[43] Pevsner and Hubbard, *Cheshire*, p. 78.
[44] B. R. Mitchell and Phyllis Deane, *Abstract of British historical statistics* (Cambridge, 1962), p. 64.
[45] Sulley, *History of ancient and modern Birkenhead*, pp. 318–19.
[46] *Ibid.*, p. 324.
[47] 'Joseph Baylee' (1807–83), *ODNB*; see also Sheridan Gilley, 'The Garibaldi riots of 1862', *Historical Journal*, 16 (1973), 697–732, at 720–4.

been established at Holy Trinity by Baylee, who had taught himself Welsh, and then resumed in the 1890s.[48] When English dissenters were also considered – spread between twelve different denominational chapels – Henson estimated that no more than a third of the population were actual or potential church members (1: **14**).

The weakness of the church in Birkenhead underlined the limitations of the parochial system, as a conversation with William Makin (1853–1929), the local agent of the Charity Organization Society, made clear to him. First, it had failed to develop an equivalent of the Wesleyan 'class leaders' who maintained regular contact with chapelgoers and provided support in times of need. (This said, he noted Makin's observation that the Wesleyans were themselves 'losing their hold on the people', perhaps because of the regular subscription or attendance required for Wesleyan church membership even in difficult times.) Second, the parochial system made little sense in the North where the people were always 'flitting' in search of work (1: **81–3**; 3: **10**). A local leader, H. K. Aspinall – to whom we will return presently – estimated that during the trade depression of 1885, the population of Birkenhead had been reduced by 13,000 to judge by the number of empty houses. Workmen sought employment in other shipyards: for example, in Barrow-in-Furness, to the north or on the Clyde (3: **102**). Henson toyed with the idea of introducing commendatory letters which migrants would take with them, thus ensuring continuity of church membership (1: **81–3**). Here, already, we see him drawn to the 'flock' theory of the church that was to underpin his case for Establishment, against growing pressure for church 'self-government' from the 1890s rooted in the parish; in his view, the 'flock' theory represented a broader, more fluid ideal than its rival – the 'little fold' – both in territorial and spiritual terms.[49]

Clearly, within days of his arrival, Henson had found much in Birkenhead that had fuelled his resolute opposition to protestant sects. A striking feature of volumes 1 and 2 of the Journal is the zeal with which he set about 'heresy hunting' on Merseyside, avidly seeking out 'schism shops'. One such target was the Salvation Army; the Journal provides a detailed account of a meeting in which the participants 'testified' to their 'salvation' before the 'Captain' and each other. He managed to contain his scorn on this occasion, chastened by the organization's success in reclaiming habitual drunkards. In contrast, his visit to a meeting of an unnamed sect that purported to engage in faith healing of the body resulted in a public altercation with what he egregiously termed the 'shepherd'. While they parted on friendly terms, his engaging account in the Journal of the 'wonderful production of schism' he had witnessed was written from a clear if unacknowledged position of intellectual strength (1: **135**). The irony is that while he condemned another 'shepherd' – the grocer turned mission worker, Charles Thompson (1842–1903) – for confining his religious teaching to 'Jesus' (1: **107**), this was not far from the position he eventually adopted himself towards the end of volume 4 (4: **319, 322**).

Indeed, this position was already emerging in his work for the mission attached to Holy Trinity (3: **93–6**), which took place in the school room.[50] Missions and mission churches were a widespread feature of urban parishes from the mid-nineteenth to the

---

[48] Sulley, *History of ancient and modern Birkenhead*, p. 326.
[49] H. H. Henson, 'An appeal for unity', in *Godly union and concord: sermons preached mainly in Westminster Abbey in the interest of Christian fraternity* (London, 1903), pp. 127–8.
[50] Other Birkenhead churches had their own mission churches, for example St Peter's and St John's: Sulley, *History of ancient and modern Birkenhead*, pp. 327–8, 331.

mid-twentieth centuries, growing out of 'special missions' of the kind that Henson had witnessed in Broadstairs.[51] They were designed to draw more of the inhabitants of the parish into the church, although a study of religious life in Croydon concludes that there, at least, Anglican missions were less effective than their nonconformist counterparts in increasing attendance at religious services.[52] In contrast, at the Holy Trinity mission, where Henson preached regularly, attendance trebled within two months (3: **52, 95**). Notwithstanding the length of his sermons (up to twenty-five minutes), and a concern that they went over the heads of his audience, he noted in the Journal that he succeeded in holding their attention. Henson was pleased that the rector, Thomas Sheriff (1855–1923), was willing to take over the mission's work when he returned to Oxford. Tellingly, he wrote: '[i]n the Mission Service Sheriff has the means whereby to form for himself a Catholic minded congregation wherewith in time to leaven, or overawe, the Protestant majority, which now forms the mass of the congregation' (3: **95–6**).

His views on disestablishment and disendowment aside (1: **53**), Sheriff was congenial to Henson as a fellow Oxonian who was close to the bishop of Chester and Henson's teacher in the School of Modern History, William Stubbs (1825–1901); Henson had been a founder member of the Stubbs Society at Oxford. However, he developed firmer and more lasting ties of friendship with Sheriff's curate – Edward Watson (1859–1936), later professor of ecclesiastical history at Oxford – who had introduced him to Holy Trinity (1: **15**). Four years his senior, Watson had coached Henson for his finals in Modern History in June 1884, before becoming ordained the following year.[53] Henson later described his many walks and talks with his former tutor – they are much in evidence in the Birkenhead journals – as 'among the best educative influences of my life'.[54] He admired his intelligence and learning: the first entry in the Journal records that he 'looked up Watson & found him reading the Odyssey!' (1: **14**). Watson was clearly the model of the clergyman to which Henson aspired, despite his limitations as a preacher and lack of interest in the mission (3: **54**).

Most of all, perhaps, he envied the security of Watson's broad churchmanship, untroubled by Rome's continued refusal to accept the validity of Anglican orders, which was to be reaffirmed very publicly in Pope Leo XIII's apostolic letter *Apostolicae curae* in 1896.[55] In contrast, Henson agonized over the church's uncertain status, which affected his attitude towards protestants as well as to the church. While a 'logical anathema' on them seemed the only appropriate course, it would lack 'moral justification' issued from such an isolated Anglican position. He was strongly tempted to adopt his erstwhile tutor's broad church affiliation, not least to preserve his intellectual independence, which mattered to him a great deal, and which he suspected would be lost if he was to become '"a Catholic"'. However, having 'played with the Catholic idea so long to spite the Low Church people', he felt his hands were tied, despite being 'bored at being considered a Rit:' (1: **28–30**).

---

[51] J. Cox, *The English churches in a secular society: Lambeth, 1870–1930* (Oxford, 1982), p. 25.
[52] J. N. Morris, *Religion and urban change: Croydon, 1840–1914* (Woodbridge, 1992), pp. 59–60.
[53] Journal, 18 Aug. 1936.
[54] Henson, *Retrospect*, I, 8.
[55] See his reference to the 'loneliness of the Anglican position' (V1, **30**); for Henson's damning response to *Apostolicae curae*, see his *Christian liberty and papal claims: a sermon preached before the members of the Canterbury Diocesan Church Reading Society, in Folkestone Parish Church, on Thursday, October 1st* (Canterbury, 1896).

For the time being, then, he continued to keep up his Catholic appearances. He attended St Agnes' church in Toxteth, Liverpool – the citadel of high Anglicanism on Merseyside – on several occasions and heard Cardinal Manning (1808–92) preach from the altar steps to a packed congregation at St Anne's Roman catholic church at nearby Rock Ferry (3: **15**). His attraction to Catholicism perhaps most served to disguise the uncertainty of what he believed. At the same time, it enabled him to distance himself from the local *élite*, particularly the Aspinall family, protestant to the core, whom he enjoyed 'fetching' on the reformation (2: **121**; 3: **70**).

The Aspinalls feature prominently in the Birkenhead journals; he certainly seems to have spent more time in their company and paying similar calls than in visiting the poor, contrary to the suggestion in the *Retrospect* that his afternoons were divided equally between these activities.[56] His account in the Journal of his visits to the Aspinalls provides a revealing insight into the operation of class in a provincial setting. While Henry Kelsall Aspinall (1824–1908), a businessman and improvement commissioner in Birkenhead and Henson's neighbour in Hamilton Square, and his relative Clarke Aspinall (1827–91), coroner of Liverpool and magistrate who lived two to three miles away in Higher Bebington, were useful sources of local knowledge, they swiftly determined the social ranking. On one occasion, an unnamed member of the family inquired condescendingly about Henson's undergraduate college, undoubtedly aware of his non-collegiate status and perhaps his sensitivities on the subject, too. Instead of proudly proclaiming his achievement in securing a first in Schools against all the odds followed by a prize fellowship at All Souls, he was duly cowed into making what he called 'the usual inevitable "confession" of my academic misfortune' (3: **70**).

The success of the male members of the Aspinall family in maintaining the upper hand is also clear at Holy Trinity. As a churchwarden, H. K. Aspinall judged Watson purely by his preaching ability, leaving Henson to defend his friend as best he could (2: **121**). He was vexed by the family's 'absolute contempt' for the clergy, all, that is, except their relatives (3: **102, 108**); but while inclined to 'burst out' (3: **70**), he never did.

General Gordon

A related feature of the early journals is the inspiration Henson drew from General Charles Gordon (1833–85), both in relieving the strain of his duties with Lyle, and in overcoming religious doubt. Following Gordon's assassination by Mahdist forces in the siege of Khartoum in January 1885 while awaiting troop reinforcements, his irreverent Khartoum diary was published on 25 June 1885, to much critical acclaim in *The Times*. Henson was quick to purchase a copy, followed by Gordon's earlier journal, *Colonel Gordon in Central Africa, 1874–79*.[57] He also purchased a photograph of his new hero (3: **21**). Like many, he believed that Gordon had been betrayed by Gladstone in delaying the dispatch of relief to the besieged garrison at Khartoum (3: **107**); this added to his dislike of the Liberal leader and what he regarded as his empty speeches (3: **60**; 4: **29**). A revealing insight into Henson's 'aloner' status is clear in his comment

---

[56] Henson, *Retrospect*, I, 8; see also Journal, 17 and 20 April 1943 for his memories of the family, prompted by a letter from a resident of Birkenhead in appreciation of the *Retrospect*, and with a memory of him at the time..

[57] *Colonel Gordon in Central Africa, 1874–79: from original letters and documents*. Ed. George Birkbeck Hill (London, 1881).

on finishing the Khartoum diary, that Gordon had 'entered into my life as nobody has ever done' (1: **75**), a response which found little echo among his acquaintances, either in Birkenhead or Oxford (1: **104**; 2: **64**).[58] Gordon so possessed him that he would ask not 'What would Jesus do' but 'What would Gordon do?' in resolving the difficulties he faced, helping 'to strengthen one to a decision' (1: **75**).

Imbued with Gordon's 'power of inspiring to great deeds' (1: **75**), Henson lectured on him to working-men's clubs in London when he returned to Oxford to much acclaim, in contrast to the indifference if not hostility of his peers. He explained in a note to the published version of the lecture, that this was in his capacity as 'one of the lecturers on the staff of Oxford House', the university settlement in the East End established by Keble College (3: **139, 147, 149**). He was encouraged to print the lecture by his friends, the note continued; almost certainly, these would have included Anson, chairman of the Oxford House Council.[59]

To his audiences he emphasized Gordon's character rather than his career as the main focus of his interest; to that extent, his hero's achievements in Africa would receive the greatest attention, for there 'his liberty of action was more absolute, and therefore his actions more accurately reflected his intentions'.[60] He commended Gordon's self-suppression, his lack of personal ambition and his disinterestedness, particularly in China in supporting the Ming dynasty in a bloody civil war against the Taiping rebels, for whom he nonetheless negotiated safety in return for their surrender, only to be betrayed by his imperialist commanders. Most pertinently for this edition, he praised Gordon's staunch Christian faith that had sustained him in his 'martyrdom' at Khartoum: 'It was on his knees by the side of that bed, whereon he rarely rested, that he gathered his heroic fortitude and triumphant patience.'[61]

He rejoiced at the avenging of Gordon's death following the defeat of the Mahdist forces at the battle of Omdurman in 1898;[62] generally though, he ceased to draw moral and spiritual strength from this quarter following his ordination, and was dismayed by Lytton Strachey's revelations of his erstwhile hero's vices in *Eminent Victorians* (1918).[63] However, Gordon's influence was more lasting in other ways. First, it provided an example of journal-keeping that lent insight into its author's motives and provided 'an authentic and intensely interesting account of his achievements'.[64] Second, it enhanced his patriotism; in his lecture on Gordon, he cited approvingly the comment of Sir Frederick Bruce (1814–67) – envoy to the Chinese emperor – in a letter to Earl Russell, that Gordon 'had elevated our national character in the eyes of the Chinese'.[65] The English rather than British focus of Henson's patriotism is apparent in the amusing account he gave in volume 1 of an encounter with Kuno Meyer (1858–1919), a renowned German scholar and lecturer

---

[58] However, the Khartoum journals proved absorbing to other young and rebellious readers, such as the future Irish secretary, George Wyndham: Richard Davenport-Hines, 'Gordon, Charles George' (1833–85), *ODNB*.

[59] Henson, *Gordon: a lecture* (Oxford, 1886).

[60] *Ibid.*, p. 3. See Stefan Collini on the salience of the Victorian language of character and its contrast with the Georgian language of virtue in 'The idea of "character" in Victorian political thought', *Transactions of the Royal Historical Society*, 35 (1985), 29–50, at 42–3.

[61] Henson, *Gordon*, p. 30.

[62] All Souls Coll., Anson MSS, Henson to Anson, 7 Sept. 1898, fo. 310.

[63] Journal, 29 June 1918; although see his critical remarks on Strachey's attempted demolition of Matthew Arnold's reputation in his Journal entry for 17 July 1918.

[64] Henson, *Gordon*, pp. 2–3.

[65] *Ibid.*, p. 9.

in Celtic and Teutonic studies at the University College of Liverpool (1: **34**); and of a visit to a 'Scotch colony' at nearby Wallasey, with whose members he engaged in furious political argument, fuelled by a sense of their respective national differences and superiority to the other side (1: **65–8**).

Poverty and its treatment

If Henson quickly proved a more effective preacher than Watson, he was indebted to his friend for, as he later recalled, 'lift[ing] for me the veil that commonly shrouds from view the squalid mystery of industrialism, and introduc[ing] me to the sorrows and hardships of the poor'.[66] These are set out in vivid and often harrowing detail in the journals reproduced here, and suggest that Henson came to regard Watson's response as superior to his own. For example, while Henson could not bring himself to shake hands with those living in filth and squalor, Watson showed no such scruples (1: **22, 52**). Unlike Watson, too, in Birkenhead he became wedded to a view of poverty that emphasized the personal responsibility of the poor for improving their position. He was a stalwart supporter of the Charity Organization Society, and Makin, in distinguishing between the 'deserving' and the 'undeserving' poor (2: **65**).[67] He noted the bitter hatred of Makin among the unemployed, and Makin's contempt in turn for those who responded to their appeal at a town meeting for donations that could be distributed independently of the Society. The contributors included the Laird brothers – William Laird's grandsons – who donated fifty pounds, despite the sarcasm of one member of the crowd when John Laird (1834–98) ventured to express his sympathy for the unemployed (3: **8–9**). Nevertheless, Henson assured Makin of his support if the 'roughs attacked the office' (3: **12**).

Henson immediately recognized the injustices suffered by the poor when brought face to face with the economic realities of Birkenhead, including the exploitation of young people. He was struck by the monotony of their work, their lack of prospects and the pressures they faced if they were to survive in the Victorian equivalent of the modern gig economy (1: **17, 26**). He was moved when Watson reported to him the regular deaths of those constructing the Mersey tunnel that would connect Birkenhead to Liverpool by rail. Watson also reported how rapidly workers in construction died of typhoid, a fate to which they were resigned. Henson observed that 'there can be no doubt that these big works on which we plume ourselves have a horrent record of murder locked up in their recesses' (3: **99**).[68]

He found the irregular nature of employment for the mass of those currently unemployed especially vexing. For Clarke Aspinall, it represented an ineradicable feature of the existing economic system in which the supply of labour barely sufficed during times of excessive demand, and must therefore continue to be available, even at the price of periodic unemployment. On hearing this explanation, he

---

[66] Henson, *Retrospect*, I, 8.
[67] Although this distinction was by no means exclusive to the Charity Organization Society; for the fears that were aroused by the 'residuum' of the poor in conjunction with perceptions of urban degeneration in London in the 1880s, and the different solutions that were advanced on the basis of the distinction; see G. Stedman Jones, *Outcast London: a study in the relationship between classes in Victorian society* (Oxford, 1971), ch. 16.
[68] This is echoed later in the Journal, for example in the entry for 19 Apr. 1934 following an explosion at the chemical works in Billingham in his diocese and the death of three men.

wrote despairingly that 'a great section of the people are always confined to the moral degradation of living on odd jobs: now there is not work enough to keep the ordinary hands busy.' He had no answer at the time, other than to declare only half-jokingly that he would become a socialist if he stayed in the town for a further six months (1: **24**). However, as we shall see in the following section, he continued to develop his ideas concerning the relief of poverty and unemployment in other settings.

Return to All Souls College

Henson returned to Oxford from Birkenhead slightly earlier than expected, relieved that his responsibility for Lyle had at last ended and heartened by William Rathbone's warmth towards him in his farewell interview (3: **113**). As well as his interaction with students and prominent Oxford scholars, and his early attempts to make a living by teaching and lecturing in modern history, the closing entries in volume 3 and much of volume 4 record his activities as founder and secretary of the Oxford Laymen's League for the Defence of the National Church in 1886. Centred upon Oxford where he believed the rival Church Defence Institution was weak (4: **43**), the organization sought to oppose Joseph Chamberlain's calls for disestablishment and disendowment in his Radical programme of July 1885.

These volumes also record his unease following a vow he made at the altar of Iffley church to dedicate himself to God and the service of the church immediately after his return to Birkenhead (3: **122**). Apart from the problem of religious doubt, he was ambivalent about the Anglicanism of those who sought to draw him into the church. On the one hand, he relied on Charles Gore (1853–1932), principal of Pusey House and a leading figure in the anglo-catholic wing of the church in the aftermath of the Oxford Movement and its Tractarian offshoot,[69] to hold him to his pledge.[70] He had made Gore's acquaintance through Henry Offley Wakeman (1852–99), another prominent high churchman, fellow of All Souls and history tutor. He stated in the *Retrospect* that Gore, Wakeman and other church leaders at Oxford convinced him of Anglicanism as 'a reasonable, coherent, and attractive version of Christianity'. On the other hand, however, he placed greater emphasis on the nation at the core of the church than his mentors. For example, in the *Retrospect* he recalled 'reading the literature of the Oxford movement, and shar[ing] the general enthusiasm for *John Inglesant*', a novel published in 1881 by the writer Joseph Henry Shorthouse (1834–1903), whose high church sympathies recognized the tensions between Anglicanism and Roman catholicism. He continued, 'the conception of a National Church, Catholic and free, appealed to my historic sense, to my patriotism, and to my local loyalty'.[71]

---

[69] For the tensions in the high church wing of the church that were born of the Oxford Movement and Tractarianism following the end of the confessional state in 1828 and 1829, and even more so after 1870 and the development of anglo-catholicism; see Robert M. Andrews, 'High church Anglicanism in the nineteenth century', in *The Oxford history of Anglicanism*, III: *Partisan Anglicanism and its global expansion, 1829–c. 1914*, ed. Rowan Strong (Oxford, 2016), 141–64.

[70] According to Chadwick, Henson's vow acquired a clearer commitment to ordination a few weeks later following his return from Rome: *Hensley Henson*, pp. 29–37. Chadwick's sources here, as elsewhere, are unclear.

[71] Henson, *Retrospect*, I, 11.

The conflict between Henson's Anglicanism and the churchmanship of those who had helped to secure it is evident in a reference in volume 4 to his endeavour to free himself from the 'chains' of the 'pseudo-Catholic' theory of the church before his diaconal ordination (4: **337**). Although not amplified, he clearly meant the spread of Roman catholic practices in the Church of England, so-called 'Ritualism', and the sacramental beliefs that accompanied them, a subject to which we shall return. Hostility towards the League in Oxford and the Establishment it upheld also lowered catholic Anglicanism of a Roman hue in his esteem (4: **172, 184, 276**); this centred upon the enforcement of ecclesiastical law by a secular state to curb the growth of 'Ritualism' among anglo-catholics, often in open defiance of the Public Worship Regulation Act (1874), which Henson defended.[72] Increasingly, anglo-catholic aversion to confronting modern forms of knowledge and inquiry also set him apart from his mentors. His differences with Gore on this account became apparent in 1889 with the publication of *Lux Mundi* which Gore edited, and which contained Gore's controversial essay defending the need for biblical criticism, but only in relation to the Old Testament. Coupled with the essayists' socialist sympathies, Henson dismissed the work as an attempt to save Tractarianism from its 'social and theological rigidity' by administering a mild dose of Modernism, while retaining its commitment to ecclesiastical independence.[73]

He continued to be drawn to 'Romanism' outside of the Church of England, while recognizing the source of its attraction in the restlessness of his mind (4: **66**) and what he called his 'insurmountable objection to Evangelicalism' (4: **147**). However, his Romanist leanings were checked by a heavy sense of duty to support his family financially, preventing them from dropping out of gentile poverty into something much worse (4: **66**). It is unclear why he felt obliged in this way given that three of his brothers had followed their father into business. Certainly, though, they would not have underwritten the Oxford education with college membership he planned for Gid. This was before he received reports of Gid abandoning his religious beliefs as soon as he reached India in 1883 – where he had accompanied his elder brother, Arthur, on a business trip – and general lack of application, which suggested that his ambitions for him were misguided (4: **124, 132, 136**).

Beyond the problem of Gid, the journals included in this edition provide insight into the financial pressures to which college fellows of limited means were subject; Henson's constant and frequently unavailing attempts to rein in his expenditure, despite support from Thomas Raleigh (1850–1920), another older friend at All Souls,[74] and his anxieties about securing sufficient pupils in the School of Modern History to make ends meet suggest that for all his academic success, his early life continued to haunt him. His non-collegiate status added to the heavy shadow of a past that failed to lift (4: **34**). It prompted his efforts to abolish a dual system that would spare students of poorer backgrounds the humiliation that he, at least, felt sharply (3: **32, 71**).

What of his wider views on poverty, that of the working class especially? Once back in Oxford, he continued to resist socialism, particularly in the form of the broad

---

[72] For the controversy over the legislation, see J. Bentley, *Ritualism and politics in Victorian Britain: the attempt to legislate for belief* (Oxford, 1978); and Nigel Yates, *Anglican ritualism in Victorian Britain, 1830–1910* (Oxford, 1999), 213–76; for Henson's defence of the Act, see his pamphlet *Cui bono* (London, 1898), p. 42.
[73] Henson, *Retrospect*, I, 155.
[74] Davenport-Hines, 'The trimming of Herbert Hensley Henson', p. 86.

Christian interest in developing an ethic of social morality – 'Christian Socialism' – that had made large inroads into Anglicanism during the late nineteenth century. As Jane Garnett has shown, much of this was driven by critical engagement with classical economics under a range of cross-cultural influences and within different sections of the church.[75] Part of Henson's interest for historians derives from his failure to share this hostility towards classical economics. He distanced himself from the Christian Social Union (CSU), an organization founded in 1889 by Gore, Henry Scott Holland (1847–1918) and James Adderley (1861–1942) to enhance the moral and religious dimensions of debate about contemporary social problems. He particularly disliked its bias towards collectivist action against perceived economic injustice. In a revealing letter to a friend, Leslie Hunter (1890–1983), later in life, he recalled his first clash with Hastings Rashdall (1858–1924), one of the leaders of the Oxford branch of the CSU and later a prominent historian and theologian who became a friend and ally. Their dispute centred on the 'principle and policy' of the 'White Lists' campaign against employers who were deemed exploitative, which Hastings supported and Henson opposed. Henson's principal objection was that, especially in trades that were unorganized and lacking in agreed standards, the CSU as a private society would sit in judgment, often on the basis of limited understanding of the industry in question.[76] Still, Henson commented, Rashdall was 'far less socialistic than the rest'.[77] 'The rest' included Adderley, whose extensive influence at Oxford through his novel *Stephen Remarx* (1893) Henson noted in his letter to Hunter. This was part of a wider spate of religious novels in the 1880s and 1890s that sought to reinforce the secularization of religion in modern thought; in Adderley's case, it was an attempt to resolve the tension between the Marxist concept of alienation and a Christian-inspired ideal of human love.[78]

In contrast, Henson defended what he termed an 'alternative conception of Christian social obligation', one he associated with the Anglican basis of Oxford House against the secularist and undenominational creed of Toynbee Hall, the rival settlement in the East End attached to Balliol College.[79] As documented in volume 4, he resided at Oxford House in the autumn of 1886 and again during December of that year (4: **139–60, 216–67**), working closely with Adderley ('the Abbot'), its then head, in the neighbourhood and with the clubs associated with the settlement. There are already hints in the Journal of their differences, although it is unclear whether these were primarily political or religious in nature (4: **327, 337**). Certainly, Henson's approach to social reform was rooted in a belief in the importance of moral change in the individual inspired by the teachings of Jesus as the precondition

---

[75] Jane Garnett, 'Anglican economic and social engagement', in *Oxford history of Anglicanism*, III, ed. Strong, 456–80.
[76] Henson, 'The C.S.U. policy of white-lists', in *Light and leaven: historical and social sermons to general congregations* (London, 1897), pp. 325–9.
[77] Henson to Leslie Hunter, 21 Mar. 1943, Hunter papers, B164, HH21, Sheffield Archives and Local Studies Library; for an account of the limits to Rashdall's advocacy of equality, see Gary J. Dorrien, 'Idealistic ordering: Hastings Rashdall, post-Kantian Idealism, and Anglican liberal theology', *Anglican and Episcopal History*, 82 (2013), 289–317, at 303–9.
[78] Lynne Hapgood, '"The reconceiving of Christianity": secularism, realism and the religious novel, 1880–1900', *Literature and Theology*, 10 (1996), 329–50.
[79] Henson to Hunter, 21 Mar. 1943; for Henson's conception of the distinctiveness of the two settlements, see 4: **192** below; see also Journal, 14 July 1932, for a letter from Canon Thory Gardiner of Canterbury, recalling his envy of Oxford House with Henson as its head while he was at Toynbee Hall.

of social progress, reinforced by regular church attendance.[80] A strict interpretation of the ethos of the settlement as he understood it informed his headship of Oxford House when he succeeded Adderley in December 1887. He recognized that scepticism of wider programmes for change ill-equipped him for this post given the degree of squalor and deprivation in the area: this prompted his resignation within a year.[81] However, he continued to uphold the basis of his 'alternative conception to Christian obligation' in Barking, a large working-class parish which he served as rector from 1888 to 1895. In one of his annual sermons to the gas workers of the town, he insisted that Christianity was devoid of specific solutions to social problems; it was, though, he insisted, keenly interested in maintaining what he called 'the temper of good citizenship' through voluntary collective provision and support for measures that would reduce the likelihood of unemployment such as longer-term contracts and technical instruction.[82]

The high premium that Henson attached to citizenship co-existed with a conception of world markets as the determining factor in employment and prosperity at home, the force of which he thought that working men – under the influence of their leaders – failed to appreciate.[83] However, while he believed this meant that poverty could not be eradicated entirely, the causes that were known and treatable could and should be addressed. After setting out his theological grounds for intervention in a contribution to an 1899 discussion in the letters page of *The Saturday Review* centred on poverty, he agreed with one correspondent that in practical terms what was needed was 'wise, gradual, continuous betterment of the condition of the poor by individual effort or by legislation, as seemed best'.[84] Once again, what he termed the 'lowering effect on citizenship' of poor social and economic conditions remained his primary concern. Four years later, in reviewing Charles Booth's monumental *Life and labour of the people in London*, he concluded that before Christianity could bring its unique spiritual message to the poor, it should first address the conditions of their existence, particularly squalor and overcrowding. Otherwise, as Booth's study made clear, the different Christian churches and sects competing for influence would continue to be associated with the relief of distress alone.[85] This emphasizes the distance he had travelled since Birkenhead towards a more flexible response to poverty, entailing a measure of public provision rooted in good citizenship. He maintained this approach throughout the rest of his life, for example in 1934 when admonishing the then archbishop of York, William Temple (1881–1944), for invoking '"Christian duty"' when pressing for an extension of the school leaving age and more state assistance for the unemployed: why, Henson asked, in a tone of exasperation, 'cannot he be content to argue the case of civic obligation on grounds of reason & expediency?'[86]

---

[80] Henson, *Retrospect*, I, 27.
[81] *Ibid.*, 29; an entry in his Journal several decades later (16 June 1935) refers to a growing sense of discord between himself and the 'ecclesiastical tone of the Oxford House Committee', with Bishop Talbot of Southwark – later of Winchester and a close ally of Gore – as the 'choragus' being the reason for his departure.
[82] Henson, 'Sermon to working men' (1891), in *Light and leaven*, pp. 269, 272–3.
[83] *Ibid.*, 290.
[84] Henson, 'Rich and poor', letter to the editor, *Saturday Review*, 21 Jan. 1899, 81–2, at 82.
[85] Henson, 'Religion and the poor', *Quarterly Review*, 198 (1903), 230–45, at 235–6, 245.
[86] Journal, 23 Jan. 1934.

Church, faith and nation

These first four volumes are crucial to understanding Henson's formation as an outstanding churchman of the twentieth century, particularly the rapidity with which the basis of some of his life-long positions developed following his visit to Birkenhead. Freed from the discipline of being in constant examination mode for the first time in four years, and with greater opportunities for leisure, he was able to examine himself closely instead. He also avoided the social pressure that was beginning to shape him at All Souls; he was essentially on his own again, except for the friendship that had taken root at Oxford when Edward Watson had tutored him successfully for his final examinations. Being on his own enabled his social character to develop at its own pace. Also, before his Birkenhead time was complete, he was aware that he was acquiring the gift of oratory (2: **125–6**; 3: **72–3**), while recognizing that it could not be deployed to maximum advantage in a small mission room. This left him free to cast his career over a wide, public stage.

The beginnings of maturity emerge in these four volumes, assisted by Henson's habit of writing a regular, often daily journal entry. He used it to record the lesson that this part of England's industrial heartland was largely unchurched, that something came between the church and the constant movement of people in and out of towns and regions in search of employment, but that Christianizing the nation was the overall responsibility of the Church of England, and that it was achievable. He clearly felt that God had called him to this great task.

In readiness, he used the Journal to clarify his thoughts on salvation. His brother Gid's lapse underlined the truth of the Gospel that 'Strait is the gate and narrow is the way, which leadeth unto life and few there be that find it'.[87] He reflected ruefully that 'Jesus Christ must mean what he says: yet we marvel at the defection of a single person' (4: **136**). On the other hand, he believed that the church could no longer use the 'weapon' of eternal punishment in saving souls; 'perfect love' had to get the better of fear (4: **312–13**). In a similar vein, he toyed with the idea that those who rejected creeds as the embodiment of truth but who nevertheless followed Jesus might be disadvantaged but not excluded from salvation.

However, without pursuing this possibility further, he brought himself back to the question of the authority of the creeds, and its basis in the church. This raised further questions concerning the nature, constitution and function of the church that Christ had founded, and where it could be found in the present (1: **18–21**). His discussion of the creeds was clearly informed by John Henry Newman's conception of the Roman catholic church as the infallible authority on their meaning, not as established permanently by the fathers in the early church but as part of the historical development of the conscience of humanity. Yet unlike Newman, Henson did not think that the church's authority was beyond the scrutiny of reason.[88] Undoubtedly, this was because he continued to be exercised by the problem of how dissenters should be treated. Early in 1887, he concluded that Christianity is wider than the church, certainly the Roman catholic church (4: **277**).

During the following decades, Henson upheld a liberal Anglican conception of

---

[87] Matt. 7:14.
[88] For an excellent account of Newman's concept of development in the meaning of the creeds, and its historical context, see Joshua Bennett, *God and progress: religion and history in British intellectual culture, 1845–1914* (Oxford, 2019), ch. 2.

the relation of religious truth to history focused on the spiritual past of all mankind, and within a clear developmental conception of Revelation.[89] This played into broad church ideals, heavily focused on the nation, as shaped by Thomas Arnold (1795–1842), reforming headmaster of Rugby in the 1830s. For Arnold and those he influenced, a unified, critical conception of truth across all domains of knowledge, including biblical studies, held the key to overcoming divisions in both church and society.[90] In the same vein, Henson assimilated the church into the broad sweep of English thought and history, with the publication of *Ecclesiastical polity* (1593–7) by Richard Hooker (1554–1600) a seminal moment. In a striking passage in a lecture of 1919, delivered at a time of heightened pressure within the church for 'self-government' through the establishment of a church assembly,[91] he spoke proudly of a nation that had restored the self-confidence of the church at the end of sixteenth century following the vicissitudes of the reformation. Unwilling to allow the church to remain in the low place to which it had sunk in English society, he maintained,

> the Nation reacted on the Church, to which it lent the *éclat* of its own triumphs. Politics and controversy were the twin influences under which this naked framework of a national church became substantial, intelligible, and self-conscious. Hooker's '*Ecclesiastical Polity*', composed in the years of patriotic exultation which followed the defeat of the Armada, discloses a version of Christianity, avowedly and almost proudly Anglican, which is no longer tentative and hesitating, but commands the deliberate assent of reflecting and learned Englishmen, stirs a grave and tenacious loyalty and secures a permanent and honourable place in the world-scheme of Christianity.[92]

His support for the reunion of the Church of England with the other protestant churches in England from 1901 emphasizes the importance he attached to recovering a form of national Christianity that had been established at the time of Hooker but had been ruptured by the Act of Uniformity in 1662.[93] The authority of the Church of England, it seems, lay squarely with the nation.[94] This conformed with his tendency, as he remarked

---

[89] He recalled his sceptical reading of Newman's essay as 'a very young man' in his Journal, 1 Dec. 1934; he read F. D. Maurice's criticism of Newman's *Essay on the development of Christian doctrine*, as noted in his Journal, 12 Jan. 1908. See also his acute criticism of Ronald Knox's defence of the 'Papal theory of salvation' in Knox's popular tract *Caliban in Grub Street* (London, 1930), in Journal, 10 Aug. 1932.

[90] Mark D. Chapman, 'Liberal Anglicanism in the nineteenth century', in *Oxford history of Anglicanism*, III, ed. Strong, 212–31; for the philosophical idealism that lent support to Liberal Anglicanism from an 'agnostic' standpoint, see Timothy Maxwell Gouldstone, *The rise and decline of Anglican Idealism in the nineteenth century* (London, 2005), ch. 5; for the 'national' focus of liberal Anglicanism, invariably projected through a communal view of the state in the early decades of the twentieth century, see M. Grimley, *Citizenship, community, and the Church of England: Liberal Anglican theories of the state between the wars* (Oxford, 2004), ch. 1.

[91] For his resistance to this pressure, see Julia Stapleton, 'Herbert Hensley Henson, J. N. Figgis and the Archbishops' Committee on Church and State', 1913–1916: two competing visions of the Church of England', *Journal of Ecclesiastical History*, 73 (2022), 814–36.

[92] Henson, 'The Anglican version of Christianity', in Henson et al., *The Church of England: its nature and its future* (London 1919), p. 75.

[93] Henson, 'Appeal for unity', pp. 126–43; for his attack on the Restoration settlement of the church, see Journal, 22 May 1910.

[94] For context, see Arthur Burns, 'The authority of the church', in *Liberty and authority in Victorian Britain*, ed. Peter Mandler (Oxford, 2006), pp. 179–200.

in another context, to 'hold lightly to ecclesiastical forms', reflecting the influence of his stepmother's religion which was 'strongly ethical and "mystical"'.[95] That tendency is also evident in his concern below for a monastic revival infused with study at the expense of 'Celebrations' (4: **151–3**).

If this grounding echoed of the authority of the church in the nation marked the resolution of his struggle with sects in his early life, reinforced by his schism hunts in Birkenhead, it also owed much to his opposition to the 'Ritualists' ('the Rits') following his return to Oxford.[96] Aside from his considered position on the twin principles of 'decency' and 'instruction' that should inform Ritual practices (4: **103–6, 108**), this opposition had crystallized in two ways. First, against the Ritualists' conception of the Sacraments as the sole means of grace he maintained that non-Catholics were not 'obviously' the moral inferiors of Catholics in this regard, and that a 'Catholic priesthood' was not integral to the concept of a church. Instead, he invoked Christ's words, 'Ye shall know them by their fruits' (4: **278–9**).[97] This position informed his later assertion that the nonconformist churches had received the 'plenary blessing' of the Almighty as 'His instruments for far-extended evangelisation', as confirmed by 'Time'. In contrast, the descendants of Tractarianism remained wedded to episcopacy as the basis of ecclesiastical authority, among other factors shaped by a misguided conception of nonconformists in the early nineteenth century as 'powerful rivals' to the church, rather than its 'separated brethren'.[98]

His second difference with the Ritualists arose from their pursuit of what he derisively termed the 'Chimerae of ecclesiastical independence'; if successful, it would in the history of the world represent more a 'great Secularist victory' than a 'great act of clerical enfranchisement' (4: **40–1**). Even when he embraced the cause of voluntary disestablishment after parliament rejected the revised prayer book in 1927–8, he continued to emphasize the importance of the church's national status and responsibilities, particularly in the volatile circumstances of the 1930s. If it could no longer maintain the pretence of an identity with the political nation, newly democratized, the church would be able to make common cause with dissent in upholding the value of spiritual freedom. Together encompassing much of the religious nation, they would spare the wider nation the turmoil of an anti-religious campaign against Establishment, with revolutionary implications.[99] A recognition of the importance of unity between the two streams of protestantism in England marked a step forward from the hostile position towards the sects that he had assumed during his stay in Birkenhead, but which he now directed against the insular vision of the Church upheld by the 'Rits' (4: **39**). It was a lesson that he applied both to the external and internal threats to the church as a national institution during the decades that followed, and documented extensively in a Journal which ranks among the great diaries in the English language.

---

[95] Journal, 26 July 1924.
[96] His opposition echoed that of the wider shift in Anglican thought towards an acceptance of culture and civilisation as gifts of the same spirit as the church; see Gouldstone, *Anglican Idealism*, p. 181.
[97] Matt. 7:16.
[98] Herbert Croft, *The naked truth* (1675), introduced by Herbert Hensley Henson (London, 1919), p. xx. Croft was one of Henson's predecessors as bishop of Hereford (1661–91), whose interest in a 'comprehensive' church his successor shared fully.
[99] Journal, 28 Aug. 1932, 31 Aug. 1932.

Editorial policies

Every effort has been made to preserve the features of the original text in producing this unabridged edition of the first four volumes of Henson's journals. In most cases, Henson's inconsistencies and idiosyncrasies of spelling, punctuation and abbreviation have been retained, subject only to minimal formatting in some respects and silent editing in others. Use of [*sic*] has been kept to a minimum.

While Henson's practice varies, the following changes have been made: each entry follows the preceding entry instead of commencing on a new page; original page numbers are placed between square brackets and given in bold; dates at the head of each journal entry have been ordered uniformly: anniversary/feast/Sunday in the church calendar (where relevant): day of the week: month and date of the month: year. For example, **2nd Sunday after Easter, April 24th, 1887.** Paragraphs are given in 'block' style instead of having an indented first line; quotation marks are placed inside punctuation except where a sentence is quoted in full; occasional missing words and missing quotation marks are placed in square brackets.

Henson returned later to his journals to assist him in the writing of his autobiography, *Retrospect of an unimportant life* (3 vols, 1942, 1943, 1950). To try to reproduce this within the constraints of a monochrome print-run, Henson's mark-ups have been rendered differently than in the original. No attempt has been made to discriminate between the different colours he used in the categories of editing given below. Instead, passages which are underlined in coloured crayon are rendered in **<u>bold with underlining</u>**; passages with coloured strokes in the margin are rendered in *italics*; and passages with both coloured underlining and marginal strokes are rendered in ***<u>bold and italics with underlining</u>***; coloured square brackets and associated symbols (e.g. **/** and **|**) are rendered in **bold**, although bold square brackets are also used for editorial comments at the head of a new page if required by the physical appearance of the text that follows, or base of a page as appropriate. Henson's occasional use of double, dashed, and wavy underlining has been retained. His use of symbols to assign passages in the Journal to relevant volumes and sections of the *Retrospect* is indicated by the word 'symbol' beneath the date of the entry.

Annotation guidance

The journals have been annotated extensively to enhance the reader's understanding of the text and the diverse social settings in which it unfolds.

The most numerous class of reference is to persons. These have been compiled using a variety of sources, from information on leading figures in British national life in the *Oxford dictionary of national biography* and *Who was who* through the lists of Oxford graduates in *Alumni Oxonienses* and *Oxford men and their colleges* and Cambridge graduates in *Alumni Cantabrigienses* to *Crockford's clerical direchotory* and census returns, as well as newspaper obituaries. Specific sources such as these are credited in the notes. The annotation also includes selected references to Henson's later journals where these are deemed of interest and significance to the material in this edition. Readers are encouraged to use the Persons search facility in the online edition of Henson's journals between 1900 to 1939 for further references: www.hensonjournals.org.

The editorial notes provide full references to Henson's reading, emphasizing its range and extent and providing context for the ideas that provided the basis of his developing religious and political views, as outlined in the journals reproduced here. In addition, the notes provide details of the speeches and campaigns of politicians he reported and commented on in the entries, and of other items in newspapers that caught his eye. The notes draw further on the *Oxford English dictionary* to clarify the meaning of archaic words and usage in the Journal. They also include short passages from the biblical references in the text, as rendered in the King James Version that Henson would have used before becoming a life-long advocate of the Revised Version from his time at Barking in 1888. The notes also identify biblical allusions in the text. These references make clear his intimate knowledge of the Bible, most likely emanating from the nonconformist atmosphere of his home and his central aim from an early stage of his career to strengthen Christian faith and morals in England, particularly among the poor.

Table of sources and abbreviations

AC	J. A. Venn, *Alumni Cantabrigienses*, 1752–1900 (10 vols., Cambridge, 1922–54)
Anson MSS	Papers of William Anson, All Souls College, Oxford
AO	J. Foster, *Alumni Oxonienses*, series 2, 1715–1886 (4 vols., Oxford, 1891–2)
barr.	barrister
B.N.C.	Brasenose College, Oxford
Bt	baronet
C	Conservative
CCD	*Crockford's Clerical Directory*
Ch. Ch.	Christ Church (Coll.)
Classical Mods.	Classical Moderations
Coll.	College
ECU	English Church Union
FBA	Fellow of the British Academy
FRS	Fellow of the Royal Society
Henson Journals Online	www.hensonjournals.org
hon.	honorary
Journal	The Journals of Herbert Hensley Henson, Durham Cathedral Library
JP	justice of the peace
Kt	knighted
L	Liberal
letter	letter to the editor
Lit. Hum.	Literae Humaniores
LU	Liberal Unionist
MA	Master of Arts
matric.	matriculated
MD	Doctor of Medicine
N	Nationalist
non-coll.	non-collegiate student
OED	*Oxford English dictionary*
ODNB	*Oxford dictionary of national biography* (2004–)

OLL	Oxford Laymen's League for the Defence of the National Church
OMC	*Oxford men and their colleges: matriculations, 1880–92* (2 vols., Oxford, 1893).
ord.	ordained
Pedersen, *Eleanor Rathbone*	Susan Pedersen, *Eleanor Rathbone and the politics of conscience* (New Haven, 2004).
QC	Queen's Counsel
Retrospect	H. H. Henson, *Retrospect of an unimportant life* (3 vols., Oxford, 1942–50)
WWW	Who was who

Books of the Bible cited in this edition

Old Testament

1 Sam.	1 Samuel
Ps.	Psalms
Isa.	Isaiah

New Testament

Matt.	Matthew
Luke	Luke
Acts	Acts of the Apostles
1 Cor.	1 Corinthians
Gal.	Galations
Eph.	Ephesians
Col.	Colossians
Heb.	Hebrews
Jas	James
John	John
1 John	1 John

Illustrations

1. The Stubbs Seminar, Oxford, 1882–3. From Charles Oman, *Memories of Victorian Oxford and of some early years* (London, 1941), p. 106.   2
2. Interior of Holy Trinity Church, Birkenhead, taken before demolition in 1970: nave to East. Royal Commission on Historical Monuments of England, reproduced by permission of Historic England Archive.   7
3. Journal, vol. 1, 18 June 1885, 59–60: dock scenes, Birkenhead. Durham Cathedral Library, reproduced by permission of the Dean and Chapter of Durham Cathedral.   20
4. Journal, vol. 1, 27 June 1885, 132: sketch of 'The Shepherd', faith healing meeting, Birkenhead. Durham Cathedral Library, reproduced by permission of the Dean and Chapter of Durham Cathedral.   41

THE JOURNALS

1 The Stubbs Seminar, Oxford, 1882–3: Henson as an undergraduate, first row, second from right, the only surviving photograph of him in the 1880s. Charles Oman, *Memories of Victorian Oxford and of some early years* (London, 1941), p. 106.

Volume 1
12 May – 20 July 1885

[The first entry of the Journal (1: **14**) is preceded by an account of a fictional clergyman, Richard Andrew, rector of a fictional parish, 'Clarkleigh'. There is no indication of precisely when or why it was written; however, its similarity with passages on religious sects in Birkenhead and Liverpool in the entries that follow suggests its nature as a prologue. Its central concern is not only the divisiveness and 'heresy' that Henson associated with such groups but widespread misunderstanding of what 'a church' and 'the Church' entailed, a theme to which he quickly returns. While Birkenhead clearly provided the model for the religious divisions of Clarkleigh, Thomas Sheriff, vicar of Holy Trinity, Birkenhead, may have been the inspiration behind Richard Andrew, in part at least. Later in the volume, Sheriff is chided for encouraging the grocer Charles Thompson in the work of the mission he established for children, despite his absence from church, and in volume 2 for enabling Thompson to procure Bibles from the British and Foreign Bible Society, regarded by Henson as doctrinally unsound (1: **108**; 2: **79**). Henson may have become aware of Sheriff's indulgence of sectaries such as Thompson – 'a shepherd of schismatics' (1: **108**) – during the three-week interval between his arrival in Birkenhead and his commencement of the Journal: like him, both Sheriff and Watson lived in Hamilton Square and it is probable that he would have discussed local matters of a religious nature with them at an early stage.]

[1]

The Rev. Richard Andrew was a short, stout man with fine blue eyes, and heavy reddish moustachios. His hair was very grey, though he had not yet reached the age of 40. At once impracticable and easily led, obstinate and wonderfully ignorant, bigoted but prepared to sacrifice anything for effect, proud of his preaching & unconscious of its defects, worshipping the good opinion of others, & jealously excluding every influence which either directly or indirectly could be a rival to his own.

On the whole the rector was not well fitted for his post. Had he been a layman his character would more or less have been hammered into ~~conformity with his surroundings~~ some measure of improvement **[2]** by the steam hammer of circumstance. His self-conceit would perhaps have been destroyed or at least rendered less offensive if his ignorance had been brought home to him by contact with other men. **But as Rector of Clarkleigh he was placed in a position exactly calculated to develope & make inveterate all his characteristic faults**. The clerical life is admirably adapted to create the most contradictory types of character. On the one hand it forms the pedestal on which the good man may be elevated into sainthood: on the other it acts as a platform upon which the weak man, the vain, & the bad may exhibit to the world his faults.

[3]

The Rev. Richard Andrew was not a bad man: but a weak one, subjected to unwholesome influences.

The essence of the clerical position is its lofty responsibility: but that has a two-fold influence on character. On the one hand it humiliates & saddens, on the other it elevates & dignifies. In some men both these results appear in their due correlation – then we have a true saint a S. Anselm or a S. Hugh: but more often we observe that one or other of these results has an exaggerated position: and in the place of saints, the world beholds autocrats or fools. – despots or cringing serfs – priests or "shepherds".

[4]

The rector of Clarkleigh would, if he had been free to display himself truly, have appeared as an autocrat, despot, priest, but the peculiar condition of his parish forced him to suppress himself. It made him a hypocrite.

Clarkleigh was by no means an ideal parish. As far as morality is concerned it was probably neither worse nor better than most parishes. It had, perhaps, rather more than the average number of public houses, and hence was not distinguished for temperance: but on the whole one could not complain. The monstrous vices of cities were not found, for the causes which generate civic vice did not exist.

[5]

But while the morality of Clarkleigh was hardly to be complained of, its orthodoxy was at a very low ebb. The inhabitants were habituated to schism: they had lost all sense of church-membership.

Sect followed sect in raising its chapel, and organizing its ministry. Sect split off from sect as if revelling in the fresh delight of unbounded schismatic liberty. Social anathemas multiplied with the sects: the whole social life of Clarkleigh was honeycombed with sectarian bitterness.

Solidarity there was none in the place. Religious life only stirred in the direction of subdivision of existing sects, & introduction of new ones.

[6]

Now the Rev. Richard Andrew was a pronounced Anglican. He was far too ignorant to justify his position on grounds of history or theology: but **he had a profound admiration for the mysterious position of a Roman priest: and therefore "took up" with the nearest parallel within his own Church**.

To the Anglican mind nothing presents an aspect more grievous and irritating than the sight of sects. It grieves by the historical reminiscences it brings up: it irritates by the unreasonableness of its present attitude. Dissent is the veritable "thorn in the flesh" of the Anglican. His relations to the Roman church [7] are theoretically friendly: and it is only occasionally that this theory receives a sharp reminder that its practical value is not great: but towards Dissent his logical position is simply one of internecine war. The desire of his heart is the annihilation of Dissent.

He may "for practical purposes" assume towards Dissenters a genial and sympathetic attitude; but behind these deceptive exhibitions which as a rule have their chief effect in degrading his own churchmanship & marring the efficiency of his own work, there **exists in its unmitigated sternness, the fact that his sole wish with regard to Dissent is to see it annihilated**.

[8]

There is a natural tendency among many excellent persons to minimize all differences between the church & the sects. It is questionable how far such conduct is even prudent. Honourable it cannot be. It must be better for both that the real nature of the difference between them should be known and frankly acknowledged. The present system has some undeniably bad results. It not only tends to conceal the truth, but directly countenances error. It creates or continues an artificial relation between the belligerent parties, which must some day terminate with disastrous results.

[9]

What then are the real relations which exist between the Anglican Church & the sects? **They are those of fundamental difference**. There is so much ambiguity in current religious phraseology, that some definition of terms is here necessary. When we speak of the Church, we mean the Church of England considered not as a state organisation for public worship, but as a branch of the Holy Catholic Church. It is the more necessary to insist upon this, because probably the majority of churchmen do not recognise at all, or only recognise insufficiently this all-important distinction. The Dissenters [10] insist upon regarding the church merely & exclusively as a State Organisation for Public Worship: a sect which has been set apart & endowed with a national position & enriched with national funds by the National Parliament. Take away these privileges & endowments & the Dissenters readily extend the hand of patronising fellowship to a brother sect, no longer obnoxious.

Here then is one fundamental difference between Anglicans & Dissenters – they look upon the Church from different standpoints: when they talk of the church they mean different things. But the difference is even more fundamental. [11] The difference between their conceptions of the Anglican Church is only the outward manifestation of the deeper difference between their whole ~~ideal of Christianity. To the Anglican the work of Christ's~~ conception of a church.

[12]

Two questions present themselves: the answers to which determine our religious position

1. What is the Church?
2. Where is the Church?

The first question is more or less theoretical, the second is painfully practical.

[13] [Sketch of a man's profile: overleaf, the following.]

Causes of the Low State of the Church in Liverpool & Birkenhead.

1. Presence of the Irish
2. Paucity of Varsity men
3. Rapid growth of population
4. Presence of a great body of intellectual dissenters
5. General commercial atmosphere of the place

[14]

Tuesday, May 12th, 1885.

Looked up Watson[1] & found him reading the Odyssey! We went round his parish: which to be sure is sufficiently monotonous. Long straight streets of 2 storied houses peopled by dockyard-workman and artisans – side lanes narrower & dirtier – pavements covered with unclean women & children – filled with Irish. These latter form a great part of the population, & with them the clergy have no dealings whatsoever. Further, Watson says there is a huge lot of Welsh people here who can't speak English, & who are Dissenters to a man: almost necessarily for there is no Church service in Welsh. Deducting Irish Papists, Welsh Dissenters, & English Dissenters there remains probably scarcely more than 1/3rd of the population to be ministered to by the Church.

[15]

Watson took me to his church, and what a church – blue whitewash & stucco – with hideous plaster Angels presiding over the hideous columns. No cross or candle-sticks on the altar which, to be sure, is not of first rate importance, yet, just as a protest against the building they ought to be there. And that is the only Anglican Church in Birkenhead![2] and Liverpool in just as bad a state, or worse if that be possible.

Moreover Watson took me to the ruins of an Abbey, part of which are Norman[3] – the mass seemed decorated, but was a mere fragment – yet how precious in this modern

---

[1] Edward William Watson (1859–1936; *WWW*, *CCD*, *AO*), St John's Coll., Oxford (1st class Classical Mods.; 2nd class Lit. Hum.; 1st class Modern History); ord. 1885; curate, Holy Trinity, Birkenhead, 1885–7, and St Paul's Chester, 1887–8; professor of ecclesiastical history, King's College, London, 1904–8; canon of Christ Church, Oxford, and professor of ecclesiastical history, Oxford, 1908–34.

[2] Holy Trinity, Price Street, Birkenhead, opened in 1840 and closed in 1975. Contrary to Henson's claim, it was not 'the only Anglican Church in Birkenhead'; the others were St Mary's, the mother church, St Anne's, St John's, St James', St Paul's, St Peter's and St Matthew's.

[3] Henson was mistaken that this was an abbey. He is referring to Birkenhead Priory, a Benedictine order founded probably in the 1170s. In 1330, Edward III granted the Priory exclusive right to run the ferry across the Mersey and to charge tolls. This was the basis of its wealth. The parish church of Birkenhead, St Mary's, was built in 1819–21 immediately east of the ruined priory. This would have functioned fully in Henson's time. The church was closed and in 1975 most of it was demolished, leaving the tower and the west face, including the transepts as a broad screen.

2 Interior of Holy Trinity Church, Birkenhead, taken before demolition in 1970: nave to East, see 1: **15**. Royal Commission on Historical Monuments of England, Historic England Archive.

wilderness of workshops, little houses, artisans, & Low Churchmen. Even here, new as the place is **[16]** there may be met with some gross cases of overcrowding. Watson told me of a case he met with the other day. Father, son of 21, daughter of 16, &, I think 2 younger children living & sleeping in <u>one</u> room. The mother had recently died: and no doubt in the Irish streets there are many worse cases to be met with.

Moreover the Middleman exists in all his abominable oppressiveness. Laird[4] told me of a case wherein the Middleman paid rent £10, & extracted over £80.

---

[4] Two of the sons of John Laird (1805–74; *ODNB*)–Birkenhead's first MP, and son of William Laird –were politically active in the town for many years. John Laird Jnr (1834–98) served on the council from Incorporation as a borough in 1877 until 1898. He was mayor of Birkenhead from 1877 to 1878, and 1878 to 1879 and then again from 1885 to 1886. His brother William Laird (1831–99) served on the council from 1877 to 1899. He was mayor of Birkenhead from 1880 to 1881 and from 1881 to 1882 and then from 1886 to 1887. John Laird Jnr represented the Claughton ward which was then a much more prosperous ward than the Argyle ward represented by his brother William Laird. The probabilities suggest that, as the Argyle ward was 'downtown', and the parish of Holy Trinity likewise, that Henson would have been referring here to conversations with William Laird.

The dockyard labourers who load & unload ships are tyrannised over by a sort of middlemen called "stevedors [*sic*]". the name sounds Slavonic

[17]

Stevedores are of two classes. First there is the contractor who loads & unloads ships. Secondly there are foremen, two of whom preside over each gang, & who are really only superior workmen, receiving ½ as much again in wages as the rest.

Watson had a conversation with an "Echo"[5] boy. This youth made 10$^{\underline{d}}$ on "good nights". He paid 4½ per doz. for the Echoes: thus earning 1½ on every doz that he sold. Thus to make a profit of 10$^{\underline{d}}$ he would sell about 7 doz. This seems a great number especially when one thinks of the great number of men, women, boys, & girls who are engaged in selling the "Echo".

[18]

What is the importance of Dogma? What is the value of the Creed? What does disbelief in the Creed involve?[6] **Is it a sin to disbelieve the Creed? Is Belief in the Creed a sine qua non for Salvation? If so, what ought our attitude to be towards non-believers**?

Is it satisfactory to say that given a ^definite^ creed exists, given that the Nicene symbol embodies that creed, that the importance & value of holding the Nicene Creed is merely that which belongs to the possession of the truth about religion? That there is no necessity to believe the creed in order to be saved, but only a distinct advantage in doing so? Thus non-believers in the creed would appear in a more or less disadvantageous **[19]** position. They possess the truth only in part, or combined with error. In fact, they haven't reached the first standard.

This attitude might be possible if one only had the creed to deal with: but alas **the creed cannot be isolated from its basis of authority, the Church**. What is the meaning & value of membership? How are we to treat Dissenters?

1. Did Christ found a Church in the ordinary sense at all?
2. What is the nature, constitution, & function of that Church?
3. Where is that Church?

[20]

I do most sympathetically protest against the conduct of many Anglican clergy in that they abuse the word "Church" sadly. Let us take heed not to be deceived.[7] It

---

[5] The *Liverpool Echo* was launched in 1879 by Alexander Jeans. It was the evening paper to the *Liverpool Daily Post* which was launched in 1855 by Michael James Whitty (1795–1873; *ODNB*).

[6] These questions anticipate the controversy raised by Henson's suggestion in 1903 that subscription to the creeds of the church should cease to be a condition of ordination: *Sincerity and subscription: a plea for toleration in the Church of England* (London, 1903), pp. 19–46. He was duly denounced by the bishop of London, Arthur Foley Winnington-Ingram (1858–1946; *ODNB*), from the pulpit of Ely Cathedral.

[7] Gal. 6:7: 'Be not deceived; God is not mocked; for whatsoever a man soweth, that shall he also reap.'

is one thing to believe in the adequacy of the Authority of an Æcumenical Council, it is another thing to have Pseudo-Dyonisian Angelology palmed off as a portion of the Church's teachings. In fact many of the more ignorant Anglicans seem to consider that the authority of the Church is centred in the individual priest. They talk all manner of disputable things in their pulpits, & resent any criticism of their utterances as rebellion against the authority of the church. This appears to me very much the same sort of blunders as that made by Protestants, who **[21]** predicate of the single Christian all that Christ promised to the whole Church in its collective capacity.

"We must not resign our reason, says Mackay,[8] *at all regards we must retain that fully free." Yes, I can't but think that is right: yet what is the province of Reason: plainly not to supersede Revelation: nor yet to tamper with Revelation. It is then a restricted province.*

I am almost tempted to confine Reason to an examination of authority. Reason may ask "why do I hold the Creed"? but, hardly, is the Creed true? If the authority for it be adequate, it must be true. The truth is involved in the validity & adequacy of the authority.

[22]

Monday, May 18th, 1885.

Watson took me to see an "<u>interior</u>" 3 storied house: enter narrow passage, & knock at door. Dirty woman opens, & we pass thro' to a little stair-case about 2 feet wide, & go to the floor above: where – in one small low room – dwells an old woman – sailor's widow. As we enter she is bending over the tiny grate cooking over some sticks some abominable-looking pieces of fat bacon. The window is happily open: & a lot of flowers –faded – are in tumblers – broken of course. In the corner is a single bed though the old creature shares the room with 2 children, her grandchildren I think. Watson shook hands bravely, but I barred the thick layer of soot & bacon fat which covered them. This, I am told[,] is far above the average of single room tenancies.

[23]

There's a sad mystery about some of the very poor. Watson showed me a note which had just reached Sheriff.[9] It was written on a dirty page torn out of an expensive book. Yet both writing and spelling were perfectly correct: and the composition would not have disgraced a lady. It was merely a request that the Rector would call & see a daughter, who was dying. Watson says that the poor woman speaks excellent English without a touch of dialect. Who can say what mystery is here?

---

[8] Henry Falconar Barclay Mackay (1864–1936; *WWW*), Merton Coll., Oxford; ord. 1888 (Cuddesdon); curate, All Saints, Margaret Street, London, 1889–91, and vicar, 1908–34; described as 'one of the most influential of the anglo-catholic clergy in his time': *Times*, 21 Apr. 1936, 16.

[9] Thomas Holmes Sheriff (1855–1923; *WWW*), MA (Cantab.), ord. 1877, vicar, Holy Trinity, Birkenhead, 1883–7; lived at 15, Hamilton Square; surrogate of Chester diocese, 1885; vicar, St Paul's Stalybridge, 1887–1923; hon. canon, Chester Cathedral, 1911; friend of Bishop Stubbs and of his successor, Bishop Jayne (*Church Times*, 30 Nov. 1923).

The dreadful thing about these very poor is that there is just one step, only one, between respectability & the abyss. And poor things! Their livelihood is terribly uncertain. And just now the depression in trade is causing awful suffering.

[24]

Probably between 2 & 3000 men are without employment from the practical stopping of Laird's Yard. It is the same in the other yards. A great section of the people are always confined to the moral degradation of living on odd jobs: now there is not work enough to keep the ordinary hands busy.

Surely something must be wrong somewhere in the body politic, that this state of things should exist. I'm afraid if I stay here for the next 6 months I shall become a Socialist. As it is I'm beginning to reconsider my life projects. But I will try not to be rash: & old Watson, who's as cautious as brave, shall show me some more interiors.

[25]

Wallasey is blessed with a fine new church: and the tower of an old one. The old church was burnt somewhere about 30 years ago.[10] The parson's an Anglican,[11] **more pronounced than ever since Stubbs' arrival**.[12] Got eastward position since that happy event. From Wallasey churchyard there's a splendid view of the open sea, & the Estuaries of the Dee & Mersey: the Welsh Hills look very fine.

[26]

Tuesday, May 19th, 1885.

I went to dine with the Hubbacks[13] at New Ferry. Returning by tram I found myself the sole occupant of the vehicle. Accordingly I **began to talk to the conductor, a boy of about 15**. He told me that he worked from 9 to 11.30 every day, Sundays (with a few

---

[10] St Hilary's, Claremount Road, Wallasey Village. The medieval church was destroyed by fire in 1857; its thirteenth-century tower remains, while the new church was built at the top of the churchyard in 1858–9.

[11] Andrew Edward Phillimore Gray (1853–95), Brasenose Coll., Oxford; ord. 1877; rector, Wallasey, 1885; son of Robert Henry Gray (1818–85), Christ Church, Oxford, rector of Kirkby, Liverpool, 1850–85, and canon of Chester Cathedral, 1867. Henson seems to consider only a certain type of Anglican as an Anglican proper, i.e. high church Anglican.

[12] William Stubbs (1825–1901; *ODNB*), historian and bishop of Oxford from 1888 until his death; regius professor of modern history, 1866–84; bishop of Chester, 1884–8; editor of *Select charters and other illustrations of English constitutional history from the earliest times to the reign of Edward I* (Oxford, 1870); author of *The constitutional history of England in its origins and development* (3 vols., Oxford, 1873–8). Henson was taught by Stubbs at Oxford: sermon preached on the fiftieth anniversary of his ordination, Trinity Sunday, 1937, Durham Cathedral, in *Ad clerum* (London, 1937), p. 49.

[13] John Henry Hubback (1844–1939), corn merchant, lived with his wife, three children and four servants at Oak Lawn, 34, Stanley Road, New Ferry (1881 census). His grandfather was Sir Francis Austen, brother of Jane Austen. His son, Sir John Austen Hubback (1878–1968), was the first governor of Orissa (now Odisha) in India.

exceptions) included. He had no holidays. He was a Catholic. His parents were Irish. His father was an Irishman & had been 9 mos [months] out of work. He received for his work on the tramcar 15/–. The driver 27/– per week. I asked him what he hoped to rise to & he said he didn't know. He felt awfully tired & when he **[27]** got home he went off to bed, & slept until he had to get back to the tram. He was not supposed to sit down at all through the day. If he did so he was liable to fines or dismissal. I had ascertained this much when our conversation was broken up by the entrance of passengers. For the rest of the way I mused, & when I got out I gave him 2/6: because I was so sorry for him: & he was so unfairly treated. 14½ hours work and no holidays! God help me: but this is a monstrous & an abominable thing.

[28]

If I could get a satisfactory attitude towards Protestants I would take up definitely the Anglican position. As it is I can't see any escape from the logical anathema. *This would not be so hard to arrange if the Anglican Church were in communion with the rest of the Church Catholic: but standing alone what is the value of her anathema, what is the moral justification for such an inadequate curse. In fact I am rather alarmed at the position of the Anglican Church. If only the Roman Anathema were removed it would be tolerable but now it is wretched. Cut off from sympathy with the only people who will have dealings with us, we have to rest content with an imaginary Catholicism & a theoretical communion.*

[29]

I wonder whether I shall turn out a Broad Churchman after all. *I'm awfully bored at being considered a Rit:* & *I can't complain if people put the only reasonable interpretation on my words. If they knew me better they wouldn't do so, but as it is, it is hardly blameworthy.* **I do feel caught in a perfect net. I've played with the Catholic idea so long to spite the Low Church people that I can't resume my freedom now I want to do so.** *The idea of the Church has seized me, and I can't shake it off: and yet I worship intellectual freedom: & I suspect – & the suspicion gains force – that if I am to be a "Catholic" I must say goodbye to my intellectual freedom.*

[30]

Watson says that I shall become a Roman Catholic unless I take care: he blames me for thinking so much about these bothering questions of the bases of the creed, & the meaning of the Church &c: practical work will bring about a cure. I don't know what to do. Watson seems to me quite illogical: and astonishingly happy: laughs at poor me cruelly: and yet what can I do? There's an awful lot to swallow in becoming Roman: and even the gain doesn't seem certain: yet the loneliness of the Anglican position is tormenting.

[31]

In sober verity I am in a perplexing position. From 6 in the morning until 5 in the evening Lyle[14] is engaged in the shop. After he returns he must wash, get a meal, take some open-air exercise and go to bed about 9. **Clearly there is very little time left for study**.

The question for me to answer is twofold[.]

1. How much time can I extract out of Lyle for study?
2. How can that time best be utilized?

Now with regard to getting time for study the difficulties are very great: at most about an hour from 8 to 9 can be counted on. How ought that hour to be employed? It is obvious that the question must be answered by a reference to Lyle's special needs.

So far as I can now see, he is **[32]** singularly lacking in continuity in interest. He blows hot & cold alternately. It seems advisable then that some continuous work should be undertaken so as at least to try to force him to carry his interest from day to day on one subject.

Further, that will be an historical subject (1.) because for his station in life a knowledge of history will be extremely valuable (2.) because the study of history is the subject which I can, & which I undertook to teach.

What then, shall be the continuous subject in history which shall form the basis of our work? And in respect of this question I enquire (1.) What will be most useful, and (2.) What will be best calculated to arouse & sustain Lyle's interest.

[33]

After such thought as I could give to the point it seemed to me that the wisest course to take was viz – to begin and go through English History in the most entertaining way possible. The attempt has scarcely yet been fairly tried, but certainly, as yet, there is small prospect of success.

[34]

Kuno Meyer[15] *is an ardent Bismarkian with a healthy scorn for English constitutional ideas. Dear to his soul is the military system. Many who flee from it are feeble, and*

---

[14] Acheson Lyle Rathbone (Lyle) (1868–1923). Little is known of Lyle's career, except that he served as a Liverpool city councillor later in life. At the time Henson made his acquaintance, he had been dispatched to Birkenhead to earn his living in Laird's shipyard as an apprentice. His father, concerned about his indolence and lack of aspiration, had engaged Henson on the recommendation of Sydney Ball to provide an elevating influence in his leisure time. The terms were that for six months he would live with Lyle in his rooms in Hamilton Square as a tutor and companion in return for a stipend payable at the end.

[15] Kuno Meyer (1858–1919; *WWW*), Celtic scholar and lecturer in Teutonic languages at University Coll., Liverpool, 1884–95, and professor, 1895–1915; founder of the School of Irish Learning, 1903; brother of the distinguished classical scholar, Eduard Meyer; left Britain for the United States at the outbreak of the First World War; vilified in America and Britain for stirring up anti-British sentiment

their departure a gain to the country. The army, he regards as the great unifying force. The Catholics from the south forced for 3 years to serve, side by side with the Prussians of the north. For 3 years to know no leader but the Emperor are in spite of themselves compelled to be loyal. To the army Germany owes her attitude of repose: the fact that she need not worry herself though the nations of Europe clash their weapons, & become threatening.

To honest Kuno we English people are strangely incomprehensible **[35]** with an [*sic*] uniquely glorious Empire, and no interest in it. There is not the intensity of national feeling among Englishmen, it would seem, as there is among the Germans and the French.

Parliamentary Government in Germany would never work. To begin with the people have had no long constitutional training. Then the majority of the Reichstag is Catholic and anti-Prussian. If the unity of Germany be an object to be conserved at all hazards: if that unity be bound up with the supervising of Prussia – then a free Reichstag cannot be thought of until a Prussian majority can be secured. When that will be no one can say. The army will make it possible.

[36]

"In Germany["], quoth Kuno, "we date everything from 1870. *You English don't understand that, because you have a long history behind you: but we haven't. Old people are to us quite out of practical politics. Many of them hate the present régime. Many had their own little plans before 1870, they can't consent to see that Bismark's plan was the only possible one.*["]

Kuno looks forward with some anxiety to the death of the Emperor. The Crown Prince doesn't like old Bismarck, & then the Liberals and Reactionaries (strange combination) will have their chance.

[37]

Trinity Sunday, May 31ˢᵗ, 1885.

I persuaded Mackay to accompany me to S. Agnes[16] for evening service. A stranger preached. I ascertained afterwards that his name was Clark. He was a well-built man, apparently the shady side of 50, with a rasping, unpleasant voice, and an offensive manner. He took for his text, "And who is my neighbour" – he preached "extempore". After a slip-shod, rambling account of the parable: he told us that England had reached her zenith some years ago & was now on the decline: quoted Prince Bismarck that England had had 200 years the rule of other nations.

---

in Ireland in speeches and letters: 'Death of Kuno Mayer: the German professor at war', *Times*, 15 Oct. 1919, 11.
[16] St Agnes, Toxteth Park, Liverpool; consecrated in 1885 and built by Douglas Horsfall in memory of his father Robert Horsfall; interior modelled on Truro Cathedral.

[38]

Emigration he incidentally informed us was the curse of the evils which weighed us down. Then he returned to the idea of his text, and urged the claims of the poor as human beings & ergo our neighbours. The reason for England's greatness was the fidelity with which she performed her neighbourly duties e.g. to the negroes.

The scandalous indecencies of this man's discourse cannot be recollected. They were infamous, and made me furious, and Mackay sardonic. [later insertion] *(Aug 14th 1885)*

[39]

Saturday, June 6th, 1885.

Saw Kuno Meyer at Mackay's room. He was well started on philology, talking away at a terrible pace; I can't help laughing out at him but he takes it in excellent good part & is never offended at anything goodhumoured [sic]. I asked him as to the numbers who attended his lectures. He said that he got nobody at all for Celtic and Anglo-Saxon, for German, 15 or thereabouts. These latter are mostly persons who have knowledge of German – in some cases are Germans, or half Germans. There seems room for surprise that so few people attend. There are hosts in Liverpool.

[40]

Meyer, like Mackay, finds the want of a good library a great hindrance to work. Thus Lesley Stephens [sic] asked Meyer to write Lives of Irish saints for his Dictionary of Biography(?).[17] Meyer consented: but had to withdraw from his engagement by want of materials. Then he was asked to find a substitute. He wrote to a German friend in a German University: and the reply he got was a regretful refusal for lack of materials. It really is a great shame for the University to be without such indispensable things as the Rolls Series,[18] the corresponding series in France & Germany, Migne[19] &c. They form part of the necessary machinery of our University.

[41]

Meyer is editing some Irish romance for the Clarendon press.[20] It is to appear very shortly. He seems rather disgusted with the work. The M.S. is 15th century, & copied – so the modern character of the Irish compels one to think – from one not much older.

Meyer says that 6 Pictish words have been discovered.

[17] Leslie Stephen (1832–1904; *ODNB*), distinguished man of letters and first editor of the *Dictionary of national biography*, 1881–91.
[18] *The chronicles and memorials of Great Britain and Ireland during the middle ages*, commonly known as the Rolls Series, published as 99 works in 253 volumes between 1858 and 1911, under the direction of the Master of the Rolls. William Stubbs edited 19 volumes.
[19] Jacques Paul Migne (1800–75), French Catholic priest who made accessible through cheap editions a wide range of theological and other works relating to the church to equip priests with a universal library.
[20] *Merugad uilix maice leirtis: the Irish Odyssey*, ed. with English translation, notes and glossary by Kuno Meyer (London, 1886).

Also that the Flemish colony in S. Wales has left no traces on the language.

Also that Caesar's treatment of Celtic names – making them of different declensions – was not arbitrary: but followed a Celtic arrangement by the root vowel, closely analogous with the Latin.

[42]

1st Sunday after Trinity, June 7th, 1885.

I have failed completely: and I don't wonder at it. There are causes enough for failure. The conditions under which the arrangement had to work made success difficult. Lyle's character and mine made it impossible. He is vain, rude, stupid & lazy: without any desire to learn: nor any appreciation of his Father's liberality; nor any grasp of my position. To him it appears a monstrous injustice to demand that he should work after his day's toil – me as the concrete embodiment of that injustice he holds in detestation. If it were not for my hated presence, he would be free to enjoy himself with the other apprentices.

[43]

This afternoon I went to the Salvation Army Barracks. The room was not in the least full: in fact it was nearly empty. The Captain (Gore) informed us that the attendance was the smallest he ever remembered. This seems strange considering that this was the farewell meeting of the Captain. The proceedings began with a blare of trumpets, followed by a prayer by the Captain's wife, then one by the Captain, then one by a young woman, & another from a middle-aged man. The last was a most passionate performance. This soldier engaged[,] flung himself into various attitudes & shouted.

[44]

His excitement evoked that of the rest of the band. Shouts of Amen, Alleluia &c broke in again & again. The whole "service" appears to consist of two parts (1.) in which the officers are the principal actors (2.) when the meeting is thrown open for experience. Some variety is caused by solos interspersed at intervals. Mrs Gore read the 10th ch. of the Acts, and commented as she read. One remark of hers was repeated by several other speakers, viz that **General Booth[21] only failed when man came between him & God**: which remark was simplified into something like infallibility. The Experiences were very tame indeed.

[45]

One individual announced that he was 75 years old: 73 years he had served the devil – "That was pretty well – wasn't it" – groans – now he was a member of the Salvation Army – Halleluia.

---

[21] William Booth (1829–1912; *ODNB*), founder of the Salvation Army in 1878.

One speaker said that he had always regarded the Army as a nuisance in the former times. Now what was the object of the army? What was the good of all this marchin, & drummin, & singin & preachin & prayin. If they looked beyond all that what should they see – loud shouts of God. "Ah. I love him with all my heart."

[46]

After the service I made up to the Captain and asked him about the work. **He said that Birkenhead was the worst place he had worked in: the results of his labour were abnormally small**: moreover many people who seemed "softened on the penitent form, lost their grace almost as soon as they left the barracks".

Had the Clergy been friendly? No, far from it. I asked about Sacraments. "We don't allow them now, replied the captain, we used to, but found them abused so the Army decided to abandon them completely.["] Personally he regretted the fact, but no doubt it was necessary. However the Salvation Army don't refuse baptism by [47] immersion to adults. Infant baptism was quite unscriptural. "I have been baptised, I felt the need of it first." I enquired whether the army intended to continue in Birkenhead, & if so, how they kept their people together. He said that the Army certainly intended to continue & had purchased their hall: their chief means of keeping people together were constant services and visiting. 17 services held, & 60 families visited every week. "Look at me. I am only 34: yet already an old man: 7 years work has nearly worn me out. The Lord's work is not easy." I then asked about the army generally. Hereupon he [48] became at once enthusiastic. The Salvation army was destined to evangelize the world, to do what never had yet been done – the "work of the Acts". The General's death would not hinder the work; there were plenty in "the Family" to continue his power. Had Booth any doctrinal positions? No, there was a "Schoolmaster": and a Catechism was used: otherwise the offices were doctrinally free.

[49]

Monday, June 8th, 1885.

I went out with Watson to see Wood Church, about 4 miles from Birkenhead. It is a perpendicular building, low pitched with hateful modern windows, some fragments of excellent 15th century carving in the choir stalls, a modern screen of very simple design. The tower is supported by 2 huge, unsightly buttresses projecting from the angles, & looking like flights of difficult stairs. Over the porch there was an empty niche. Also, in the Church, fastened to the west wall of the South aisle there were 2 small carved oak cases – like little book-cases – on which there was an inscription declaring them to be the gifts of certain individuals, & [50] the date was added – c. middle of 17th century. I suggested to Watson that they might be relics of the old parochial library.

On my way to Mackay I was on a tram and lighting on a sociable old fellow plainly a merchant. He told me that Lewis[22] (that enemy of Gods & men) had paid £1000 a

---

[22] David Lewis (1823–85; *ODNB*), retailer and philanthropist, who started in business in Ranelagh Street, Liverpool, in 1846, selling men's and boys' clothes made in his own workshop; built up a chain of 'universal provider' stores in the north of England, the prototype of the modern department store; shrewd in his advertising tactics.

year for the monopoly of advertising on the cars: that he had done so for several years until he had gained the notoriety he wanted; then he made difficulties about payment and ceased to advertise in that manner. I commiserated the hard fate of car-drivers & conductors, and delivered a diatribe against share-holders. He evidently suspected my **[51]** designs at that: and said that if the men didn't like their work there were plenty who would be glad to take their place: as to the share-holders they had no responsibility, the directors alone were responsible.

Then I made mention of the proposed cathedral. Would it be ever built? My companion smiled incredulously and said there was no money. The site, too, was bad because it was in a low neighbourhood; "of course, we are all sinners, (with another incredulous smile) but then they <u>are</u> sinners down there". The bp. too was a very good man, but nobody seemed to like him.[23] He wasn't "High" enough for one thing: & his public utterances were offensive.

[52]

Tuesday, June 9th 1885.

I made my way to the Picton Public Reading Room,[24] and asked for Palgrave's Normandy.[25] It was not in the Library. In my opinion the promoters of education in Liverpool should without delay remedy this great want viz. of a really efficient Library. Good work is nearly rendered impossible without that.

Wednesday, June 10th, 1885.

Watson has discovered an abominable piece of tyranny on the part of the "stevedores mirrores [*sic*]**"**. They simply levy blackmail on the men. There are always a number of men out of work. These precious stevedores cause the work that turns up to be given to those men who pay them 6$\underline{d}$ a day out **[53]** of their wages (4/–) as commission. It is difficult to see how this patent piece of oppression could be put down. Nothing less than an organised opposition of all the men would suffice.[26]

---

[23] John Charles Ryle (1816–1900; *ODNB*), prominent evangelical and first bishop of Liverpool, 1880. An act of parliament in 1885 authorized the building of a cathedral on the site of St John's Church adjoining St. George's Hall; but this proved unsuitable and plans for a cathedral were abandoned. Following the appointment of the second bishop in 1900 – Francis James Chavasse (1846–1928; *ODNB*) – and a new act of parliament, work began on the present site on St James Mount in 1902 to a design by Sir Giles Gilbert Scott; it was completed in 1978.

[24] The Picton Reading Room was built between 1875 and 1879 as part of the set of splendid public buildings on one side of St George's Hall (opened in 1854). The Room's circular plan resembled that of the British Museum's Reading Room, completed in 1857. It was named after Sir James Picton (1805–89), chairman of the William Brown Library and Museum in the city, and designed by Cornelius Sherlock (1823–88).

[25] Francis Palgrave, *The history of Normandy and of England* (4 vols., London, 1851–64).

[26] The exploitation of casual labour described by Henson continued until Ernest Bevin (1881–1951; *ODNB*) began his offensive through the formation of the Transport and General Workers' Union. The Dock Workers (Regulations of Employment) Act in 1946 that resulted from this endeavour outlawed casual labour in the docks. Bevin became minister of labour in Churchill's wartime coalition government and foreign secretary in the post-war Attlee government.

In the evening I went to the school room[27] **and gave a short mission address on Heb 12. 1,2**[28] **to the scanty assemblage which had come together**. Afterwards – having heroically shaken hands with some appalling old creatures – I went with Watson to Sherriff and had a long talk on church affairs. **I am sorry to find that he can bring himself to regard without horror the prospect of disestablishment & disendowment**.

[54]

Saturday, June 13th, 1885.

I went out with Watson for a walk. He took me to some really beautiful country – Upper Bebington or thereabouts I think. We actually succeeded in losing sight for a few moments of that torturing sequence of red brick houses. There was a splendid quarry of sand-stone, deep, long, & broken, with its upper cliff covered with fir trees, in a deep, dense dark mass.

[55]

Tuesday, June 16th, 1885.

A wet day until 4 o'clock. Watson came in and we went for a stroll round the docks. Encountering Capt<u>n</u> Wilson, the dock master, an ex-merchant captain, we had a chat with him about the shipping and the docks. He has to be at his post when the tides allow the docks to be opened for the ingress or egress of vessels. Hence it results that he scarcely ever gets 3 full nights rest in a fortnight. We saw some wooden sailing vessels unloading their cargo – wheat. It was brought over in bags, which were weighed, and then emptied on to the floor of the warehouses. Of these we saw several heaped high with corn: such a sight as one can conceive of in an Oriental country, where the Government [56] granaries would be bursting with the offerings in kind, wrung from the myriads of toiling serfs, by the exertions of an immemorial & half-religious despotism.

These docks are a marvellous sight. One huge & hideous brick erection contains the engines which work the whole of the machinery of the network of docks. The quays are appropriated to various trades e.g. cattle, &c have their respective quays. One noteworthy feature of the scene is the perfect fleet of "flats" which come with salt from Cheshire, and Merchandise from Manchester.

Watson abuses the Fathers in a shameless manner, as possessing "neither grammar, sense, nor style". He accuses them of obscuring the faith by their orthodox labours.

---

[27] The school still exists at the entrance to Birkenhead Park and is now called Priory Parish Church of England School.

[28] 'Wherefore seeing we also are compassed about with so great a cloud of witnesses, let us lay aside every weight, and the sin which doth so easily beset *us*, and let us run with patience the race that is set before us, Looking unto Jesus the author and finisher of *our* faith; who for the joy that was set before him endured the cross, despising the shame, and is set down at the right hand of the throne of God.'

[57]

I can't understand this. Watson is orthodox himself, though inclined to give & claim the largest liberty in some departments. I adore liberty, but Athanasius[29] dominates me. *But compare him with oily, bombastic, collapsible Eusebius Pamphili.[30] The sight of them side by side would be a tableau of the Temptation.[31]*

[58]

Wednesday, June 17th, 1885.

Agricultural show somewhere beyond Oxton. **I went with the Rathbones** and observed with ignorant wonder the beasts & the machinery.

In the evening I took the Mission Service for Watson, who had to preach at St Anne's. Sheriff is at Southport with his mother. My text was S. John 8.12.[32] and I talked for about 20 minutes. They listen extremely well – these Birkenhead people.

The shaking hands with them afterward is a painful performance, but no doubt, highly politic. In the process I acquired that which has troubled me since, but happily been slain this morning in a glutted condition.[33]

[59]

Thursday, June 18th, 1885.

I went with Watson for a walk all round the docks. I am gradually getting to know my way about them. First comes the Morpeth dock where the big steamers load. Then the Wallasey dock. Then the Albert dock which leads into the Great Eastern Float, beyond which is the Great Western Float. All these have been formed out of a tidal brook called Wallasey Brook, which formed the boundary of Wallasey parish & ran into the Mersey.

The Western Float was very lively this afternoon. One ship was loading with salt, probably for India, from where she will return with a cargo of wheat. Another **[60]** was being loaded with Guano – bags upon bags were emptied into here. Another was receiving Copper ore, and another was being unloaded of her burden of some sort of stone.

In the dry or "growing" docks there were 3 "cargo boats" being done up – one was a wooden 3 master: one was a "China boat" and the other was a big steamer. I forgot

---

[29] Athanasius of Alexandria (b. 296–8, d. 373), archbishop of Alexandria; defended Trinitarianism against the Arians; regarded as one of the four great theologians of the East in the Roman catholic church.
[30] Eusebius Pamphili (b. 260–5, d. 339/40), bishop of Caesarea, theologian and historian.
[31] The Temptation of Christ during his forty days in the desert.
[32] John 8:12: 'Then spake Jesus again unto them, saying, "I am the light of the world: he that followeth me shall not walk in darkness, but shall have the light of life."'
[33] Henson could have meant an aversion to hand shaking with strangers, undoubtedly due to fastidiousness, which he recognized could no longer be maintained in a public role. That 'slain this morning' is presumably a flea.

> June 18th 1885;—
> I went with Watson for a walk all round the docks. I am gradually getting to know my way about them. First comes the Morpeth dock where the big steamers load. Then the Wallasey dock. Then the Albert dock which leads into the great Eastern Float, beyond which is the great Western Float. All these have been formed out of a tidal brook called Wallasey Brook, which formed the boundary of Wallasey parish & ran into the Mersey. The Western Float was very lively this afternoon. One ship was unloading with salt, probably for India, from whence she will return with a cargo of wheat. Another

3 Journal, vol. 1, 18 June 1885, 59–60: dock scenes, Birkenhead, see 1: **59–60**. Durham Cathedral Library.

was being loaded with Guano — bags upon bags were emptied into here. Another was receiving copper ore, and another was being unloaded of her burden of some sort of stone. In the dry or "graving" docks there were 3 "cargo boats" being done up. — one was a wooden 3 master; one was a "China boat" and the other was a big steamer. I forgot to say that an old wooden 3 master was unloading a lot of barrels of petroleum from the United States. Side by side with all this activity the thing which strikes one most is the terrible amount of enforced idleness. Lots of men are sitting & standing about the quays waiting for work.

to say that an old wooden 3 master was unloading a lot of barrels of petroleum from the United States. ***Side by side with all this activity the thing which strikes one most is the terrible amount of enforced idleness***. *Lots of men are sitting & standing about the quays waiting for work.*

[61]

Saturday, June 20th, 1885.

Watson took me to see Makin,[34] the official of the Charity Organisation Society.[35] He is a very intelligent and interesting person, whose speech is quite free from any obedience to the laws of pronunciation, yet is seasoned with strangely original expressions and quaint constructions. He is full of information about the poor: and full of indignation against the ignorant & undiscriminating charity of the pious. **"Giving ought to be made a punishable crime."** He says that the worst cases come from people who earn good wages: in fact that not actual poverty, but rather want of thrift creates the demand for assistance. He gave us some **[62]** frightful descriptions of filth e.g. the case of a single room tenement so dominated by vermin as to compel self-defensive action on the part of the inhabitants of the house. The door had to be stopped up to prevent the egress of the creatures in question. One woman – a wife & a mother – could do nought motherly: she drank & smacked: and never washed herself: "it came off in cakes sometimes" that was all: she couldn't comb her hair, or if she could she didn't. The worst thing of all was the common lodging house "where they all lie down together, lads and lasses, & never take off their clothes for weeks together". Just now the idle & worthless were reaping a **[63]** wealthy harvest. "Out of work" was a very taking cry.

Sometimes the Society lent money: but often lost on the proceeding: because the borrowers rarely repaid the loans: and the Society could not prosecute because of the "Upper Few" who would withdraw their subscriptions. Thus the loans often became changed into donations in the balance sheet.

The boiler-makers won't allow a man to be taken on to work unless he is a member of their provident Society. The society allows 12/– a week for 14 weeks in the year, when men are out of work, and 3/– a week for an additional 7 weeks. This struck me as an excellent arrangement **[64]** but Makin said it gave too much power to an unfair secretary.

The docks of Birkenhead really owe their existence to the Lairds. They bought up the banks of Wallasey Brook, and resisted the jealous hostility of Liverpool. The docks on both sides of the Mersey are now under a common management. The cost of the Birkenhead docks is said to have exceeded £5,000,000 & this great outlay has

---

[34] William Makin (1853–1929); labourer (iron works); lived with his wife, two daughters and a lodger in Meadow Street, parish of Holy Trinity (1881 census); in *Kelly's directory of Liverpool and Birkenhead* (1894), listed as agent to the Birkenhead Charity Organization Society and Provident Society, 46, Hamilton Square.

[35] The Charity Organization Society was founded in 1869 to assist the 'deserving' poor. It emphasized the link between poverty and character, and the exercise of the rational will rather than indiscriminate giving as the key to overcoming destitution. Its leading lights were Helen Bosanquet (1860–1925; *ODNB*), Octavia Hill (1838–1912; *ODNB*) and Sir Charles Stewart Loch (1849–1923; *ODNB*).

prevented Liverpool becoming a free port. For anchoring in the Mersey, the ships have to pay dues.

[65]

Thursday, June 25th, 1885.

Mackay looked me up, & brought the ghastly news that he was about to depart for Edinburgh, there to spend 3 mos [*sic*] **of his Long Vac.** We went to Egremont, & visited a perfect colony of Scots – fine fellows on the whole though besottedly attached to the G.O.M.[36] As was inevitable I got into a tremendous argument on the Church & on the late Government. This however was broken into by a walk to Wallasey, wherein there is an old inn, shortly to be pulled down. It dates from the 17th century. Here Charles II is said to have slept: though in truth, the accommodation must have **[66]** been scanty enough, for the house appears to have consisted of but 3 rooms: a parlour, with a glorious old settle & a huge chimney: a kitchen, and one bedroom above it. An old cupboard, also, of some size projected from the parlour. In a neighbouring & apparently coeval cottage the chair in which His Majesty had sat was preserved – a most ordinary piece of furniture, without any carving. I was far more struck with the 2 boys of the cottage – keen clever looking fellows – one of them had got a certificate of some sort or other hanging on the wall. Mackay of course **[67]** at once perceived this piece of unrecognised merit: and drew attention to it. The other boy who in mine eyes was much the best looking, brushed my hat for me, & received 1/– for the job, to the infinite scandal of the Scotchies, who dilated in an exhaustive manner on the servility of the English as contrasted with the independence of the North. Really I felt very much in the position of a criminal convicted of bribery. On our return to the Settlement, the political argument was fought with fierceness. Mackay backed me up, against the Scotchies: & we continued until we lost the 11.30 boat, & the result was that **[68]** I didn't get back to my rooms until close to 1 o'clock: thus annihilating the good effects of my lecture to Lyle on the duty of industry & early hours. **I must confess that these young Scots are far better fitted to push their way than the young Englishmen, who are pitted against them**. Fine fellows are they, & admirable but the most besotted Gladstonians, and the most indurated Schismatics – glorying, forsooth, in that precious Reformation of theirs as quite the bravest fact of their history: & loving that miserable church of theirs with an absolutely blind affection.

[69]

Wednesday, July 1st, 1885.

I spoke to the people at the Mission Service for about 20 minutes on Cor. 1. 27–29.[37] They are splendid listeners, but I doubt whether they understand what they hear.

---

[36] Grand Old Man: William Ewart Gladstone (1809–1898), Liberal politician and prime minister, 1868–1874, 1880–5, 1886 and 1892–4.

[37] 1 Cor. 27–9: 'But God hath chosen the foolish things of the world to confound the wise; and God hath chosen the weak things of the world to confound the things which are mighty. And base things of the world, and things which are despised, hath God chosen, *yea*, and things which are not, to bring to nought things that are.'

Afterwards I went a walk with Sheriff, and talked with him in his rooms until past midnight.

["]—Could you & I conspire to grasp the sorry scheme of things entire. Would we not shatter it to bits? & then Remould it nearer to the hearts desire.["][38]

[70]

Thursday, July 2nd, 1885.

Went with Watson to Chester by the 9.30 train, and got back by about 2: had 3 clear hours in the city. First we walked round the city walls, inspecting a little museum which filled one of the Towers, & contained amid a majority of silliest rubbish, a few relics of Roman and feudal times. The tower was built (so said the museum-keeper recipient of the 3d fees) in 1332. Then having completed the circuit of the walls we proceeded to inspect the old city itself, enclosed within them. The most astonishing thing is the system of Rows. I conceive these to be unique.

[71]

"They are formed by two lines of shops, one above the other, the upper line communicating with the street by steps, while the lower line has a covered arcade in front."

Through the city are scattered sundry ancient houses: dating for the most part from the middle of the 17th century.

Having "done" the "Rows" and Houses we went on to the Cathedral which is still in a sadly dilapidated state. S. John's Church which formerly was the Cathedral Church of the see of Chester and Lichfield, is really architecturally far more interesting, presenting a really splendid specimen of Norman work. Alas only half the church stands.

[72]

The Norman tower in its fall carried down 3 bays (eastern) and the fall of the perpendicular tower at the west end involved in destruction the early English doorway. In the East End there is a wretched modern window in a pseudo-Gothic style, put up (as said one guide) to commemorate the marriage of the prince & princess of Wales.

The crypt had been long used as the kitchen of the sector of the Church.

---

[38]   Ah, Love! could thou and I with Fate conspire
       To grasp this sorry Scheme of Things entire!
       Would not we shatter it to bits – and then
       Re-mould it nearer to the Heart's Desire!
   The Rubáiyát ['Quatrains'] *of Omar Khayyam*, transl. Edward Fitzgerald (privately printed, 1859). Khayyam was an eleventh-century Persian poet whose agnosticism resonated with Fitzgerald.

Then we returned into the city & **I bought some photographs & Gordon's diary**:[39] after which we returned to Birkenhead.

[73]

I strolled with Watson round the docks, and saw there the City of Canterbury – **the very ship in which Arthur**[40] **and Gid**[41] **went to India in April 1883: more than 2 years ago**. How slowly the time passes it seems an eternity since they went: and yet it's only 2 years or so. When they will return, God knows, not I.

I wonder whether they are much changed: sometimes I fear they may be: Arthur specially troubles me: yet I will not be hopeless, but trust that they shall be kept safe by the Lord X[t], to whom both they and I have sworn obedience not once or twice. The City of Canterbury was a finer vessel than I expected.

[74]

5th Sunday after Trinity, July 5th, 1885.

With extraordinary precautions to ensure waking, I managed to get down to 8 o'clock service. At 10', I took a class in the incipient Sunday School for ½ an hour. Very nice little boys, neatly dressed with bright clean faces (of course exceptions) a credit to their parents, all of whom are, I believe, working people of some sort or another. I do like to see the children nicely turned out: when they are left, there is little hope of the parents. If I continue to teach these little boys I shall give them all a book of some sort or other to remember me by. I wonder whether I can teach or not. Lyle has shaken my faith.

[75]

I finished Gordon's Journal today for the first time: I shall be slower going through it again, stopping to realize the connection of the ideas often as startlingly sudden in their abandonment & resumption. One thing is certain, that **Gordon was a hero**

---

[39] Charles George Gordon (1833–85; *ODNB*), army officer assassinated by Mahdist forces during the siege of Khartoum in January 1885; dispatched reluctantly to Sudan by Gladstone's government in response to the wave of popularity he enjoyed following W. H. Stead's interview with him in the *Pall Mall Gazette*; experienced an intense religious awakening in the years before his death, exacerbating his instability.

[40] Arthur Edward Henson (1862–1938), Henson's brother, who had taken their youngest brother Gilbert to India with him on an extended business trip; m. 1891 in Calcutta, Eleanor Templeton Blaney. On his death, Henson recalled his kindness to his brother Gilbert, his sister Marion and his stepmother – also his employees; but added 'I think that he was uncomfortable with me. He didn't like my prominence, nor did he have any feeling save suspicion towards Bishops, and Ellie was jealous of my wife's indisputable superiority. So, although we regularly corresponded and he always expressed himself in words of affection, we were never on easy terms, and latterly he made it apparent that neither he nor his wife desired to see me. These estrangements are regrettable, inexplicable, and irremovable. They darken life, and probably they damage character, but it is to be doubted whether they are wholly within the control of those whom they affect. We are in bondage to our temperaments, and from that bondage men can only be set free at a heavy price': Journal, 20 Aug. 1938.

[41] Gilbert Aubrey Henson (1866–1947), Henson's youngest sibling; emigrated to Canada in 1886, where his eldest brother, Walter, had settled.

indeed, possessed of that peculiar property of heroes, the power of inspiring to great deeds. He has entered into my life as nobody has ever done. What would Gordon do? is the question that turns up at every puzzle, & helps to strengthen one to a decision. And he was murdered – betrayed to his death by these hypocrites at home, but it was rueful that the parallel with His Master should be complete.

[76]

Watson had to preach at Wavertree[42] and so Sheriff asked me to read the lessons, which I did, attired in a surplice short enough to display terribly secular trousers, and his B.A. hood, a most filthy object, weighted with the accumulated dust of years.

Watson tells me that Biggs[43] objects to me as insincere: well, perhaps he is right: at least it is a disinterested insincerity: it is not "because of advantage" as a deal of faith is, & most orthodoxy, except of course the faith & orthodoxy of Biggs himself, which is entrenched in the most transparent sincerity.

[77]

Tuesday, July 7th, 1885.

Received a letter from Podge[44] saying that **the Mater[45] & Jennie[46] started yesterday for Germany**. I hope very much they will have a good time. It has been terribly rainy today, but of course it may be fine enough further south. I feel glad they have at last definitely started: as a matter of fact I was sceptical up to the last moment. It now remains to be seen whether I shall be able to hold out here for the remaining 15 weeks of my time. I cannot say that I have found a satisfactory modus vivendi yet. Hitherto my greatest efforts have just succeeded in managing to exist. For ever so many reasons it will be terrible to fail disastrously in the middle of my engagement.

[78]

Watson and I looked up Makin, and had a long palaver with him. He is a most interesting man: among his strong points one would hardly reckon political economy,

---

[42] There still is a fine parish church at Wavertree, Holy Trinity, the parish church, built in 1794 and reordered in 1911.

[43] Arthur Worthington Biggs (1846–1928; *WWW*), Kt 1906; active in the volunteer movement, particularly as a major with the VI Lancashire Artillery Volunteers; appears in the 1881 census as a cotton broker living in Oxton; conceivably, a prominent member of Holy Trinity's congregation. There is a tradition in the town, and possibly elsewhere as well, that residents who have made their money move to outlying parts of the town but continue to worship in town.

[44] Henson's younger sister Marion Edith (1865–1923) nicknamed 'Podge'; devoted her life to looking after her stepmother.

[45] Henson's stepmother, Emma Theodora Parker Henson (1841–1924), nicknamed 'mater' and later 'Carissima'; on the death of Marion (see note above), cared for by Henson's wife at Auckland Castle, *Retrospect*, I, 67.

[46] Henson's elder sister Emma Ann (1859–1896), nicknamed 'Jennie'; Henson was greatly affected by her death. On the death of his sister Marion, Henson wrote: 'I cannot recall any lives more entirely surrendered to the claims of others than those of my two sisters. Jennie's death in 1896 left an incurable wound on my heart: & now poor Marion's death in 1923 renews the anguish in a more poignant form': Journal, 8 July 1923.

for he was able to advocate with conscious pride the following original plan for the abolition of pauperism. Beer drinking should cease, & the money spent in beer should purchase calico, which the purchasers should destroy: the demand thus created would supply work for all, ex-brewers & bar men included (!). Makin is loudly bewailing the probability that a Home for Destitute Children was to be built in Birkenhead. A man named Thompson, formerly a grocer's assistant who fell ill, & was assisted by a subscription to open a grocers shop on his own behalf **[79]** has started a sort of institution for waifs and strays: this threatens to become established as a home.[47]

Now an institution of that nature, says Makin, degrades a town, first by giving it a bad name, then by giving an impetus to the evil which it is designed to abolish. There is a far better arrangement at Liverpool, the Children's Defence Society[48] (?) which acts on the principle of working in and through the family. In fact it is a little more than a Vigilance Committee to assist the Law. Whether with fair cause or not, Makin throws doubt on the motives of Thompson. Of course he is an bête noir to his brother-grocers: that is only to be expected.

[80]

I asked Makin about drunkenness. What percentage of working men were intemperate? More than half, his experience decided: there was a great deal of home-drinking e.g. one family earning 28/– a week spent 7/– or 8/– weekly in liquor sent to the house.

Of course there were great complaints of the deceitfulness of the poor: and indeed Makin mentioned cases of the grossest deception. Especially does it seem impossible to recover loans from borrowers. I asked whether landlords exacted unfair rents in Birkenhead. Rents were higher in Birkenhead than elsewhere, but the prospect of payment was very uncertain **[81]** and the destruction to property by no means inconsiderable. Thus it was not unusual for tenants to pull up the stairs and use them for fire-wood, making shift with a ladder to ascend to their rooms.

The parochial system in Makin's opinion had broken down. Dissenters claimed and exercised equal rights with the Clergy. He himself had once been a Wesleyan. I asked about the system of that sect. He said the strong point in the Wesleyan system was the close connection which existed between the members of the congregation, every one of which was enrolled under a class leader, bound to see him once a week. Tickets of membership were issued quarterly by the **[82]** minister, and were only granted to regular subscribers or attendants at chapel. Thus every Wesleyan was *looked after: no one could fall into poverty unknown or unassisted. In the church, on*

---

[47] Charles Thompson (1842–1903), described in the 1881 census as a grocer living in Price Street, Holy Trinity parish; he appears in the 1901 census as a missionary living in Hemingford Street, Holy Trinity parish. The Thompson Mission in Hemingford Street still thrives as the body in Birkenhead that caters for many of those who are homeless and destitute.

[48] There is no reference in the Liverpool Reference Library to a Children's Defence Society in the city. There was however, founded in 1883, the Liverpool Society for the Prevention of Cruelty to Children. The Liverpool Society was the first of its type to be founded in the country and within a few years a number of similar societies had been formed, including in London, Manchester, Edinburgh and Glasgow. The London Society became known as the National Society for Prevention of Cruelty to Children in 1889 and took responsibility for cases in England, Ireland and Wales, except Birkenhead, Liverpool and Bootle, where separate societies existed.

the contrary, there was no such individual care. "I've attended S. Mary's church, 3, 4, 5 years, and I haven't a single friend there yet." However Makin thought the Wesleyans in Birkenhead, if not elsewhere, were losing their hold on the people. Therefore he had become a church man. There is a great deal worth attending to in what Makin said about the Church's lack of fraternity. I wonder whether an efficient **[83]** system of Guilds would meet the want: or, still better, a sort of religious frankpledge, under its "borhs-ealdor".[49] Commendatory letters should go from one parish to another on behalf of those who migrate. Here in the North the people are always flitting: bound by the necessity imposed on them by economic law. They must follow work: & work is now on the Clyde, now at Barrow, now on the Mersey &c. **Thus the clergy have no hold on them as long as they stick to the territorial idea of the parish: & ignore the unfixed personal idea.** *It is a case of the flock v. the fold: & a system of parochial intercommunication by letters commendatory might do something.*

[84]

Wednesday, July 8th, 1885.

Watson says he has discovered a Christadelphian[50] at last: and from him learnt that the mysterious Schism Shop at the corner of Price Street is the assembling place of the sect. **I must lose no time in going & learning all I can**.

I suppose the idea of the sect is what the sectaries call "unsectarian", like the "I of Christ" in the Church of Corinth, which obtained equal denunciation with the less imposing-sounding parties at the hand of the Apostle.[51]

I wonder whether these Christadelphians have split off from the Plymouth Brethren. It is not unlikely. The Phraseology of that sect would suggest that it was so, but I must go and see.

[85]

Thursday, July 9th, 1885.

This day brings to an end 11 weeks of my probation, & in good truth what shall I say of the hopes suggested by their history for the tenor of the remaining 15. – only this, that I will try my best to act with fidelity, wisdom, & courtesy in a position for which I am unfitted by age, character, and training. I have to guide me the example of

---

[49] A clause in the laws of Edward the Confessor required all men to associate in groups of ten (a tithing) under a headman, a borhs-ealdor, and bring before the local courts any of their number who had been party to wrong-doing, on penalty of a fine: William Stubbs, *The constitutional history of England: in its origin and development* (1873; 6th edn, 3 vols., Oxford, 1893), I, 94–5.

[50] A Christian millenarian sect which developed in the nineteenth century in Britain and America from the teachings of John Thomas (1805–71); it rejects the doctrines of the Trinity and the Immortality of the Soul, and in the nineteenth century opposed the organization of congregations into churches.

[51] Acts 18:4–6: 'And he reasoned in the synagogue every sabbath, and persuaded the Jews and the Greeks. And when Silas and Timotheus were come from Macedonia, Paul was pressed in the spirit, and testified to the Jews *that* Jesus *was* Christ. And when they opposed themselves, and blasphemed, he shook *his* raiment, and said unto them, Your blood *be* upon your own heads; I *am* clean: from henceforth I will go unto the Gentiles.'

Gordon at Khartoum – of course this is fanciful, but it helps me to hold on. Again & again when questions of difficulty arise, pressing for immediate answers, there comes the thought of direction & invigoration—What would Gordon have done now? and I try to do likewise[.]

[86]

Truly I am not satisfied with the state of affairs: and I know not where to turn for a better arrangement. Ball[52] said that to go for regular work from Lyle would be only vexation of spirit. He recommended that he should read for himself, the books of my suggestion, and, accordingly, I presented him with "Napier's Peninsular War",[53] and he has apparently taken to the book with tolerable appreciation. Yet I don't feel prepared to drop the work altogether. Just a little to witness to my position ought perhaps to be maintained. My main difficulty at present is the tendency to keep late hours, and have nothing to do with me: which is puzzling.

[87]

Today the "Ireland" went on her trial trip, and Lyle went with her. Watson and I took our usual turn round the docks, which were comparatively empty.

A Beaver Line Boat – the Lake Huron – had just disembarked between 5 & 6 hundred cattle from Canada. The wretched beasts were stowed under the deck (from which position they emerged through a doorway cut in the ship's side) and on the deck itself. The stench arising from the vessel & the lairage[54] was horrid. There are two lines which carry cattle – the Beaver, and Leyland lines – from Canada & the U.S.A. respectively.

[88]

I wish I could remember the colours of the funnels of the liners – these are some –

City Line (to India) – buff & black
Pacific Line (to S. America) – black
Beaver Line (to Canada) – black & 2 white bands
Hall Line – buff
Holt's (to China) – blue

I don't think there are any other lines that dock on this side of the river. A great many vessels don't start from Liverpool, but come into the river for a few days to get a cargo of Manchester goods.

---

[52] Sidney Ball (1857–1918; *ODNB*), lecturer and fellow in philosophy, St John's Coll., Oxford, 1882–1918; socialist and campaigner for educational reform at Oxford.

[53] William Napier, *History of the war in the peninsula and in the south of France from the year 1807 to the year 1814* (6 vols., London, 1828–40).

[54] Lairage (2a) *OED*: 'Place where cattle may lie down and rest.' Lairage at Birkenhead was approved by the privy council in 1881 (*Daily News*, cited in *OED*). By 1911, Birkenhead had become the principal port of entry in mainland Britain for Irish beef cattle: www.martinsbank.co.uk/11-078%20 Birkenhead%20Woodside%20Cattle%20Trade%20Branch.htm, accessed 25 Apr. 2024.

[89]

Friday, July 10th, 1885.

This day I finished going through the Hebrews in Alford[55] (as a scholar he is excellent, as an exegete infamous). Miss Aspinall[56] brought back my Gordon's Journal which I forthwith took over to Sheriff according to promise. There came a note from Miss Aspinall begging for a contribution towards the School Treat.

I hate school treats as being bribery to a greater or lesser degree. However to avoid the shadow of consistency I sent 2/6.

I went with Watson to see Charles Thompson, the grocer who keeps the Children's Mission going; I must say that I don't like his looks. He has the cut of a "Shepherd" & the sniffle of an incipient Stiggins.[57]

[90]

Worst of all he doesn't look one in the face. Gordon judged the blacks by their eyes & found himself justified in regarding the test as a fair one. If the test be applied to Thompson he won't come out very well. I feel more inclined to think that Makin (who does look you in the face) has some ground for his suspicion of C.T.s motives.

Then we visited a court[58] *"house to house". Houses dirty and dilapidated; inhabitants ditto: little or no furniture, & proprietors peering round corners and through half-opened doors: a general atmosphere of evil secrecy over everything: lies a necessity in this environment: truth quite inconceivable.*

[91]

I wonder whether any good results from this visiting.

Parson enters a court, & knocks at a door: after a considerable interval during which we may suppose the curiosity to see what it is has been overcoming the guilt-derived abhorrence of self-exhibition – the door opens a little way, and a female party reveals herself, in the aperture.

"Good afternoon, I want to know as many people as possible in this place so I've come to see you. How long have you been here?" — 3 mos — "Are you Church? "Ayes["] — "Do you attend church?["] When I can: to tell you the truth I go to the Salvation Army sometimes." — "What is your name?["]

---

[55] Henry Alford, *The Greek Testament* (4 vols., London, 1849–61).
[56] Henson refers to two Miss Aspinalls, the two daughters of H. K. Aspinall (see p. 34, n. 66 below): Sophia Maude Aspinall (1863–43) and Ada Isabella [Bella] (1857–1913), both born in Birkenhead.
[57] Reverend Stiggins is the hypocritical alcoholic deputy shepherd of the Brick Lane branch of the United Grand Junction Ebenezer Temperance Association in Charles Dickens's *Pickwick papers*.
[58] These are the tenement blocks for the poor, or 'dock cottages'; those in Birkenhead were the first of their kind in England.

[92]

"Mrs—". Are you the landlady? Yes. "How many other people live in the house?" One. "Well Mrs— I must be going. I hope you'll come to church regularly. Goodbye." Exit Parson.

That is a fair example of house to house: and what good comes of it? As far as the people are concerned, none at all. The parson perhaps learns something. Sometimes the reception is not so friendly. **Especially insulting, Watson says, are the Evangelicals: which is, to say the least, sufficiently suggestive**. I must confess I think that such visiting is practically valueless.

[93]

Saturday, July 11th, 1885.

Dicks,[59] a ponderous retired master mason, in his enthusiasm for church-going has reduced himself to the brink of death: by getting rheumatism and falling down. This in Birkenhead to be noted.

[94]

Sunday, July 12th, 1885.

[symbol]

This morning I went on my tour of inspection to the Christadelphians. On entering an "upper room" nearly empty, I perceived a venerable looking individual, whom I reckoned to be in authority. So I went for him & held out my hand, said I was a stranger & would be glad to know something about the Christadelphians. He very kindly – officiously – took my hat & stick, & showed me into a place, informing me at the same time that **though free to spectate, I could not participate in the breaking of bread not being a member**. This of course I was very glad to hear, not being desirous to do what the Church Times would call – excommunicating myself.

[95]

The congregation amounted to about 50 persons, equally distributed between the sexes. The service began with a hymn which was sung to the accompaniment of a harmonium. Then followed a prayer – all standing. Then the "minister" said – "The first Lesson is taken from Jeremiah II. Brother – will read it" – whereupon the designated brother rose in his place & stumbled as he best could through Jeremiah II. After he had finished the Minister set another brother to read the 2nd Lesson S. Matt. 13. Then came another hymn after which it was announced that "Thanksgiving for the Bread would be asked by Brother Lea."

---

[59] Not identified.

[96]

The said thanksgiving consisted of an extemporary prayer, without much special connection with the breaking of bread.

After this the Minister took the Bread – a hard biscuit – in his hands & spoke as follows.

"God our master when he was about to be betrayed took bread & blessed it & broke saying 'This is my body which is given for you, do this in remembrance of me.[']" And in another place ["]Except a man eat the flesh of the Son of Man & drink his blood, he hath no life in him.["] And (laying his hand on the bread which he had been breaking in the meantime) He said **[97]** ["]this was His body". Then taking a piece himself he passed the platter to the nearest Christadelphian, from whom it passed through the mediation of the venerable man whom I addressed on my entrance, to the members of the system. Having first been blessed by an extempore prayer by a brother nominated by the minister, afterwards the cup was passed round in a similar manner, the Minister repeating the words of consecration with sundry additions by way of comment and explanation e.g. "The Lord said 'This is the cup of the New Testament in my blood which is shed for many – **mark many not all** – for the remission of sins.[']" In both cases the Christadelphians received sitting.

[98]

After the distribution had come to an end a hymn was sung, and then the Minister said, "It is Brother Eastlake's privilege to address to us the word of exhortation, but he will wave his privilege if any other brother have ought to say. Therefore if there be anyone who has any word of exhortation to give us, let him step up here and speak.["] After a short interval (during which a collection was made from the communicants) as no brother proffered, B. Eastlake stepped up to the table and began an exhortation of considerable length. Beginning with the question of the Bread-breaking he emphasised **[99]** the spirituality of the participation. It was not possible really to receive X^{ts} Body & Blood, but by faith we could be made partakers of his glorious Body. Our bodies could be easily broken, & our blood soon shed. It wasn't so easy to break Christ's body, &c.

Then he said that he had been struck by a passage in the morning's lesson viz 12th S Matt (as the lesson read was the 13th the worthy brother must have been asleep during the lection). The point which struck him was the condition of the religious people of the day. We needn't go back so far to see the same thing. Wesleyans stuck **[100]** to the teaching of Wesley, whether it were right or wrong. So did Baptists, Church of England, Buddhists & all these sort of people. What we read of is what they call profane 'istory. Mahometans also followed Mohamet. Nothing was so dangerous as tradition.

Then he diverged into a confused comparison of the Two Covenants out of which he emerged to plunge into the question of personal responsibility. "We know that once saved, always saved." Nobody would be saved in the family or sect or church, but only alone &c &c. He concluded with some struggling exhortations towards endurance.

[101]

Then came another hymn, & then Brother Robertson broke up the meeting by an extemporary prayer.

As soon as the service was ended, my grey-headed friend hastened towards me: and I thanked him for his kindness & made some enquiries about the Christadelphians. How long had they existed? About 30 years. Who was their Founder? Dr Thomas, M.D. of Edinborough [*sic*]. What had he previously been? A Baptist or Independent. I forget which. Then my friend turned inquisitive in turn. Who was I? I gave him my card & address. What did I want? To collect **[102]** information about Christadelphians in whom I was interested. What was I in faith? A churchman, intending to take Orders in due time. Would I read their "Twelve Lectures"[60] if he lent it to me? I should be most happy to do so. However as the "Library" did not contain the "Twelve Lectures" he promised to send it, and also to lend me any other books I might want. "You'll see something in these. X^t said this is life eternal to know God & Jesus Christ whom he had sent: he didn't say believe the Athanasian Creed, which was utterly senseless & without meaning["] &c &c.

[103]

Thus terminated my encounter with the Christadelphians.

Apparently **their strong point is their complete republicanism**. They appear to look forward to a setting up of God's kingdom on earth: to regard all existing Churches, and the sects as hopelessly in error: to believe in a return of the Jews to Palestine, and a conversion of the Universe from that land & by their agency – but on that point I am not clear.

One thing is certain that they are fully organized as a sect, and hopelessly opposed to the Church.

[104]

I stumbled out of the Schism Shop right into the arms of Porter, the organist,[61] who was amazed at finding me in such company.

In the afternoon I walked with Watson to Bebington and had tea at Clarke Aspinall's,[62] who drove us most of the way back. In the evening, at Sheriff's request I read the lessons in church & then went to him for supper: got back to my rooms about 12.45.

Sheriff has been reading my Gordon's Journal, and actually tends, therefore, to regard the late Government with sympathy as having had to deal with an impracticable creature (!).

---

[60] Robert Roberts, *Christendom astray: popular Christianity (both in faith and practice) shewn to be unscriptural, and the true nature of the ancient Apostalic faith exhibited: eighteen lectures [on Christadelphian doctrine]*, originally published as twelve lectures on the true teaching of the Bible (Birmingham, 1932).

[61] Billinie Porter (1839–1916), commercial clerk and organist, St Mary's parish, Birkenhead (1881 census).

[62] Clarke Aspinall (1827–91), solicitor, JP and coroner of Liverpool, and philanthropic supporter of social improvement projects in Liverpool; popular platform speaker; lived at Laurel Bank, Lower Bebington; son of James Aspinall (1795–1861; *ODNB*), incumbent of St Luke's, Liverpool, 1831–44, and Althorpe, Lincolnshire, 1839 until his death; grandfather and great-grandfather merchants active in the Liverpool slave trade; assumed to be a cousin of H. K. Aspinall: see n. 66 below.

[105]

Sheriff cut a paragraph commentating on the recent promotion of the Bp. of Chester, out of the Birkenhead News, and sent it to Stubbs. For security sake I wrote the address on the envelope.

Clarke Aspinall says that he has been told by Liverpool merchants that the mass of unemployed labour is required by their trade: because although there is not nearly enough work to employ them constantly, yet at intervals they hardly suffice for the work in hand. There seems absolutely no remedy for this evil, since it is begotten of the very economical conditions under which commerce has to be conducted.

[106]

Monday, July 13th, 1885.

Started the Romans this morning with Olshausen[63] & Alford as commentaries. *Neither the one nor the other came up to my idea of what commentators should be, they are so ruinously Evangelical. How I wish Lightfoot[64] had written a Commentary on this Epistle.*

Watson & I strolled round the docks about sunset. They were really beautiful, the calm water reflecting the light of the sun setting. The tall masts with their texture of rigging standing out against the illuminated sky, the silence of the place from which the toilers had departed, combined to render the docks for once beautiful.

[107]

Tuesday, July 14th, 1885.

I went to Liverpool to the Athenaeum[65] to **make a beginning of my lecture on "Spain in America" which I promised to the Kilburn Liberal Club.** On the Ferry Boat I fell in with H. K. Aspinall[66] who forthwith attacked me on the subject of Thompson's Mission: especially as to the famous visit of Watson's & mine: which seems to have scandalized the pious. That Thompson – shuffle-eyed Stiggins as he is – must have a considerable element of the sneak in him to[o]. He has been whining most pathetically over our want of sympathy. I asked H. K. what teaching **[108]** Thompson gave to the children. H.K. said that he taught them Jesus only. Aha, thought I, you've hit on a formula comprehensive enough to include all the heresies that have been or shall be.

---

[63] Hermann Olshausen, *Biblical commentary on the New Testament ... translated from the German. Containing the Epistle of St Paul to the Romans* (London, 1846).

[64] Joseph Barber Lightfoot (1828–9; *ODNB*), biblical scholar, and bishop of Durham, 1879–89; advocate of the Revised Version promoted by Henson from his time at Barking, and an original member of the New Testament revision company, 1870–80.

[65] The Liverpool Athenaeum was founded in 1797 and opened two years later in Church Street as a place where merchants and professionals could read newspapers in quiet surroundings. A library was added in 1800. Its opening preceded that of the Athenaeum in London – of which Henson was a member – by twenty-seven years.

[66] Henry Kelsall Aspinall (1824–1908), brewer turned ship broker, son of a sail maker; churchwarden at Holy Trinity; lived at 43, Hamilton Square, Birkenhead; in the 1881 census, the household included a cook/domestic servant and a housemaid.

The hymn book used was Sankey & Moody.[67] After that, how is it possible to do ought with this man. That hymn book is chok-full of heresy as an eff of meat [*sic*]. How can Sheriff encourage Thompson who is neither a Communicant nor an attendant at church, but in very truth, a shepherd of schismatics, a Stiggins, squinting & a sneak.

[109]

Wednesday, July 15th, 1885.

Watson took me up to the School and introduced me to Mark, one of the Masters: a very unclerical person but a good fellow enough.

Lyle as usual went to the theatre tonight – a proceeding which I entirely condemn, but have conceded on one day in the week; amongst other ominous signs he has become careless about being at the works in due time. This morning he was more than an hour late, and this is not the first time he has been late this week. He cares nothing at all about the matter, I think, & nothing I can say will make him care, I fear, which makes it worse. Then he has such a **[110]** tendency to be out late. Thus tonight he didn't get back until ¼ past 1 o'clock. Truly he said that he had missed the midnight boat, & then had fallen asleep in the Waiting Room, but then, if he had wished to be back he w^d not have done either. Late hours at night, I vainly remind him, mean, sooner or later, late hours in the morning. It is of no use, he will have to learn from experience I suppose; but then, what about my responsibility? I hold to the belief that I should not be here unless God had some purpose to be fulfilled by my presence. Once more I will beg to do my duty, like Gordon.

[111]

This is S. Swithun's day, and it rains. The saint is not lacking in shrewdness; according to the analogy of recent years it is not unduly risky to expect a sufficient amount of rain during the next 6 weeks to justify in the eyes of the many the position of the saint.

[112]

Thursday, July 16th, 1885.

Rain, rain, rain, to the glory of S. Swithun, the annoyance of mankind, & the hidden delight of credulous females.

Walked round the docks with Watson: all very slack: a Beaver Boat – the Lake Winnipeg – was unloading a cargo of dead meat. A whole gang of men were busily occupied in carrying the quarters of meat from the vessel into the Lairage-house – truly a most hateful sight! men in the image of God, bowing their heads under a burden of carrion, the very touch of which once defiled men. For this labour they get 6/– a day: generally being employed ½ a day at a time.

---

[67] Ira D. Sankey (1840–1908) and Dwight L. Moody (1837–99); American evangelical preachers who held revivalist meetings in the United States of America and the United Kingdom in the 1870s attended by large crowds; their hymn book *Sacred songs and solos* was published in 1877.

[113]

Harry Rathbone[68] **looked us up about 6 o'clk**. He is now staying at Hoylake for change of air. Terribly wet evening: the flags which have been set up for the Rose Show look sufficiently melancholy. Lyle came in in excellent time, but was so conversational as to be hard to get to bed. However he went off about 11 o'clk, which, though late, is an improvement on yesterday.

[114]

Friday, July 17th, 1885.

Received Vine's Grammar[69] from Thornton,[70] & a vast lot of envelopes from college. Also letters from the Mater & Jennie, who seem very chirpy, which is a great blessing. In the afternoon I played lawn tennis with Miss Aspinall at the house, or rather, on the court of M<u>rs</u> Livingstone, who lives up at Oxton.[71]

Then went out a short stroll with Watson: after which gave an hour's instruction to Lyle.

This evening is very wet: so far S. Swithun is all square.

Lyle went to bed at 10.

[115]

Saturday, July 18th, 1885.

Rain, rain, rain to the destruction of the Rose Show & the glory of S Swithun.

I went over to Liverpool and got Liddon's[72] *Sermon on the Episcopate*.[73] *Otherwise I have been cabined all day: reading most of the time – the Romans: Socrates*[74], *de*

---

[68] Henry [Harry] Gair Rathbone (1857–1945), third son of William Rathbone by his first wife, Lucretia Gair, and half-brother of Lyle; lived off inheritance from his mother and £10,000 marriage settlement from his father; purchased a London home, travelled and maintained an American wife; a disappointment to his father, as reflected in the smaller share of William Rathbone's inheritance he received relative to that of his siblings: Pedersen, *Eleanor Rathbone*, pp. 29, 56, 66–7, 156; died in Switzerland.

[69] Not identified.

[70] Joseph Thornton (1809–91), bookseller in Oxford since 1835; rented 11, Broad Street, Oxford, in 1870 and remained in business as the family firm until 1983; the name survives and Thornton's bookshop is now situated in Faringdon, Oxfordshire.

[71] Not identified.

[72] Henry Parry Liddon (1829–90; *ODNB*), Ireland professor of scripture, Univ. of Oxford, 1864–75; canon, St Paul's Cathedral, 1870–90. Christ Church, Oxford; high churchman, ritualist and controversialist; leading figure in the anglo-catholic movement between Pusey and Gore. Henson had attended Liddon's Sunday evening lectures on the Greek Testament in Christ Church, Oxford, in the early 1880s: see Journal, 3 Sept. 1911.

[73] H. P. Liddon, 'A Father in Christ', preached in St Paul's at the consecration of the bishop of Lincoln and the bishop of Exeter on the Feast of St Mark, 25 Apr. 1885, in *Clerical life and work: a collection of sermons with an essay* (London, 1894), 288–310.

[74] I.e. Socrates of Constantinople's *Historia ecclesiastica*, which covers the years 305–439 and is one of the few early sources for Hypatia, the female mathematician and philosopher of Alexandria.

Broglie[75] *&c, broken by Pepys,*[76] *the Standard, and Liddon. I'm sorry to say* **Lyle has bought that filthy publication of the Pall Mall**,[77] *which will have to work much good to justify the harm it is doing.*

Wrote to the Pater[78] & Podge: & to the Mater & Jennie.

[116]

Sunday, July 19th, 1885.

Went to early Service in a soaking rain, which fell steadily until about 9.30 to the glory of S. Swithun & the discomfort of his orthodox admirers. Then to the Sunday School, where I hammered the first part of S. Matt. 8[79] into a class of restless little boys, who are not however, on the whole, a discredit to Birkenhead. I wonder whether I did the boys any good: I am not a good teacher, that's plain: yet boys do not dislike me, and I think in time I should get a good hold of them. However probably even so much confidence is unwarrantable in my case.

[117]

Sheriff asked me to read the lessons always when free to do so: of which I am glad, though I gave occasion to the adversary (i.e. Watson) to speak scornfully this morning by saying Patára.[80]

In the afternoon I went to the Salvation Army Barracks on another cruise of inspection. I was rather vexed to see there the very old crone, whom I had joined Watson in exhorting to go to church. She saw me too, which was the worst part of the business. Henceforward my orthodox exhortations to attendance at church will be to her a case of Satan rebuking sin.

---

[75] Jacques Victor Albert de Broglie, duc de Broglie, *L'église et l'empire Romain au IVe siècle* (6 vols., Paris, 1856).

[76] Samuel Pepys (1633–1703; *ODNB*), naval official and famous diarist. Perhaps surprisingly, Henson's engagement with Pepys's diary was minimal, and critical in places: see Journal, 20 May 1929.

[77] *Pall Mall Gazette*: sensationalist newspaper under the editorship of the campaigning journalist William Thomas Stead (1849–1912; *ODNB*) from 1883 to 1890. As a nonconformist with an enhanced social conscience, Stead specialized in exposés, particularly concerning the living conditions of the poor. Henson's hostility to the newspaper was notwithstanding its central role also in organizing public pressure on Gladstone to dispatch Gordon to Khartoum in January 1885 to relieve the besieged garrisons. On Stead, see Stewart J. Brown, *W. T. Stead: nonconformist and newspaper prophet* (Oxford, 2019).

[78] Thomas Henson (1812–96), Henson's father; businessman and evangelical.

[79] Matt. 8:1–4. 'When he was come down from the mountain, great multitudes followed him. And, behold, there came a leper and worshipped him, saying, Lord, if thou wilt, thou canst make me clean. And Jesus put forth *his* hand, and touched him, saying, I will; be thou clean. And immediately his leprosy was cleansed. And Jesus saith unto him, See thou tell no man; but go thy way, shew thyself to the priest, and offer the gift that Moses commanded, for a testimony unto them.'

[80] Once a large commercial town opposite Rhodes, possibly founded by the Phoenicians, from where St Paul embarked for Jerusalem at the end of his third missionary journey (Acts 21:1–3).

[118]

As soon as I got inside the Barracks **I was requested to sign a petition in favour of vindictive measures against the perpetrators of the Pall Mall outrages:**[81] **which I very readily consented to do & signed in full**. H. Hensley Henson B.A. (Oxford) wherat they opened their eyes. The service was about the same as before: rather more lively: a new captain, very young: who went in for gesture to an alarming extent. The testimonies were a trifle more interesting. One old fellow had been a drunkard, liar, & swearer for 73 years: now he was saved. He was watched by a woman **[119]** who had been a drunkard for 6 years: but had been brought to the Salvation Army & thus to salvation, by reason of the death of two of her children in succession of scarlet fever. Now she had been kept straight for 4 years, & though the devil often tried to pull her back into sin, she was confident of final victory. Then came the testimony of another man, whose story was diminished in value by the jaunty and "professional" mode of delivery. "Yes I'm saved. Bless the Lord! There's been a great alteration in me since I was saved. The money that used to go to the publican was now brought **[120]** home to supply the 'little ones' with food."

I should not omit to make mention of the sermon which was delivered by an old man of striking appearance. He started by asking the people whether they knew how often the word Calvary occurred in the Bible. Then he proceeded to comment in an estatic & fanciful manner on the import of its sole occurrence. "Calvary fills the world." Then he rambled on to an account of our Saviour's Sufferings drawn from the 22nd Psalm: which he declared to be a convincing proof of the **[121]** authenticity of the Bible.

Turning from the subject of our Lord's Passion, he went on to describe the character of God. God was Omnipotent, omnipresent, & omniscient: the Bible never said that He was Omnipotence, omnipresence, & omniscience. It did say that He was Love. That was his essence, the rest were only attributes. It also said God is light: but that, when considered came to the same thing as love.

Then the preacher turned to the consideration of the dignity of the redeemed. They were ambassadors: and they were princes. Jacob had wrestled **[122]** with the infinite. "Let me go, Jacob, let me go" cried God: but Jacob kept hold "I will not let thee go until thou bless me.["] Therefore he became Israel the victor over God: the Prince: and thus Christians were Conquerors of God – Princes. They were more. He hath made us unto our God kings and priests. "We're a fine set of fellows aren't we?" Shouts of Amen. Bless the Lord: &c &c.

Among the testimonies was one which is worth noting. A young fellow of rather pre-possessing appearance said he was an organ-grinder, & **[123]** bore witness to the Army in the society of organ-grinders. Since he had been in the Army his conduct had been changed.

Then a man rose from among the people: & declared that he was a Salvationist from Seacombe, where the Army was thriving: healing of the Body by Faith, & healing of the soul. He wound up his testimony by the following story which was received with

---

[81] Public outrage following the exposure of the London vice trade in the *Pall Mall Gazette* in July 1885 forced the government to pass the Criminal Law Amendment Act in August. The Act raised the age of consent to sixteen and created new offences linked to juvenile prostitution.

breathless interest. "Before I sit down, I'll tell you about my little girl. The other day she struck her nail and hurt<u>ed</u> herself. She **[124]** came to her mother, and her mother put a piece of plaster on it. This morning she came to her again & said "It hurts" but her mother told her she could [do] nothing for it. Her wrist was quite inflamed. "Yes, mother, you can tell Jesus" she said: & then she went with her Father into a room, & had ½ of an hour's prayer. When she came out it was much better. The inflammation had disappeared, & the pain ceased. There that's faith for you"——

"I believe it from the bottom **[125]** of my heart, I believe it that I do" – shouted that man whose theatrical testimony had annoyed me.

A poor little boy was put forward to blow the cornet; and in his zeal nearly blew himself out of existence to the delight of the Host.

One of the most striking portions of the Service was the appeal to the Holy Spirit. On their knees they sang a sort of invocation; then one & another – now a brother, now a sister poured forth incoherent petitions – then the singing was resumed. It was strange to observe **[126]** how, during this invocation, some of the soldiers flung themselves into astonishing attitudes: & I observed that man, with the stage-testimony particularly ostentatious in his method of receiving the "divine" infusion. The sisters positively looked demented. Their lips quivering hysterically. *The captain is apparently of a jovial disposition, for I observed him playfully slap the head of an elder brother in token of his "happiness". Shortly after the brother who had received the happy slap betook* **[127]** *himself to smelling salts. On the whole* **there was a great air of unreality about the proceedings**.

I went up to the Captain at the close of the service, & said that I should be glad to learn more about the Salvation Army. He blushed; somewhat; and was very polite: I promised to look them up again.

I feel that one can't pass over the movement with a sneer. The reclamation of habitual drunkards is said to be a fact. Sheriff says he has known cases.

[128]

To church. Watson preached about charity, giving H.K. Aspinall & Thompson, some very hard hits, which didn't have their full effect owing to the impassive way in which they were delivered.

I was pleased to have Sheriff give the people some straight talk about the Bazaar. I really think he's a little ashamed of the business, as indeed he might well be.

He & I had an argument about the parochial system: against which he pours forth railing accusations. He would substitute congregationalism under the bps: with the parochial system continued for relief purposes, in the hands of lay deacons.

[129]

He would have a church army in every parish. I told him that he would thus reproduce the state of things which was brought about by the Franciscan friars, who traversed the country with portable altars, being emancipated from all obedience to parish priests, and hopelessly damaged the parochial system, to the great & permanent injury of the church.

[130]

Monday, July 20<u>th</u>, 1885.

This afternoon I went on a hunting expedition after an anomalous sect, which goes in for Faith-healing of the Body.

It had been announced that a public meeting w<u>d</u> be held in the Craven Rooms, Chester Street, and I thought it as well not to miss the chance of getting a glimpse at Schism in action.

There were gradually collected about 100 persons – respectable little shopkeepers, several Salvation-Army officers, about a dozen dock-labourers & some very evil looking females.

The proceedings began with a hymn: in which the "trained" voices of the S.A. officials were very **[131** – Henson sketched the profiles of two of the speakers on this page] observable. Then prayer-extempore by 3 several individuals. First, a little thin old man, who poured forth a rhapsodical petition with tremendous excitement which proved contagious. "Amens" followed the petitions. Especially unctuous ones came from the Shepherd, who simply wriggled in a prostrate condition & emitted the said unctuous Amens. The old gabbler, was followed by a calmer individual, considerably his junior, whose effort to be ecstatic met indeed with every encouragement from the audience, but were very **[132** – Henson sketched the profile of the shepherd on this page] laborious. Not so were the voluminous outpourings, which came from the raised form of the prostrate shepherd. His supplication evoked of course the most passionate Amens. I should make mention that all the prayers made mention of a certain "lady" who wished to be "raised["] from a bed of sickness.

The prayers were followed by another hymn, sung with extraordinary fervour. The number of people being considered, the volume of sound was exceedingly great, & the effect singularly unmusical.

[133] [Henson sketched the profile of another speaker on this page.]

Then an elderly person whose age I gathered from his subsequent remarks to be the shady side of forty, read a few verses of S. John 14 and commented as he read, especially laying emphasis on v. 12, and 14. In the course of his remarks he mentioned that he had been converted 2½ years. He owed his salvation to the Salvation Army: for 39 years he had led what the S.A. called "an up & down life, sinning and repenting". He was engaged in **[134]** the "Lord's work", and he modestly added "I was reckoned a very good man." Yet he met with no success to speak of. "I could count my converts on one hand." He was discontented with his position, & fell to praying. "I said 'O Lord God, if this is all thou'st got for me, I'll have nothing more to do with you': but there was heaps more to come. One night I went down on my knees & said 'O Lord God, I'll die on my knees, if thou dost not give me the Holy Spirit'" – this last attempt had been crowned with success.

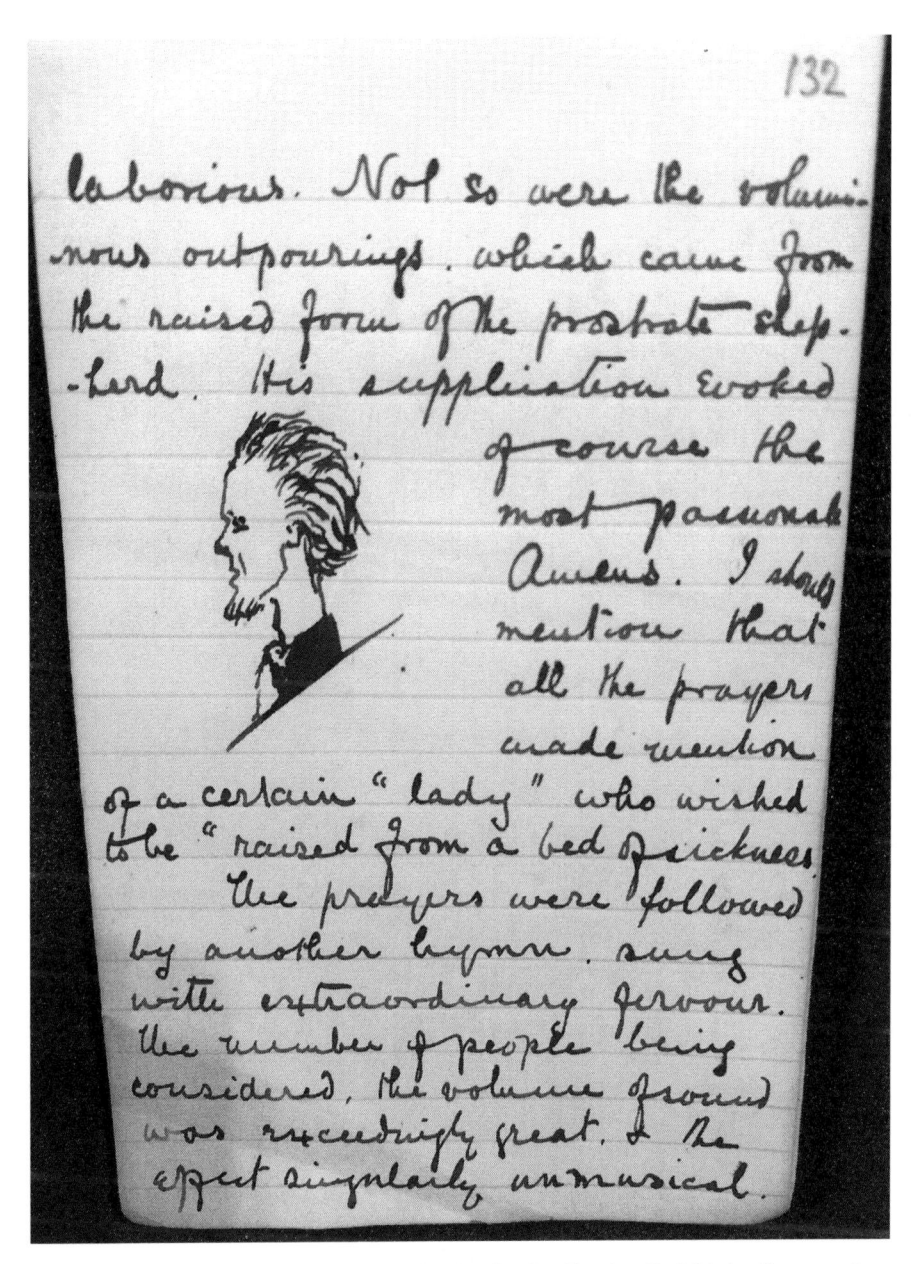

laborious. Not so were the voluminous outpourings, which came from
the raised form of the prostrate shep-
-herd. His supplication evoked
of course the
most passionate
Amens. I should
mention that
all the prayers
made mention
of a certain "lady" who wished
to be "raised from a bed of sickness.
The prayers were followed
by another hymn, sung
with extraordinary fervour.
The number of people being
considered, the volume of sound
was exceedingly great, & the
effect singularly unmusical.

4 Journal, vol. 1, 27 June 1885, 132: sketch of 'The Shepherd', faith healing meeting, Birkenhead, see 1: **132**. Durham Cathedral Library.

[135]

The next thing that followed was the address by the aforesaid prostrate, unctuous Shepherd. To give an adequate account of the mingled folly and fraud, the combined blasphemy and ignorance of this address is quite beyond my powers. I can only say that if I had seen the words in print I should not have brought myself to believe that they represented the actual public utterances of any man, professing the Christian name. Yet it is advisable to attempt some inadequate sketch of the doctrine of this wonderful production of schism.

[136]

He said that the "Reign of the Holy Ghost" had begun. Since the day of Pentecost until now the Holy Ghost had been on earth in the plenitude of power: yet since the 4th century, until the 19th He had been practically inactive. The Church had for all intents & purposes ceased to exist. Even now the majority of Christians had no conception of the H.G. as a Person.

Three stages in the Christian life were stated.

1. The reception of Christ into the heart: the acceptance of Him as Saviour – Conversion
2. The reception of the Holy Ghost into the heart as an indwelling **[137]** Person – Sanctification
3. The coming of the H.G. upon the sanctified, endowing him with the plenitude of His powers – the Baptism of Fire

This latter was administered by persons who have been "set apart by the Holy Spirit" & the authorized means was the laying on of hands. It was blasphemy for people to pretend to have "Apostolical Succession" who had not received the Baptism of Fire. Look at the Ministers of the Church who claimed it: where were the signs, which the Lord promised should follow upon them that believe. (S. Mark. 16)

[138]

The results of the "Fire Baptism" were then detailed. To the baptized was given the "fulness of the Godhead bodily". – Bodily!. "Its [sic] 4 years since I was converted. Somebody asked me once whether, when you got the H.G. you'd know it. Certainly you would. I shall never forget the moment when I received the H.G. It shot like fire through my body from head to foot. I felt it tingling in my finger ends: and (then he stretched out his long, lean claws) I feel it now." He brought his address to a close by remarking on the distribution of the Spirit's gifts, and the obligation to make use of them when possessed.

[138] [Misnumbered 139.]

[140]

Then the bearded man arose & after a few remarks asked those who wished to be converted to hold up their hands. Four persons did so 2 men & 2 women – but eventually it turned out that one of the men had misunderstood the point at issue, & as a neighbouring sister vicariously explained "Please Sir, Brother— has been converted long ago. He made a mistake.— ["] The 3 persons were then told to kneel down, and repeat after the bearded-man a short petition, which briefly stated that they accepted Christ as their saviour, and believed in Him. After which they were informed that they were **[141]** henceforward ["]safe for eternity["].

Then a similar invitation was addressed to those who wished for sanctification. About a score rose in their places. They in like manner repeated a petition, & were informed that they were henceforward "sanctified".

[Henson included three further sketches at the foot of this page, with the caption 'types of the sanctified'.]

[142]

After this the sanctified were invited to testify to their having experienced the coming of the Holy Spirit. About 6 did testify, among whom was one of the newly converted: for sanctification was given to them as well as to the others. This man seems in his vulnerable state to have been especially tempted to commit the heinous crime of smoking. On one occasion he flung his pipe & pouch as far away as he could. One of the sanctified declared that he had been in the Lord's work for over 40 years & hadn't found peace till that moment.

[142] [Overleaf.]

Benedict XII elected Dec 20$^{\underline{th}}$ 1334

in some sense a reformer – he declared against the practice of heaping benefices on the favoured few.

"He had the moral fortitude to incur unpopularity with the clergy by persisting in his slow, cautious, & regular distribution of benefices."

Milman Latin X$^{\underline{ity}}$ book 12.[82]

[Back cover.]

Mackay, 37 Peel Street
Mrs Hubback, Oaklawn, New Ferry.
Watson, 26 Hamilton Square, Birkenhead.
May 12th—July 20th

---

[82] Henry Hart Milman, *History of Latin Christianity, including that of the popes to the pontificate of Nicolas V* (London, 1855).

Volume 2
July 20th – August 31st 1885

[1]

Monday, July 20th, 1885 (continued).

The testimonies having come to an end, an individual arose and congratulated the newly converted, & sanctified, and proceeded to give some account of himself. For 12 years he had been a colporteur[1] in Birkenhead & Rock Ferry. He had believed in the doctors for a long time; but at length he had thrown them off. He had been afflicted with a bad leg. The doctor had said that if he used it, he would not undertake to be responsible for the results. He had prayed to the Lord, & used his leg for a month without causing injury. Nay, the damage to it had got all right. And, contrary to custom, he had not been troubled with Rheumatism. **[2]** Then a hymn was sung and the meeting was dismissed with a "benediction" from the Shepherd.

As was inevitable my wrath had been kindled by the proceedings of the afternoon, esp. the conversion and sanctification business: so I went for the Shepherd, & asked of what sect he was. "Of none, was the hostile reply.["] "I am sorry, I said, not to be able to supply a name to these scandals." This roused the shepherd: & when I followed it up, by telling him that he had deceived the people, & had misquoted Scripture, he turned greasy & whiter, & hissed with rage. At first he tried to swamp me by talking big. He was a Ph.B. of Upsala: his training was infinitely valuable. I was a mere boy: grossly ignorant of religion. **[3]** "My good boy, go home & read your Bible." I reminded him that it was not a question of my age or learning, but of his sincerity. He had converted Christianity into an impious jugglery. Hereupon he challenged me to prove from the Scriptures my charge against him. I turned to the Col. and showed that the words "in him dwelleth all the fullness of the Godhead bodily"[2] were spoken of X[t], and not of believers. Hereupon he fumed & quoted a multitude of texts very rapidly without giving me a chance of answering. Then I raised my voice & turned to the people who had collected. "Do you for one moment believe what this man has dared to tell you – that God has forsaken His **[4]** Church for 1500 years[?]." The wrathful shepherd angrily interposed with an admonition to me to read my Bible &c. "Yes, I said, turning sharply to him; yes, and when I have done reading, God grant, that I may have succeeded in retaining enough conscience to prevent me from talking the lies & blasphemies that you have talked today." And I turned to depart: but he felt he looked rather small, & so went after me, and asked me to come aside for him to talk to me. "Don't trouble about a private room, I said, these good people may like to hear what we have to say." Then for about 20 minutes we argued: & he displayed the most astonishing ignorance of logic inspite [*sic*] of his Ph.B. **[5]** Suffice it to say that

---

[1] Colporteur (*OED*): 'A hawker of books, newspapers, etc, esp. (in English use) one employed by a society to travel about and sell or distribute Bibles and religious writings.'

[2] Col. 2:9.

among other astonishing heresies, he put forth these that the validity of Sacraments depended on the moral character of the clergy; that every part of the Bible was of equal importance e.g. the minutest ceremonial enactment of the Levitical law was equally important with the words of Christ: that there was no visible Holy Catholic Church in the sense of the Creed.

It was amusing to see how he changed his tone as the argument proceeded. His blustering gave way to argument which became almost apologetic.

He said that he himself had cured by laying on hands, cases of heart disease, and cancer: which I couldn't believe.

[6] Finally, I gave him my card and he gave me his name and address:–

>Rev. J.H. Garside, Ph.B.
>106 Queen's Road
>Liverpool.

He said he would correspond with me. I said I should be glad to answer his letters, which is true.

Thus ended a most amusing episode, which has done more to open my eyes to Dissent, than all the experience of my life before.

This sect which for convenience sake I call the Bethshanites boasts of the fact that they are in the van of the sects, even the S. Army has not yet attained their level.

[7]

Tuesday, July 21st, 1885.

This morning I received from the Christadelphians this book:–

> — Christendom Astray –
> or Popular Theology (both in Faith and Practice) shown to be unscriptural.
> and
> The True Nature of the Ancient Apostolic Faith exhibited in 18 lectures by Robert Roberts.

> Birmingham. R. Roberts.
> Athenaeum Buildings
> Edmund Street
> 1884.

The book was accompanied with the following note:–

[8]

Dear Sir,

I am leaving you the book "Christendom Astray" as promised on Sunday morning week at our room in Price Street.

I hope you will find it interesting & after you have given it a perusal I should be glad to have your opinion respecting its contents.

Hoping that you & I may be constituents of God's Kingdom to come.

I am,

Yours faithfully,

J.M. Millman.

68 Camden Street,
Birkenhead.

To this I have sent the following reply.

[9]

41 Hamilton Square
Birkenhead
21st July 1885

Dear Sir,

I have to thank you for the loan of "Christendom Astray". I will find time to read the same, and give you my opinion on it. Heartily re-echoing the wish with which you close your note.

I remain,

Yours faithfully H. Hensley Henson.

I wonder what the ultimate outcome of this piece of play will be. I shouldn't wonder if my tussle with the shepherd gets spread abroad.

[10]

As I went to the Station for my diurnal Standard: I encountered the School children starting for their treat: & Sheriff persuaded me to go to Bromboro with them. I had a lively time in the train, with a carriage full of choir-boys in a madly riotous state.

The country about Bromboro seems sufficiently beautiful.

Sheriff and I went for a walk and had a long talk, leaving the School to fare as best it might. Then I walked to New Ferry & took the train back to Birkenhead, having first given Sheriff 4/6 to procure donkey-rides for the choir.

Harry Rathbone drove Lyle & me to Hoylake; where we **[11]** went for a stroll, and afterwards had dinner. Then caught the train to the docks, from which by train to the Square, where we arrived shortly after 10 O'clk.

This day I have done hardly any reading: and I find Schism-hunting sadly destructive of my time. However there certainly is some compensation.

[12]

Wednesday, July 22nd, 1885.

Didn't get up until 9.30: Lyle's cough kept me awake great part of the night, which troubles me both on his account & on my own.

Watson & I went to Liverpool to look up Bigges [Biggs], who, however, had just left, when we arrived at the School. During the afternoon, however, he turned up, and we went for a stroll about the docks. He was suffering from a bad tooth-ache.

During the afternoon I did my best to think of something to say to the mission-people, not however with any great success.

In the evening I went to the Mission Room, and Sheriff **[13]** took the service, while I gave the address. My text was S. Matt. II. 28–30, [*sic*][3] and I did my best, but the audience was abnormally small, the weather was sultry, and I myself rather slack: being annoyed by the failure of my attempt to dissuade Lyle from going to the theatre tonight, on account of his cough, which was alarming last night.

After service Sheriff and I walked round the docks. We agreed in ascribing the small number of the audience at the Mission Service to the fact that today Thompson has been giving his children a treat, to the horror of Makin & the orthodox.

[14]

Then I went to my rook & fetched sundry books to shew Sheriff, and, fetching Watson on the way, I came back to Sheriff for tea & talk. I am sorry to see no traces of the bright, nice-looking, little Irish page – Daniel, who is ill.

I left Liddon's Sermon "A Father in God", and Froude's "Luther"[4] for Sheriff to read: and showed him my note-book containing the account of my tussle with the Shepherd. Sheriff says he saw the Shakers. Mrs Gurling (?) professed to have the stigmata, & readily pulled off her stocking to show them, but he could see nothing remarkable.

Watson says that in **[15]** Westmoreland the current word for a clergyman is "priest": only schismatics talk of "ministers", which, it is much to be desired were the general state of England.

---

[3] Perhaps Henson was misremembering Matt. 28:18–20, on which he preached at St Margaret's Westminster, 21 Sept. 1902: 'And Jesus came and spake unto them, saying, All power is given unto me in heaven and in earth. Go ye therefore, and teach all nations, baptizing them in the name of the Father, and of the Son, and of the Holy Ghost: Teaching them to observe all things whatsoever I have commanded you: and, lo, I am with you always, *even* unto the end of the world.'

[4] J. A. Froude, *Luther: a short biography* (London, 1883).

Recently Watson has been bothered by persons professing to be Roman Catholics who have read the Bible, and are in doubt. This of course is only a pretext for begging, &, no doubt, efficacious enough with Protestant old ladies. Makin recognised the people as well-known rascals.

*Sheriff told me yesterday that since he had been in Birkenhead, **he had never had to attend a single infectious case**: such are immediately isolated: and* **[16]** *thus if cholera comes it will not affect parochial machinery unless it is very bad, and exceeds all the means in hand for isolating its victims.*

The disease is spreading in Spain, & is said to have got into Portugal. The Riviera and Italy seem to escape this year.

This day I have done no reading, which is terrible. I felt awfully tempted to buy Hake's life of Gordon[5] 24/– but I can't afford it.

[17]

Friday, July 24th, 1885.

Didn't come down until nearly 10 o'clock which is shameful & calls for reform.

Received letters from home & from Denham.[6]

In the afternoon played tennis at Mrs Livingstone's. I won 3 sets to Miss Aspinall's 2. On my return I lent her Gordon's journal.

Lyle was in by 8.30 and we did some work. He went off to bed about 10.30: but came down in a very little time saying there was a fire. So we both sallied out, & went to the bank of the river. The fire was on the Liverpool side, probably some corn-warehouses or cotton.

[18]

Saturday, July 25th, 1885.

Went to Hoylake with Harry Rathbone. Train hatefully crowded with cheap trippers. We drove from Hoylake to Neston, calling on the way at Backwood, the residence of Mr Theodore Rathbone,[7] a magistrate & a very active one though confined to his chair with paralysis. He is an ardent Liberal, whereupon I informed him that I was an ardent Tory. We chatted amicably-hostilely for the space of ½ an hour. On the road we had a glorious sunset; & Harry Rathbone caused great delay by insisting on getting a lot

---

[5] E. A. Hake, *The story of Chinese Gordon* (2 vols., London, 1884–5).
[6] Thomas Denham (1856–1939; *AO*), non-coll., Oxford, matric. 1881; Queen's Coll., Oxford, 1883; BA Modern History, 1885; son of John Barden Denham, general dealer, Islington; m. (1892) Helen Duncan Moss in Madras, India; educational advisor to Krishnaraja Wodeyar IV, Maharaja of Mysore; played an instrumental role in the establishment of the University of Mysore, 1916. See Introduction, p. xii.
[7] Theodore William Rathbone (1832–90), Trinity Coll., Cambridge; JP and farmer; Backwood Hall, Neston, Cheshire; grandson of William Rathbone IV (1757–1809).

of honeysuckle from the hedges. We got back to Hoylake about 9.30; & wound up the day by carrying a portion of the honey-suckle to M̃ʳˢ Warr,[8] who lives next door.

[19]

Sunday, July 26th, 1885.

We walked to West Kirby, & arrived at the Church (S. Bridget's) too late for service: so we sat in the porch with Mʳ & Mʳˢ Warr[9] who were in the same plight. Service Anglican but not very well managed: church crowded, but several females must needs come out during the service, which is very horrid. During the Litany, I observed a queer spelling of West Kirby on a gravestone – we skerby. We didn't wait for the sermon but strolled off: the church is a decent little building of red sandstone. The tower is its best feature, with corner buttresses, better shaped than those at [20] Wood Church. The hill which rises behind W. Kirby preserves it from the winds: & it is quite a place for invalids, a sort of Northern Torquay. One could feel the change of temperature very markedly, when coming over the hill into the town. Then we walked back to Hoylake along the beach. Hilbre Island looked very nice: there are numbers of sea-birds there. During the afternoon we slumbered, the evening we spent with the Warrs. **Warr told me about the Pythagoreans,[10] of whom 11 exist in Liverpool, living in common**, both sexes together, very secret: & subtle in adding to their society, sparing no time & pains to secure a victim.

[21]

Warr is immensely "struck" by the completeness of Romanism. He seems, however, to have but an inadequate comprehension of Anglicanism. I did my best to enlighten him on the subject. Mʳˢ Warr declares herself "a Christian apart from any Church". I told her the position was impossible. By the single fact of Baptism she was committed to Church membership. How horrid it is to hear women talk so slightingly of the Church! I can hardly allow them a voice on the question, & predictably let Mʳˢ W. know that.

Warr says the Horsfalls[11] are genuine Catholics, & do their great work without thought of self-elevation. Surely it is some little relief to the darkness of Religious Liverpool – this pure enthusiasm of the Church.

---

[8] Possibly Henrietta Warr (née Gorrell), sister of the judge Sir John Gorrell Barnes, 1st Baron Gorrell; m. (1885) Augustus Frederick Warr (see below).
[9] Possibly Augustus Frederick Warr (1847–1908; *WWW*), Liverpool solicitor and MP (C) Toxteth, 1895–1902; son of Rev. George Winter Warr, rector of St Saviour's, Liverpool, 1846–70, and vicar of Childwall, Liverpool, 1870–95.
[10] Religious cult based on the teachings of the sixth-century mathematician, Pythagoras; its members live in communities and practise strict loyalty and secrecy, observing codes of conduct and eating; the cornerstone of their faith is a belief in the transmigration of souls and the mathematical nature of reality.
[11] George Henry Horsfall (1824–1900), shipowner and JP, and his wife Sarah Jane (née Hodgson) (1833–1927). Horsfall and his twelve siblings built Christ Church, Everton, in honour of their father, Charles Horsfall (1776–1846), merchant and mayor of Liverpool, 1832–3.

[22]

Monday, July 27th, 1885.

Harry Rathbone drove me over from Hoylake; when I entered my room I found it given over to that horror – cleaning. So I fled from the dust, & disorder & dominant damsel, crossed the river, and subsided in the Athenaeum, from which I wrote letters home. The place was very uncomfortable, owing to the existence of painters &c: so I withdraw into the Picton Reading Room, & spent an hour over a small French history of S. America by Deberle.[12]

Watson came in, and we went for a stroll round the docks. The Clan line (black funnel with 2 red stripes) is said to be on the eve of bankrupcy [*sic*]: the only **[23]** part of their traffic which pays is that which goes on between the Cape and this country. We saw a vessel loading with metal routing for the Cape. The Clan line is said to be carrying goods from India at the rate of 18/– a tow, of which 12/– has to go to the Suez Canal, and port-dues be paid at both ends of the journey, besides the expense of the crew & vessel & officials.

It is strange but true that while the great ocean lines pay no dividend to the Shareholders, the managers & certain officials are making big fortunes. Their commissions, it seems, are a first charge. The last thing to be paid is the dividend. And yet the shares are very popular all the same: which I can't understand.

[24]

I am sorry to see that the cholera is rapidly spreading in Spain. Yesterday's death roll was over 1100 against about 700, this day last week. The authorities, here, are beginning to prepare in the usual useless manner, by issuing admonitions to the people.

[Half of page torn off.]

[25]

Tuesday, July 28th, 1885.

Received letters from the Mater and Jennie in Teinach, Wurtemburg. They send their photos, very well taken indeed at München.

In the evening Watson & I walked to Bebington, & spent the evening at Clarke Aspinall's. He & I had a long talk on Church matters. He is full-filled with a virile dislike of ritualism, largely if not exclusively based on the contemptibility – physical & intellectual – of ritualists. He championed Bishop Ryle in a most heroic manner.

The Aspinalls are an ideal family, simply full-filled with love for one another.

We walked back to Birkenhead & got back soon after midnight.

---

[12] Alfred Joseph Deberle, *Histoire de l'Amérique du Sud depuis la conquête jusqu'a nos jours* (Paris, 1876).

[26]

Wednesday, July 29th, 1885.

This day Watson departed for the first part of his holiday. He will return about the middle of August. I accompanied him to the Central Station in Liverpool, from whence he took ticket to Sheffield.

I read the service and Sheriff preached at the Mission service: only 15 persons besides Sheriff & myself present. This is very bad: there were only 10 last week, but we ascribed it to the fact that Thompson's treat was returning about the time: a few weeks back as many as 25 attended. If the district visitors (of whom there are 16) would do their duty, & whip up the people, we should get a decent number, 4 apiece would bring us up to about 70: & that is sufficiently small.

[27]

Went to Sheriffs [sic] rooms for coffee & talk. We prolonged our discourse until after 12.30 p.m. First, we discussed the state of the parish: then, we got on to an argument about Episcopacy v. Presbyterianism, in which Sheriff propounded and vigorously defended the notion that the presbyters had the power of ordaining presbyters: that the bishops were par excellence governors, necessary to the maintenance of the Church's unity, indispensable to its bene esse: not its esse[13] as Liddon boldly declares. It appears to me that this view gives no adequate basis to Episcopacy: though it might make out a decently strong case historically. Ordination by presbyter seems to have been common enough before Cyprian,[14] & occasional afterwards.

[28]

Thursday, July 30th, 1885.

Class List (Lit. Hum.) came out yesterday & appeared in the Standard of today: as **did also the announcement that Pember[15] had got the Craven [prize]. I'm awfully glad, & have written to congratulate him**.

In the afternoon I made my way to 19 Mersey Road, Aigburth, in order to free myself from the obligation of calling on Lee. M[rs] Lee is a hateful creature: a "spikey" Protestant with an adequate canting sniffle: and a tremendous desire to chatter, & a vile sanctimonious expeditionary innuendoism – altogether a beastly hag. Lee himself is subdued: as well he might be: the pecking of such a hen might well render living impossible.

---

[13] *Bene esse* (Latin): well-being; *esse*: essence.

[14] For Henson's later repudiation of the intolerance of St Cyprian in defining the episcopalian parameters of the Christian Church, and Cyprian's followers in the Oxford Movement, see his sermon 'S. Cyprian', preached in Westminster Abbey on St Cyprian's Day, 26 Sept. 1909, in *Westminster sermons* (London, 1910), pp. 97–111.

[15] Francis William Pember (1862–1954; *WWW*), barr.; Balliol Coll., Oxford; elected fellow of All Souls Coll., Oxford, at the same time as Henson, November 1884; succeeded Sir William Anson as warden of All Souls, 1914–32. Henson later described his friendship with Pember as 'strong enough to withstand the passage of time, and the divergence of our careers. I officiated at his marriage, and baptized his children' (*Retrospect*, I, 169).

[29]

On my way back I lighted on Herbert Rathbone,[16] and H.K. Aspinall, both on the ferry-boat. H.K was tremendously excited about the newly discovered swindling of Farqhuarson, a manager of the Munster Bank.[17] He says that lots of banks are in a shaky condition: during the whole period of depression in trade, the banks have continued to pay high dividends: they have been drawing on their reserve funds according to H.K. He says that an astonishing number of Scots are managers & directors of banks in England. Their superior education secures employment: their calm self-reliant demeanour inspires confidence. Hence their swindling has widely disastrous results.

[30]

In the evening I introduced Lyle, in the garden, to H.K. Aspinall & his son: & to MacMaster.[18] I want to get him to play. Then we did some reading until 10.30, when Lyle went off to bed.

14 weeks of the 6 months are completed today: there yet remain 12 to be gone through. Mr Rathbone comes to Liverpool on Saturday, & I shall meet him. I wonder what the result will be. One must be content to wait and see the end.

Miss Aspinall tells me that Thompson had the Bethshan notices stuck about his place: and a schismatic evident to hold forth. Even H.K. was scandalized and is going to protest.

[31]

Friday, July 31st, 1885.

Went to Liverpool and bought Gordon in Central Africa by Birkbeck Hill.[19] It is mostly letters, and promises me as much enjoyment as the journal. (cost 7/6 i.e. 6/3).

In the evening played lawn tennis with the Aspinalls, in the new court which is indeed level, but with hardly any grass, as sandy as the bed of the Wash.

Afterwards I read my new acquisition for about 3 hours, and then went to bed, still possessing the headache which lawn-tennis & Gordon had failed to remove.

[32]

Saturday, August 1st, 1885.

Cholera is increasing at an awful pace. 2650 deaths in last 2 days, making total for the month in 17 provinces of Spain 61320 cases & 26839 deaths. Yet nobody takes any

---

[16] Herbert Reynolds Rathbone (1862–1930), Lyle's cousin; New Coll., Oxford, BA 1885; barr., local Liberal politician and mayor of Liverpool, 1913–14.

[17] Robert Farquharson, assistant manager of the Irish bank, the Munster Bank, absconded on 28 July 1885, embezzling more than £70,000.

[18] Thomas McMaster (b. 1858), marine engineer.

[19] *Colonel Gordon in Central Africa, 1874–79: from original letters and documents*, ed. George Birkbeck Hill (London, 1881).

notice: though we were all panic-stricken at the mortality in France & Italy last year which, all told, didn't much exceed half the deathroll in Spain for 1 mo. [month] but sentiment can't be brought into play for the Spaniards.

Lyle went off to Wales to meet his father at Bangor.

I played tennis with the Misses Aspinall & McMaster for about 2 hours: and then went in to H.K.'s for 5 o'clock tea. The glib old humbug was as gushing as ever, though still a trifle inebriated in manner.

[33]

Then went over to Sheriff and dined with him and D[r] Knox,[20] the vicar of S. Anne's, a nice fellow able to look one in the face. He makes the most serious charges against the Salvation Army, & as to Thompson he fully endorses all Makin says. His grandfather, Canon Knox, was vicar of Birkenhead for 56 years.[21] He says my landlord – Worrall,[22] is a rabid, political Dissenter: in fact he expressed the deepest sympathy for me, when he heard that I was lodging with him. In justice to Worrall, however, I must say that I am not annoyed. Knox is in great fear of the cholera; he says he had it once on board ship in the Mediterranean: in a few moments after the panic seized him, he turned blue and become almost unconscious **[34]** yet he could hear the captain say: "He's gone: fetch the carpenter" – He recovered sufficiently to beg them not to throw him overboard, but carry him to Lisbon. Ultimately he got well and retained ever a horror of the disease, the agony of which he says is indescribable.

He travelled with Philip Rathbone[23] to Bordeaux on one occasion, & found him rather given to very broad jokes in the smoking room. I am not surprised at this. Aesthetes slip into sensualism very easily.

[35]

Sunday, August 2nd, 1885.

Managed to get up to H.C. at 8: Sheriff came stumbling into church ½ awake about ¼ past 8: I was in an awful state of suspense lest he should fail to put in an appearance, for I knew his affection for his bed.

Sunday school at 10: very scanty attendance: but good order on the whole.

Service at 10.45: I read lessons. Sheriff preached a very good sermon.

---

[20] Andrew Knox (1850–1915; *WWW*), Trinity Coll., Dublin; principal curate and vicar of St Anne's, Birkenhead, 1876–1915; hon. canon of Chester, 1901–15. The patron of the curacy was the vicar of Birkenhead, and of the vicarage, the bishop of Chester.
[21] Andrew Knox (1791–1881), Trinity Coll., Dublin; curate-in-charge, St Mary's, Birkenhead, 1828–34; first vicar of Birkenhead, St Mary's, 1834–81; hon. canon of Chester Cathedral, 1868.
[22] Samuel Worrall (1837–1916), shopkeeper and time-keeper; living in the parish of St Peter, Birkenhead, 1881 and 1891.
[23] Philip Henry Rathbone (1828–95), underwriter; youngest sibling of William Rathbone VI.

At 2.30 I took Watson's Bible-Class for ½ an hour. Acts xi.

I fear I've demolished S. Peter's character in their minds by referring to Galatians.[24]

At 3.15 children's service. I catechized with my usual want of success. I evidently **[36]** am not possessed of the gift of getting into children: & yet I am not a child hater or child-hated. Children take to me very readily e.g. Mrs Aspinall's little nieces this afternoon – but I can't catechize. It's awful work. Every idea you have, naturally grouped into a sentence, must be watered down to the infantile comprehension, & in the process the beauty of the sentence gets hopelessly damaged. I showed the Aspinall's [*sic*] my photos, and gave Sophie her pick. She chose the Abp of Canterbury. Won't Bella be jealous? Old Mrs A. is rather shocked at my levity, I think.

[37]

I had great fun with some children who are staying with the Aspinalls, especially two boys. I walked to church with Mrs A., Sophie, & the two boys: & talked rot all the way to the delight of the boys. After Service one them asked where I had been: & said he hadn't seen me, though I read the lessons. So successfully had I adopted a Sunday face.

After church to supper with Sheriff, who has asked me always to come to supper with him when in Birkenhead. **I addressed an envelope to Stubbs, enclosing "scathing criticisms" on his management of patronage.**[25]

[38]

Monday, August 3rd, 1885.

This is Bank-Holiday: & accordingly a day of Fetes. Father Nugent brings over all his guilds, and organises a great outing. They all assemble in the square, with bands & banners: & then march out into the country to spend the day. The order of the multitude (several thousands) was excellent. They returned between 8 & 10 in the evening by detachments.

Played tennis with Miss Aspinall & others, in all about 10 sets, in most of which I was "smashed". Afterwards I had supper with the Aspinalls: & spent the evening until 10.30 at their house. Afterwards I read Gordon in Central Africa until 1 a.m.

---

[24] Gal. 2:11–14.
[25] Letter by 'A lay churchman' on 'Church patronage', *Liverpool Echo*, 20 July 1885, 6. The letter was provoked by the appointment of Andrew Gray as rector of Wallasey (see 1: **25** n. 11); it raised accusations of 'nepotism' on the grounds that Gray had enjoyed patronage principally for being 'the son of his father', having served in the diocese for two years only. The criticisms were answered by the letter of 'Laicus', on 'Church patronage', *Liverpool Echo*, 21 July 1885, 6, which defended the practice of Stubbs's predecessor–William Jacobson (1803–84; *ODNB*)–in appointing 'new blood' from outside the diocese against criticism from the 'dominant school' among the Liverpool clergy, i.e. the extreme evangelical party; he commended Stubbs for maintaining the same approach. Jacobson had been regius professor of divinity at Oxford, and as bishop had been mobbed by Orangemen in Liverpool on two occasions.

[39]

Tuesday, August 4th, 1885.

Very wet day until about 5 o'clock. Cholera definitely known to have broken out in Marseilles. In Spain yesterday 1364 deaths reported.

Went over to Liverpool, and read the papers in the Athenaeum.

Llewelyn Davies*[26] *has been sitting on the bps for their conduct in this Pall Mall business, in fine style. I heartily agree with him. He urges the formation of Vigilance Committees. The most disgusting thing about the Pall Mall agitation is the way in which the Salvation Army has tried to make capital by usurping a monopoly of the agitation. I wish I hadn't signed their petition.

[40] [Torn out.]

[41]

Wednesday, August 5th, 1885.

Very wet day. About 5.30 it became so dark that the gas had to be lighted.

Received a letter in pencil from Jennie addressed from Mainz telling me that Mother had been detained at Stuttgart by the critical state of Herr Hausmeister, & that she had come off alone. This information was confirmed and extended by a letter from the Mater. There seems no hope for the poor fellow. It is a sad end to a holiday to have to mourn with a sister over her husband: yet it is infinitely well that the Mater is with Aunt Marie. In her presence sorrow loses half its sadness by ceasing to be lonely.

[42]

I myself am seedy today. I haven't been myself since Sunday: which is a bother, & destroys all reading. **I went to Liverpool and got tickets for Lyle & me to see Mikado on Friday**. I don't want to go a bit: but I promised & can't run word.[27]

Lyle has gone off to the theatre tonight. The fact that I shall go with him on Friday changes Mikado into work!!! I never met with such shameless indolence as Lyle's. I have almost given up fighting it: until this walking tour is over.

How Lyle's swagger does annoy me! My temper was never marked by angelic patience: & it is sorely tried now every day.

---

[26] John Llewelyn Davies (1826–1916; *WWW*), Trinity Coll., Cambridge; vicar, Christ Church, Marylebone, 1856–89, appointed by Lord Palmerston; close personal friend of Frederick Denison Maurice; writings include introduction to Henson's *The national church: essays on its history and constitution and criticisms of its present administration* (London, 1908).

[27] Word (7a) (*OED*): 'A promise, a pledge, an undertaking; a guarantee. Almost always with possessive.' M. Bishop, *The life and adventures of Matthew Bishop* (London, 1744), 'They ... did not fly from their Words but stood firmly to what they first proposed' (p. 130).

[43]

Cholera still increases in Spain. Over 1500 deaths yesterday. Rumour declares that it has appeared in Paris.

How that beastly "Christendom Astray" weighs on my mind! I haven't read it, and ought not to keep it longer. This is the Nemesis that follows on playing with heresy.

I addressed the Mission Service. Though the rain came down in torrents, there were 17 people there besides Sheriff and me. My text was Eph. 6.11 and I spoke for about 25 minutes to a very attentive little audience.

Then I went to Sheriff's and had coffee, and kept talking until 12.30: after which I turned in.

[44]

Thursday, August 6th, 1885.

Lyle very ill in the night. Natural result of vast quantities of bad lemonade & worse ices at the theatre! This morning I sent a note to Heron,[28] saying he was too ill to come to the works. Thus he is loafing about today doing nothing, but reading novels.

Went to Liverpool, to the Athenaeum, and to the Picton Reading Room. Wrote to Thornton for Deberle's Histoire de l'Amerique du Sud: read the papers, & returned about 1 p.m.

Cholera again increased 1570 deaths in Spain: and 35 in Marseilles.

Chamberlain[29] has been making a big speech at Hull,[30] putting out a vast programme of social reform: extremely generous but scarcely [45] practicable. He is led astray by his practice of isolating classes. He forgets that as long as the masses are more or less dependent on the spending power of the rich, any measures which tend to reduce that spending power must react unfavourably on the masses.

***I go with him in his attack on the land laws. I think their action clearly disastrous, tending** to set up an artificial inequality in the place of the natural. Equality of wealth or land-holding cannot be in this world: but the natural inequality is alone economically defensible. An inequality based on an obsolete legal system cannot be looked upon as satisfactory. Why should one generation bind another? Their only legitimate power is that of education.*

---

[28] William Heron (1841–1914), foreman, marine engine works (1891 census), living in the parish of St Mary's, Birkenhead; (1911) retired works manager.

[29] Joseph Chamberlain (1836–1914; *ODNB*), industrialist and leading Liberal turned Unionist politician, instrumental in the divisions within the Conservative party over protectionism in the early twentieth century; MP (L) Birmingham, 1876–85, and Birmingham West (LU), 1885–1914.

[30] At a large election gathering in Hull on 5 August 1885, Chamberlain called for a graduated income tax to 'elevate the poor, to raise the condition of the people', as well as land reform: *Times*, 6 Aug. 1885, 6. His speech echoed the radical programme he had promoted with other leading Liberals in 1885.

[46]

15 weeks of my exile end today. 11 weeks yet remain to be endured.

Did an hour's work with Lyle this afternoon.

In the evening played tennis for the space of 3 hours.

From 10.30 to 11.30 a thunderstorm. One very loud clap.

Read Socrates[31] from 9 to close on 1 p.m. when I retired to bed.

[47]

Friday, August 7$\underline{^{th}}$, 1885.

Rainy in the morning: afterwards fine. Spent about 4 hours in getting out a list of Councils and Creeds under Constantine.

In the afternoon went to Liverpool & met Sheriff on the way. We went to the Wildbeast-shops in Manchester Street.[32] A beautiful pair of Marmosets was offered at 35/–: a Spanish goat which had been saved from a wreck, & which was supposed (on insufficient evidence I think) to be in an interesting condition, for 50/–: Ostrich eggs ranged from 7/6. Then we went to Cross's "Nursery" or menagerie, & on payment of 6$\underline{^{d}}$ apiece were permitted to go through it.[33] In a box about 6 feet long: 3 wide, & 4 high there was a splendid lion, 18 mo$\underline{^{s}}$ old recently arrived from **[48]** Central Africa, & already sold for £320. We saw the cage in which it travelled to England: which was about double the size of its "parcels post" arrangement. **The "officials" who appear to be Germans were trying to get a Bengal tiger into a packing case**. They succeeded after many failures in coaxing the beast into the trap by the bail of raw flesh, & water. The attendant told me that the tigers only wanted drink twice a day. When the sliding door was slapped down, the imprisoned tiger looked so sold. The price of a tiger is £175. A whole lot of harmless snakes – 153 in number & some of great size, all piled on the top of one another – were in another case. They came from Calcutta. **[49]** The manager (or master for aught I know; he talked as if he were a member of the firm: by his speech he was a German) took out a big snake 10 or 12 feet long, and tried to show us its teeth: it wriggled violently, & Sheriff tried to hold it, but vainly, it was too strong for him. I felt its skin: not a bit slimy, but dry & soft like silk.

A kangaroo & a young one were for sale: the one was priced at £40: the other at £5: it was very tame & would be a charming pet. Sheriff was much tempted to buy it.

A pair of llamas, several antelopes, wolves, jackals, tapirs, monkeys of all sorts, & a multitude of birds made up the rest of the collection.

---

[31] See 1: **36 n.74**

[32] On the flourishing trade in wild animals in Victorian Britain, especially in major ports, see Helen Cowie, *Exhibiting animals in the nineteenth century: empathy, education, entertainment* (London, 2014), 83–4

[33] Cross's menagerie and museum was established in 1878 and the following year moved to Earle Street, close to the docks; its proprietor, William Cross (1843–1900), was a leading importer of animals for the zoological gardens of Victorian Britain, employing agents across the world; the business was badly damaged by fire in 1898.

[50]

There was a zebra "packed" in a case so small as to give one the idea of being built on it.

Ravens were from 35/–:

Cross has an enormous trade in wild beasts with all parts of the world.

It is comical to see how the poor people take Sheriff for a Roman priest. The Irish navvies, & boys took off their caps to him.

In the evening I went with Lyle to see Mikado[34] at the Royal Court Theatre. It is a very funny piece: & I'm glad I went. Some of the songs are capital.

We got back to our Rooms about 11 o'clock, after which I wrote until about 1. o'clock.

[51]

I see the conduct of the Rev$^{\underline{d}}$ Coker Adams in excommunicating M$^{\underline{r}}$ Joseph Payne, a parishioner aged 82,[35] was brought into Parl$^{\underline{t}}$ last night by Picton.[36] Cross[37] said the Bishop would look into the matter.

Sir Moses Montefiore's will[.] Personality over £350,000. About £30,000 goes to charitable institutions in Jerusalem & the Holy Land: and £15,000 to ditto in London & Ramsgate.[38]

Cholera still increasing. Deaths in Spain yesterday, 1638: in Marseilles, 30: in Aix, 3. The average mortality in Spain from Cholera during July was 865.7. The average for the last 4 days has been 1518 nearly double.

[52]

Saturday, August 8$^{\underline{th}}$, 1885.

Read de Broglie all the morning. Received letters from home. Jennie has safely arrived, & sends me 7 photographs of Munich, with which I am much pleased.

---

[34] Comic opera by Arthur Sullivan and W. S. Gilbert, which had opened in London at the Savoy Theatre on 14 March 1885, and which quickly became of the most frequently performed pieces in musical theatre. Set in a fictional Japan, it was a satire on British institutions.

[35] Coker Adams (1828–92), rector, Saham Toney, Norfolk, 1876–92; combative member of the ECU; excommunicated Joseph Payne at the communion rails on 26 July 1885 for 'persistent neglect of the Church's ordinances and refusal of its ministrations'; Payne may have become a dissenter who advocated the abolition of tithes; the excommunication was lifted following widespread criticism.

[36] James Allanson Picton (1832–1910; *WWW*), MP (L) Leicester, 1884–94; minister in the Congregational church.

[37] Richard Assheton Cross (1823–1914; *ODNB*), 1st viscount Cross (1886); home secretary, 1874–80, 1885–6; ecclesiastical commissioner 'keenly interested in the affairs of the Church'.

[38] Moses Haim Montefiore (1784–1885; *ODNB*), financier and prominent figure in Anglo-Jewry; Kt 1837; Bt 1846. Henson lived close to Montefiore's country estate, East Cliff Lodge, Ramsgate, when the Henson family moved to the town (see Introduction, p. xii). He referred to this connection in supporting a motion in the Church Assembly in 1935 expressing sympathy with Jewish people in Germany against Nazi persecution: *Church Assembly: report of proceedings* (Autumn session, 20 Nov. 1935), XVI:3, 476; see also Journal, vol. 67, 220.

A sailor died of Asiatic cholera yesterday in Bristol.

I played tennis both in the afternoon & in the evening (from 3 to 8.30) with the Aspinalls, and Cecil[39] & Noel,[40] two funny boys, their relatives.

Then I read until past midnight.

[53]

Sunday, August 9th, 1885.

Woke too late for Early Celebration: thereupon went to sleep once more, and nearly got [up] too late to open the Sunday School at 10. However I managed to get down in time through a pouring rain. Read the lessons very badly owing to hoarseness. At 2.30 I took Watson's Bible Class: 11 were present. We read the account of S! James' Martyrdom & S. Peter's escape from prison. I remembered to tell them Eusebius' story about S. James: also I dwelt on guardian angels: and talked at some length about S. Mark. Unfortunately I had to hurry off to the afternoon Sunday School, wherein I took a class of 6 boys, whose names were:–

Whittaker.[41]	Roose[42]
Ed. Weston.[43]	Forrester[44]
Baxter.[45]	

[54]

It is an awful nuisance to me that I can't remember names or faces. For example I scarcely know the names of half the choir-boys. All I can vouch for are

1. Williams[46] (comes to Bible-class)
2. Whalley[47] (nice quiet boy)

---

[39] Cecil Faber Aspinall-Oglander (1878–1959; *WWW*), army career; served in the South African war and the Great War; chief general staff officer Dardanelles army in the evacuation of Gallipoli; brigadier-general, 1920; son of Henry Edmund Aspinall (b. 1849, 'general agent', Streatham, London – 1881 census) and Kate Williams (b. 1853, Wrexham, Denbighshire); grandson of Henry Kelsall Aspinall; changed his name to Aspinall-Oglander following his second marriage to Florence Joan Oglander, 1927.

[40] Edmund Noel Aspinall (1874–1956), stock broker; brother of Cecil Aspinall; changed his name to Edward Trevor Aspinall.

[41] Edmund Whittaker (1874–1926), apprentice boilermaker; son of a boilermaker; Holy Trinity parish (1891 census).

[42] Not identified.

[43] Edward Weston (1878–1971), son of a hydraulic engine driver; Holy Trinity parish (1881, 1891, 1901 census); secretary, meat importers and exporters, Birkenhead (1911 census).

[44] Benjamin Forrester (1877–1953), son of a general labourer; Holy Trinity parish (1881, 1891 census); assistant in a newspaper shop (1901 census).

[45] Thomas Baxter (1875–1945), son of a general labourer; Holy Trinity parish (1881, 1901 census); clerk (1911 census).

[46] Not identified.

[47] Percy William Whalley (1872–1907), son of a land agent, surveyor and valuer; Holy Trinity parish (1881 census); apprentice ironmonger in Liverpool (1891 census).

3.	Price[48]	"the boiled nigger".
4.	Tibbits[49]	Nice boy: superior to the others: knows it: and brings an umbrella when it rains: horrid effeminacy in the eyes of the rest.
5.	Whittaker	(comes to Sunday School.)
6.	McGowan[50]	healthy young Oirish boy
7.	Weston	Sheriff's favourite

There are about 18 choir-boys, yet I can think of no more names.

Of the men I know not one.

At 6.30 Service, I read Lessons. Walked back with H.K. Aspinall & **[55]** Thompson, discussing the prospects of Conservatism in Birkenhead. The great want is an adequate candidate. Neither William nor John Laird will stand: and their influence is not what it used to be. In good times they can command 3000 votes: with an empty yard not 1/10th of that number. Kennedy the Liberal candidate is a strong man:[51] Moreover the Conservatives are disorganized: they have no club.

Aspinall says that the tunnel under the Mersey will have cost nearly £1300,000 [*sic*] instead of the £750,000 of the contract.

Went to Sheriff's for supper. Daniel is back all right. He [Sheriff] has become lukewarm about the kangaroo, & displays little zeal about the mongoose & marmosets. Stayed with him till about 1 o'clock a.m.

[56]

Monday, August 10th 1885.

During the first week in August there occurred in Spain 29612 cases of cholera & 10832 deaths: an average per diem of 1547.4. On Aug. 8th there occurred 1638 deaths.

In France the cholera slowly extends its domain. It has spread to Toulon where 2 deaths occurred on Saturday: 30 deaths at Marseilles.

Went over to Liverpool, met Clarke Aspinall. He said he had had a light crime-list this Monday. He ascribed it to the rain yesterday. When the Sunday is wet the people send for their liquor: and don't stand about the public-house doors, to quarrel and fall into the hands of the police. Thus the rain has an external "moral" effect.

---

[48] Albert Edward Price (1877–1946), son of a railway guard; St Peter's parish (1881 census); Holy Trinity parish (1891, 1901 census).
[49] William Elwood Tibbits (1873–1940), son of a freight clerk; baptized Holy Trinity, Birkenhead; emigrated to Canada.
[50] Not identified.
[51] Sir William Rann Kennedy (1846–1915; *ODNB*), judge; Pembroke Coll., Cambridge; QC, 1885; contested Birkenhead, 1885, 1886; judge of the King's Bench division of the High Court of Justice, 1892–1907. In 1903, Henson and Kennedy were dinner guests of Lord James Bryce, historian, jurist, politician and fellow Scot: Journal, 15 May 1903.

[57]

Lyle was in early but did no work: read novels: chatted: wrote letters & so spent the time until 11.

The religious question turned up tonight. He declared that he would be an Unitarian: Very well, I said, then you cease to be a Christian. "Do you mean to say, my father isn't a Christian." Certainly, whoever denies the Deity of Christ is not a Christian. Christianity is a definite, historic, objective reality: quite apart from and external to preferences of individuals. I do not blame a man for being an Unitarian if his conscience bad him to that unhappy position, but I only state a fact when I say that he is not a Christian. It makes no difference who it is that says the contrary.

[58]

Afterwards I wrote letters home to Jennie, and turned into bed about 1.30 a.m.

I finished the 3rd volume of de Broglie this evening: & began the 3rd book of Socrates. Eccl. Hist.

[59]

Tuesday, August 11th, 1885.

Received dolorous news from Germany: and indifferent from home. General effect depressing. Wrote letters to Germany, home, Jennie, and **that impatient dis-creditable brute Welden,**[52] **who wants his money, only 6 mos. due**. I told him it wouldn't be convenient to send him a cheque until next quarter: that he might add 5% to his account if he liked: and that I wanted an Inverness Cape. The effect of writing these epistles was to prevent my doing any reading.

In the afternoon Sheriff and I went to Liverpool, and looked over the picture-gallery.[53]

Returned & read de Broglie, and wrote until 1 o'clock.

Cholera. Sunday. 1504 deaths. 2 cases at Avignon: & a death at Gibralter.

[60 & 61] [Torn off at the top but showing that some writing had commenced.]

---

[52] His tailor; not identified.
[53] The Walker Art Gallery opened in September 1877 and benefited from a further extension in 1884. Named after its founder, the brewer and former mayor of Liverpool, Sir Andrew Barclay Walker (1824–93), it housed the collection that Liverpool City Council had purchased on the proceeds of its annual Autumn Exhibition at the William Brown Library and Museum since 1871. This was supplemented in 1893 by the collection that the Liverpool Royal Institution placed on long-term loan to it. The Autumn Exhibition still exists.

[62]

This afternoon I played tennis with Cecil & Noel & Miss Aspinall. The ground was not very wet: and it rained at intervals.

In the evening I addressed the Missions [*sic*] Service on S. Luke 7.14. "Young man, I say unto thee, arise." There were nearly 30 people present, including the two Misses Aspinall. The service went off very well indeed.

After service Sheriff and I attempted a stroll, but were compelled to abandon the attempt by the rain. Then we had coffee, and talked until nearly 1 o'clk. He gave me a fez which he brought from Tunis.

The cholera appears to have slain over 1600 persons in Spain on Monday among whom the Abp of Seville. To bed at 1.30 (a.m.)

[63] [Torn off at the top; no writing visible.]

[64]

Received an answer from Wellden, who accepts my ultimatum, and sends patterns for the Inverness Cape. **Also received a very jolly letter from Pember, who alas sees in my hero Gordon little to admire**[.]

> "That the man had some great qualities I don't pretend to deny, but it was a very narrow, though intense mind, and he was little better than an insubordinate impracticable fanatic" (!!)

I am sure Pember can't have read his journal & letters: for if he had, his mind must have conceived a different opinion of Gordon.

This afternoon I went out a walk with Miss Aspinall, and Noel, & "Theta" (little girl from Wavertree): How I hate walking with women!

[65]

At 5 o'clock I went as alter ego for Sheriff to the Charity Organisation Society. There was only one other member of the Rota there – Miss Cook, a sensible female.[54]

We had about a dozen cases to decide on; which were disposed of rapidly; **I always advocating severity, & receiving the grim smile of Makin's approval**. Then we chatted for awhile [*sic*] with Makin, who looks very knocked up. He told us some of his ghastly revelations in his characteristic style –

> "I found the old creature sitting in a corner, smoking a short cutty pipe, and never resting her hands for filth. I always carry away filth (i.e. vermin) from that place" –

---

[54] Maria Cook (1851–1926), school teacher; living in Holy Trinity parish, 1881, 1891, 1901 and 1911 census.

Makin delivered a diatribe against **[66]** private charity. There is a vicar on the Birkenhead Rota, who privately as clergyman assists people, whom he has, as member of the Rota, declared to be undeserving of assistance. I consider that unprincipled. In S. John's parish a cart is loaded with coals, and potatoes, and these are delivered in stated quantities to a number of people, whose names on a list are placed in the hands of the driver. So little supervision is there in that parish. Elsewhere the district visitors go & ask the people to receive presents of coals. All this is very bad & one doesn't see how to stop it. It would be of some use perhaps if the following rules were adopted in large towns:–

[67]

I. All the clergy shall be members of the Rota.
II. No "charity" shall be performed except through the agency of the Charity Organisation Society.
III. District visitors shall be bound to refer all cases of distress to the Society, and not to give money privately.
IV. Private giving shall be discouraged and subscription to the Funds of the Charity Organisation Society encouraged as a substitute.

Thus the parochial system would be for relief purposes supplanted by an inter-parochial system. The fund-raising power of the clergy would be united with the fraud-avoiding organisation of the Society: & thus both would be utilised.

[68]

Miss Cook was very anxious to have my name placed upon the Rota in order that I might inform the Committee of "my views" at their quarterly meeting. **Makin promised to cause my name to be added: though as I shall leave Birkenhead for good in a few weeks, I don't see what good can thereby be effected**.

Played one set of lawn-tennis against Sophie Aspinall & Noel, winning by 6 games to 2. Being attired in my Tunisian fez I was an object of interest to the populace of the gardens.

Cholera. Tuesday. 2109 deaths in Spain, a great increase. In France it does not seem to get worse.

[69]

Friday, August 14th, 1885.

Beautiful day. Played tennis with Noel: he plays quite as well as I do, which isn't saying much, yet he only began to play during the last fortnight.

The Misses Aspinall both unwell, & unable to play. That beastly creature, the bull-terrier, which I hated is now dead: died this morning. R.I.P.

[70–7] [Torn off at the top but showing that some writing had commenced.]

[78]

11th Sunday after Trinity, August 16th, 1885.

Happily managed to get up for Early Celebration: I found Miss Aspinall there also.

I turned down to the Sunday School with Watson: no teacher appeared: so we had to divide the work between us.

Morning Service – I read lessons with a horrid cold.

In the afternoon I took Miss Aspinall's Class in Sunday School. Nice boys in good order. Two of them are choir-boys viz. Magee[55] and Weston.

Spent the rest of the afternoon in the Gardens with Miss Sophie and the children – Edith,[56] Meta,[57] Hilda,[58] and the famous Noel.[59]

[79]

I am sorry to know that Sheriff has been prevailed upon by H. K. Aspinall to sign a recommendation to the Bible Society of that Thompson, who has thereby succeeded in procuring a grant of Bibles.[60] I think Sheriff very much to blame: for he knows quite well that those Bibles will be employed in the dissemination of false doctrine & schism.

If clergy won't be true to right ideas where they have them there is an end of hoping for the Church. The only result of Sheriff's conduct is to make it more difficult to quench Thompson, when the crisis comes. The retort is so ready – You yourself once recommended & assisted him whom you now denounce.

[80]

Evening service: good sermon: full church: collection above the average £2.5. The morning collection was 30/–: & the Early Celebration 6/1 i.e. total = £4.1.1. After service Porter[61] played Chopin's Funeral March in honour of a certain Mrs Jones,[62] who recently died under sad circumstances.

Sheriff, Watson, Bella & Sophie Aspinall, Noel & myself walked round the docks. They were really beautiful. The dying light of the Sunset gave such a background:

---

[55] Not identified.
[56] Possibly Edith Storrs Aspinall (1867–1915), daughter of Clarke Aspinall.
[57] Not identified.
[58] Hilda Gardyne Snowdon-Smith (1882–1971), daughter of Charlotte Smith (née Aspinall), third child of Henry and Margaret Aspinall; teacher in a preparatory school (1939).
[59] Noel Lake Aspinall (1861–1934; *WWW*), son of Clarke Aspinall; St John's Coll., Oxford; ord. 1886; archdeacon of Manchester, 1916–34.
[60] The British and Foreign Bible Society was founded in 1804 to disseminate translations of the scriptures throughout the world, 'without note or comment', a principle that pleased evangelicals but among other churchmen often raised misgivings about the lack of guidance this provided. See Leslie Howsam, *Cheap Bibles: nineteenth-century publishing and the British and Foreign Bible Society* (Cambridge, 1991).
[61] See 1: **104 n. 61**.
[62] Not identified.

against which the masts & rigging stood out with rare distinctiveness. All that was horrid was not there. The filth & dust & disorder of the warehouse quays had gone into the deep darkness: the noise of dock-labour, the scream of the engines were not heard; all was silent and so calm: hardly a ripple stirred the face of the water: which **[81]** reflected back in its peaceful mirror, the whole mystery of shipping & docks.

Then we three turned in to supper and prolonged our discourse until about 1 o'clk: I being overwhelmed with sleep, so that I could hardly keep my eyes open: the result of recent worries.

Birkenhead has been mapped out into wards, and doctors appointed to each in preparation for the cholera, quod Deus avertat.[63]

[82]

Monday, August 17th, 1885.

Played tennis with the Aspinalls. Met Lily, the wife of a parson named Heath.[64]

In the evening did an hour's work with Lyle.

[83]

Tuesday, August 18th, 1885.

Went to Eastham with the Aspinalls, and Noel & Cecil. Menagerie there, very poor: only good thing was the Lion & 2 lionesses: which were really fine specimens. Horrid lot of people about the place. The "sail" thither was very pleasant, though the boat was inconveniently crowded. We got back about 5.45 and I had tea with the Aspinalls. Mr A. showed me a letter from Albert Brassey,[65] refusing to stand for Birkenhead in the Conservative interest. Miss Bella gave me her canary, which has a damaged foot, and doesn't sing (!) but I have to buy a cage. The expedition to Eastham cost me 1/– which I can ill spare at this moment.

[84] [Torn out at top; no writing visible.]

[85]

Today I finished the 3rd book of Socrates: and read a chapter (110 pages) of De Broglie. He is splendid on Julian.[66]

In Spain yesterday 1627 deaths from cholera.

---

[63] *Quod Deus avertat* (Latin): which [may] God avert.
[64] Charles Heath (ord. 1872, Chester; *CCD*), Emmanuel Coll., Cambridge; curate of St Nicholas, Liverpool, 1875–6; vicar of Walkden Moor, Lancashire, 1876–98.
[65] Albert Brassey (1844–1918; *WWW*), military officer; University Coll., Oxford; high sheriff, Oxfordshire, 1878; MP (C) Banbury, 1895–1906.
[66] Flavius Claudius Iulianus Augustus (c. 331–63), Roman emperor, 361–3, the last non-Christian emperor; known as 'Julian the Apostate' for his renunciation of Christianity and reversion to Paganism.

Germany sticks to the Carolines.[67]

The docks tonight were again rendered beautiful by a splendid sunset: though the effect was not so perfect as on Sunday because of the noise of dock activity.

[86]

Wednesday, August 19th, 1885.

Watson came in and asked me to speak at the Mission Service. So that I abandoned de Broglie in order to write a short sermon, merely as a means of evoking ideas. In the evening I went to the Mission Service, and spoke on Rom. 14.7,8[68] for about 25 minutes. There were 23 persons present besides Sheriff, Watson, and myself. The Aspinalls being in London, failed to put in an appearance.

Afterwards we walked about the docks though it was quite dark: then had coffee at Sheriff's. I returned to my rooms about 11 o'clock.

Sheriff has set his mind at rest about the cholera. It has to traverse Germany yet: it will not come from Spain direct.

[87]

Walkington[69] slapped me on the back after service[.] "An excellent discourse Sir" (!!!) Such demonstrations are decidedly embarrassing. Sheriff and Watson are amused at my talking about the stigmata of S. Francis:[70] the people probably haven't the faintest notion of the meaning of stigmata: but I think with Sheriff that they rather like to hear things they don't understand. They admire "<u>larnin</u>.'"

[Torn out at top; no writing visible.]

[88]

I am sorry Meredith[71] wasn't there tonight. This makes the 2nd week of his absence. We can't afford to lose any of our men. There were 4 there tonight. Walkington, Jones, the ex-Policeman,[72] and a young man who is a Baptist. I must get Watson to look up

---

[67] In an early imperial stand-off on 21 July 1885, Kaiser Wilhelm II had sanctioned the German occupation of the Caroline Islands in the western Pacific, against Spanish claims on the territory. In response to anti-German riots in Madrid and the threat of war with Spain and its ally, France, Bismarck agreed to independent arbitration under Pope Leo XIII as a goodwill gesture following Germany's *Kulturkampf* against the Roman catholic church in Germany. In October, the pope found in favour of Spain.

[68] 'For none of us liveth to himself, and no man dieth to himself. For whether we live, we live unto the Lord: whether we live therefore, or die, we are the Lord's.'

[69] John Walkington (1834–99), seaman, Holy Trinity parish (1881 census); born Isle of Man; father of seven children.

[70] Stigmata: manifestations of the Five Wounds of Christ on the cross; they were reportedly given to St Francis in 1224, two years before his death.

[71] Thomas Meredith (1821–1906), baker/shopkeeper; widowed, Holy Trinity parish (1881 census); born Cardiganshire; father of one child.

[72] Not identified.

Meredith. Most probably the silly old fellow is worrying himself into a belief that he is neglected by the clergy. I think it quite worth while to make a fuss with such old creatures. After all they haven't very many opportunities of feeling important.

11.30 p.m. Lyle returned from the theatre and gone off to bed.

[89]

Thursday, August 20th, 1885.

Lyle failed to get up again this morning. I don't like to blame him for I know he would get up if he were only awake: but the alarm quite fails to wake him.

Today ends 17 weeks of my exile: there yet remain 9 to be endured.

I received a kind letter from Jennie. This morning I went with Watson on an expedition ostensibly to West Kirby, by way of Frankby and Greasby: but he lost the route & strayed nearly to Bebington so that we found that time would not permit us to go to W. Kirby. We got back to the Square about 1 o'clk. Thus was wasted the morning.

I received a letter from Lewis[73] telling me that de Quincy[74] matriculated at Worcester about the end of 1803 and never took a degree. [90] Also I had a letter from Denham. He is now staying at Lynton in North Devon.

I wrote a letter home: and as I went to post it I fell in with Miss Aspinall and Noel: and went with them as far as the house of the Relieving Officer,[75] who is a huge and hateful creature. On my return I played tennis for about an hour and a half.

In the evening I went for a long walk with Lyle over Bidstow Hill. We started about 6.30 & got back about 9 o'clk. The moon was beautiful. On our return we sat and talked over tea & biscuits for the space of an hour. *Our conversation turned on religion. Lyle says that since his Confirmation, he has twice communicated – at the* [91] *Unitarian Chapel. His father requested him to do so. I am very sorry to hear this. If Lyle is going to be religious at all, he is already committed to that terrible heresy. I talked to Lyle about principle in life, and came down hard on cynicism. I told him that cynics generally became such* by crediting all men with their own baseness. Therefore cynicism augured no good of the cynic's character & conduct. I was the more anxious to emphasize this because Lyle has adopted a revoltingly cynical style of talk recently. Everything is a "fraud" with him, especially the "British Working Man". I'm afraid my remarks were very personal at times, [Script on up to two bottom lines of page torn off.]

[92]

There is a change in Lyle's conduct. He is far more obliging than he has ever been before. He gives me the impression of trying to "make it up".

---

[73] Not identified.
[74] Thomas Penson De Quincey (1785–1859; *ODNB*), essayist; best-known for his autobiography, *Confessions of an English opium eater* (London, 1821).
[75] Under the Poor Law Amendment Act (1834), relieving officers in Poor Law Unions adjudicated on applications for poor relief, either awarding emergency funding or requiring entry into the workhouse.

Tonight I bought a Douay Bible in English,[76] & the Garden of the Soul for 1/6.[77]

The harvest has well commenced about this district.

The Aspinalls had not gone to London yesterday but to Llandudno. On the passage Noel was very sea-sick. Miss Aspinall says it was ludicrous to see him without a lingering trace of bumptiousness. He has recovered every bit of it today.

[93]

[Torn out.]

[94]

This morning I read de Broglie for 2 hours, and then went through Acts XI with Alford: but to little good purpose, I fear, though Julian's death seemed to me terribly sad: I felt more kindly towards him than ever when I reached the last act of the tragedy. The fact is I am done for the present: I cannot read: as soon as I look at a book I want to go to sleep. This is wretched: and is besides a nuisance. **What my Theology School will come to between my various troubles I don't know**.

This afternoon I played 4 sets of lawn-tennis with Noel: winning 3: at the end I was so fagged that I could hardly move about the court.

[95]

I walked over to Watson's and saw his brother Miles;[78] he strikes me as rather a "moke":[79] but I shall be better able to form an opinion tomorrow morning, when I go a walk with him to Thurstaston in order to see the moot stone.

At 9 o'clk I returned, and found Lyle engaged on Napier. We had tea & talked until 10.15 when he went off to bed: leaving me in peace to finish the 4th volume of de Broglie.

[96]

Saturday, August 22nd, 1885.

I made an expedition to Thurstaston with Miles Watson: he is a most terrible moke, and I foresee no great eminence for him. He will be a feeble edition of Watson all his

---

[76] The Rheims-Douai Catholic Bible, translated from the Latin Vulgate: The New Testament, first published by the English College at Rheims, 1582; The Old Testament, first published by the English College at Douay, 1609.

[77] Richard Challoner, *The garden of the soul* (London, 1740), a work which 'even after 1850, with additions, … continued to be the staple devotional text for the vast majority of Catholics living in England' (M. Heimann, *Catholic devotion in Victorian England* (Oxford, 1995), quoted in S. Gilley, 'Richard Challoner (1691–1781)', *ODNB*).

[78] Miles Walker Watson (1868–1916), civil service clerk, estate duty officer, Somerset House (1901 census); inland revenue (1911 census).

[79] Moke (1b) (*OED*): 'a person who is stupid, awkward, or incompetent; a dolt, a fool'.

life through. He plays nothing: and therefore presumably loves reading. He is saturated with heresy: and pretends to deride the stage, albeit he confesses never to have entered a theatre. His profession is to be the law: and I wish the lawyers joy of an acquisition: meanwhile I must be civil to him for the sake of Watson who is distinctly superior all round. His little brother may pro tem[80] remain a moke.

[97]

We reached Thurstaston by way of Woodchurch, and Irby. The mootstone lies on the moors about 3 or 4 hundred yards off the high road between Thurstaston & West Kirby. It is a huge block of Red Sandstone 60 or 70 feet long, by about 25 feet wide: and in height about 20 feet: though it is much buried in the sand. It is certainly a notable stone: as such it is polluted with tourists' names. As we enquired our way to it, we were informed that it was the altar whereon in the days of yore the Jews sacrificed in order to fetch fire from heaven. This is all gammon:[81] but it may have been associated with Druidic worship.

[98]

From Thurstaston we made our way to West Kirby, and there endeavoured to inspect the church, but of course it was fast locked against the orthodox. **How I loathe locked churches**! We caught the train from W. Kirby to the docks: and then came into Birkenhead by tram. In all the expedition cost me ½ [crown?]: an offering to my friendship with Watson.

In the afternoon Lyle and I made our way to Greenbank. There we played lawn-tennis 6 sets: every one I was beaten

(1) 6 games to 1
(2) 6 games to 2
(3) 6 games to 4
(4) 6 games to 1
(5) 6 games to 0
(6) 6 games to 4

[99]

I should have done better with my own racquet & tennis-shoes. Lyle is a horrid person to play with. Every game he loses by his generous folly, not by the superior play of his adversary! Moreover his language is too low altogether: and he can't bear being beaten. I think less of him than ever.

---

[80] *Pro tempore* (Latin): for the time being.
[81] All gammon (2) (*OED)*: 'Talk or patter designed to persuade someone of something or to flatter or cajole someone into a particular course of action in order to further one's own interests.'

Ashton Rathbone[82] arrived from the Engadine[83] just in time for dinner. He is growing a beard & moustachios: the resolution is 3 weeks old: and looks appalling.

Miss Rathbone[84] is back from the lakes & Harry is at home.

[100]

12th Sunday after Trinity, August 23rd, 1885.

I went to church at S. Agnes. Beautiful service, and very good sermon from a stranger.

Morning prayer and choral celebration. I communicated. More pleased with S. Agnes than before. Noticed in the porch designs for stained-glass in apsidal windows £75 each. In the evening I went to Mossley Hill church, and heard a very good sermon from the rector – Diggle.[85] I was however surprised to hear him address his remarks to drunken husbands & sluttish wives. I supposed that Mossley Hill knew them not: but Miss Rathbone says there is a poor part.

[101]

The Mossley Hill congregation offend me excessively. Hardly any of them kneel during the prayers. The whole of the middle of the Church is given up to seat-holders, the aisles alone are free: which is a shame, inasmuch as the original agreement was that ½ the sittings should be free.

The moral interpretation of that arrangement will not allow that it is satisfied by a merely numerically correct division.

[102]

Monday, August 24th, 1885.

I reached Hamilton Square about 10.30 A.M: and found a letter from home, & a packet of photographs of Stuttgart and Cologne. My cape arrived from my tailor & pleases me very well: though it is unduly heavy.

Watson told me that the local name for hemlock in Westmoreland is "kesk", from which is derived the name of Keswick i.e. the place of hemlock. There is another Keswick in Norfolk I think.

---

[82] Thomas Ashton Rathbone (1856–95), second son of William Rathbone from his first marriage to Lucretia Gair; half-brother of Lyle; partner in the Liverpool branch of Rathbone Brothers; philanthropist in whom William Rathbone had invested much hope for the future of the business; his early death from blood poisoning devastated his father: Pedersen, *Eleanor Rathbone*, p. 56.
[83] The Rathbone family enjoyed travel, including to the Swiss and Austrian Alps: Pedersen, *Eleanor Rathbone*, p. 29.
[84] Eleanor Rathbone (1872–1946; *ODNB*), daughter of William Rathbone and his second wife, Emily Acheson Lyle; social reformer, best known for her campaign for family allowances during the inter-war years, culminating in the Family Allowances Act, 1946; Independent MP, Combined English Universities, 1929–46.
[85] John William Diggle (1847–1920; *WWW*), Merton Coll., Oxford; vicar of Mossley Hill, 1875–97; bishop of Carlisle, 1905–20. Henson and his wife stayed with Diggle and his family at Rose Castle, home of the bishops of Carlisle, Dalston, Carlisle: Journal, 8–9 Aug. 1910.

In the afternoon I played tennis with the Aspinalls: and afterwards went out a walk with Lyle.

[103]

Went with Lyle to Wood Church [sic], and then struck across the fields towards Oxton. The valley through which "flowed" the "Fender" was very wet. The damp mist hung over it like a sheet, so dense as to make it impossible to see more than a few yards in front of one. I was glad to leave the valley. We got home about 9 o'clk having walked at a tremendous pace for about 2½ hours without once stopping: and this after an afternoon's tennis.

Then we had tea & Lyle went to bed at 10.30.

I wrote a "sermon" for 2 hours being too slack to read: & thinking it might come in useful for Wednesday.

[104]

Tuesday, August 25th, 1885.

I went to Liverpool and had my hair cut: then to the Athenaeum & wrote letters to Home & Jennie, and read the papers.

In the afternoon I went with Miss Aspinall & bought a bird-cage for 9/–: at least twice as much as I had intended to give.

Then I made my way to Greenbank to dinner.

Ashton Rathbone says that there is far more extravagance among Liverpool merchants than formerly: in fact the "standard of comfort" has been raised. The depression of trade he regards as in a certain sense permanent i.e. in spite of episodes of prosperity the tendency is constantly downwards. He ascribes this to foreign competition mainly.

[105]

The "Clan Line" will not smash, although it is losing heavily. Last year, Ashton Rathbone says the firm lost £240,000: but the shareholders are immensely rich, & they will be able to wait for better times. The reason of the practical bankruptcy of the shipping merchants is the excessive lowness of freights caused by keen competition. In 1879 the ocean liners began to run: their profits were large, 30%: a steamer paid for itself in 3 years. The result was a rush of capital into the trade. For several years the ship-building yards worked night & day: a multitude of steamers were built: soon it was discovered that supply had far exceeded demand: but orders had to be executed, & it was not **[106]** until the end of 1884 that production ceased. Since then few if any vessels have been built.

Ashton says that few fortunes are now made in regular trade. Vast fortunes are accumulated by men who obtain a monopoly of an article of general demand: & such fortunes are being multiplied inasmuch as the demands of the masses are becoming multiplied, e.g. Bass's Ale, Horax's (?) & C⁰'s Shirts, Bryant & May's Matches, Holloway's Pills, &c, &c.

Miss Rathbone tells me that Diggle personally had nothing to do with the repudiation of Gore:[86] as he had no share in inviting him. **He only lent his church for the Retreat, & acquiesced in the action of the clergy who formed it**.[87]

[107]

Then we (i.e. Ashton, Harry, Frank,[88] Lyle & I) went to the Alexandra Theatre, and saw "Jo". Miss Jennie Lee plays the part to perfection. The piece is most pathetic. The death of Jo is almost too sad: I was affected, nearly to tears.

I reached my rooms about 11.15 P.M. and wrote this short record of a wasted day, & then retired to bed.

[108]

Wednesday, August 26th, 1885.

I had hardly sat down to work before Watson rushed in to ask me to speak to the people tonight. He seemed rather wretched on the whole. I fancy his sermon last Sunday displeased **Sheriff & I think he is recognising the fact that he is not suited for parish work**.

I received the canary from Miss Aspinall: the servant has just told me that the house cat is a terrible bird-hunter, & has recently annihilated the pigeons. This sounds well for the domestic peace of my canary.

Lyle started to the lakes for his fortnight's holiday. I am glad to be alone, though annoyed at the slight put upon me by the arrangements.

---

[86] Charles Gore (1853–1932; *ODNB*), leading anglo-catholic churchman. Balliol Coll., Oxford; vice-principal, Cuddesdon Coll., 1880–3; co-founder, Community of the Resurrection, 1887; canon, Westminster, 1894–1902; bishop of Worcester, 1902–4, Birmingham, 1905–11, and Oxford, 1911–19; editor of *Lux Mundi* (London, 1889), a major figure in the development of liberal theology and social concern within the tradition of high churchmanship; as bishop adopted orthodox position on the creeds; assisted Henson's ordination, but they were later sworn foes on theological and ecclesiastical matters; submitted a formal protest against Henson's appointment as bishop of Hereford in 1918.

[87] The 'Retreat' may have followed the sermon preached by Gore at St Margaret's Church, Liverpool, on 2 August 1885, while the curate, James Bell Cox (1838–1923), a committed ritualist, was on holiday. At the time, a private prosecution had been brought against him for offences under the Public Worship and Regulation Act (1874); see 4: **293** n. 295. In his sermon, Gore defended Bell Cox, emphasizing the special role of St Margaret's in repudiating the authority of the state in spiritual matters: *Liverpool Mercury*, 3 Aug. 1885, 6. For the 'Bell Cox case', see Nigel Yates, *Anglican ritualism in Victorian Britain, 1830–1910* (Oxford, 1999), pp. 269–73.

[88] Francis Warre [Frank] Rathbone (1875–1939), youngest son of William Rathbone by his second wife, Emily Lyle; brother of Lyle Rathbone; educated at Oxford; entered the family firm and single-handedly managed its dwindling resources into the inter-war period: Pedersen, *Eleanor Rathbone*, pp. 162–3.

[109]

In the afternoon I played tennis with the Aspinalls.

At 7.30 I went down with Watson to the Mission Service, and spoke for about 25 minutes on S. Luke 6.46. "And why call ye me, Lord, Lord, & do not the things which I say?" There were about 30 people present, including the two Miss Aspinalls, and a choir boy – Tibbitts. The singing went off far better than usual: & on the whole the little service was fairly good. Meredith was not there to my great sorrow. Jones & Walkington were faithful. I slagged the people for not going to church in the morning of Sunday: also had a fling at the Schismatics. Sheriff was not there.

[110]

After service Watson and I walked out for about an hour. Capt<u>n</u> Wilson[89] told Watson that the labourers get 2½ a ton for throwing salt from the flats into the ships. Also that a dock-labourer last week worked 6 days & 5 nights: earning no less than £3.12.6 as he would be well accustomed to live on 30/- he would have 2/6 to spend in drink, & no doubt would so spend it.

I am beginning to lose faith in Giff**ord**'s [*sic*][90] statistics. No doubt the wages of labour are higher than ever, that food is cheaper, and hours shorter. The trades-unions & such defensive organisations are without doubt strong enough to prevent wages falling. All this is true. Yet there is another and darker side to the question. **[111]** Even trades-unions can't create labour: and as a matter of fact the numbers of men out of employment, or working at half time is very much greater than heretofore.

Ashton Rathbone told me that it was common practice to employ 2 men 3 days in the week rather than 1 man for the whole 6 days. Thus though wages are so high as 4/6 a day: the net earnings of masses of men are only 13/6 a day: So much for Giff**ord** [*sic*]. Statistics can never give a case truly. They can always be traversed.

[112]

Thursday, August 27<u>th</u>, 1885.

The first instalment of my proof sheets arrived from the Clarendon Press.[91] The asses have put everything that I underlined in italics. Yet I suppose I ought to blame my own carelessness.

Watson and I went over to Liverpool by the 9.35 boat and made our way to the police court where we sat on the bench with M<u>r</u> Clarke Aspinall. There were only about 70

---

[89] Not identified.

[90] Robert Giffen (1827–1910; *ODNB*), economist and statistician; assistant secretary, Board of Trade, 1882–93; president, Royal Statistical Society, 1882–4; ardent advocate of free trade as central to the prosperity of the working classes, which he supported with a wealth of statistical evidence in papers such as 'The progress of the working classes' (1883); later embraced protection on political and imperialist grounds; Knight Commander of the Bath, 1895.

[91] Henson, 'The Stamford schism: letters relating to Oxford in the 14th century, from the originals in the Public Record Office and British Museum', in *Collectanea*, first series, ed. C. R. L. Fletcher (Oxford, 1885), pp. 1–56.

cases most of whom were women. The thing that struck me most was the admirable perfection of the machinery. Rapidity and justice were not in opposition. As soon as an offender was placed in the dock an officer turned out his record of previous convictions. It was **[113]** consolatory to perceive that the great crime list of the year was largely swollen by repetitions of offences by individuals. Thus individuals had been previously convicted as many as 56 times. This again shows how perilous statistics are. The recognition of this fact of repetition traverses annual statements of the amount of crime. Clarke Aspinall said he made a rule of being severe on recently convicted persons, more easy on persons whose offences were more remote. On the whole I was very much pleased at the way justice was done. The only thing wanted was more elasticity in the matter of penalties.

[114]

In the afternoon I walked out in the wet with Miles Watson who showed less of the moke and more of the heretic.

About 7.30 I was making my way to Watson when the Misses Aspinall ran into me, and dragged me to church *vi et armis*.[92] Meredith was there, & I went for him after service, and asked him why he wasn't at the Mission Service. He professed great regret but had been ill; & indeed I believe him: I wish Watson looked him up more.

After service I turned in to the Aspinalls, & had a long discussion on ecclesiastical and theological matters with the old people. I have to **[115]** steer my way with considerable prudence among them: for they are schismatic to the core. The girls at present are quite orthodox; but under different circumstances they would no doubt be schismatic. Fred. Aspinall[93] the "Doctor" is a more revolting being than ever. I don't know when a person has offended me so much. A cad in appearance. Every word he says, every gesture he makes supports your first impression. Leering like a bull dog: with a strange fondness for doing little hurtful things, a moral bully i.e. one who tramples on sentiments &c. The "Doctor" is a sad person to have any dealings with.

[116]

This day brings to an end 18 weeks of my exile, and leaves 8 still to be endured. Great mystery surrounds the attitude of Mr W. Rathbone. "<u>Young William Rathbone who never was young</u>" as Mrs Aspinall says he used to be called. For myself I have but one wish viz. to terminate the connexion without loss of honour, & to forget all about it. Though I fear that neither one nor the other part of my desire will be given me.

I am glad to have seen a little of the Church in the north: & to have made the acquaintance of these people. I am a strange creature. To most young fellows in my position to get to know a man like Rathbone would be quite a step up in their career: to me I think it will be just the opposite: Is it because I can't conform?

---

[92] *Vi et armis* (Latin): by force and arms.
[93] Frederick Aspinall (b. 1859), apprentice shipbuilder.

[117]

Friday, August 28th, 1885.

I sent off my proof sheet with a note about the italics to the Clarendon Press: also a note to Lewis acknowledging his information about de Quincey; also sent off 3 shirts & 3 collars to Lyle according to request.

Read for about 2 hours in the morning.

In the afternoon I went over to Liverpool and read the papers in the Athenaeum; also wrote a letter to Denham.

Returned & had tea: after which I settled me down for a good evening's work: but hardly ¾ of an hour had passed before Clarke Aspinall called to give me what he is **[118]** pleased to call final instructions about the service next Sunday evening [at Tranmere]. I can see he is diffident about my youthful appearance, & has misgivings, which would be offensive were they not natural. However, there is only one way of dealing with misgivings – disprove them.

This visit disturbed my mind, & abandoning reading I fell to writing a sermon for next Sunday, and spent about 3 hours in that manner. Then I turned me to writing my diary: which I faithfully keep although I have nothing of importance to put down: & have had none for many days.

[119]

Saturday, August 29th, 1885.

Hardly had I settled down to work before Miles Watson came in to return my cape which I lent him last night. With him I squandered the morning, going to see the little "church" where I am to hold forth tomorrow evening.

The afternoon was spent in lawn tennis with the Aspinalls: with whom I had tea, & squandered most of the evening.

A large body of men out of work have been tramping the streets both yesterday and to-day, collecting money, which by a concerted arrangement they send to the Charity Organisation Society for distribution. This afternoon they brought their collection to the Society's office in Hamilton Square & demanded distribution. But **[120]** Makin the Agent was away for his fortnight's holiday at Blackpool. It was at first attempted to put the people off until next week: but this failing, Makin was telegraphed for, & arrived with admirable promptitude. D[r] Miller[94] told me tonight that there is a great deal of humbug in these proceedings of the men out of work. The majority of the processionists being loafers, and many of the regular working men standing aloof. This he was told by a respectable man now out of work but until recently employed in Laird's works. The number of men out of employment in Birkenhead alone can be reckoned by thousands.

---

[94] Hugh Miller (c. 1846–92), surgeon, MD, Glasgow; lived at 25, Hamilton Square, Birkenhead (1881 census).

Watson tells me on the authority of Captⁿ Wilson that the Indian **[121]** lines are about to combine for the purpose of raising freights. They will agree to take off some of their ships. This looks rather caddish: & will be a bad thing for the dock-labourers.

I had a long conversation with the Aspinalls: in **which I vigorously condemned bazaars, with special reference to the work Sophie is doing for the Holy Trinity Bazaar, which comes off next winter**. I fetched[95] old Mʳˢ Aspinall by talking of the Reformation as a "great disaster". I am sorry to find Mʳ Aspinall very hostile to Watson, chiefly on the score of his preaching. I fear it hinders his chances a great deal that he has the church-wardens opposed to him. I did my best to defend him.

[122]

Aspinall spoke with great bitterness about the want of honesty which marks commercial transactions.

"I have been a brewer, & when I was a brewer I heard a great deal of abuse showered upon the trade in liquor as debasing the people. Now I'm a ship-broker, buying and selling ships, loading & chartering them, and **I can safely say that there was not a tithe of the dishonesty in the brewing trade that there is in ship-broking**. One man said to me "There's no sentiment in trade"; another, who is a well-known, wealthy Roman Catholic said that "on Sunday he attended to his soul & gave no thought to business, but as soon as Monday came, & throughout the 6 days of the week, he gave himself up to making money, & trying to get advantage over others."

[123]

13ᵗʰ Sunday after Trinity, August 30ᵗʰ, 1885.

I went to the early Celebration at 8 o'clk: and on the return journey introduced Miles Watson to Bella Aspinall. I took a class of boys in Sunday School at 10: & had to turn out of school by the coal-cellar a demoralized stable-boy, known as the Senior Pickles.[96] The Junior Pickles[97] I suffered to remain, though he is more harm than good to a class.

No organ in services today. The instrument is being transported to Liverpool for dissection to be replaced in a new position. So Porter presided over the harmonium, where are wont to operate the indolent digits of Miss Lawrence.[98]

In the afternoon I first sped down to the church & fetched Sheriff's hood for my evening operations: & then went out a walk with Noel & Cecil: during which we trespassed on the fields between Wood **[124]** Church Road and Oxton. Lo a boor armed with a formidable ash stick, and with a face in which sensuality struggled with ferocity for the position of predominance. He proceeded to order us off with vile language

---

[95] Fetch (4) (*OED*): 'To move to interest, admiration, or goodwill by some happy contrivance or telling feature; to attract irresistibly.'

[96] George Thomas Pickles (1875–1944), son of John E. Pickles (horse keeper) and Sarah Pickles (nurse); living in Holy Trinity parish (1881 census); slaughterman (1901 census).

[97] Matthew Oliver Pickles (b. 1875), son of John E. Pickles (horse keeper) and Sarah Pickles (nurse); living in Holy Trinity parish (1881 census).

[98] Not identified.

& threatened to use his stick. I told him that I was quite willing to go off the field because I knew I was trespassing; but as to his stick, two could play at that game: and I wouldn't move an inch for any threats: whereat the rustic looked astonished & swore at me: so I very leisurely walked off the field, feeling every minute tempted to go back & cudgel the brute, or at least, try to cudgel him.

In the evening accompanied by Miles Watson, Cecil Kingcome,[99] & Noel Haselden[100] **I walked down to S. Barnabas. There was quite a big surpliced choir, & choral service though I told the "choir-master" before I went in that I should read the [125] service.** *As a compromise I monotoned to the best of my ability. One of the choirmen read the lessons. The sermon was delivered from the altar.* I took for my text 2.Kings 6.16[101] & **preached for about ½ an hour**. *The little place was crowded. I suppose it would contain nearly 150 people. They listened very attentively: and when I came out I received quite a little ovation. "We wish you was our clergyman." "Come again, Sir" was the cry: I, having signed my name in the preaching book, and said good-bye to the people, went my way: back to Birkenhead.*

Miles Watson pleased my foolish soul by telling me that I reminded him of Liddon!

On my return I was rejoiced to find Watson's sermon had been a success. Church full & good collection.

[126]

Then I went in to Sheriff with the Watsons, had supper, & talked until 11.30, when I left them & retired to my rooms & to bed.

On the whole I think I ought to be satisfied with my reception at Tranmere. Certainly the people were quite enthusiastic at the end, running up to me eagerly as soon as I appeared. **Noel says I looked so awfully fierce during the sermon: & Cecil that I was almost theatrical: so that considerable deductions are to be made from Watson's compliment**. However, I tried my best.

[127]

Monday, August 31st, 1885.

I went to Liverpool by the 9.25 boat, & made my way to the Court where Clarke Aspinall deals justice. After a little delay he arrived, & I established myself by his side. Suddenly he remembered that the Sessions were on under his brother, the Recorder,[102] which I should see: so he wrote a note to his brother: & sent me round under the care of an official to the Sessions Court in S. George's Hall[103]. We first went into the

---

[99] Cecil Kingcome (b. 1870), attended Bancroft Hospital Drapers Company School for Boys, Mile End Old Town (1881 census); son of Charles Kingcome (1819–73), general merchant.
[100] Ewan Noel Haselden (1873–1918), born Alexandria, Egypt; m. (1900) Evelyn Margaret Aspinall; died on the way to Alexandria following the bombardment of his ship, SS *Djemnah*, in July 1918.
[101] 'And he answered, Fear not: for they that be with us *are* more than they that *be* with them.'
[102] John Bridge Aspinall (1818–86) QC, recorder of Liverpool from 1861.
[103] A striking Neoclassical building opposite Lime Street railway station; opened in 1854, it housed both the Assizes Court complete with prisoners' cells and a magnificent concert hall.

Recorder's private room & found him robing. He is a finely made man, tall & with considerable presence, looking however very ill. He very kindly allowed me to sit by his side during the morning's proceedings. First of all came the sentencing **[128]** of several wretched people, who had pleaded guilty to various charges. The sentences were based more on considerations of character than of the actual offence. Some women on receiving their sentences wailed piteously, whereat the policemen cried "Order"!!! One case struck me as very bad. An ex-bailiff of most villainous appearance pleaded guilty to extorting money under false pretences. His method was to feign himself a bailiff sent by the landlord for the rent: thus he had extorted much money from many poor people. He got 18 mos. with hard labour: which I believe is equivalent to 7 years penal servitude; indeed criminals prefer the latter. A nice-looking boy was sent to a reformatory training ship for 5 years. He seemed **[129]** very pleased at the idea: and said "Thank you, sir" with an appearance of real delight.

Then came a bothering case of an Oil-manufacture. Was it a nuisance or was it not? On Saturday about 30 people swore to ghastly stinks: today a number of witnesses swore to the astonishingly sweet state of the atmosphere inside & outside of the Works!! A parson looked an awful ass in the witness box.

At 1'o'clk the case was adjourned & I took leave of the Recorder with many thanks, & returned to the Coroner, & said goodbye.

On my way to the Ferry I met Harry Rathbone. He entertained me at the Reform Club. Then I read the papers at the Athenaeum: & afterwards returned to Birkenhead: about 4 'o'clk: played tennis for 2½ hours: then read until the small hours of the morning.

Volume 3
September 1ˢᵗ – December 12ᵗʰ 1885

[Inside cover.]

From
> September 1ˢᵗ

To
> December
> 1885

Including a period of about 100 days spend mostly at 41 Hamilton Square, Birkenhead, and All Souls' College, Oxford. Three days in London, and three in Cambridge make the sole exception.

> H. Hensley Henson

Tuesday, September 1ˢᵗ, 1885.

[1]

I went with Miles Watson to the Picture Gallery, and there bought 2 photographs of pictures which struck me especially.

In the evening, according to request, though much against my will I went to Wombwell's Menagerie[1] with Bella & Sophie, Will & the Doctor,[2] Mr Holden & a cousin called Bell, & Noel & Cecil. I was vexed at the hour, and ashamed of my companions.

The "Doctor" with his hat set back on his head, a pipe in his mouth, and with Bell, (a young person very much like a bar-girl in dress, face, and manner) hanging on his arm, were soon displaying themselves to my shame & horror before the eyes of everybody. Bella stuck to me **[2]** like a leech, &, of course, in a crowd of cads I could not desert her, but my wrath was extreme, and when the barbarities commenced I insisted on retiring.

Wallace is a splendid beast still: and the tigers are very fine. A bear, a jackal, and a hyena were placed together in one cage, they worried each other frightfully.

My wrath at the events of the evening was a little mollified afterwards by my meeting Noel's father, Mr Haselden,[3] who has recently returned from Egypt, & who knew

---

[1] One of the leading menageries that continued to tour Britain while zoological gardens were established; founded by George Wombell (1777–1850; *ODNB*), and divided into three parts after his death.
[2] Fred Aspinall; see 2: **115** n. 91.
[3] Joseph Haselden (1823–87), born in Walton, Liverpool; m. (1863) Emma Maria Saunders (1838–1907), Alexandria; died at his home in Ramleh, Alexandria.

Gordon. He told me that Gordon's face reminded him of two men – Raleigh (?)[4] the famous horse-trainer, & Speke, the traveller.[5]

[3]

When Gordon was appointed Governor General of the Loudau he was offered the sum of £10,000 a year: which had been the salary of his predecessor. He at once cut it down to £2000 [sic]. Though transparently honest he did not escape the baseless slanders of the base: it was whispered that he was "feathering his own nest". When he returned to Alexandria he visited Haselden, & took him aside and quoted the words of Samuel. "Whose ass have I taken?" &c. (1.Sam. 12.3)

[4]

Wednesday, September 2nd, 1885.

Very wet day. In the evening I took the Mission Sermon: with S. Matt. 8.20[6] for text. Though it was pouring rain there were 29 people present.

After service Watson and I turned in to Sheriff, and had coffee, & talked until 1.15 a.m. after which Watson & I walked several times round the Square and then went to bed.

[5]

Thursday, September 3rd, 1885.

I wrote a letter to Milman, the Christadelphian commenting on "Christendom Astray".

In the afternoon I took Miles Watson to Wallasey, from whence we walked to New Brighton, and took the boat to Liverpool, & from thence to Birkenhead. Miles Watson strikes me as a greater moke than ever: I can't understand him when he does speak. He emits a sort of cackle intermingled with hisses, which is absolutely unintelligible.

In the evening I went to Church & carried back Sheriff's hood, & read the lessons inaudibly. Afterwards went in & had **[6]** coffee with him & talked until nearly 1. We arranged to spend next Easter vacation in Italy: and to be at Rome for Holy Week. Our expenses will not exceed £40 apiece, which is a vast sum to spend on oneself, but I don't think it will be wasted. It will be very pleasant travelling with Sheriff. In order to justify the holiday then, he will only take a short holiday now.[7]

I have been much annoyed today by Bella Aspinall presenting me with a little prayer-book & asking me not to let the rest of the family know. I am getting suspicious of that young woman: surely she can't **[7]** be so very silly as to suppose I care for her.

---

[4] Not identified.
[5] John Hanning Speke (1827–64; *ODNB*), explorer in Africa, after his death credited with having discovered the source of the Nile after much disputation following his return in 1863.
[6] 'And Jesus sayeth unto him, The foxes have holes, and the birds of the air have nests; but the Son of man hath not where to lay his head.'
[7] Henson went to Rome with Arthur Headlam, not Sheriff: see 4: **283**.

I do all in my power to place relations in a safe position by emphasising Celibacy of clergy & so forth. Yet I don't like the way Bella goes on at all. She asked me for my photo: & I said I'd see if I had one left. She shan't have one. It would be comic if it were not annoying to see how jealous she is of Sophie if I look at or speak to her. I am glad to hear she is going away for a fortnight.

[8]

Friday, September 4th, 1885.

Received a letter from Jennie: and a box containing 4 bunches of grapes, some plums, and a fig from home. I sent 2 bunches to Mrs Aspinall, 1 and 4 plums to Watson, and have kept the rest for myself.

I wrote to Jennie and Home.

Went to Liverpool & bought "Gordon's private diary of his Exploits in China by Sam Mossman["] (6/3) [6s 3d].[8]

On my return I was soaked through by a thunder-shower: & had to change my clothes.

Last night there was a meeting of the unemployed. When John Laird began his speech by saying "Times are hard" one [9] of the men cried out "Don't seem like it, to look at you." Various subscriptions were paid in, among others £50 from Messrs Laird.

One speaker who said that the married men must be helped, & the single men left to themselves, was terribly hooted.

It is unfortunate that the men have got it into their heads that the Charity Organisation Society have ample funds to relieve the unemployed. Therefore they prefer to be unemployed. Makin is awfully savage against the people who have subscribed.

The working men hate Makin with a bitter hatred.

In the evening I felt chilly [10] and therefore got Watson to take a walk with me: after this we had cocoa in my rooms, & talked on religion until midnight. We are agreed that the parochial system as at present worked is not adequate to cope with the evils of society. Sheriff & Horton would go in for its abolition. I & perhaps also Watson, would see the system reorganised. One thing comes home to me more thoroughly every day & that is the **enormous waste of clerical work involved in the present system**. Sheriff says that 35% of his people change their residence every year: they go he knows not where: & such influence as he has gained is dissipated. An efficient inter-parochial system is more what we want.

---

[8] Charles George Gordon, *General Gordon's private diary of his exploits in China: amplified by S. Mossman* (London, 1885).

[11]

Saturday, September 5th, 1885.

I sent back the proof sheet to the Clarendon Press telling them to go on with the printing. If it all is wrong Fletcher[9] is to blame for having the proof-sheets sent to me without giving me a hint as to what ought to be done.

I bought myself a pair of blue braces price 1/–: my red pair have at last perished.

I read de Broglie, and began the 5th book of Socrates: also I wrote to Thornton for Ammianus Marc[10] and Zosimus.[11]

I received a note from Edward Rathbone[12] asking me to come over for Sunday, which invitation I wrote to decline **[12]** because I had previously promised Watson to take his Bible Class next Sunday.

In the afternoon I played lawn tennis on a soaking-wet ground with the Aspinalls, with whom also I had tea.

I saw Makin, and told him that I would back him up if the roughs attacked the office. Two working-men were detailing their sorrows to old Mrs Aspinall; I asked them whether it was true that the men refused work when it was offered to them. They strongly denied it: yet Makin, & young Wilson, & Dr Miller, & Porter all say that it is true: and no doubt the men were interested witnesses.

[13]

Yesterday I went to 68 Camden Street but found the house empty, and on enquiry at a neighbouring shop, ascertained that Milman had removed to Tranmere: so I shall leave the books & my letter at the Christadelphian Schism-Shop tomorrow: unsealed in order that they may read it: it fills 3 sheets: and has been approved of by both Sheriff and Watson: though it may evoke an abusive letter from the Sectaries: about which I care nought.

---

[9] Charles Robert Leslie Fletcher (1857–1934; *ODNB*), historian and fellow of All Souls Coll, Oxford, 1881–8; Magdalen Coll., Oxford; tutor of Magdalen, 1883–1906, and fellow, 1889; staunch protestant Anglican, Conservative and imperialist; publications include *Introductory history of England* (5 vols., London, 1904–23), and (with Rudyard Kipling), *School history of England* (Oxford, 1911).

[10] Ammianus Marcellinus (*c*. 330–*c*. 391–400), Roman soldier and historian; his *Res gestae* chronicled the history of Rome from the accession of the Emperor Nerva (96) to the death of Valens at the battle of Adrianople in 378; it is the penultimate last major surviving history of antiquity, although only the section covering the years 353–78. An English translation by Charles Duke Yonge appeared in 1862.

[11] Zosimus, Greek historian who lived in Constantinople during the reign of the Eastern Emperor Anastasius (491–518); author of *Historia nova* in six books. A translation was published in London in 1814.

[12] Edward Lucretius Rathbone (*c*. 1859–86), youngest son of William Rathbone 6th by his first wife, Lucretia Gair; partner at Ross T. Smyth, a Liverpool firm established to oversee the Rathbone Brothers' trade in grain; drowned in Derwentwater; described by Susan Pedersen as 'the sunny and charming Ted' (Pedersen, *Eleanor Rathbone*), p. 26.

I went in to the Aspinalls about 8.30 and stayed there until 11 o'clock. After awhile [*sic*] Willie[13] came in, and then a cousin named Raymond, a schoolmaster & a Cambridge graduate:[14] a clever looking & pleasant enough fellow.

[14]

I have promised to go with Willie Aspinall to Rock Ferry **to hear Cardinal Manning**[15] **preach**. I don't relish the prospect of his company, but I can't allow the opportunity of hearing the Cardinal pass by.

Then I looked up the chapters in the Acts which I shall take tomorrow with Watson's Bible Class, after which, I turned in to bed, bringing thus to an end a most indolent week, the net result of which is nil, except the arrangement with Sheriff about the Italian trip next Easter.

[15]

14th Sunday after Trinity, September 6th, 1885.

I got up in time for early Service. In all, at the two celebrations, there were 43 communicants today.

Then I went with Willie Aspinall to S. Anne's R.C. Church to hear Cardinal Manning. The church was filled to its utmost capacity at least ½ being English Churchmen. I should think the Cardinal pleaded for funds for the R. C. Schools. His text was Heb. 2.14[16] and he preached from the altar step. **He is a splendid looking man, tall & thin, with a magnificent presence & a persuasive voice. In his cardinal's robes [16] he looked most effective. He gave us 100 days indulgence for being present: the brute of a priest who read out the indulgence dropped hs & was altogether a vulgar beast**.

"Our lot, brethren, is cast in a land where unfortunately faith is dim: I give you joy in that you have preserved unbroken the continuity of Catholic Christianity."

The cardinal denounced the Board Schools as an attempt to educate without Christianity. He made an indirect reference to the Recent Revelations into which he looked.[17]

---

[13] William Christian Aspinall (1853–1917), commercial clerk (1881); son of Henry Aspinall; lived at 43, Hamilton Square.

[14] Alexander Raymond Aspinall (1854–1934; *AC*), son of Joseph Aspinall, merchant; St John's Coll., Cambridge; school teacher at private schools in Lytham, Lancashire, and Eastbourne, Sussex; served in South African war with the Cape Colony Cycling Corps; founded Park Town School, Johannesburg.

[15] Henry Edward Manning (1808–92; *ODNB*), Roman catholic convert, 1851, and archbishop of Westminster, 1865–92; cardinal archbishop, 1875; influential in establishing Roman catholic schooling in Britain, and campaigned against poverty, degradation and exploitation; concentrated his preaching activity in churches in poor areas of his diocese.

[16] 'Forasmuch then as the children are partakers of flesh and blood, he also himself likewise took part of the same; that through death he might destroy him that had the power of death, that is, the devil.'

[17] Manning had maintained that the provisions for rate-supported education in the 1870 Education Act denied to parents the religious education for their children that the majority sought; also, that the provisions favoured board schools to the detriment of voluntary schools, which were usually church-run, as well as burdening the poor disproportionately in payment of the rate: 'Is the Education Act of 1870 a just law?', *Nineteenth Century*, 12 (Dec. 1882), 958–68.

On the whole I was much pleased with Manning: I wish I could hear Newman.[18]

[17]

I dined with the Aspinalls at 1.30: and at 2.30 took Watson's Bible Class. Only 6 boys present. I stayed to the children's service and heard Sheriff catechize. He does so admirably.

Had tea with the Aspinalls and explained at length the reason why it is wrong to call the Church of England protestant.[19]

Read lessons at church: had a walk round the docks with Sheriff & the Misses Aspinall: had supper with Sheriff: & turned in to bed shortly after midnight.

I forgot to say that **[18] I delivered my letter to the Christadelphians**. It was on our return from evening service that I found the Schism Shop open, &, on rushing upstairs, discovered 4 "elders" just putting things to rights for the night. They received me with great urbanity, & took my letter with alarming delight: which will undergo a change during the perusal I suspect.

[19]

Monday, September 7th, 1885.

I read de Broglie & Socrates until 12.30, & then bought a Standard. Cholera has appeared at Cardiff. In the afternoon I played lawn tennis with the Aspinalls & had tea with them.

In the evening I went with Watson to Clarke Aspinall's at Bebington & spent the time there very pleasantly until about 11 o'clk. Clarke insisted on my reading the article in the Times on Lord Ebury's[20] letter & Bp of Carlisle's[21] answer.[22] He is very suspicious of

---

[18] John Henry Newman (1801–90), leading figure in the Oxford Movement in the Church of England; received into the Roman catholic church, 1845; defended his conversion in *Apologia pro vita sua* (1864); guarded in his support for Ultramontanism; cardinal, 1879; canonized in 2019.

[19] At this stage, Henson held fast to the Catholic understanding of the English reformation, reinforced by the Oxford Movement, as a rejection of papal authority rather than of catholic doctrine. He departed from this position increasingly from the mid-1890s, emphasizing instead the protestant nature of the reformation but institutional continuity of the church: see Henson, 'The continuity of the Anglican church', in *The Official Report of the Church Congress, held at Manchester*, ed. C. Dunkley (Manchester, 1908), pp. 331–5; and the response of T. A. Lacey – a member of the council of the ECU, which campaigned for reunion of the church with Rome – pp. 343–5.

[20] Robert Wellesley Grosvenor (1834–1918; *WWW*), 2nd Baron Ebury, military officer; MP (L) Westminster, 1865–74.

[21] Harvey Goodwin (1818–91; *ODNB*), bishop of Carlisle, 1869–91.

[22] Ebury had written to *The Times* five weeks earlier, expressing his concern about the increasing lawlessness of ritualist clergy and the blessing they apparently received from church leaders, embodied – he thought – in the appointment of Edward King to be bishop of Lincoln, which Ebury saw as repudiating the principles of the reformation. In his response, Goodwin maintained that he did not recognize Ebury's portrait of a 'Romanized' Church of England, beset by serious ritualist or other problems; Ebury then turned on Goodwin's complacency: Goodwin, letter to the editor, *Times*, 7 Sept. 1885, p. 10; Ebury, letter to the editor, *Times*, 7 Sept. 1885, p. 10.

my conduct at S. Barnabas,[23] though I assured him that my sermon contained nothing controversial.

[20]

Mrs Clarke Aspinall investigated my religious opinions: though indeed she & all at Bebington seem to have made up their minds **that I am on the eve of going over to Rome** (!) *She asked me point-blank what I thought of the Reformation. Now I try make it a rule never to shirk point-blank questions: so I forthwith answered that I regarded the Reformation with infinite regret: it was the outcome of the follies & errors of centuries: inevitable no doubt, but it had permanently damaged the Church: her unity seemed for ever gone.*

To which Mrs C. A. replied nothing but looked volumes (!)

[21]

Tuesday, September 8th, 1885.

I received a letter from Jennie. While still sitting at breakfast, Noel came in to beg me to help him with his maps, which he has to do as a Long Vacation Exercise. So I squandered an hour in No 43.[24] Then I read Socrates & de Broglie for 2 hours: after which I walked out & bought a Standard, & a photograph of Gordon "The Last Slumber". Watson came in about 2 o'clk, & as it rained all the afternoon he stayed in my room: and we chatted in a desultory manner: until about 5, when we strolled about the docks for an hour.

[22]

After tea I spent about 2½ hours in finishing Socrates book 5. Then from 9.30 to 12 I wrote a "sermon" for tomorrow evening.

Thus ends my fortnight of freedom-from-Lyle: he will return tomorrow, and I shall enter on another stage in the campaign. All has been black failure so far, but what the end will be I dare not say. At least there is the comfort of knowing that the time is comparatively short.

[23]

Wednesday, September 9th, 1885.

Hardly had I finished breakfast before David appeared with a note from Sheriff asking me to go to Liverpool with him and spectate the Museum. I therefore went over to No 15: and while waiting in his rooms, for him to attire himself: behold Macdona[25]

---

[23] See 2: **117, 123–4**.
[24] Home of Henry Kelsall Aspinall, Noel's grandfather: see 1: **107** n. 66 below.
[25] John Cumming Macdona (1836–1907; *WWW*), former clergyman (rector, Cheadle, Cheshire, until 1873), turned dog breeder, barr., and MP (C) Southwark, Rotherhithe, 1892–1906; resident of West Kirby, Cheshire.

arrived: and desired Alford on the Acts[26] for his son now at Eton. Sheriff not possessing the book, I lent mine: & we then proceeded to Liverpool. The passage over the Mersey was very rough. The ferry-boat rocked so that one could hardly walk the upper deck.

[24]

Macdona told me about his Iceland trip, which – though he had but 5 days on the island – he enjoyed immensely. His party numbered 12, and they hired 50 ponies & 6 guides, taking with them all the equipment of Expedition. Macdona sent an account of his experiences to the Field, which I read with much interest. On the whole, Iceland would be a splendid place for a holiday, were it not for the 5 days sea-passage there & 5 days sea-passage back: the people are honest, & the country grand, & unique. The clergy & farmers entertain well and cheaply.

[25]

Leaving Macdona at Lime Street Station, Sheriff and I went to the Museum & looked through it: as I had been over it twice before there was nothing very striking to behold: not so was the case with the Picture Gallery, to which we next wended our way. The Autumn Exhibition[27] – admission 1/– – was in full swing. We spent about 3 hours in looking at the pictures. Those which most struck me were.

Absolution for the Lost at Sea
—Notre Dame d'Afrique Algiers by Andrew C. Gow. R.A. price £800. The priest in his vestments swinging a **[26]** censor, with a group of boys in crimson cassocks, surplices, & tippets, & carrying a crucifix & candles, while the rough sailors & their wives & children stand and kneel around, all in the presence of the Sea – is very fine.

Queen of the Tournament
by Frank W. W. Torphane. £1000 the scene from Ivanhoe, wherein he selects Rowena to be the Queen of Beauty & Love. The blush on Rowena's face is beautiful.

John Knox at Holyrood
By W. P. Frith R.A. £1200. Foreground – group of courtiers of both sexes sitting in a circle playing kiss in the ring. Knox just **[27]** leaving, a fiddler with a serio-comic face is opening the door to him. In the background Queen Mary weeps.

The Last Stand at Isandlwana
– Jan. 22nd 1879 by Chs. E. Fripp. £600.

Last hours of Chopin by P. S. Holland £210.

Love & Life by G. F. Watts R. A.

Gordon's Last Messenger by Fred Goodall R. A. £800.
A waste desert, horrible with skeletons & hyenas: and one lonely figure, rifle in hand, hurrying on his way, urging his camel, nearly fagged out.

---

[26] Henry Alford, *The Greek Testament* (4 vols., London, 1849–61), II: *The Acts of the Apostles, the Epistles to the Romans and Corinthians* (London, 1865).
[27] See 2: **59** n. 52.

[28]

Chatterton – morning of the 25th Aug. 1770 by J. K. Ferguson. £120

Gen. Gordon & the Slave Hunters of Darfour by Stanley Berkley. £250

S. Dorothea. 2 companion pictures by F. Hamilton Jackson £367.10 cash. They are in sections.

I. { 1. The Refusal
      2. The Procession of Aphrodite

II { 1. The promised sign
      2. The sign promised
      3. The passing of Theophilus
      4. Before the Throne

It is the Lord by Audley Mackworth £80.

After the Battle (of Tel. el. Kabir) by Mrs Eliz. Butter.

[29]

Hypatia by C. W. Mitchell. It is the last terrible moment when the poor hunted girl gains the altar, & stands up before it naked & white, stretching out her hand in mute appeal to the "great still Christ".[28]

The World, the Flesh, & the Devil
By Wm Weekes £36.15.

A group of slumbering swine, a World newspaper lying in the straw, & a raven looking on.

Freedom by Walter Crane £400

The Track of a Hurricane. By J. Mc Whirter. A.R.A., R.I.

Hamlet – Polonius by J. Yates Carrington £200

(1.) How now? A fox terrier regarding a cage hanging wherein a rat.

[30]

(2.) "A rat!" The dog on tip-toe ascertaining what is in the cage.
(3.) "Dead for a ducat, dead!["] The cage down amid rain, and the rat slain.

The Royal Fugitive by W. W. Wynfield – £300

Œuoue, by Philip H. Calderon R. A.
My heart is breaking & my eyes are dim
And I am all aweary of my life. £800

---

[28] A quotation from Charles Kingsley, *Hypatia, or New foes with an old face* (2 vols., London, 1853), II, 329.

Death of ~~Juncitia~~ Turciton[29] [at Beverley] by E. H. Corbould R. I.

Prince Ch. Ed. at Versailles on the anniversary of Culloden by Alex Davidson. £65

The Tithe Pig by Joseph North. £80

[31]

This morning I received a letter from Burrows[30] at the Oxford House asking if I would lecture. I have written back to say that I am awfully busy, though eager to work for the House: that I will gladly give a lecture on Gordon.

In the evening I went to the Mission Room, & "preached" on Col. 3. 17.[31] There were 34 people present, exclusive of Walkington who is engaged in night work, Williams the ex-policeman, & Jones. If they had turned up we should have done well. This is the first time we have been well over 30. There was only one Miss Aspinall.

[32]

Lyle has returned and thus I am once more tete-à-tete with my permanent puzzle.

Watson came in to my rooms & saw him: after his withdrawal to bed I went over to № 26: and Watson & I talked until 1 o'clk. We got talking about *the Varsity*, & ***I told Watson what my ideas are about the future of the collegiate system and the non-collegiate students***.

Two things are clear to me.

1. *Whatever happens Education must always tend to get cheaper.*
2. *No system which divides the students into two classes according to their wealth* **[33]** *can be regarded as either satisfactory or permanent.*

The question is really this –

Can the college-system adapt itself to modern needs? If so then establish it thus adapted as the only system in Oxford. *If not, then abolish it, and establish another that can satisfy modern needs.*

The present arrangement which divides elements into two sorts: ranking one above the other: thus placing a stigma of reproach on honourable poverty is contrary to the tradition of University life, at once unjust & unreasonably opposed to right feeling and common sense.

---

[29] Or Turcitin.
[30] Winfrid Oldfield Burrows (1858–1929; *WWW*), tutor, Christ Church, Oxford, 1884–91; ord. 1888; bishop of Truro, 1912–19; bishop of Chichester, 1919–29; high churchman.
[31] 'And whatsoever ye do in word or deed, do all in the name of the Lord Jesus, giving thanks to God and the Father by him.'

[34]

Thursday, September 10th, 1885.

The 20th week of my exile ends today: there remain at most 6 weeks yet to be endured.

Tomorrow being the Birthday of Jennie & Aunt Long,[32] I wrote letters to both, sending to Jennie a photograph of Gordon sleeping. Thus passes my time until 11.30 a.m.

Then for an hour I read Isaiah in Cheyne's Commentary.[33]

In the afternoon I played tennis with Bella, Noel, & Cecil. The latter goes back to school tomorrow morning; probably I shall never look on him again.

[35]

After tea I read de Broglie for about an hour: then did about 1¼ hour's work with Lyle, and I talked with him until about 10. After which I went back to de Broglie, and read for about 1½ hours; by which time feeling abnormally sleepy, I wrote this and then went to bed.

This makes only 10 hours reading in this week as yet, an average of 2½ (!!!!!!!!!!!!!!) [sic]

[36]

Friday, September 11th, 1885.

[Page torn out.]

[37]

"Magistrate"[34] tonight.

In the afternoon I read variously for about 1½ hours.

In the evening Lyle & I went to the "Magistrate" & laughed very much. We got back about 11: he went to bed & I read for about 2 hours.

In all 6 hours reading today: 16 this week so far, an average of 3⅓ per diem (!!!!!!!!!!!!) Then I went to bed about 1 o'clock a.m.

---

[32] Emma Hensley Long (née Henson) (1829–1912), younger sister of Thomas Henson, Henson's father, and from whom he derived his middle name; m. (1864) Samuel Long; held by Henson in high esteem (*Retrospect*, I, 1); paid his fees on his appointment to Westminster Abbey: Journal, 22 Jan. 1912.

[33] Thomas Kelly Cheyne (1841–1915; *ODNB*), biblical scholar; Oriel professor of the interpretation of holy scripture, 1885–1903, and canon of Rochester; his first work was *The Book of Isaiah, chronologically arranged* (London, 1870); increasingly, he embraced biblical criticism.

[34] Arthur Pinero, 'Magistrate', a play that was first performed in March 1885 at the Court Theatre, London, and proved a box-office success; Pinero's first attempt at farce, it centred on a magistrate who becomes caught up in a series of events that almost leads to his downfall.

[38]

Saturday, September 12th, 1885.

At 5.30 I was awaked by Lyle's alarm which passed scathless over him. After a few minutes I woke him up, but he was soon asleep again: whereupon I renewed the operation & this time effectually. So he <u>did</u> get down to his work at 6. this morning, for which he is very grumpy with me. Such is human gratitude.

It is a very wet morning & I anticipate another "barker" from Lyle.

Then I read de Broglie from 9 until 12.40, but hardly had I started Isaiah before behold Watson with a headache, & a proposal for a **[39]** walk: to which I weakly consented: and remained out until 2 o'clk: walking & talking in a violent wind.

After lunch I packed such things as were needful: then lent Lyle 2/– which may the Gods grant that I come not to want!

I received a letter from Burrows this morning accepting my offer of a lecture on Gordon: I must therefore turn my odd moments to account in designing a plan, according to which to write an eulogy on my hero. I don't want it to be a mere chronological affair, like the average lecture in a Methodist schoolroom: but a realization of Gordon.

Read Cheyne's Isaiah for awhile [*sic*]. About 3 hours reading today.

[40]

Total for the week 19 hours, or an average per diem of 3⅙ hours. This is scandalous, less than ½ of my proper average.

Then went to Liverpool, & reached Greenbank about 5. Miss [Eleanor] Rathbone was at home. At dinner there were 5 guests – Warren,[35] Osborne, Williams & two others. Osborne is in the army, & is busily engaged in getting up a "Gordon Memorial", towards which he has collected £6000. It is to take the form of Night-Schools for boys. He told me that Gordon was variously regarded in the army: some looking on him as fanatic, some as a truly religious man. He was very eager & proud of his success: & I fear tends to become Schismatic. Open air meetings are perilous always.

Willink[36] & I had a long talk **[41]** about church matters. He is apparently orthodox. Ed. Rathbone seemed suspicious: "Henson has such an invincible distrust of Dissenters" he said: whereat I merely bowed assent.

Willink told me Mackay's lecture on Gordon was badly arranged. He found so much to say about his early years that the time was gone before he had reached his career.

Went to bed about 11.15 p.m.

---

[35] Possibly one of the three sons of George Warren (1819–80), merchant and shipowner, Toxteth Park (1861) and Little Woolton (1871).
[36] Possibly William Edward Willink, JP (1857–1924).

[42]

15th Sunday after Trinity, September 13th, 1885.

Warren stayed over Sunday like myself; and being of the same way of thinking went with me to S. Agnes, where, as usual, a beautiful service, and execrable sermon.

In the evening we went to Mossley Hill Church: & found it crowded to excess for the Harvest thanksgiving. Diggle preached a long & foolish sermon, marked by pantheism and poverty of ideas, involving of necessity absence of doctrine and repetition ad nauseaum [sic] of phrases.

[43]

Ashton and I had a discussion about the merits of the R.V.[37] in which it was strange to find him taking the Conservative side, & me the Radical.

Everybody went to bed at 10.15 except me. I stayed up reading George Eliot until 11 & then also retired to bed, but not to rest: why I know not, but I passed great part of the night in testing the relative comfort to be derived from various positions: arrived at no satisfactory conclusion.

[44]

Monday, September 14th, 1885.

Pouring wet day. At breakfast hot discussion on the respective merits of sundry historians: and the true theory of English history.

Reached Hamilton Square by 10.15 only to find the room given over to the 7 devils of cleaning. Driven, therefore, out, I went over to Watson, who was on the eve of taking a marriage. I decided to await his arrival in his rooms; but after a while, becoming irritated at his delay, I went to the station & bought a Standard: becoming more mollified by the news of the death of the Abp of Aix:[38] I returned to 16 & found Watson [45] returned from Church. He tells me that on Saturday night, a drunken woman knocked him up to see her sick daughter, who was dying. Albeit doubting the truth of the statement, he accompanied the beast to a slum: & found there 2 drunken men: & a wretched girl dying from the effects of her confinement. She had given birth to an illegitimate child. Her father & seducer were the adjacent drunkards. – a horrid story.

I noticed announcements on the walls: inviting the unemployed to get work from the Corporation in <u>Stone-breaking</u> & <u>Oakum picking</u> at wages ranging from 2/– to 6^d a day according to number of dependencies.

---

[37] Revised Version. The work of revision, by members of various protestant churches in England, Wales, Scotland and Ireland, began in 1870 in the Jerusalem chamber of the abbey: Mark D. Chapman, 'New Testament revision company (act. 1870–81)', *ODNB*. Henson advocated use of the Authorized Version throughout his life as a more accurate rendering of biblical texts. See Journal, 13 Nov. 1932 and 24 Sept. 1933.

[38] Monsignor Théodore-Augustin Forcade (1816–85), archbishop of Aix-en-Provence, 1873–85; Ultramontane; death caused by visit to one of the cholera areas of his diocese: *Times*, 14 Sept. 1885, 6.

[46]

In the afternoon I attempted to read but had to abandon the attempt in about ½ an hour. Then I tried to sleep with no better success: after which I turned in to the Aspinalls & spent the afternoon there.

There came in Rosie Brook, and the Rev. Snowdon Smith[39] & his wife, (Mrs Aspinall's daughter, the mother of Hilda the Fair).[40]

Smith, brother to him of S. Aidans,[41] is not a prepossessing man, tall, dark, ungainly, with a black moustache, and white tie – unctuous & hypocritical – I like him not. Mr. Haselden was also present, looking as much like Don Quixote as ever.

In the evening I began to get out a list of books for Lyle: and afterwards from 9.30 to 10.45 read with him. He went to bed about **[47]** 11, and I read on then until 12.45. Thus the reading for this day scarcely attains 2½ hours: the result of the wretched slavy's cleaning the room, and my post-prandial somnolence.

[48]

Tuesday, September 15th, 1885.

I received letters from Mr Rathbone, Gid, Jennie, Aunt Long, & home: & *consequently squandered the morning in concocting an epistle to the M.P.*[42] **which should be approximately truthful, and as little offensive as possible**. *In this I am afraid I succeeded but ill: yet I at least did my best: to be honest & courteous, & if I give offence why it can't be helped. Watson approved of my letter.*

The Pater's 2nd box of fruit arrived this morning: I reserved 1 fig 2 pears & ½ a bunch of grapes for myself: the rest was divided between Watson and the Aspinalls: the big fig going to the former, and the big pear to the latter.

[49]

The afternoon was passed in an expedition to Bidston with Watson, who had a parochial obligation there. In the evening the rain descended & Lyle & I were confined to our room: but I had too bad a headache to work & therefore wrote letters: Lyle being wretchedly fidgetty.

About 10 he went to bed: I spent the next two hours in finishing "Gordon in China", and trying to knock out some sentences for a Latin Speech. Then I went to bed.

Work done – None

---

[39] Edward Snowdon Smith (1849–1896; *AC*), Sidney Sussex Coll., Cambridge; 2nd son of Rev. Richard Snowdon, vicar of All Saints, Brighton; curate, St Saviour's, Liverpool, 1875–7; curate, St Mary's, Wavertree, Liverpool, 1878–80, and rector, St Mary's, Wavertree, 1880–6.
[40] Charlotte Snowdon Smith (née Aspinall) (b. 1855), daughter of John Bridge and Eliza Aspinall.
[41] William Saumarez Smith (1854–1909; *WWW*), Trinity Coll., Cambridge; principal, St Aidan's Coll., Birkenhead, 1869–90.
[42] William Rathbone VI (1819–1902; *ODNB*), partner in the family shipping firm, Rathbone Brothers & Co., from 1841; active in philanthropic work in Liverpool from 1849 and in the Liverpool Select Vestry from 1867; MP (L), Liverpool, 1868–80, Caernarvonshire, 1880–5, North Caernarvonshire, 1885–95.

[50]

Wednesday, September 16th, 1885.

I received a letter from Hutton.[43]

From 9 to 12 I read Socrates.

From 12 to 1.30 I played tennis with the Aspinalls.

From 3 to 5.30 I played tennis with Noel: with great effort managing to give him two sets out of 3: & so to gain the 1/– staked. The games were

my 6 to his 7
my 6 to his 1 } =16 to his 14
my 4 to his 6

At 7.45 I went to the mission-service. There were present no less than 43 persons exclusive of Watson & me. I repeated the address I gave at Tranmere with variations. Watson complains that I spoke for 35 minutes. Two small hitches **[51]** occurred. Rutter,[44] the Sunday School Superintendent omitted to send the keys of the hymn-book cupboard, and harmonium. As several people brought their own hymn-books, and Tibbits produced a key able to open the harmonium, this hitch was partially rectified.

The second incident was more serious. In showing Watson the lesson to be read I pointed to a verse in the chapter (2 Kings 6) as the end of the lesson. He took it as the beginning: & detailed, by consequence, with ghastly deliberation, the squabble of two indigent females of Israel over a boiled baby (!). This lesson was neither pertinent to the occasion, nor in any way edifying. It secured close attention (!)

[52]

The hand-shaking is becoming quite a big operation. The numbers at the Mission Service since I kept count are as follows:–

July 22nd	I preached		10
July 29th	Sheriff	"	15
Aug. 5th	I	"	17
Aug. 12th	I	"	30
Aug. 19th	I	"	23
Aug. 26th	I	"	28
Sept. 2nd	I	"	29
Sept. 9th	I	"	34
Sept. 16th	I	"	43

---

[43] William Holden Hutton (1860–1930; *ODNB*), fellow of St John's Coll., Oxford, 1884–1923; ord. 1886; like Watson, tutored Henson for his finals in the Modern History School; urged Henson to compete for an All Souls fellowship in October 1884 (*Retrospect*, I, 4); reader in Indian history, Univ. of Oxford, 1913–20; dean of Winchester Cathedral, 1919–30.

[44] Hugh Smith Rutter (1837–98), railway ticket collector, Holy Trinity parish, Birkenhead (1891 census); b. Warrington, Cheshire.

Watson tells me that Clarke Aspinall received a letter from somebody at Tranmere thanking him for sending me to take the service. This is satisfactory so far as it goes, which isn't far.

[53]

Watson & I turned in to the Aspinalls & spent 2 hours. H. K. had been attending a meeting of the unemployed workmen, of whom, he says, the number is no less than 5000. Their great fear is that the landlords will insist on their rents. The charity organisation funds & the stone-breaking & oakum-picking promise to supply them with sufficient to eat. The problem is to find money for the rent. They strongly urge that the Corporation should start public works e.g. the enlargement of the Cemetery which will have to be done before long.

[54]

Meredith, Williams, & Sherry[45] (I have learnt his name this evening for the first time: his face I know, he has attended the last three times but one) also several female faces I missed. Thus the 43 was really a very legitimate increase on the previous reckoning.

I can't help fearing that the *numbers will fall back to their old level when Watson resumes the preaching. The reason is twofold.*

(1) he cannot, even at his best, make himself attractive to the people as an extempore preacher.
(2) he does not try his best, in fact, he takes no interest in the Mission Service.

I shall urge Sheriff to take the service regularly.

[55]

[Page torn out.]

[56]

Thursday, September 17th, 1885.

I spent an hour in trying to knock out that terrible Latin Speech: which hangs over me like a thunder cloud. Then – according to promise – I went with Jones over Laird's works – which are a melancholy sight, all empty, except for 2 small tugs. I gave him 3/–, which seemed more than he expected. How my money does fly! Lyle came back "seeding"[46] from his morning work: & went over to Greenbank. I shall be glad when I've done with him: for he is an unhealthy creature, & causes me endless anxiety. After "dinner" I played tennis with Miss Aspinall until about 6.30: winning 3 sets out of **[57]** 4 before tea, and 1 set afterwards. Then finished the "Last Days of

---

[45] George Sherry (1849–1907), dock labourer, Holy Trinity parish, Birkenhead (1891, 1901 census).
[46] Seeding (adj.) *OED*: 'That seeds: running to seed.'

Pompei",[47] & resumed my hopeless attempt at that speech. I shudder to think of its probable reception.

About 9.30 Lyle returned.

At 10.20 he retired to bed.

For an hour & a half I was engaged in reading Stubbs' Lecture on Cyprus & Armenia.[48]

About 12 o'clk to bed.

Work done.	1½ hours
Total this week.	7 hours
Average per diem.	1¾ hours

[58]

Friday, September 18th, 1885.

Read Socrates and Cheyne's Isaiah from 9 to 12.30: then bought my diurnal Standard.

I played my match with Miss Sophie for a pair of gloves. Happily she won: though indeed I tried my best: but was at some disadvantage, having the sun in my eyes in two of the three sets. The games were thus:–

My 7 to her 6
My 3 to her 6   } my 14 to her 18
My 4 to her 6

After tea I went across to Watson and fetched Finlay's Greece under Foreign rule,[49] of which I forthwith read the 1st chapter, thus expending 2 hours.

[59]

[Page torn out.]

[60]

Saturday, September 19th, 1885.

Read Finlay & Socrates for 3 hours. Fetched my Standard which contained *Gladstone's Manifesto to the Electors – all froth, no substance anywhere:*[50] Chamberlain's speech

---

[47] Edward Bulwer-Lytton, *The last days of Pompeii* (London, 1834).

[48] William Stubbs, *The medieval kingdoms of Cyprus and Armenia: two lectures delivered Oct. 26 and 29, 1878* (Oxford, 1878).

[49] George Finlay, *The history of Greece under the Ottoman and Venetian dominion [A.D. 1453–1821]* (London, 1856).

[50] Gladstone's morally charged address to his electors in Midlothian on 18 September 1885 included the reform of land ownership, electoral registration, parliamentary procedure, local government and education, and the enhancement of local self-government in Ireland: *Times*, 19 Sept. 1885, 8.

at Inverness on the land question – a most inflammatory production.[51] *Goschen*[52] *at Hastings.*[53] *Not a sound from the Tories.*

Read Jules Verne[54] in the afternoon: then bought Sophie her gloves (3/6). Afterwards had tea with the Aspinalls. Then finished my "sermon" for next Wednesday: & read Cheyne's Isaiah for about an hour. Then Daniel brought a request from Sheriff to go to see him: so I went & spent with him the time **[61]** until midnight. He managed to see Oban, Iona, Staffa, Lochs Awe, Lomond, Catrine, the Trossachs, Stirling, Dunblane. He attended services at the Established Kirk, the Free Kirk, & the Episcopalian Church. With the latter he was pleased. The Presbyterian Service struck him as inferior to the Mission Service.

I am glad to say that he has resolved to take the Mission Service himself.

Work done	4 hours
Total for week	16½ hours
Average per diem	2¾ hours

I despair of doing any serious reading in this place.

[62]

16th Sunday after Trinity, September 20th, 1885.

I went to Holy Communion at 8: to morning Service – Watson preached. I took his Bible Class at 2.30: there were present 9 boys.

Toby.
Geo Long[55] – slim, dark boy that comes to H.C. son of an engineer.
Sherwood[56] – horrid, fat, stupid, eating lips & jowls.
Holmes.[57]
Daintree Sen^{r58} – sensible and reverent but red-haired.

---

[51] In his speech in Inverness on 18 September 1885, Chamberlain had seized on the plight of the crofters in inveighing against the concentration of land in a few owners and the injustices of much existing law in relation to land: *Times*, 19 Sept. 1885, 6.

[52] George Joachim Goschen (1831–1907; *ODNB*), 1st viscount Goshen (1900), financier with the family firm Fruhling and Goschen; director of the Bank of England, 1858–65; Liberal politician, 1863–85; moved progressively towards the Conservative party, which he joined in 1893; chancellor of the exchequer, 1887–93; MP (LU) Ripon, 1880–5; (LU) Edinburgh East, 1885–6; (LU then C) St George's, Hanover Square, 1887–1900.

[53] Goschen's moderate Liberal sympathies were in evidence in his speech at St Leonard's on 18 September 1885: *Times*, 19 Sept. 1885, 6.

[54] Jules Gabriel Verne (1828–1905), French novelist, poet and playwright, credited with assisting the birth of science fiction through novels such as *Twenty thousand leagues under the sea* (Paris, 1870).

[55] George Charles Long (1868–1943), railway porter; Holy Trinity, Birkenhead (1891 census).

[56] William Richard Shearwood (1869–1922), railway worker (1901, 1911 census); son of a police officer; Holy Trinity, Birkenhead (1881 census).

[57] Not identified.

[58] Thomas Wilkinson Daintree (1866–1954), painter (1891, 1911 census); son of ferry toll collector, Woodside; Holy Trinity, Birkenhead (1881 census).

Daintre Jun[59]

E. Williams.[60] The choir-boy with the sad home history – nice fellow.

[63]

Wedgwood.[61] Short, stumpy & stupid.
Moorhouse.[62] ditto but better.

This morning Tibbits came not into choir but sat in the congregation. Wilson had told him that he sang wrong & had been supported by the others. Tibbits' amour propre was wounded. He was not appreciated. He retired (!). I wanted to go & fetch him back but Sheriff wouldn't let me. However this afternoon Tibbits came to me, & I put my arm round his shoulder & talked to him **[64]** about his conduct. I told him that God had given him the work of singing for him in the services of the Church: and that in leaving the choir, he had sinned. In the evening he came back all right: & hung about me in that queer, pathetic sort of way peculiar to penitent boys.

Watson & I walked up Holt Hill, vehemently discussing methods of preaching. In the evening we alone were present, as Sheriff retired to Southport about 2 o'clock. Watson preached on S. Matthew. Fair sermon shockingly delivered. Collection 28/4.

[65]

After having with difficulty got rid of the Aspinalls we had supper in his rooms & talked on until 12.30, **reading Matt. Arnold[63] & Wordsworth[64] as a sleeping draught**.

Haselden told me today that in Egypt it was strongly felt that the Soudan [*sic*] was necessary to Egypt. The abolition of the stick was a mistake: the Assembly of Notables a farce. He believes that we shall have to stick in Egypt, or hand the country over to some other power. Germany would be best, anything better than France.

[66]

Haselden was present at the Bombardment of Alexandria; he witnessed it from a ship in the harbour. He says that 500 men could have saved Alexandria from destruction, & relieved Egypt of £400,000 to pay. On the day following the bombardment he saw a

---

[59] Samuel John Daintree (1869–1936), architectural draughtsman (1901 census), engineer (1911 census); son of ferry toll collector, Woodside; Holy Trinity, Birkenhead (1881 census).
[60] Not identified.
[61] John Wedgwood (1871–1934), dock labourer (1891, 1901, 1911 census); son of a dock labourer; Holy Trinity, Birkenhead (1891 census).
[62] Albert Ebby Moorhouse (1870–1945), assistant water manufacturer (1891, 1901 census); water manufacturer (1911 census); son of a chlorinated water manufacturer; Holy Trinity, Birkenhead (1891 census).
[63] Matthew Arnold (1822–88; *ODNB*), poet, writer and inspector of schools; best remembered for *Culture and anarchy* (London, 1869), which sought to frame a common culture around all that was best in human thought and feeling, of which church and state were instruments.
[64] William Wordsworth (1770–1850; *ODNB*), poet.

number of unexploded shells: 3 shells from the Inflexible[65] lay side by side unexploded in the main street: another had penetrated through 5 stone houses & not exploded.

[67]

Monday, September 21st, 1885.

Hardly had I well settled down to work before Watson appeared & suggested a walk: so we went by train to Hooton & from there walked to Neston, and Parkgate with intent to reach West Kirby & take the train from there to the Docks. Finding that we could not catch the train, we resolved to strike across the peninsula to New Ferry, which we did by way of Brimstage, & Higher Bebington. We didn't get back before 3.30 p.m. The view across the Dee of the Welsh Hills was splendid; & the air was delightful. Flocks of gulls and sand crows were flying over the fields.

[68]

Wood[66] came to see me. He is in good spirits, having just obtained a post as assistant master at Exeter Grammar School, I think. Rooms, food, £100 per annum. He will take orders as soon as possible. He was bold enough to say he could sing.

Then I went in to the Aspinalls: they say that Thompson had a crowded room last Sunday evening when Holy Trinity was so empty: H.K. Aspinall, churchwarden forsooth, was "preaching" – it is scandalous. Sheriff should put his foot down.

Noel came in to bid me good-bye. He returns to school tomorrow. I shall miss him.

[69]

I read Finlay for 1½ hours & Socrates for about ½ an hour. I worked with Lyle for the space of an hour.

Total work —— 2 hours

[70]

Tuesday, September 22nd, 1885.

I read Finlay & Socrates for 3 hours.

Played tennis with Bella Aspinall, winning 3 sets out of 5:

---

[65] Victorian ironclad battleship built in 1876; fired eighty-eight shells in the bombardment of Alexandria, 11 July 1882.

[66] Edward James Wood (b. 1861; *OMC, CCD*), son of John Wood, Chatburn, Lancashire; non-coll., Univ. of Oxford; ord. 1886, Exeter; assistant tutor and chaplain, Exeter Diocesan Training Coll., 1885–8; vicar of Whiston, Liverpool, 1893.

My 6 to her 4 ⎫
My 5 to her 6 ⎪ my 17 to her 18
My 6 to her 2 ⎬
My 0 to her 6 ⎭
The other set I can't remember.

Then Watson & I went to Bebington & found the whole family at home. Noel was sent for, & arrived. I shocked Mrs Aspinall more than ever by my Romanism. The whole [71] family are wonderfully bigoted in their Protestantism.

They look with absolute contempt on the clergy: it is very aggravating: one feels inclined to burst out.

Moreover my evening was spoilt by the usual inevitable "confession" of my academic misfortune. "I believe your first college was Balliol, Mr. Henson." (!!!!!) This of course is pure babyish weakness, of which I am ashamed: yet let the scorner know that the confession is hard to make.

Work done	3 hours
Total for week	5 hours
Average per diem	2½ hours

[72]

Wednesday, September 23rd, 1885.

I read Finlay, Socrates, & Cheyne for 3½ hours.

Edith & Hilda arrived from Wavertree & charmed me with their appearance.

I read Victor Hugo's The Bellringer of Notre Dame[67] for the greater part of the afternoon.

In the evening I went to the Mission Service & preached from S. Matt. 17.19.[68] To my great sorrow the numbers had fallen to 33. Strangely enough the decrease was mainly made up of the abstentions of the regular attendants. Mrs Kempster[69] was away from the town. Meredith, Jones, Williams, Mrs Davies,[70] Sherry, & the Baptist were all away. That makes 7 whom we cannot [73] reasonably regard as lost: still it is very disheartening to have the number go down. In other respects I was pleased. The attention was admirable: & the people were unusually affectionate to me personally. Walkington said that if I would come to the parish, he would guarantee that the room should be crammed in a very little time. (!) Lazonby (?), an Irishman, who, with his wife, has attended for at least two times, gripped my hand fervently "Goodnight, I said[,] I am very glad to have seen you." "Goodnight, Sir, nobody who'se heard you once, would miss hearing you afterwards" (!!!). One little, white-faced, wrinkled old creature held my hand, & looked at me fixedly, [74], then slowly remarked "God bless you, Sir." I thought that I had done but poorly tonight, though Watson says I

---

[67] Victor Hugo, *Notre-Dame de Paris* (Paris, 1831); Frederic Shoberl, transl. *The hunchback of Notre Dame* (London, 1833).
[68] 'Then came the disciples to Jesus apart, and said, Why could not we cast him out?'
[69] Not identified.
[70] Not identified.

was more "eloquent" than ever before (!!). Therefore I must, perhaps, not grumble about the small number.

Watson came in & talked until 12.15: then he & I went for a walk round the docks. Beautiful moonlight silvered everything. The docks were almost deserted: night-labour only going on at two ships.

I got back at 1 a.m.

Work done	3½ hours
Total for week	8½ "
Average per diem	2.50 "

[75]

Begin by dissolving the circumstances under which the text was spoken: then lay emphasis on the eternal significance of the words of Christ. Reason why we must watch & pray, because

(1) We are ignorant of the future
(2) ~~our enemies are many & mighty~~. We are exposed to temptation
(3) ~~Failure is bound to follow our disobedience~~. This is the only way to gain heaven.
(4) ~~Our duty the Church. Wind up by mentioning some sins peculiarly fashionable today. 1. Unreality. 2. Selfishness. 3. Indolence.~~

How shall we best obey Christ's command?

1. By realizing the importance of religion.
2. By not being spasmodic in our efforts.
3. By realizing Church membership.

[76]

Thursday, September 24th, 1885.

I finished Victor Hugo's novel: and then went over to Liverpool with Watson and saw the pictures for the 2nd time. In the afternoon I wrote a letter home: and caused a fire to be lighted in our room for the first time this autumn. It was a terrible rough evening: Watson & I went round the docks in a furious wind. Rain dashes against the window & the wind blows in violent gusts as I write this. I did an hour's work with Lyle, & read Socrates & Cheyne for the space of 3 hours: making total for week 11½ hours: average per 2. 52.30. To bed at 12.45.

[77]

Friday, September 25th, 1885.

Read Finlay & Socrates from 9 to 12.30. Strolled up to the Park, which is lovely with autumn tints: and not as crowded with people. Walked round the docks with Watson: there is considerable activity among the dock labourers just now: and I hear, that the

America is having her old fittings replaced, and that Laird sends several hundred men over to Liverpool for that purpose. The streets were refreshingly free from loafers this afternoon.

I lent Lyle 5/– which may I not come to want!

[78]

[Page torn out.]

[79]

Saturday, September 26th, 1885.

Received letters from home with bad news about Jennie: the Mater has gone to Appleby: of which I am glad: if the net result of the disaster be her finally taking up her residence at home I shall be glad.[71]

I read for 3 hours: translating Cyril's 2nd letter to Nestorius.[72]

Then I walked round the docks with Watson: after which I went over to Greenbank: Lyle followed later.

Had rather a warm discussion with Ashton & Edward about the Church. **They both rail at Chamberlain**.

Miss [Eleanor] Rathbone says that there is much distress in her district. The mistress of the Board School showed her a class of "infants" all suffering **[80]** from want of food. They were not made to stand up lest they should get giddy & faint. How horrible! in that plethoric Liverpool too.

Work done	3 hours
Total for week	21 hours
Average per diem	3½ hours

[81]

17th Sunday after Trinity, September 27th, 1885.

I went to S. Agnes and was roused to fury by the priest: a miserable creature who made all his rs, ws: & preached a sermon so marvellously silly that I couldn't stay to the Celebration. I was in a rage: such a man would drive a whole congregation into schism.

Edward Rathbone and I walked together to hunt up Strong[73] for lunch: on our way we met with Ashton: so we paired, Edward & Strong, Ashton & I. Our talk naturally

---

[71] Perhaps Jennie had entered domestic service, for which her frail constitution was ill-suited.
[72] St Cyril of Alexandria (c. 376–444), patriarch of Alexandria, best known for his controversy with Nestorius, bishop of Constantinople, who maintained that Christ had two natures and was thus two persons, God and man; Cyril insisted in his second letter that Christ was one unified person.
[73] Not identified.

turned on questions of religion, and I laboured to show the illogicality of identifying Catholicism with Romanism.

[82]

"If I ever become a Christian, I shall be a Roman Catholic" he had said: and I earnestly strove to show him a wider Catholicism than that supplied by Ultramontanism.[74] He is very ignorant: and seemed very much surprised at what I said as if it were all new to him.

Later in the day the discussion resumed round the fire: Miss [Eleanor] Rathbone & Ashton v. me: Lyle spectating. I developed the Catholic argument at some length: especially showing the novelty of Romanism. Again I was astonished at the ignorance they showed: they seemed interested at what I said as if it were all new to them: may it not be useless!

[83]

In the evening I went to Mossley Hill, & heard a sermon on the Book of Wisdom, which somewhat pleased me. I think that that beautiful book is far too much neglected by English Churchmen. He mouthed his quotations in a hateful manner, but made some amends by having a fling at the Irish Church – "That misguided Irish Church [.]" [H]e referred to the recent disastrous action of that mongrel synod in "reforming" the prayer-book.[75] They have abolished the public reading of the "Apocrypha" among their other Reforms.

[84]

Monday, September 28th, 1885.

I came over from Greenbank: & on my arrival found a parcel awaiting me. It came from home, & contained a number of woollen-knitted "shawlets" & "mittens" for the old women at the Mission. There was also a letter from the good Mater. Jennie is in a bad way: and my anxiety is increased. I carried the contents of the bundle into the Aspinalls, in order to take counsel about the distribution. Old Mrs Aspinall is alarmed lest the "Mattins" and "Evensong" on the Harvest-Thanksgiving Notices means another advance towards Popery!

[85]

Sheriff has not managed to screw up courage enough to accept my offer of an Altar-Cross.

---

[74] A term first used between the reformation and the French revolution to assert the church's obedience *ultra montes* (across the mountains) to Rome. But while initially it represented a protest at Gallican absolutism, it became an instrument of ecclesiastical absolutism in turn. Lord Acton had attempted to construct a version of the 'wider Catholicism' to which Henson referred, but narrowly avoided excommunication in 1874–5.

[75] See Introduction, pp. xii–xiii, for Henson's exposure to the controversy at the home of a leading Irish bishop.

In the afternoon I played 3 sets of lawn-tennis with Bella & Sophie: and then saw old Haselden off: he leaves for Egypt on Wednesday from London.

I talked to Lyle for more than an hour about Richard I's reign, and managed to get him a little interested over St Hugh of Lincoln.[76] I wish I had the "Magna Vita"[77] here.

Lyle says that his people possess 7 steamers, & 2 sailing vessels: that represents an enormous amount of capital.

Read Cheyne for awhile [*sic*], & then to bed.

Work done 1 hour.

[86]

Tuesday, September 29th, 1885.

I dissipated this day in a sad way: in fact my mind is too unsettled for work. Watson fetched me out for a walk to Bidston, & this caused me to squander half the morning.

The afternoon went with Bella & Sophie: I managed to write home.

In the evening I received from Thornton "Isaiah, Chronologically Arranged": and read that until Lyle came a little before 8, when I spent 2 hours in talking to him on sundry subjects: after which he went off to bed, leaving me with a very dull, tired, helpless, sleepy feeling not able, at least, without sufficient energy to do anything for 5 minutes.

[87]

Lyle says that we shall leave here at the end of the week. I must get Mrs Worrall[78] to allow my things to stay at the house until I fetch them. It is very worrying this uncertainty about everything, especially when there is no necessity demanding it.

__How delighted I shall be to see the last of Lyle with his senseless, swaggering talk, & rude, boisterous manners! Ugh, how he revolts me – it destroys my appetite to see him eat & mangle the meat he "carves" – under any circumstances he is objectionable: and I shall rejoice to see him no more.__

In despair, I went over to Watson, and as he had no fire, brought him back to my rooms, where we sat and talked until **[88]** past midnight, & then walked round the square several times until it was nearly 1 o'clock, when we retired to bed.

---

[76] Hugh of Lincoln [St Hugh of Lincoln, Hugh of Avator] (1140?–1200), bishop of Lincoln, 1186–1200; formerly prior of the Carthusian monastery in Witham, Somerset; wielded immense personal and spiritual authority with Henry II and his successor, Richard I. Henson would have been drawn to his independence of mind in standing up for the church against both kings' demands upon it.

[77] *Magna vita* is the principal biography of St Hugh, written by his chaplain and fellow monk, Adam, of the Black-monks' monastery in Eynsham, and completed soon after 1212; it was commissioned by the Carthusians of Witham.

[78] Hannah Worrall (née Richards) (1820–1916), m. (1862) Samuel Worrall; daughter of an agricultural labourer, Newtown, Shropshire.

Thus passed away a melancholy day without having so much as one single delectable reminiscence, only this vain intolerable process of killing time. Worry about Jennie, worry about Lyle, worry about Gid, worry about home – was ever a poor wretch so burdened as I. And I foresee a passage to some sort of rest only through the avenue of new worries.

[Sketches on back of p. 89; profiles of the faces of three men, with a large bird in top left corner with a human face and a chick in the centre of the page.]

[89]

Wednesday, September 30th, 1885.

A letter from the Mater tends to increase rather than allay my alarm about Jennie. I can't understand quite this sudden collapse, just after one had hoped that she had been pulled together by the trip to Germany. If she manages to pull through, I'll take precious good care she isn't put into any position of labour again. Everybody will cry shame upon me, as it is: though, indeed, everything has gone against my will. I wrote to Podge urging her to draw on my purse ad libitum for the arranging of Jennie's room.

Then I turned me to Finlay, & had read about 50 pages, when Watson & Noel Aspinall stumbled in, & broke up my reading.

[90]

In the afternoon I persuaded Watson to come with me to the Liverpool Docks. We made our way from the Woodside landing-stage right up the North End. The arrangements of the older docks appear to be of a much more primitive description than those of the newer Birkenhead docks. The amount of shipping of all sizes and kinds is immense. We saw the Umbria, the Oregon,[79] and the America – which are being returned to the service by the Government. They are superb vessels. From the Oregon, cannon, & ammunition, and stores were being removed. It does seem a pity to undo all the work as soon as it is finished. And we may want the Cruizers tomorrow.

[91]

The docks form one long strip by the river bank. Then comes a long strip of timber yards: and then the huge, hideous warehouses: & then the cramped & crowded city. The quantity of timber of every description passes belief. Acres of ground are covered & high-heaped with it. Corn in sacks & poured out on the ground, & bales of raw cotton fill the warehouses. Huge packages of Manchester goods encumber the quays. Marvellous to behold are the divers kind of seamen: yellow & brown & black & white.

Everywhere there is motion and bustle, mainly unintelligible to the wretched on-looker. Nor are lacking the tormented lowings of tortured cattle, & the unmelodious protests of suffering Irish pigs.

---

[79] The *Umbria* and the *Oregon* were chartered as armed cruisers by the British government following a war panic concerning Russia's expansion south-eastwards towards Afghanistan and India in March 1885.

[92]

Oppressed by a bad headache I made my way back to my lodgings & reached them about 7 o'clock.

Hastily snatching some food, and **sending Lyle away with another loan of 10/–: he owes me 15/– which may I once more behold**! Then to the Mission Service, still with a cruel headache. Sheriff came & Watson. There were 41 people there: of whom 6 were men, viz. Walkington, Jones, Lazenby,[80] Spate (?),[81] the Baptist & his friend. Of decent people there were an undue proportion, viz. 2 Misses Aspinall, M^{rs} & Miss Hamilton,[82] 2 Misses Roose,[83] & at least 2 more i.e. 8, reducing the number of bona fide Mission folk to 33: but the decent folks, perhaps, bring the others.

[93]

Miss Lawrence came strolling in after the M^{n} hymn had been sung without any music. It is too bad: Sheriff should reprimand her.

However the service went off very well. Sheriff read the prayers: Watson the lessons: I preached. My text was S. Luke 21.36[84] and I spoke for *about ½ an hour or more. The attention was admirable. Old Walkington's distress at the prospect of my departure was great.* "Ah Sir, I felt a sort of frightened at Church last Sunday when you were not present." Then marking a space with his stick: "Look you, sir, I feel as if I would like to follow you from there to there". I had intended to give away my "shawlets" & cuffs [94] but owing to some mistake, Miss Aspinall failed to stop the requisite old dames. However I gave some to old Mrs Davies, & a pair of cuffs to Walkington. So I have rendered the stuff to <u>Bella</u> & Sophie to distribute next Wednesday. I stayed with Sheriff & Watson until 11.30: & then went to bed.

Lyle came in soon after, & soon began to groan as if ill: then to be sick recklessly over the room!!: to my fear & horror! When he is in the least degree ill he has no self-command whatever. Thus passed the melancholy and un-savoury (!) night.

Thus ends my connection with the Mission Service: a connection which has conduced perhaps [95] more than anything else to make my existence with Lyle endurable. **I leave the service with trebled numbers, and perchance, with more interests engaged in it**. I don't know what will happen to it: but I am certain that schoolroom could be crammed before the winter is over: but **this will only be by throwing enthusiasm into the work, and thinking it worth while to do it well**. There is much to make the Mission Service important. There, at least, one is free to speak the truth without humiliating considerations as to whether offence will be given. In the Mission Service

---

[80] Matthew Lazenby (1850–1906), b. Ireland; general labourer, Holy Trinity parish, Birkenhead; married with four children (1881 census).
[81] Not identified.
[82] Christina Hamilton (née Cairns) (1848–1903), born Dumfries; m. (1868) William Hamilton, general labourer; Agnes Hamilton (b. 1874); Holy Trinity parish, Birkenhead (1881, 1891, 1901 census).
[83] The family of Edward Roose (c. 1820–87) had moved to Birkenhead from Herefordshire in the early 1880s; in the 1881 census, his occupation is listed as 'late of Lincoln's Inn'. He and his wife Alice had six daughters.
[84] 'Watch ye therefore, and pray always, that ye may be accounted worthy to escape all these things that shall come to pass, and to stand before the Son of Man.'

Sheriff has the means whereby to form for himself a Catholic minded congregation [96] wherewith in time to leaven, or overawe, the Protestant majority, which now forms the mass of the congregation. Then hereby, a close acquaintance with a section of the parishioners is made possible. As soon as anybody once sets foot in the Mission Room, he ought to be secured: this must be done by the clergy and district-visitors: had it been done thoroughly during the past 2 months only we should have been well over 50.

It must be remembered that this evening was wild & wet: & that, therefore, 41 was all the more creditable.

[97]

Thursday, October 1st, 1885.

This day marks the completion of 23 weeks of my exile. Wearily have the days passed by: at most there only remain 3 weeks more ere I am released.

Miss Aspinall brought back my Gordon's Journal: & again preferred her request for a photograph, which I again replied with an evasion: but since she appears to have escaped her foolish idea, I feel more leniently towards her. Her request to be suffered to keep one of my sermons was benignly granted: & I even condescended to visit the church during the afternoon, & look on at the putting up of the harvest decorations.

[98]

I found Sheriff & Watson in the church before me, & soon succeeded in committing their reverent persons to all manner of scandalous conduct. Tea was provided in the vestry for the workers. Mrs Roe[85] being the presiding genius. Thus I squandered the afternoon in all manner of follies: and after service in the evening renewed the same conduct to the wonder of the churchwardens & sidesmen &c. I chaffed old Thomson,[86] & Porter until they were mad: & had no end of a game with the choir boys. So I passed the time until 10, where I returned to my rooms & wasted my energies on scribbling divers things.

[99]

Watson told me that the Woodside ferry-boats are subjected to a Government inspection every 6 weeks: that a body of 150 men are regularly employed in the repair of the same.

The men engaged in the Mersey tunnel works[87] are said to die rapidly from typhoid. One fellow told Watson that he had seen 3 men die before him, & he expected soon to go himself. There can be no doubt that these big works on which we plume ourselves have a horrent[88] record of murder locked up in their recesses.

---

[85] Alice Maud Roe (b. 1860), m. William James Lyon Roe (1849–98), Board of Trade examiner in navigation seamanship, Oxton, 1891 census.
[86] Andrew Ross Thomson/Thompson (1819–89), cotton porter, docks; born in Dumfries, resident in Holy Trinity Parish since at least 1851.
[87] Construction work on the Mersey railway tunnel commenced in 1881; it opened in January 1886.
[88] Horrent (2) *OED*: 'shuddering; feeling or expressing horror'.

Jones told me that very many men have accepted the offer of the Corporation viz. to break stones and pick oakum at rates varying from 2/ to 6d a day.

[100]

Thomson, the Churchwarden, told me that a few days ago he received from Germany a "circular" offering all manner of degrees for sale. I had supposed that this odious & contemptible traffic had expired.

Sheriff has been appointed a Surrogate[89] by the Chancellor: by which he hopes to increase his income: because he is well placed for the sale of marriage licenses.

I went to bed at 12.45 after another squandered day.

[101]

Friday, October 2nd, 1885.

I walked round the great float with Watson: absolutely nothing going on.

Lord Shaftesbury[90] died yesterday. R.I.P.

I received a letter from home: no news about Jennie, more than I know already. Then I went to the Church, and fooled about among the decorators.

Hardly had I sat down from returning from church before Miss Sophie came rushing in to ask me to dinner. So I went & met Charles Heath, & the unmarried sister. He is tall & thin, with a slight flaxen moustache, hideous mouth mercifully hidden as a rule by the said moustache, pleasant expression on the whole: kindly blue-grey eyes, & pleasing manner.

[102]

The harvest festival went off fairly. The church was well filled: the choir did their part creditably: anthem "Blessed be the Lord" by Gadsby:[91] Sheriff monotoned the first part of the service: Watson read the second: I read the lessons: Heath preached a most disgusting sermon, wanting in good taste as in suitability to the occasion. He rambled, and mixed his metaphors, & broke up the construction of his sentences: paucity of ideas combined with carelessness of composition: its length was as objectionable as its disconnection & poverty. Yet H.K. Aspinall was flowing over with praise of the sermon: and forced me into endless lies!

Collection £5.1.2.

---

[89] Surrogate (1b) *OED*: 'The deputy of an ecclesiastical judge, of a bishop, or bishop's chancellor, especially one who grants licenses to marry without banns.'

[90] Anthony Ashley-Cooper (1801–85; *ODNB*), 7th earl of Shaftesbury (1851), Anglican evangelical and social reformer.

[91] Henry Robert Gadsby (1842–1907; *ODNB*), organist and composer; professor of harmony, Guildhall School of Music, 1880–1907; his many works included the harvest anthem, 'Blessed be the name of the Lord' (1878).

[103]

Sheriff, Watson, & I went to the Aspinalls after service, & had music & singing with the ladies: then to the smoking room, where conversations turned on the existing trade depression. There are 2600 houses empty in Birkenhead: representing a population of at least 13000: some will have gone into single room tenements: most have left the town. The depression is making itself felt in various ways, e.g. the receipts of the Woodside Ferry have fallen off £100 a week. Tonight the unemployed are holding a mass meeting to consider the conduct of the Corporation. Aspinall says that public works ought to be undertaken: so say the men: I am in a fix on the matter.

[104]

Then we talked about ships. The Great Eastern is again for sale: she can be bought for any sum not under £12,000. Last time she fetched £28,000. Her shell is as good as ever, & it would, perhaps, pay to put engines in her, & twin-screws & run her as a passenger steamer. There would be plenty of passengers because of the comparative immunity from sea-sickness. The growing dock in Birkenhead is large enough to take her: but it would be necessary to destroy a large portion of the dock to enable her to enter. Some years ago she was done up at Rock Ferry by Laird Brothers, who haven't recovered their expenses said to amount to £5000.

[105]

There are 160 steamers lying idle in the Tyne. Of the greater Lines, only the White Star (Ismay, Imrie & Co?) pay. Even Hoult's China line is working at a loss. The Cunard line is in a bad way.

Sailing ships are being produced at an excessive pace now: they are said to pay better than steamers. San Francisco is said to be chock-full of sailing vessels without employment. In the construction of these sailing vessels rumour says there is no end of jerry-building.

Shortly after midnight I returned to my rooms: and found Lyle. He has seen his father: who is coming over here tomorrow (!) when I suppose I shall see him. **[106]** I try to think sometimes about the probable results of the interview. What will be Rathbone's line of inquiry? For myself, there is nothing to be rendered but the record of failure: I wish he would pay me, and let me go off on Monday next: but this is more than improbable.[92] I do hope – though this too, I feel, is chimerical – that we shall secure an amicable parting. At Oxford there await me "explanations" with Ball & Raper:[93] every discussion of my disaster will be torturing. Yet any settlement of the matter will be welcome, even because it is a settlement. O for rest, and the end of worry! Gordon, I invoke thee.

---

[92] Using information in 2: **30**, Henson's six-month appointment was due to end on 22 October 1885.

[93] Robert William Raper (1842–1915; *ODNB*), Balliol Coll., Oxford; fellow and classics tutor, Trinity Coll., Oxford, 1871–1915; influential in securing positions for students at Trinity and other Oxford colleges as tutors, secretaries and scholars; his extensive contacts enabled him to establish the Oxford University Appointments Committee in 1892 to place students in appropriate professional openings.

[107]

Saturday, October 3rd, 1885.

Lyle didn't go to work this morning: so we had breakfast at 8.45: after which I took back to Watson the books I had borrowed: & then went with him for a walk: which occupied the time until 12: I then bought a Standard, which contained an excellent account of the Fall of Khartoum by Major Kitchener.[94] It didn't fall by treachery after all: as the Rads have been so eager to assure us: but by <u>starvation</u>. Someday, please God, the English people will view the murder of Gordon with just indignation.

I received a note from Ashton Rathbone asking me to come over this afternoon as the M.P.[95] would like to see me!! So the encounter is fixed for tonight: preliminary skirmish, perhaps, this afternoon.

[108]

I met Redding[96] the Superintendent of the Girls Sunday School, he is flowing over with wrath against Heath for his wretched sermon: in which wrath – with more honesty than prudence – I agreed. It is to be hoped that Feilden[97] will be a better preacher. Nevertheless, I am sure that Charles Heath congratulates himself on his brilliant success, and receives with a sense of merit, the brainless laudations of his relatives. Such is human nature!!

*I went over to attend the opening of Term.[98] Earl of Derby[99] – **fat, pussy,**[100] **prize-fighting, sensual, conceited,** [word illegible] – **presided**. Bradley[101] made a good speech, as usual, invective against specialism. Rathbone seconded vote of thanks to Earl of Derby – ignoble task.[102]*

[109]

I shook hands with the M.P. and then re-crossed the water to get my clothes. Hardly reached Greenbank in time for dinner. The M.P., Sam Rathbone,[103] his daughter,[104]

---

[94] Horatio Herbert Kitchener (1850–1916; *ODNB*), earl of Khartoum (1914), field-marshal (1909); intelligence officer of the relief expedition sent to rescue Gordon.

[95] I.e., William Rathbone VI.

[96] William Redding (1857–1930), accountants' clerk/manager (1881, 1901, 1911 census); St Catherine's parish, Birkenhead (1881 census).

[97] William Leyland Feilden (1825–1907), Christ Church, Oxford; ord. 1849; perpetual curate, Knowsley, Lancashire, 1856–83; hon. canon, 1880, and chaplain from 1880 to the bishop of Liverpool.

[98] William Rathbone had played a major role in the founding of University Coll., Liverpool, in 1882, and served as president in 1892.

[99] Edward Henry Derby (1826–93; *ODNB*), 15th earl of Derby (1869), politician and a founder of University Coll., Liverpool.

[100] Pussy (adj.) (now rare) *OED*: 'fat, pot-bellied; (also) short-winded'.

[101] Andrew Cecil Bradley (1851–1935; *ODNB*), literary scholar; Balliol Coll., Oxford; professor of modern literature, University Coll., Liverpool, 1881–9 (a chair founded by William Rathbone and his two brothers); professor of poetry, Oxford, 1901–6.

[102] The speeches were reported in *Liverpool Mercury*, 5 Oct. 1885, 8.

[103] Samuel Greg Rathbone (1823–1903), William Rathbone VI's brother and merchant and partner in Rathbone Bros & Co.; Liberal councillor in Liverpool in the 1860s; JP for more than forty years; campaigner for the improvement of elementary schools in the city.

[104] Samuel Rathbone had five daughters.

Ashton, Harvey, Edward, Lyle & Elsie[105] at dinner. Everybody very courteous esp. Rathbone himself.

Went to bed at 11.15.

Rathbone told a good story about Sherbrooke.[106] Thomson[107] is a very deaf member: & makes pertinacious efforts to hear: roving about the house for good positions, & swinging his ear trumpet with energy. Lowe from the gallery beholding him remarked "I never saw a man more anxious to divest himself of his natural advantages."

[110]

18th Sunday after Trinity, October 4th, 1885.

After breakfast the M.P. took me for a stroll in the Garden & discussed Lyle. As I expected Lyle lied about the smoking. I told Rathbone exactly my attitude. Concluding scene[:]

M.P. I do not regard the time as wasted. I think you acted rightly. I tried my best, & I failed.

Then went to Unitarian chapel: heard a capital discussion of American extinct volcanoes from Beard,[108] which I had for courtesy sake to call a sermon. In truth there was no religion in it at all.

[111]

To be fair to Beard, I allow that he is eloquent, and impressive: but I cannot consent to call his discourse religious.

In the afternoon I went over to Birkenhead, & packed a box of books. Then in to the Aspinalls for tea & talk. To church and read the lessons. Canon Feilden preached a mildly good sermon. He couldn't see his manuscript, the light in the pulpit is so bad. Sheriff introduced me, but we had no converse: as I hurried away to chat with the people & bid them goodbye. They all professed great sorrow at my departure, & great desire to have me for curate, Mrs [word illegible], Venables,[109] Thompson, & Rutter especially.

---

[105] Elizabeth Lucretia Gair (Elsie) (1851–1920), daughter of William Rathbone and his first wife, Lucretia Gair.

[106] Robert Lowe (1811–92; *ODNB*), 1st viscount Sherbrooke (1880), MP (L), Kidderminster, 1852–9, Calne 1859–68, London University, 1868–80; chancellor of the exchequer, 1868–73; opponent of political reform.

[107] Henry Thomson (1840–1916; *WWW*), MP (C) Newry, 1880–5.

[108] Charles Beard (1827–88; *ODNB*), Unitarian minister and scholar; minister, Renshaw Street Unitarian Chapel, Liverpool, 1867–88; vice-chairman of council, University Coll., Liverpool; editor, *Theological Review*, 1864–79; works include *The reformation of the sixteenth century in relation to modern thought and knowledge* (London, 1883), based on his Hibbert lectures.

[109] Frederick William Venables (1844–1907), auctioneer, Holy Trinity parish, Birkenhead (1891 census); life-long resident of the Wirral.

[112]

Then back to Sheriff for a walk and supper: after which Watson arrived from Bebington & we talked until past midnight.

I bade goodbye to the Aspinalls. They profess great affection for my person: & I confess to liking the girls, though I abhor the males.

Thus came to an end my last Sunday in Birkenhead.

[113]

Monday, October 5th, 1885.

I slept at Sheriff's. Breakfast at 9. Quite a pleasant waking to see pretty little Daniel come into the room. I gave him 1/– and M<u>rs</u> Whitehorn[110] the same to prevent jealousy. Then to 43 & packed 2 more boxes of books borrowing one from Watson.

Telegraphed to Chapman.[111]

Then I went over to Liverpool, & called at the office of Rathbone Bro^s in Water Street according to agreement. Mr Rathbone received me with great kindness. He said that Lyle had spoken of me with respect & even affection. The outcome **[114]** *of the engagement had been better than he or I expected. For his part he could only say that had he his choice again he would repeat the engagement. He hoped that I would continue acquaintance with the family:* & *if I wanted work, a curacy in Liverpool w<u>d</u> suit me well, to which he could help, as in the cases of Doyle*[112] *& Beeching.*[113] *With these words & the requisite number of bank-notes I returned: not bringing myself to mention the washing.*

Then I went by train to Mossley Hill: had lunch at Greenbank, bade goodbye to Miss [Eleanor] Rathbone who was good **[115]** enough to express a hope that we should meet again: then departed, got back to Birkenhead at 2.30: finished my packing & caught the 3.45 to Oxford, which I reached about 9.

[Remainder of page torn out.]

[116]

So ends my engagement with M<u>r</u> Rathbone – my first essay at tutoring. How shall I look upon the months spent at Birkenhead? They have not been exactly happy, nor yet altogether wretched. At least some results have followed from my engagement:–

    1. I have become acquainted with the Rathbones.

---

[110] Not identified.
[111] James Chapman (b. 1813), college servant, All Souls Coll., Oxford, parish of St Mary the Virgin, Oxford (1881 census), retired college servant (1891 census).
[112] James Borbridge Doyle (ord. 1852), curate, St Peter, Walworth, Liverpool, 1878–81.
[113] Henry Charles Beeching (1859–1919; *WWW*), curate of Mossley Hill Church, Liverpool, 1882–5; joined Henson at Westminster, 1902–11, as canon of Westminster Abbey; like Henson, a member of 'the Brotherhood', an informal dining society for liberal churchmen in London whose other members included W. R. Inge, dean of St Paul's.

2. *I have made friends of Sheriff & Watson.*
3. *I have found out something more about myself, viz. both my inaptitude for private teaching, & my ability in public work.*
4. *I have looked at the masses face to face.*

[117]

The Mission Service – small though it be – has had a great place in my thoughts & perchance, will exercise great influence on my subsequent career. Not soon shall I forget Old Walkington – I believe I could work with these people: & get them to follow me.

As far as Lyle is concerned I feel that I have failed altogether: & nothing but sadness will remain with me, whenever I think of him.

[118]

Poor old Bertie[114] has had a paralytic stroke, from which he will probably never recover. He is more than 75 years old, & hasn't much strength.

Duff[115] is going to take up his residence permanently in the College, which is a splendid good thing. There will be in permanent residence this term: the Warden,[116] Bertie, Duff, Oman,[117] myself, & the two new probationers – 7 in all: The professors & Fletcher cannot be relied on: and the rest only will come up from Saturday to Monday.

Maguire[118] & Prothero[119] are both up here.

I sent off £5 to Jennie & £10 to Arthur.

[119]

Tuesday, October 6th, 1885.

I woke up with a delightful sensation of freedom from Lyle, almost as happy as when I was first elected: to see the light coming through the mullioned window was

---

[114] Rev. Hon. Henry William Bertie (1812–93), Christ Church, Oxford; fellow of All Souls Coll., Oxford, 1836–93; rector of Great Ilford, Essex, 1844–81.

[115] Harry Duff (1855–1905; *AO*), fellow of All Souls Coll., Oxford, 1878–90; barr.-at-law, Inner Temple, 1880; Henson conducted his funeral service: Journal, 9 May 1905.

[116] William Reynall Anson (1843–1914; *ODNB*), 3rd Bt (1873), (first lay) warden, All Souls Coll., Oxford, 1881–1914; MP (U) Oxford Univ., 1899–1914; parliamentary secretary, Board of Education, 1902–5; barr. and distinguished legal scholar; father figure for Henson, who in turn wrote Anson's memoir, *A memoir of the Right Honourable Sir William Anson, Baronet* (Oxford, 1920).

[117] Charles William Chadwick Oman (1860–1946; *ODNB*), fellow of All Souls Coll., Oxford, 1860–1946; Chichele professor of military history, Oxford, 1905–46; a close friend of Henson, who became godfather to his son (b. 1901).

[118] James Rochfort Maguire (1855–1925; *WWW*), Merton Coll., Oxford; fellow of All Souls Coll., Oxford; barr.-at-law, Inner Temple, 1883; MP (N) North Donegal, 1890–2; W. Clare, 1892–5.

[119] Rowland Edmund Prothero (1851–1937; *ODNB*), 1st Baron Ernle (1919), author, land agent and politician. Balliol Coll., Oxford; fellow of All Souls Coll., Oxford, 1875–91; MP (C), Univ. of Oxford, 1914–19; president of the Board of Agriculture, 1916–19; author of *English farming, past and present* (London, 1912); member of the Ecclesiastical Committee, 1920, following its establishment under the Enabling Act (1919).

positive pleasure: **breakfast in the common room with Maguire to talk to** – what a difference from the painful daily trial with Lyle. To stroll into the common room & find all the papers to my hand – how pleasant after being wont to toil, penny in hand, to the Station at Birkenhead! Chapman & Standwick[120] & even Henry[121] all seem glad to see me. It is very pleasant this life here, but alas, it is not fair.

[120]

I sent off a cheque to Wellden, & another to Evans:[122] & then went to see Bertie. I found him in bed, & his nurse, knocking about the room: he looks very ill, but is lively & hopeful of recovery. Poor old fellow. I love him better than ever now he is ill.

Then to the hair-dresser for cutting & shampooing: when wrapped in the barbaric shroud who should come in but the Warden:[123] we were mutually astonished at the appearance of each other.

[121]

I think I shall make an effort to do without wine this term: it must come to it sooner or later, so I had better make a beginning: and the moral training won't do me any harm. Moreover there's a certain amount of money saved which I at least, cannot affect to despise.

Furthermore, I will not buy any more books this term. This will be as hard to keep as the resolution not to take wine.

Thirdly, I will be as inhospitable as possible. Thus may I lighten the quadruple burden that comes upon me next year:–

(1) Furnishing rooms
(2) Trip to Italy
(3) Gid
(4) Those d_____d m_rtg_g_s[124]

[122]

Wednesday, October 7th, 1885.

I walked along the river-bank, until I reached Iffley: then I betook me to the church: and entered. There was absolute silence: and through the coloured glass the light fell softly.

---

[120] Possibly Alfred Standwick, college servant; m. (1863) Ethel Flown at St Mary the Virgin, Oxford; marriage ceremony performed by Frances Leighton, warden of All Souls Coll., Oxford.

[121] Henry Offley Wakeman (1852–99; *WWW*), Christ Church, Oxford; fellow and bursar of All Souls Coll., Oxford; member of the council of Keble Coll., Oxford; described by Henson as a 'devout and scholarly Tractarian' who introduced him to the leaders of Oxford Churchmanship, including Edward Talbot and Charles Gore – *Retrospect*, I, 11; publications include *The church and the puritans, 1570–1660* (London, 1897); *An introduction to the history of the church of England: from the earliest times to the present day* (London, 1897).

[122] Evans & Co., linen draper, woollen draper, carpet warehouse; 12, High St., Oxford.

[123] William Anson, 3: **118** n. 116 above.

[124] Perhaps a reference to the mortgages on his father's property in Broadstairs.

I was alone, sad, and troubled. /The illness of Jennie, **the unknown fate of Arthur**, the responsibility for Gid, the poverty of home – all & more were weighing harshly on my soul, shattered by the long failure with Lyle./ I wanted rest, & I betook me to God: there in that beautiful temple, all alone I related my troubles to the All-Merciful. Then I walked to the altar, passing the cord, which would deter the approach of the unhallowed. Standing before **[123]** the altar, with my hand upon it, **I vowed to devote my life to God and the Church**. On that altar was a marble Cross: figure of my future: I felt that I was accepting a life of struggle and sorrow: it was as if the Lord Christ had raised his hands & shown the nail-prints, and pointed to the Cross, & called me to follow Him. *There in Iffley Church, & standing before the altar, with my hand upon it I dedicated myself to God and the Church. Registered in the Archives of Heaven is my vow: and here also, in the time to come, a reminder to me not to forget.*

[124]

Thursday, October 8th, 1885.

Wrote two more cheques: making 4 in all. Viz.

	£.	s.	d.
Wellden	7.	11.	6
Evans & Co	12.	11.	
J. Thornton	21.	6.	10
W. H. Gee	5.	16.	
	£47.	5.	4
In Bank	£130.	10.	
Balance	£83.	4.	8

To oblige the rest I played whist, and lost no less than 4/9: I must make that up by some means or other.

[125]

A great argument with <u>Prothero, Maguire</u>, and <u>Duff</u> about the Church, in which I failed to adequately express what I believe. <u>Duff</u> is an Agnostic: <u>Maguire</u> a Rationalist and Erastian: <u>Prothero</u> **a mere Gallic with occasional periods of seriousness: eclecticism tempered by reminisences of Newman**.

I wish there were a more adequate exponent of Catholicism in the college. <u>Wakeman</u> never opens his mouth: and <u>Cholmondeley</u>[125] even if as orthodox in doctrine as he is admirable in conduct, is never here. <u>Johnson</u>[126] is **a mere frivolous wordling**: so I am left alone.

---

[125] Francis Grenville Cholmondeley (1850–1937), fellow of All Souls Coll., Oxford, 1874–1937; vicar of Leek-Wootton, Warwickshire, 1880–1905; rector of Broadwell with Adlestrop, Gloucestershire, 1905–37.

[126] Arthur Henry Johnson (1845–1927; *WWW*), chaplain of All Souls Coll., Oxford, and fellow, 1869–74 and 1906–27; lecturer in modern history at various Oxford colleges, including Trinity College, 1876–1903.

[126]

Saturday, October 10ᵗʰ, 1885.

Watson took his M.A. Jowett[127] was in great form, & performed his part with dignity: at the Ascription to the Holy Trinity, he lifted his cap with grace as the grace of Manning.

He (Watson) returned to Birkenhead in the course of the afternoon.

I spoke to Poulton[128] about Gid. He seemed delighted with the prospect of an ardent pupil. The question is what college. In S. John's he would have Ball & Hutton among the seniors: Maynard[129] & Watson among the juniors as friends. I will speak to Jackson[130] on the subject. Exeter is a rowdy **[127]** *college: & Keble is a snivelling place at best. Balliol & New are too big. Wadham might do. Dixie[131] is a good scientist: Wells,[132] also, would befriend Gid. I think the toss up is between S. John's & Wadham. I detest the clericalism & pseudo-Toryism of the first: while the rationalism of the latter also vexes me.*

How would Ch. Ch. do? It is a scientific college, and Burrows & York Powell[133] would help Gid on. Or Trinity?

I reckon Gid will cost at least £120 a year: and to the Parents I must give, well say, £80: my own requirements are at least £150: Total = £350.

[128]

How am I to provide this sum? In one of two ways

(1) by taking pupils – Coaching
(2) by taking a curacy –

The latter will be rather a piece of self-stultification. I reckon for Gid 4 years i.e. from Mich. Term 1886 to the end of the Summer Term 1890. My fellowship ends in Oct. 1891: if, by the Grace of God, I give Gid a fair start in life: it will not have been thrown away: the sneer against the idle fellow shall not lie. On the whole – considering everything – the chances for Gid are better than they were for me in Mich. Term 1881.

---

[127] Benjamin Jowett (1817–93; *ODNB*), philosopher and master of Balliol Coll., Oxford, 1870–93; vice-chancellor, 1882–6.

[128] Edward Bagnall Poulton (1856–1943; *ODNB*), zoologist; lecturer in natural science and tutor, Keble Coll., Oxford, 1880–9, and lecturer in natural science, Jesus Coll., Oxford, 1880–8; Hope professor of zoology, Oxford, 1893–1933; FRS, 1889; Kt 1935.

[129] Sir (Herbert) John Maynard (1865–1943; *WWW*), Indian civil servant; member of the governor's executive council, Punjab, 1921–6; St John's Coll., Oxford; Stanhope Prize Essay, 1885; 1st class Modern History, 1886; Indian Civil Service, 1883; vice-chancellor, Punjab University, 1917; parliamentary candidate (Labour), 1929, 1931 (twice); member of the Fabian Society.

[130] William Walrond Jackson (1838–1931; *WWW*), censor of non-coll. students, Oxford, 1883–7; rector of Exeter Coll., Oxford, 1887–1913.

[131] Frederick Augustus Dixey (1855–1935; *WWW*), zoologist; fellow of Wadham Coll., Oxford, 1885; lecturer in physiology, Univ. of Oxford, 1883–91.

[132] Joseph Wells (1855–1929; *WWW*), classicist; fellow of Wadham Coll., Oxford, 1882, and warden, 1913–27; vice-chancellor, 1923–6.

[133] Frederick York Powell (1850–1904; *ODNB*), non-coll.; law lecturer, tutor and student, Christ Church, Oxford; regius professor of modern history, 1895–1904.

[129]

Pember and Hardinge[134] both put in an appearance at dinner. Pember won't allow that I am a politician in any true sense. I always decide on a side issue.(!) He speaks very strongly against confession, and indeed I myself think that for practical purposes it would be wise for Anglicans to let it drop out of sight. Moreover personally, I very much sympathize with Pember on the subject: and while, no doubt, the power of Absolution is real & has a legitimate exercise, yet **I cannot think with my present knowledge that Auricular Confession has any adequate basis in Catholic Antiquity**. **[130]** *I described my own position as "Catholicism tempered by a great contempt of the clerical order." Pember is ready to acknowledge such Catholicism.*

Hardinge and I had a long conversation on various subjects. On religion his attitude is a little apologetic. I call him an "unconscious Catholic": he cannot see the practical bearing of Christian doctrine: but he is good & true & humble before Revelation, & I love him dearly. How would it be beautiful indeed to see that joyous nature radiant with the consecration of Catholic devotion! He is not far from the Kingdom: not so far as I am: with my super-structure of **[131]** unbending Orthodoxy resting on the crumbling foundation of a hidden unbelief: with my Catholicism kept up by a continued & painful exercise of will: while the skeleton of scepticism is always present. For me the unthinking gladness of Hardinge is no longer possible: it was once possible, I believe, but it is not possible now the ghosts have been raised within my soul, & must be laid somehow. The only alternative to this precarious Catholicism is the bitter, aggressive, secularism of J.A. Froude,[135] or M. Arnold. Catholicism is all-beautiful or all-hateful.

[132]

I have broken my resolution about books: for I have already incurred debts for
    Grote's Greece[136]
    Newman's Athanasius[137]
    Mozley's Miracles[138]
    Westcott's Gospel of the Resurrection[139]
    Stubb's Reg. Sacrum[140]
    Delitzsch's Isaiah[141]

---

[134] Arthur Henry Hardinge (1859–1933; *ODNB*), diplomatist; Balliol Coll., Oxford; fellow of All Souls Coll., Oxford, 1881–94; Kt 1895.

[135] James Anthony Froude (1818–94; *ODNB*), historian and writer; fellow of Exeter Coll., Oxford; rejected the Christianity of his clerical home and the Tractarianism of Oxford in his semi-autobiographical novel *The nemesis of faith* (London, 1849).

[136] George Grote, *History of Greece* (12 vols., London, 1846–56).

[137] *Select treatises of St Athanasius in controversy with the Arians*, selected and translated by John Henry Newman (2nd edn, 2 vols., London, 1881).

[138] James Bowling Mozley, *Eight lectures on miracles, preached before the University of Oxford in 1865 on the foundation of the late Rev. J. Bampton* (London, 1865).

[139] Brooke Foss Westcott, *The gospel of the resurrection* (London, 1866).

[140] William Stubbs, *Registrum sacrum Anglicanum. An attempt to exhibit the course of episcopal succession in England, from the records and chronicles of the church* (Oxford, 1858).

[141] Friedrich Delitzsch, *Biblical commentaries on the prophecies of Isaiah*, transl. James Martin (Edinburgh, 1867).

And bought & paid for
 Stanley's Eastern Church[142]
 "   Corinthians[143]

So much for Dame Partington!![144]

[133]

19th Sunday after Trinity, October 11th, 1885.

I went to S. Mary's for morning service: Ffoulkes[145] preached. Then – after lunch – **went the college walk with Prothero, Duff, Hardinge, and Pember** over Shotover, by Forest Hill, Stanton, & Beckley, through Mesopotamia.[146]

Dinner in hall – 9.

Talk with Pember & Hardinge on the church. **I am not at all satisfied with my position**. I absolutely disclaimed Auricular Confession, while emphasising the power of the keys: and moreover upheld the representative as **[134]** opposed to the vicarious position of the priesthood: in both of which points I am not at all certain: in fact, I believe I am wrong.

Hardinge told me that a friend of Döllinger's[147] told him that when Döllinger expressed his astonishment at Gladstone's attitude towards establishment, the latter replied that his mind had been changed by the unsympathetic attitude of the Church towards the Bulgarian Atrocities. He realised then that Establishment "maketh not for righteousness". The Dissenters were all on his side at that time.[148]

---

[142] Arthur Penrhyn Stanley, *Lectures on the history of the Eastern church* (London, 1861).
[143] Arthur Penrhyn Stanley, *Commentary on the Epistles to the Corinthians* (London, 1855).
[144] 'Mrs Partington's broom': a figure created by Sydney Smith in 1831 to illustrate the futility of efforts to resist overwhelming forces with inadequate means, however spirited the performance.
[145] Edmund Salisbury Ffoulkes (1819–94), followed J. H. Newman into the Roman Catholic church, then returned to the Church of England as vicar of St Mary the Virgin, Oxford, 1878–94 (*ODNB* entry for his son Charles John Ffoulkes (1868–1947)).
[146] An island in the River Cherwell at Oxford, so called because like Mesopotamia, it lies between two river channels.
[147] Ignaz von Döllinger (1799–1890), Roman catholic priest and theologian; professor of theology, Munich, 1826–90; excommunicated in 1871 following rejection of the doctrine of papal infallibility; well known in English circles; visitors included Nicholas Wiseman, first archbishop of Westminster, J. H. Newman, E. B. Pusey, Lord Acton – his pupil – and Gladstone.
[148] Support within the church for the agitation that followed Gladstone's denunciation of the Turks in crushing the Bulgarian uprising in 1876 mirrored existing religious and political divisions. High churchmen supported Gladstone, moved by his opposition to the Public Worship Regulation Act, 1874, and by pro-Russian sympathies; evangelicals and broad churchmen opposed him owing to their defence of church–state Establishment and distrust of ritualists. Nonconformists lent their support, seeking a revival of the alliance with the Liberal party that had faltered with the Education Act, 1870, and pressing for Britain to take a moral stance on foreign policy issues: see G. I. T. Machin, *Politics and the churches in Great Britain, 1869 to 1921* (Oxford, 1987), pp. 104–5; J. Parry, 'Liberalism and liberty', in *Liberty and authority in the Victorian state*, ed. P. Mander (Oxford, 2011), p. 97.

[135]

Monday, October 12th, 1885.

Lord R Churchill's Manifesto appeared in the Times.[149]

Randell[150] dined with me in my Rooms: *but would not stay late. He doesn't go to Durham until after Christmas. He says that Walter Lock*[151] *is mentioned as the Conservative Candidate for Wordsworth's*[152] *late professorship. Hatch*[153] *also is suggested. In my opinion & in Randell's, the man for the post is Sanday.*[154] *I hope Lock won't get it. We have too much Puseyism as it is in Oxford: but we don't want any more of Hatch's heresy. Sanday is orthodox but untrammelled, a true student, and in fact, an independent theologian.*

[136]

Tuesday, October 13th, 1885.

Dined at Exeter and met Napier,[155] the new Merton Professor. He is tall, pale, nervous with a painful twitching of his countenance when he speaks, says very little, on the whole gives one the impression of a specialist: when quiescent countenance not unpleasing.

Paid my debt to WWJ [William Walrond Jackson] whereby reduced to Apostolic poverty, but some chirpiness of soul is compensatory.

[137]

Thursday, October 15th, 1885.

A great argument between Prothero, Duff, & me on the true means of elevating the masses: Duff takes up the non-religious I the religious side. Prothero came out

---

[149] Lord Randolph Churchill Henry Spencer Churchill (1849–95: *ODNB*), politician associated with 'Tory democracy' and gifted orator, had addressed the electors of Central Birmingham on 12 October 1885. Following Gladstone's failure to command support on the Liberal benches and his resignation in June, Churchill condemned the previous administration on many fronts, including Ireland; he set out a manifesto for policies that would unite the country and strengthen the Union and the empire. By a small margin, he lost the election to the sitting MP, John Bright.

[150] Thomas Randell (1848–1915; *CCD*), Univ. of London; non-coll. and St John's Coll., Univ. of Oxford, 1st class Theology, 1882; Kennicott Hebrew scholar, 1884; principal, Durham Training Coll. (St Bede's), 1885–91; rector of Sunderland, 1892–1911; rector of Ryton, 1911–15.

[151] Walter Lock (1846–1933; *ODNB*), sub-warden, Keble Coll., Oxford, 1881–97, and warden, 1897–20; professor of exegesis of holy scripture, 1895–1919; Lady Margaret professor of divinity, 1919–27.

[152] John Wordsworth (1843–1911; *ODNB*), Oriel professor of the interpretation of holy scripture, 1883–5; bishop of Salisbury, 1885–1911.

[153] Edwin Hatch (1835–89; *ODNB*), theologian; vice-principal, St Mary Hall, Oxford, 1867–85; reader in ecclesiastical history, 1884–9; associated with theological liberalism; scholarly contribution under-appreciated during his own lifetime and subsequently.

[154] William Sanday (1843–1920; *ODNB*), influential English gospel critic, disseminating the ideas of continental theologians, notably Albert Schweitzer; Lady Margaret professor of divinity and canon of Christ Church, Oxford, 1895–1919; ardent defender of Henson during his controversial appointment to Hereford in 1918; publications include *The gospels in the second century* (London, 1876), and *Inspiration* (Bampton Lectures) (London, 1893).

[155] Arthur Sampson Napier (1853–1916; *ODNB*), philologist; Merton professor of English language and literature, 1885–1916.

famously, with a real assertion of belief in the power of religion. He has gone up immensely in my estimation. I now think that his Gallicanism is only assumed.

[138]

Friday, October 16th, 1885.

Much to my astonishment Jack Flowers[156] **appeared & of course dined with me. I introduced him to Markby,**[157] **Duff, Oman, and the Warden, who all were very courteous & kind**. He tells me that King[158] is causing offence by his mitre & so forth. Some people have said that they wouldn't send children to be confirmed by him. I hear that some of his Oxford friends have written to advise him to stop the mitre &c. **There is a considerable element of the contemptible in all this vestment business**. Flowers says that all the emancipated rustics of Lincolnshire will vote Radical.

[139]

I have now engaged to deliver my lecture on Gordon at 5 places:–

I 1.	Oct 21st	Hanover Social Club, 33, Gilbert Street, Grosvenor Square W.
2.	Oct 25th	~~British Workmens Club & Institute, 4, Lismore Circus, N.W.~~
3.	Nov. 10th	Messrs Fred Braby & Cos Library and Club, Ida Wharf Deptford S.E.
4.	Nov. 22nd	Oxford House, Bethnal Green
5.	Feb.	Eton Mission Club

[140]

Wednesday, October 21st, 1885.

I went to London by the 9 o'clk train: & on my arrival hurried off to the Great Northern Hotel at Kings X. There I found the Mater & Jennie: whom I saw off by the Granville at 3.15. Then I made my way to the G.W.R. Hotel at Paddington, & hired a bedroom. In the evening I drove to the Hanover Club, and found nobody arrived. Presently,

---

[156] John French Flowers (1856–1926), Lincoln Coll., Oxford; vicar of Bonby, Lincolnshire, 1884; brother of Richmond Flowers, headmaster of Brigg Grammar School, Lincolnshire, who encouraged Henson to apply to Oxford as an 'unattached' student when Henson secured his first job as an usher at the school; see *Retrospect*, III, 358.

[157] William Markby (1829–1914; *ODNB*), judge of the high court of Bengal, 1866–78; reader in Indian law, and fellow, All Souls Coll., Oxford, 1878–1900; Kt 1878.

[158] Edward King (1829–1910; *ODNB*), bishop of Lincoln, 1885–1910; prominent anglo-catholic, at the centre of ritualist controversy following the Public Worship Regulation Act, 1874.

however the vicar & his brother came: and slowly about 45 people, mostly middle-aged men gathered together: a wretched audience I think, but the Warden says it was decent enough. At first they were sleepy: but soon became interested, & at the end were enthusiastic.

[141]

They applauded rapturously at the close: & in fact only stopped by the effort of the Chairman. Then came a vote of thanks. "If Mr 'Enson'll come again I'll guarantee he'll have a noble house." "By Jove! Yes. I should think so" cried out a young fellow & the rest loudly applauded. "If I'd known what was coming I'd have insisted on my two sons being here, said one old fellow afterwards. Every young man ought to hear that lecture."

I went & shook hands with them all at the end, & told them that all Gordon's admirers were my friends. They cried out "Come again, Sir!" Then a vote of thanks to the vicar, & the proceedings terminated. I returned to the hotel.

[142]

Thus ended my first lecture on Gordon: as far as I am concerned it was a success. I think I may be pleased especially: especially because I was not, as in Birkenhead, speaking to women, but to men: mostly middle-aged.

[143]

Friday, November 13th, 1885.

Received a letter from Humphrey's, the secretary of the Deptford Club, thanking me for my lecture on Gordon, which came off on the 10th. On that occasion there were about 150 people, mostly middle-aged men. The lecture went off well, in spite of the frigidity of the people whenever I dropped a political remark: but my wrath was extreme to find my whole moral-edifice reared with such care & labour, brought down with a rush by a ridiculous comic song. The faces which I had sobered into becoming sadness were writhed in a moment with idiotic grins.

[144]

This morning I breakfasted with Bryce[159] at Oriel; and met once more the "distinguished American" White (ex-U-S-Minister at Berlin, & Vice-Chancellor of an American University).[160] He brought his wife:[161] and there were 2 other ladies present, one Bryce's

---

[159] James Bryce (1838–1922; *ODNB*), politician, jurist and scholar. Trinity Coll., Oxford; fellow of Oriel Coll., Oxford, 1865; MP (L) Tower Hamlets, 1880–5, South Aberdeenshire, 1885–1907; chief secretary for Ireland, 1905–6; ambassador, Washington, DC, 1907–13; founding fellow and president of the British Academy, 1913–17; Viscount Bryce of Dechmont (1914); publications include *Modern democracies* (London, 1921). Henson first became acquainted with Bryce while teaching modern history at Oriel College before his ordination: *Retrospect*, I, 6; and maintained a friendship with him until his death.

[160] Andrew Dickson White (1832–1918), historian. US ambassador to Germany, 1879–81; co-founder of Cornell University and first president, 1865–85.

[161] Mary A. Outwater (1836–1887), m. (1857), Andrew Dickson White.

sister. Ashley,[162] **Lang**,[163] Goschen, and two more beside myself & Bryce made up the party. There is no doubt at all that Bryce can make himself a most agreeable companion: & White is undeniably a good talker. Ashley is necessarily mute: but **Lang is charming** & the ladies as good as can be expected.

[145]

Thus I enjoyed myself more than usual on such occasions.

Freeman[164] was in capital form this afternoon: I fetched him by pretending to wonder at Salisbury's[165] sensations on finding himself patted on the back by the professor.

[Back of page.]

I have dined with

1. Jackson at Exeter
2. Owen[166] " Ch. Ch.
3. Freeman " 16 S. Giles'
4. Burrows " All Souls

I have breakfasted with

1. Bryce
2. Maynard

I lunched with

1. Hutton
2. Burrows (Prof.)
3. Conybeare[167]

[This page includes a sketch in profile of a man's head and neck.]

---

[162] George Edward Ashley (1831–1904), Oriel Coll., Oxford; rector of Stretton Sugwas, Herefordshire, 1884–1904.

[163] Cosmo Gordon Lang (1864–1945; *ODNB*), archbishop of Canterbury, 1928–42. Glasgow University; Balliol Coll., Oxford; fellow of All Souls Coll., Oxford, 1888–93, 1897–28; suffragan bishop of Stepney, 1901–8; archbishop of York, 1909–28; rival of Henson at All Souls and within the church, especially as a high churchman who became archbishop after experience only as a suffragan bishop; never forgiven by Henson for boycotting his consecration as bishop of Hereford, not on personal grounds but as an act of treason to All Souls (Cyril Alington, *A dean's apology* (London, 1952), 423); Baron Lang of Lambeth, 1942.

[164] Edward Augustus Freeman (1823–92; *ODNB*), regius professor of modern history, 1884–92; a radical in politics, his works included *The history of the Norman Conquest: its causes and results* (6 vols., Oxford, 1870–9). Henson was taught by Freeman in his rooms at Trinity Coll., Oxford: *Retrospect*, I, 6.

[165] Robert Arthur Talbot Gascoyne-Cecil (1830–1903; *ODNB*), 3rd marquess of Salisbury (1868; prime minister, 1885–6, 1886–92, 1895–1902); fellow of All Souls Coll., Oxford, 1853; chancellor of the Univ. of Oxford, 1869–1903; instrumental in Henson's move from Barking to the chaplaincy at Ilford Hospital in 1895 and from there to a canonry at Westminster, 1900.

[166] Not identified.

[167] Frederick Cornwallis Conybeare (1856–1924; *ODNB*), biblical and Armenian scholar; University Coll., Oxford; member of the Rationalist Press Association, 1904–15; author of the pro-Dreyfus book, *The Dreyfus case* (London, 1898); m. Mary Emily Max Müller (d. 1886), daughter of the philologist Friedrich Max Müller; m. Jane MacDowell, 1888.

[146]

So far this term

1. Maynard has dined with me   8
2. Randall[168]   "   "   1
3. Watson   "   "   "   4
4. Hutton   "   "   "   1
5. Biggs[169] "   "   "   1
6. York Powell "   "   1
7. Flowers   "   "   "   1
8. Burrows   "   "   "   1
9. Gerard~~ld~~ Hutton[170] " "   1

[147]

25th Sunday after Trinity, November 22nd, 1885.

Already I am finding Oct 7th an enigma to me. Fewer and rarer are my moments of legitimate enthusiasm becoming: more harshly weighs on my neck this yoke of simulating what I ought in justice to myself to feel. As soon as I love ought some d—d harpy goes for it. Yesterday I would raise Freeman on a shield, when that foul vulture D—y made him ridiculous. This afternoon I am to speak about Gordon: will the old love come back to me, or is he murdered too? I will take no papers with me, but see if the gracious inspiration will come.

[148]

This is the last Sunday of the Trinities, next Sunday will be Advent Sunday: that Sunday next year, methinks, will come at a crisis of my life: for in spite of all my wild words spoken & frenzied thoughts written down, my soul has not yet lost her love for the Ideal of the Priesthood. At this moment I would still, in spite of all, bow my neck to receive the iugum Christi.[171] O but you are half an infidel, and anything but a saint in conduct, you take Orders? Impossible! Demon, avaunt: the Lord X^t has called & thy malice though so cunningly aimed shall not avail. When he holds out the robe which bears the red crusading cross, I will wear it, though it prove a very Nessus robe.[172]

[149]

My audience consisted of about 150 people, mostly men. They paid the closest attention to all I had to say, applauding at intervals: and at the end they were even enthusiastic. I shook hands with some of them afterwards, & they begged me to come again. On the whole I think I must be satisfied.

---

[168] Not identified.
[169] Not identified.
[170] Gerard Mottram Hutton (1863–1957), University Coll., Oxford; ord. 1891; vicar, St Mary's, Brighton, 1905–21.
[171] 'the yoke of Christ'.
[172] Nessus Robe *OED*: 'used allusively ... to denote any destructive or expiatory force or influence'; after the shirt poisoned with the blood of the centaur Nessus that killed Heracles in Greek mythology.

[150]

Advent Sunday, November 29th, 1885.

I got up to service in Chapel at 8. It was a Celebration: then Morning prayer at 8.45: & Varsity Sermon at 10.30. Lunch at Conybeare's at 1.30: Chapel at 6: Dinner at 7. **Maynard dined with me.**

There were no less than 22 dining including Tommy Fowler,[173] Campion,[174] Vidal,[175] & a nephew of Dicey.[176]

At 10.30 I left the smoking room having committed follies enough for this day.

[151]

Tuesday, December 1st, 1885.

This day will be memorable for good or evil: for today I have done that which cannot be undone. From 9 to 11.15 I was on my knees in the Chapel of the Pusey House: Gore knelt by me, and at intervals he spoke of the Calls of X^t, to S. Peter, S. Andrew, and S. Thomas. He prayed & bowed his head in meditation.

I was so tired of myself: so weary of keeping up this hollow show of religion: as it were crushed by a sense of defeat: my "attitude" was impossible. "Viciste, O Galilaee".[177] The calm sorrowful, majestic Murillo looked on me from the altar. There was pity as well as rebuke in his face. "Lord Christ, I cried, Thou hast conquered: **[152]** I yield me to Thee." I was so tired, there was no power of keeping up my proud independence any longer. I left the chapel, & without seeing anyone, left the Pusey House. What were my thoughts? They were not happy; nor peaceful: but sadly quiescent. I had surrendered: an issue had been attained. I went to the Union, and wrote a note to Gore: it was brief: I remember every word.

My friend

If you hear of my going wrong again, write "Traitor" on a piece of paper & send it to me; you will add one more service to the long list I owe you.

Yours affectionately ever.

---

[173] Thomas Fowler (1832–1904; *ODNB*), philosopher; Merton Coll., Oxford; Waynflete professor of logic, 1873–88; president, Corpus Christi Coll., Oxford, 1881–1908; vice-chancellor, Univ. of Oxford, 1899–1901.

[174] William James Heathcote Campion (1851–92; *AO*), tutor, Keble College, Oxford, 1882; ord. 1881; curate, St Paul's, Chichester, 1880–92; contributed chapter 'Christianity and politics' to *Lux Mundi*, ed. Gore.

[175] George Studley Sealy Vidal (1862–1928; *CCD, OMC*), New Coll., Oxford; president, Oxford Union Society, 1885; ord. 1889 (Oxford); curate of St Giles, Oxford, 1888–92, and chaplain, St John's Coll., Oxford, 1892–1901.

[176] Albert Venn Dicey (1835–1922; *ODNB*), Vinerian professor of English law, 1882–1909; Balliol Coll., Oxford; fellow of All Souls Coll., Oxford, by right of his chair; friend and mentor to Henson at All Souls; in turn, converted to Anglicanism at All Souls through Henson's influence.

[177] 'Vicisti, O Galilaee' ('You have triumphed, O Galilaean'), the supposed last words of the Emperor Julian the Apostate.

[153]

After lunch I walked to Iffley: and entered the Church: the presence of workmen hindered me from acting as I wished, but I got as near as I could to the altar, **& murmured a renewal of my vow of Oct 7th**. The same sense of sad quietness all the way: at Ch. Ch. (where I dined with Burrows), it was the same: and when I came back Maguire railed genially at my unusual gravity. It is so still, I am sad as sad could be, yet with a new sensation of quiet, as of one who has struggled hard & long and has at last surrendered. There was repose from the strife, because I was smashed.

[154]

And now before me lies the time of test and trial: how hard, God only knows. It may be that the Lord Christ will help me. How I have been humbled! that which I sneered at, that He made me do: that which I have scorned is it that which he wants me to be? O Lord Christ, who hast called me long, and I have not heeded, who hast brought me low even to the ground,[178] have mercy on me: crush not the bruised reed: quench not the smoking flax:[179] give grace to me to live truly in the days to come: and suffer me not to fall altogether for I am Thine by right of conquest.

[155]

Tuesday, December 8th, 1885.

Poor Basil's[180] death has vexed me: **and Arthur's letter has much grieved me**. Alas, how unfit am I to strengthen another by counsel! I want help myself. Why is it that all of us seem to go towards infidelity? Is it something in our early history? Or is it the sine qua non for faith: the Trial, which tests the worthiness to be Christians of every soul of man? I had hoped that *my case might remain a secret:* **when here I am informed that my Brothers have left the Faith**. *Poor fellows, they are in a bad place: God have mercy on their souls.*

[156]

I am now determined by the grace of God **to go in for Theology in June**: To that end I must work, for I have lost much time this term. Here begins the record:

Dec 8th	5½ hours
Dec 9th	4 "
Dec 10th	3½ "
Dec 11th	8½ "
Dec 12th	5½ "
	27
Average per diem	5.24

---

[178] Isa. 26:5: 'For he has brought low those who dwell on high; the lofty city, he layeth it low; he layeth it low, even to the ground; he bringeth it *even* to the dust.'
[179] Isa. 42:3: 'A bruised reed He will not break, and the smoking flax shall he not quench: he shall bring forth judgment unto truth.'
[180] Not identified.

[157]

Wednesday, December 9th, 1885.

A morning fairly spent in reading – a long walk with Duff which tired me out for the rest of the day – port wine & a futile struggle to read – despairing cession[181] to the Last of the Barons[182] – whist losing 1/6 & surprised to lose so little – and then to bed, tired, dazed, & discontent [sic].

Why do I find it so terribly hard to read? My brain absolutely won't apply itself: everything else but the necessary work: how is it going to all end?

Am I going to fall back again into my indolent & unreasoning attitude? God preserve me from so great a fall.

[158]

Friday, December 11th, 1885.

For the first time this term I did a decent amount of work, at least in respect of the time I spent at it. And I have been more interested than heretofore. Cyril & Nestorius have a great interest. At least so far as their characteristic faults are concerned I have a sympathetic contact with one if not both. ***Intense pride, an unreasoning zeal for orthodoxy conceived of as something external to the individual, a tendency to domineer by material force, hateful cruelty, instead of courage, and a certain liability to cringe on occasion – these traits of S. Cyril of Alexandria seem to appear to me as in a spiritual mirror held up before my own soul.***

[159]

Saturday, December 12th, 1885.

Shall I go home or not? Strange how absolutely callous on the subject I am. Always I was won't [sic] to be glad to go home: now I feel not a bit anxious to go, rather bored at the necessity. Shall I wait until I do want to go home? But it may be very long before the desire comes.

Something is all wrong with me still. I am still always starting at the discovery of my own hollowness. Why am I not sincere? Verily the most admirable thing in all the world is sincerity: and that flies from my presence. Why? Will Sincerity come with calling & longing & admiring. Verily I fear not. Is anybody sincere in this world? I don't know, but I can conceive such being the case – Gordon.

---

[181] Cession (noun) (1b) *OED*: 'the act of giving way or yielding to moral force, persuasion, or temptation.'
[182] Edward Bulwer-Lytton, *The last of the barons* (London, 1843); historical novel centred on the power struggle between Edward IV and the earl of Warwick – 'Warwick the Kingmaker'.

Volume 4
Journal
from
May 4th 1886
To
July 11th 1887

**Mostly in All Souls,
Oxford, and Oxford
House, Bethnal Green.**[1]

[1]

Tuesday, May 4th, 1886.

Fuller[2] came to tell me that Hassall[3] thinks it unnecessary for him to coach this term. I hope I managed to show no disappointment in my face: though I felt it keenly in my heart. This term's prospects look black for me. Welby,[4] and Sperling[5] and Blackall[6] form the whole of my pupils. They may represent £25 between them. I have no base

---

[1] Henson scribbled the following note on the recto side of the inside page of the volume:
   Under this system the arable land of the community was divided into 3 parts: two of which were sown every year, and one left fallow.
   He scribbled the following note on the verso side of the inside page:
   By commendation a freeman placed himself under the protection of some powerful person, whom he acknowledged as his lord, & from whom he received protection.
   The notes may have been inspired by William Stubbs's lectures which he attended as an undergraduate.

[2] John Michael Fleetwood Fuller (1864–1915; *WWW*), 1st Bt; Christ Church, Oxford (3rd class Modern History, 1886), MP (L) Westbury, 1900–11.

[3] Arthur Hassall (1853–1930; *WWW*), Trinity Coll., Oxford; student and tutor, Christ Church, Oxford, 1884–1924.

[4] Charles Glynne Earle Welby (1865–1938; *WWW*, *OMC*), 5th Bt; Christ Church, Oxford (3rd class Modern History, 1886); politician, landowner and public servant.

[5] Arthur Hervey Baker Sperling (1866–1949; *OMC*), St Mary's Hall (associated with Oriel College); matric. Oct. 1884; farmer; emigrated to Canada, retired to England.

[6] John Ofspring Blackall (1865–1939), Merton Coll., Oxford (3rd class Modern History, 1886); land agent.

of operations like other men, having no first college to look to: and I have not the courage to do as other men do viz. ask for pupils &c. I stand by while they secure what I want fifty times more than they. Is it cowardice? or pride? and will the crash be Nemesis when it comes? Sometimes I cannot but feel that my purposes are too high for my position.

[2]

Scarcely had [*sic*] written these foregoing words before a note from Hassall came asking if I w^d coach a man in the Charters.⁷ I wrote at once to say yes: perhaps here may be a substitute for Fuller. So far as can be seen my finance is at present as follows:

	D^b		C^d
	£ s. d.		£. s. d.
Evans & Co	18.2.6	Balance in Bank	39.13.8
Baker & Prior	74.18.3	In hand	7.5.6
Gee		Owed by Fuller	10.0.0
Thornton	15.9.3	" " Sperling	5.0.0
Book seller			
Blackwell	8.10.		
	£117.0.0	61.19.2	
		Deficit	117.0.0
			55.0.10

Gee	11.3.6
Thornton	5.18.
Boots	2.19.
Blackwell	9.19.6
	£30.

[3]

I estimate my personal expenses (including Dentist) at not less than £50 for this term and vacation[.] [T]hat represent a deficit of £105.0.10 in round figures 100 guineas. Where is it to come from?

Tuition this term, say	£30
Advance from Burser	£50
Tuition in Mich Term	£30
	£110

Leaving a surplus of £5: This does not contemplate earning anything for the Long Vacation: about which I do feel very anxious. It is clear that my finances are in a bad way, all round. And I see no way of getting them straight. Economies in battells and books w^d tell in time, but my purpose is rarely strong enough to continue them long.

---

⁷ William Stubbs, *Select charters and other illustrations of English constitutional history from the earliest times to the reign of Edward I* (Oxford, 1870).

[4]

In the afternoon I played lawn tennis in the Quad: with Watt,[8] Haines,[9] and another.

I drank no wine in Hall tonight, *afterwards I went to Museum Cottage and* **saw Vidal. He has received a long letter from Paget**[10] **in reference to the Monastery**. *As was to be expected Paget is bland, and repeats Vidal's words approvingly, and speaks sugared generalities, and leaves everything in a mist*. **In their hearts these people laugh** *at the whole scheme, but they haven't the courage to do so openly. Adderley's*[11] *ambition is too spiritual, I fear, for Vidal's: I fear, the false asceticism of the spiritual Antiquarians has laid hold on Adderley: he is a saint: & could be an apostle if he w^{d} listen to St Basil instead of the Puseyites.*[12]

[5]

[Inserted later at top of page.] *I am glad to say that Waters got his deserts in the Schools being duly ploughed, much to his own wonderment. H.H.H. 29/5/87

Wednesday, May 5th, 1886.

After Chapel I summoned up "courage" to ask Johnson to recommend men ambitious of a reading tour to come to me. He advised me to inform Hassall, which I shall do: on the whole he spoke re-assuringly.

*Waters[13] of Ch. Ch. made his appearance – affected manner, sharp look, white waistcoat, and irritating lisp – Wants a first.

I paid into the Bank, Fuller's Cheque & Blackall's "fiver" = £15. I have there the sum of £54.13.8. From 10 to 1, 3 hours, incessantly talking is rather tiring: but I wish I had it every day instead of on three days only in the week.

I walked up to Iffley, and back to Oxford through the village, tired & dusty when I got in.

[6]

I carried bundles of Prospectuses to Keble and S. John's for Bates[14] and Bastard.[15]

---

[8]   Not identified.
[9]   Not identified.
[10] Francis Paget (1851–1911; *ODNB*), bishop of Oxford, 1901–11; Christ Church, Oxford; regius professor of pastoral theology and canon of Christ Church, 1885–1901.
[11] James Granville Adderley (1861–1942; *ODNB*), Christ Church, Oxford; Church of England clergyman and influential Christian socialist at Oxford; close friend of Henson and predecessor as head of Oxford House, 1885–6, referred to affectionately in that position as 'the abbot'; defended Henson in the controversy over his appointment as bishop of Hereford – Journal, 4 Jan. 1918, *Retrospect*, I, 235.
[12] Anglican clergy associated with Pusey House, Oxford, 'the Puseyum', founded in 1892 as a centre for theological teaching and pastoral care for undergraduates in memory of Edward Bouverie Pusey, a leading Tractarian.
[13] Sampson Waters (1864–1932), Christ Church, Oxford; barr. 1889.
[14] Raymond Cooper Bates (1863–1945; *CCD*), Keble Coll., Oxford; ord. 1889.
[15] John Muston Bastard (ord. 1887; *CCD*), St John's Coll., Oxford.

Vidal came to see me about 9. O'clock, and we renewed our converse [sic] of the last night. To both of us I think there has been given a vocation to work: **he is sincere and simple: I am hypocritical and obscure***: that is the difference between us. He is really religious: I doubt my own religion much. He is free from entanglements: I am not free: how I do long for freedom, God knows. It does seem hard that right across the pathway of my holiest hopes should be thrust the impassable barrier of the poverty of the family.* The impossibility of working as I could wish to work degrades me into [7] indolence, and the cynicism *that there from flows forth.* **It is very strange that there should be any unity between such a trinity as Adderley, Vidal, and me***. The spirituality of the first, the simple purity of the second, bring out into stronger relief the hollow word-weaving deceit of the third. Yet deep down in my complex soul I believe I wish to do the work of Jesus Christ. Verily if I could but know what he would have me do I would move heaven & earth to do it. But I perish in this ignorance.*

I wrote to Hassall about the Reading Party: which I hope may come off.

[8]

Thursday, May 6th, 1886.

Letters from Prothero,[16] Watson, and Carter (Rector of Sarsden, Chipping Norton, Oxon).[17] The first said that the Isle of Wight awaited the League: the second that Cheshire would shortly make application: the third requested whatsoever printed forms existed.

I am in great doubt what to do about the Isle of Wight. We have at our command this term very few lecturers.

1. Prothero, who is good enough for anything, but could scarcely be asked to undertake the work in his own place.
2. Curzon,[18] who is scarcely a safe man to send where consiliation [sic] is required before all things. Besides he is not certainly free for much.

[9]

3. Tracey,[19] has a lecture on Tithes which is scarcely applicable to Wight.
4. Denham, whose recent affliction exempts him from work just now.
5. Holmes,[20] who is not at all adequate for any important work.

---

[16] George Prothero (1818–94), Wadham Coll., Oxford; rector of Whippingham, Isle of Wight, 1857–94; canon of Westminster, 1869–94; a chaplain-in-ordinary to Queen Victoria; cricketer.
[17] William Edward Dickson Carter (ord. 1845; *CCD*), New Coll., Oxford; rector of Sarsden, 1868.
[18] George Curzon (1859–1925; *ODNB*), Baron Curzon 1898, earl 1911, marquess, 1916; fellow of All Souls Coll., Oxford, 1883; MP (C) Southport, 1886–99; under-secretary, foreign office, 1895–99; viceroy of India, 1899–1905; chancellor, Univ. of Oxford, 1907–25; rector, Univ. of Glasgow, 1908–11; Irish representative peer, House of Lords, 1908–16; lord privy seal, 1915–16; lord president of the council, 1916–19; foreign secretary, 1919–24; lord president of the council, 1924–5.
[19] John Tracey (1862–1947), Brasenose Coll., Oxford; tutor, Keble Coll., Oxford, 1887.
[20] Richard Ellis Holmes (1863–1958), non-coll. and Trinity Coll., Oxford; member of the OLL; ord. 1888, Durham; curate of Holy Trinity, South Shields, 1887–96 and vicar, 1896–1912; vicar of Tynemouth, 1912–30; see Journal, 15 Dec. 1913, 13 Sept. 1916.

6. I have my course of 3 lectures, which must be given somewhere: but I very much wish not to undertake the work myself: because (1) my real object being to screen my individual action behind the general action of the League will be imperilled. (2) I am not old enough or well-known enough to make the proper impression.

Copies of the Prospectus were duly sent to the Rector of Sarsden[21] by the first post.

[10]

I walked up to Carfax and bought Sismondi's Republiques Italiennes[22] 16 vols. For £2.10.; I have much desired the book but I know not whether I was right to purchase it, being in so poverty-smitten a condition. If I stop short here, & buy no more I shall not materially affect my position for the worse. There seems to be a fate against my being economical in the matter of books. Of course there is an extraordinary burden on me this year through the furnishing of my rooms: a burden which really amounts to nearly £100, or nearly the whole of my deficit for this year. If only I can get straight before the crisis at home becomes acute: £500 a year is the least I can do with.

[11]

The greater part of the afternoon was spent in the vain chase after College-Secretaries: had it not so happened that I met Brassey,[23] my labours would have been quite useless. Brassey is in the Schools this term, & therefore practically hors de combat. Returning to College I ran into [Gerard] Hutton (Univ.) whom I persuaded to play tennis with me. Afterwards I went to Ch. Ch. and hunted out Yarde-Buller,[24] whose report is not encouraging. On my return I met Phelps,[25] and asked him to name the man who would serve as Secretary for S. Mary Hall.[26] He mentioned Mills,[27] to whom I must write. Then I dined at Wadham with Wells: after which I carried a bundle of [12] notices to How[28] at Merton (who was out): and wound up by calling on Jackson at Exeter, with whom I talked politics for half an hour.

---

[21] William Carter; n. 17 above.
[22] Jean-Charles de Sismondi, *Histoire des republiques Italiennes du moyen âge* (16 vols., Paris, 1807–18).
[23] Thomas Allnutt Brassey (1863–1919; *ODNB*), 2nd earl Brassey (1919); Eton Coll., Balliol Coll., Oxford; public servant; member, Archbishop's Committee on Church Finance, 1910–11; founder of the Oxford University Endowment Fund and generous benefactor to the Bodleian Library.
[24] Hon. Reginald John Yarde-Buller (1863–1950), Christ Church, Oxford; BA, 1887; ord. 1890, Cuddesdon (see *Times*, 16 June 1950, 8).
[25] Lancelot Ridley Phelps (1853–1936; *ODNB*), fellow, tutor and provost, Oriel Coll., 1872–1936; Oxford; ord. deacon, 1879, and priest, 1896; member, royal commission on the poor laws, 1907–9.
[26] St Mary's Hall in the High Street, Oxford, was founded in 1326 as part of Oriel College; its principal was the vicar of the University Church of St Mary the Virgin. It became an independent hall within the University of Oxford in 1545 but continued to maintain close institutional ties with Oriel. It was absorbed into Oriel in 1902.
[27] Edward Francis James Mills (1863–1948), b. Banghalpore, India, son of Rev. Michael Mills; St Mary's Hall, Oxford; army and university tutor (1901 census).
[28] Walter Wybergh How (1861–1932; *WWW*), classical scholar, New College Oxford; fellow of Merton Coll., Oxford, 1884–1932.

I promised Wells to draw up some Rules for the Local Leagues, which are to be founded in the Country.

[13]

Friday, May 7th, 1886.

I paid Gee's bill, which minus discount amounted to £11.3.6. a most formidable amount. Together with the £2.10. of yesterday, it reduces my balance by £13.13.6. i.e. my balance = £41.0.2.

Looking back at my old cheque-book since I was elected here, I find the following sums paid to booksellers.

		£.	s.	d.
1885				
26th May	Gee	6.		
8th Oct.	Thornton	21.	6.	10
" "	Gee	5.	16.	
9th Dec.	Richards	2.	10.	
1886				
17th March	Blackwell	3.	10.	
6th May	Slatter & Rose	2.	10.	
7th May	Gee	11.	3.	6
Total for one year		£52.	16.	4

[14]

There is yet to be added a cheque to Evans on Feb 26, 1886 £4. 7. and bills still owing to the extent of at least £3.16. 8. Which makes a total sum spent on books in one year £60. On an emergency there might be effected a saving of £50.

Analysing my cheque book still more closely, I find a cheque of £10. to Hills & Saunders: their bill was £7. 1. 6., which will not occur again. Also a cheque to Seary for £10: his bill was £9. 3. (for bedding &c.) which will not be repeated. These two together = £14. 4. 6. extraordinary.

There are also two payments for furniture in my cheque-book

| Roe (for oak table &c.) | £4. |
| Cross (for book-case) | £5.10. |

[15]

On March 13th I paid Randell for coaching me in Theology £10., which won't recur. The German trip involved an extraordinary payment of £14.

Adding these together:–

1. Books   £54. 3. 4.
2. Hills & Saunders   £ 7. 1. 6.
3. Seary   £ 7. 3. .
4. Furniture   £ 9. 10. .
5. Coach (Theology)   £ 10. . .
6. German trip   £ 14. . .
                      £101.17.10

Altogether since my Election my receipts have been as follows:

From Bursar   £19. . .
  "   "   £50. . .
" Rathbone   £150. . .
" Bursar   £88.12. .
" Coaching   £34.4. .
               £341.16.

[16]

(In the midst of these calculations came Mills of S. Mary Hall, nice Fellow very keen: will be a good Secretary I think: he paid his Shilling with zeal.)

I find 12 cheques made out to self, total in value = £72. 6. 6.

4 cheques to T. H. = £48. 10

but of this £12 has been accounted for under German Trip = £36. 10.

My Tailor expenses are likewise heavy   £   s   d

Dec 12th '84   Welden   12.   3.   6
Oct. 6th '85   "   7. 11.   6
  "   "   Evans & Co.   12. 11.
                              £32. 6.   ii

Adding these together.

Extraordinary Expenses   101. 17.   10
Self   72.   6.   6
J. H.   36. 10.
Tailor   32.   6
                          £243. 0.   4.

[17]

The remaining cheques are.

Goundry   £3
Goldsmith   £5
A.L.R.   £5
              £13
              £243.   4.

Balance in Bank	£41.	2.
Never paid into Bank but spent	£44.	4.
	£341.	4. 6.

Unexplained difference – 11–6.

The £44. 4. is a large sum not to be more particularly accounted for. It includes (1.) Railway & other Fares. (2.) Books paid for in cash. (3.) Sums given away in subscriptions, Collections, tips to College servants & others. (4.) A few articles of clothing.

Generally I conclude that under my existing regime, my normal expenses for 18 months amount to £250.

[18]

```
           £
 18  :  12  :  250.
  6  :   4      2
  3  :   2      3 | 500
```

Normal yearly expenditure   £166.13.4

And at this moment I am at least £60 to the bad.

Lawn-tennis in the Quad. —Duff, G. Hutton, Maynard, and myself—: after which I called on Hutton at S. John's and Lang Bowlby[29] (Balliol) but both were out: so again my labour was lost. Then I went to the Union and wrote a letter home.

Weather is very oppressive. Thunder-storm must be imminent. I am so "slack" as to be almost incapable of getting through any reading. As soon as my eyes light on a page I begin to nod for weariness.

[19]

Drank no wine at dinner tonight; I hope to gradually accustom the College to my teetotalism.

From 9 to 10 Blackall was with me, having been unable to come at his usual hour in the morning. We were both so slack as to do very little work. After he had gone his way I set to *work to draw up a Constitution for the proposed Local Laymens' Leagues to be dependent on the O.L.L.*

We must reform the rules of our Constitution so as to give more work & weight to the President and Vice-President. They will soon "grow cold" unless we do so.

---

[29] Henry Thomas Bowlby (1864–1940; *WWW*), Balliol Coll., Oxford; assistant master, Eton Coll., 1887–1909; headmaster, Lancing Coll., 1909–25. Henson kept in touch with Bowlby and his wife during the early years of the twentieth century; on one occasion, he invited him to preach at St Margaret's, Westminster: Journal, 12 Jan. 1907.

[20]

Saturday, May 8th, 1886.

From 9 to 11 I read Bluntschli[30] who is a very entertaining writer: though not very profound: at least he gives a skin-deep impression.

Sperling brought me a most vacuous essay: on the subject about which I had talked (as I supposed) clearly and fully on Wednesday. Not a vestige of my remarks could be traced in the production. At stupid intervals he stupidly emits a stupid "Yes Sir", to what I say: while I as stupidly continue the infernal job of filling a sieve with water "for a consideration".

Coates[31] called on me and stayed for a space of ¾ on [sic] an hour. I promised to dine with him on Tuesday at 7 (at 7, the Crescent) to meet an old buffer.

[21]

I met Alexander of Lincoln,[32] and chatted for a while about Home Rule. **He pins his faith entirely on Chamberlain, and believes that the G.O.M. will cave in**. The withdrawal of the Land Purchase Bill does not strike him as a horrible piece of perfidy. He hopes the Irish will be left to settle their own land question subject to an English veto.

Bowden[33] sent his bill for printing done for O.L.L. £6. 3. 6. Add expenses incurred for Stamps and Notebooks and the total expense incurred will approach £7 ". towards which I have so far received 7/–. The subscription must be raised to 2/6 next year: on that I have made up my mind.

[22]

2nd Sunday after Easter, May 9th, 1886.

I received the Holy Eucharist *in Chapel, together with the Warden and 2 Bible-clerks. I wish we had a weekly Celebration:* **it would help one to live a less secular life. Vidal has no doubts at all about the presence of Jesus Christ: and in that Faith, the weekly Eucharist is his stay & staff**. *To me that Presence appears occasionally: only at long intervals do I seem to believe in it, and realize it: ordinarily I make an effort and fail. Perhaps if one communicated more regularly, the Belief would grow into a continuous possession: but as yet it is far from that.*

Went to S. Mary's & heard a very interesting Bampton lecture from Dr Bigg[34] on Origen.

---

[30] Johann Kaspar Bluntschli (1808–81), Swiss jurist; prominent theorist of international law and of the state as an organic whole. Henson would have been reading his *Theory of the state* (English transl., Oxford, 1885).

[31] Allan Coates (1846–1922), non-coll., BA, 1885; ord. 1886 (Oxford); curate, St Philip and St James, Oxford, 1885–7; rector, Barsham, Norfolk, 1899.

[32] William Frederick Alexander (b. 1864, Calcutta), Lincoln Coll., Oxford; 3rd class Modern History, 1886.

[33] James John Bowden (1848–1904), printer's reader (1901 census), St Giles, Oxford.

[34] Charles Bigg (1840–1908; *ODNB*), clergyman, schoolmaster and professor of ecclesiastical history, Oxford, 1901–8; his Bampton lectures *The Christian Platonists of Alexandria* (Oxford, 1886) revived the study of Christian mysticism.

[23]

The afternoon was spent partly in S. John's Garden, partly in the Union and Coffee Room, where I wrote a paper for members in lieu of a very poor production of Wells.

At 10, the Sub-Committee of Literature & Lectures met in my rooms.[35] All were present except Hassall. A great deal of work was got through in a sitting of close on 2 hours.

Hassall and Owen are good steady people, who don't wander from the subject, and generally follow leading well: keeping the via media of moderation. Oman and Turner[36] are rather inclined to divert themselves with a time-expensive joke, they wander from the subject in hand: have to be [24] often called back to the subject in hand: but occasionally make compensation by good serviceable suggestions. Wells works capitally: perhaps his one defect is a certain lack of "go": he doesn't govern enough: yet he is very conciliating and things work harmoniously if slowly.

On the whole I am very pleased with this Committee. Its spirit is honest and workable.

Hassall recommended F.O. Wethered[37] as a good man to be a 2nd Secretary at Ch. Ch. He is an athletic man, & would reach quite a different set than Yarde-Buller.

[25]

Monday, May 10th, 1886.

Mr Tregonwell Monro,[38] a Freshman of S. John's, sent me a note to ask to join the League.

Duff and I walked round the Parks & looked at the Cricket. Baker[39] made his appearance; and said he was doing very well. Bowlby, also, was there: I had a short talk with him: and asked him to dine on Saturday at 7. He is a very good fellow, towards whom my heart has gone forth.

Wells and Lang dined with me. Dicey brought as his guest Goldwyn Smith,[40] and very kindly introduced me. *He is rather a terrible man to behold: a very skeleton: his hand scrunched in mine like a packet of dead bones.*

---

[35] Henson is referring to a sub-committee of the general committee of the League.

[36] Cuthbert Hamilton Turner (1860–1929; *ODNB*), ecclesiastical historian and New Testament scholar; New College, Oxford, 1879–84; Denyer and Johnson scholar in theology, Oxford, 1886–8; assistant lecturer to William Bright, regius professor of ecclesiastical history, Oxford, 1888–1901; his interest in the texts of early canon law issued in his *Ecclesiae Occidentalis monumenta iuris* (Oxford, 1899–1913); FBA, 1909.

[37] Francis Owen Wethered (1864–1922; *WWW*), Christ Church Coll., Oxford; chairman, Thomas Wethered & Sons, Ltd, Brewery, Marlow; lieutenant-colonel, Oxford & Bucks Light Infantry, 1908–15.

[38] Tregonwell Monro (1867–1912), St John's Coll., Oxford; political agent (1891 census); farmer (1911 census).

[39] Not identified.

[40] Goldwin Smith (1823–1910; *ODNB*), leading intellectual liberal who campaigned for parliamentary reform in Britain during the 1860s and for the removal of clerical influence at Oxford; regius professor of modern history at Oxford, 1858–66; journalist who supported the North during the American civil war and moved to the United States in 1868; hon. professor of history at Cornell, 1868–70; left most of his wealth to Cornell.

[26]

But withal a man of immense power. I can imagine him ordering a massacre and seeing his orders carried out. Black, bushy eye-brows, fierce unquiet grey eyes, a high forehead majestically arched, grizzled moustachio, and sinister white teeth; very thin face, wrinkle-furrowed. **Power written everywhere on his face. Mercy invisible**.

From 9 to 12, Sub-Committees of the O.L.L. met in my rooms. (1) The Oxford Sub-Com<u>tee</u>*: (2) The Organisation Sub-Com*<u>tee</u>*. A great deal of business got through: but my purposes not altogether carried out, especially in the matter of the formation of Local Laymen's Leagues which I had to withdraw after proposal.*

[27]

Wakeman pleased me by his practical and sensible conduct. *The absence of Brassy & Hobhouse*[41] *was very annoying.*

In practice the Executive Committee seems very unnecessary: yet I do not intend to worry the Constitution with alteration. The letter is very elastic for sensible men. **Turner's great practical defect is letter worship***: he will procrastinate for ever in order to carry out most literally the most unimportant regulations, not perceiving that a Constitution is but a means to an end: morally inoperative when it ceases to "make for" the end.*

[28]

Tuesday, May 11<u>th</u>, 1886.

I took various things to Bowden, and then spent an hour in writing letters for the O.L.L. viz. to W. Rogers (Trinity):[42] & F.O. Wethered (Ch. Ch.) asking them to be College Secretaries: to Canon Prothero & R.E. Bothus[43] respecting the proposed work in the Isle of Wight: to Garry[44] proposing work in Reading.

Wells came to propose that the College Secretaries should breakfast with him on Thursday week. This pleases me, as it will draw them together & make them know each other.

Also I issued notices for a meeting of the General Committee on Tuesday next at 5 O'clock in my rooms.

Then an hour with my vacuous friend Sperling.

---

[41] Walter Hobhouse (1862–1928; *WWW*), New Coll., Oxford; fellow and lecturer, Hertford Coll., Oxford, 1884–7; student and tutor, Christ Church, Oxford, 1887–90; ord. 1891; headmaster of Durham School, 1894–8; editor of *The Guardian*, 1900–5. Henson stayed with him at Durham in 1898: Journal, 27 Jan. 1898, noting that the school was 'charmingly placed, and now contains about 100 boys'.

[42] Walter Rogers (1864–1924), classics teacher, Uppingham (1891 census).

[43] Not identified.

[44] Nicholas Thomas Garry (1831–1907; *AO*), Queen's Coll., Oxford; vicar of St Mary's, Reading, 1875.

[29]

The rain which had threatened all the morning fell steadily through the afternoon: after wading through the debate (**Gladstone's speech[45] is simply dust-throwing-in-the-eyes of the people**: *2/3rds of it was simply "large talk" off the mark: not a single new argument was advanced. Hartington[46] had an easy task in tearing him to pieces: especially on that shameful production, the Manifesto to the Midlothian Electors: I almost think the 2nd reading will be lost), I went round to S. John's, and found everybody out.* **On Maynard's staircase I fell in with Gore, in quest of Murray,[47] who was also out. So Gore & I went to the Puseyian and chatted for half an hour.**

[30]

I went to 7 the Crescent in a hansom: and spent as "pleasant" an evening as possible under the circumstances (viz. any circumstances, for I hate dining in private houses, where females form part of the Company.) Coates is a good host, and exerts himself to interest his guests: but his female folk are a poor set. Abbott[48] and his wife were there: and a parson named Finlay[49] and his wife.

Finlay is an interesting person: an "eclectic" in politics, & a supporter of the G.O.M.: with a great fund of humour, and slightly deaf. Mrs F. offends me violently: a perfect brute of a woman, with a tongue like a mill-wheel.

So interested in every empty ma remark which your "situation" evokes from you.

[31]

Wednesday, May 12th, 1886.

Thornton's bill came in £5.18.: I expected it would be under £5: all my estimates of May 4th seem to have been too little.

Rogers of Trinity wrote declining the Secretaryship: but joining the League. It is a great bore that we cannot get a Secretary for so important a College as Trinity.

Duff and I walked the "Five-mile Grind" and on our return called on Mrs Fletcher.[50]

---

[45] The Government of Ireland Bill, second reading, House of Commons, 10 May 1886; Gladstone invoked a people whose radical sympathies were out of keeping with the law, particularly with respect to land.

[46] Spencer Cavendish, 8th duke of Devonshire (1833–1908; *ODNB*); as marquess of Hartington a Liberal cabinet minister; became a Liberal Unionist, 1886; lord president of the council, 1895–1903; instrumental in the passage of the Education Act of 1902 and in imperial defence policy; Unionist free trader.

[47] William Murray (1865–1923; *WWW*), captain 5th Battalion, King's Own Scottish Borders, 1899–1912: Magdalen Coll., Oxford; parliamentary candidate, 1895, 1900, 1910 (twice); MP (Coalition Unionist) Dumfries, 1918–22. Remained close friends with Henson throughout his life.

[48] Robert Lamb Abbott (1840–1900), non-coll., matric. 1873; tutor of non-coll. students.

[49] Not identified.

[50] Alice Katharine Fletcher (née Merry) (d. 1939), daughter of Walter Merry, rector of Lincoln Coll., Oxford; m. (1885), Charles Robert Leslie Fletcher, historian.

I went to Bowden, and got 25 copies of the paper for members, which I carried to Yarde-Buller. He, personally, is keen, but has not I think done much as yet, in College. I wrote to Holmes, & sent out many notices.

[32]

Thursday, May 13<u>th</u>, 1886.

Rain all night long, for I slept badly & heard it: rain still.

Johnson asked me to accept no engagements for Summer without first consulting him: is this hopeful of my success in getting <u>any</u>thing?

Letter from Rev<u>d</u> R. Chilton, Vicar of High Wycombe, & Rural Dean,[51] asking me for notices of the League. I sent off 20, with a short letter. Also Greenwood[52] and Cockburn,[53] 2 undergraduates of Ch. Ch. sent in their names. Also Tupper Carey[54] same of name.

I sent out copies of the Prospectus to all the Common Rooms: and also wrote to the Bible-Clerks re. the League, & after lunch took Yarde-Buller some more notices.

[33]

The rain continuing I went to the Union and wrote to Hutton accepting an invitation to dinner on Sunday at 6: also to Watson. Then called on Baker: *he tells me that the Dean of Winchester*[55] *"thinks it a pity" "to start in opposition" &c: as I never expected any countenance from mine ancient enemy, I am not disappointed: between him & me there is quite an impassable gulf fixed.* I should be almost sorry to be on friendly terms with him.

The Tutors' Association met in Ch. Ch. **and Abbott read a paper on the Non-Collegiate System**. There was a full attendance, Gore, Paget, Lock, Spurling,[56] Hind,[57] & I spoke.

---

[51] Robert Chilton (ord. 1850; *CCD*), Trinity Coll., Cambridge; vicar of High Wycombe, 1869–95; rural dean, 1882–95.
[52] Hubert John Greenwood (1867–1932), Christ Church, Oxford; JP; member, London County Council; company director (1911 census).
[53] Nathaniel Clayton Cockburn (1867–1924), Christ Church, Oxford; major, Imperial Yeomanry (Hart's list, 1908).
[54] Albert Darell Tupper-Carey (1866–1943; *WWW*), Christ Church, Oxford; ord. 1892; head of Christ Church Mission, Poplar, 1898–1902; chaplain to the king, 1938–43.
[55] George William Kitchin (1827–1912; *ODNB*), Christ Church, Oxford; ord. 1852; censor, Christ Church, Oxford, 1861–3; first censor of non-coll. students, 1868–83; dean of Winchester, 1883–94; Henson's predecessor as dean of Durham, 1894–1912.
[56] Frederick William Spurling (1844–1914; *WWW*), Wadham Coll., Oxford; ord. 1886; tutor, Keble Coll., Oxford, 1875–1906.
[57] Henry Norman Hind (1861–1945), Lincoln Coll., Oxford; ord. 1884, 1886; curate, Liversedge, Wakefield, 1884–1907; vicar, Netherthong, diocese of Wakefield, 1907.

[34]

I mainly confined myself to an invective on the migration of men, <u>and a plea for the collegializing of the system, (which of course was met by the old caste argument that it was contrary to the "ideal" of the system. What pagan letter-worship)</u>

Paget irritated me excessively by his <u>dishonest</u> manner. (<u>So</u> deeply grateful &c. such a helpful paper &c. &c.!) but I was dishonest enough, none the less to thank him.

On the whole I am glad I went though **I hate speaking of the unattached. I hate even thinking about it**. *Ah, the wretched, ruinous years of my undergraduate life! that branded into my heart a bitterness which can never be effaced! Writhing my soul into one fixed eternal* [word illegible]. *I hate the system with all my heart.*

[35]

Hind had the face to ask me for a practical recommendation to a curacy. *With my opinion as to him how can I do anything of the sort. Yet it is horrid to refuse what costs me nothing to give.* **Does it cost me nothing**? *Well, an insult to a conscience well accustomed to more serious injuries can't count for much: yet for something undoubtedly. In foro conscientiæ*[58] *can I recommend Hind? Objections:*

1) I know little or nothing of him.
2) That little I do know is not to his credit.
3) I think him an ass, & a knave.
4) I think my signature deserves respect.

[36]

Wherefore I wrote a letter refusing to do what I was asked to do: *& pleading 1) my ignorance of him* <u>practically</u>*: 2) my insignificance. Oman thought my letter too severe, so I wrote another much the same: and feel much the better for having declined his impudent request. A curious fate brings me into collision with the Tutors of the Delegacy. Abbott I refused to vote for, when Kitchin resigned the Censorship. And now I refuse to give Hind a "character" (!!)*

Oman remained talking about Church business, or rather religion generally until nearly 1 A.M.

[37]

Friday, May 14th, 1886.

Letter from <u>Cronshaw</u>[59] addressed from Green Bank, Liverpool, E. (how I remember the place & loathe it as a very Egypt of bondage.) asking about the League about

---

[58] *In foro conscientiae* (Latin): before the tribunal of conscience: a legal term contrasting private or moral obligation as distinct from a legal one.

[59] Herbert Priestley Cronshaw (ord. 1887; *WWW*), All Souls Coll., Oxford; curate of St Matthew and St James, Mossley Hill, 1886–90, living at Greenbank; William Temple's successor as rector of Piccadilly, 1917–22.

which he had heard from Mackay. It was not without a sensation of pleasure that I sent some notices about the League to that centre of Schism. It is as if I re-enter the place in my true colours: after having first posed in the garments of the Amalekites.[60] **How strangely incumbent upon me seems to be the necessity of hating the past.** *It is not tolerable to be even thought of. Everything that so much as reminds me of it is hateful to me, wherefore I am not happy.*

[38]

Cholmondeley appeared to my great delight: he was on his way to Warwickshire. He said that he didn't like my lecture on Poverty[61] so much as that on Gordon: the ignoring of the economic aspect of poverty displeased him: but some parts of the lecture met with his warm approval. For my part, I regard it as a very crude production which I should not like to repeat.

I told the Warden about Hind, and he approved of my conduct: because he suspected that Hind w^d represent my fellowship as the result of his efforts! The hound! I wish I had sent my first note.

[39]

Saturday, May 15th, 1886.

I went out a walk with [William Holden] *Hutton: and was very much vexed to find* **that he persists in regarding the League with suspicion as Erastian**: *mainly basing his belief on the names of the members of the Committee. I suspect I shall find that the Rits have been working against me. They are so strong up here that their opposition threatens the whole project with overthrow. I must think out a method of assuring its position as an outside Oxford movement. The fact is I can't give the pledges demanded by the Rits. The Church will indeed fall if she can tolerate none as her defenders but Puseyites. Heaven knows, the Dissenters are odious to me: but so long as they will consent to resist the ruin of the Church, I will not* **[40]** *only tolerate them, I will even assume an attitude of friendliness.* **Self-suppression I regard as the test and measure of loyalty: and in requiring a considerable amount of self-suppression from Dissenters, I am not so unjust as to refuse to make any myself.** *The Rits do not realize the religious significance of Disestablishment. They don't look at the question from a sufficiently lofty stand-point. If instead of estimating everything by its bearing on themselves they w^d estimate it as affecting the world, their conclusions w^d be different.* **They don't see or won't see that if Disestablishment does bring them all the liberty they covet, none the less in the history of the World it will remain a great Secularist Victory not a great act [41] of clerical enfranchisement. The Supreme interests of Religion will be sacrificed to the Chimæra of ecclesiastical independence: or can it be that they identify the two?**

Bowlby dined with me. He is a delightful fellow, charmingly simple and sincere: I hope to see a good bit of him. He purposes to take Holy Orders, **but is much troubled at the 39 articles**: *and his honest soul refuses to accept the "casuistry" with which I*

---

[60] Amalekite *OED*: 'A member of a nomadic people inhabiting the area south of Canaan in Biblical times. Also figurative: a fierce or determined adversary.'
[61] The lecture is not noted in the Journal.

am wont to overcome the difficulty. Recognise facts, say I, the whole arrangement of subscription is obsolete: but according to English custom is not abolished because of that. Therefore bow to the necessity, & go through the subscription as a mere form.

[42]

The fact is, there is a choice of evils. If I have a vocation to the priestly office – and ex hypothese[62] I have – then I am false to my vocation if I allow myself to be deterred from taking Orders by the necessity of Subscription. If I subscribe what I do not believe, then I am false to the admittedly obsolete system.

I accept what appears to me to be the less evil of the two alternatives, and remain true to my vocation. "it is casuistry" says Bowlby the Sincere: and probably – certainly – he is really right: though I cannot see my way clear to act on his principle. "It is a bad beginning" he says truly enough.

[43]

3rd Sunday after Easter, May 16th, 1886.

I heard the Bampton Lecture, *and that with morning service at chapel formed the whole of my religious history for this Sunday:* **too much for an atheist, too little for a Christian.**

Oman and I lunched with Burrows at 9 Norham Gardens, a most weary process of course. **Burrows is "sore" at the League, because he is Secretary for the Church Defence Society:**[63] **he can't perceive that it is pure self-stultification to find fault with the League for doing that which he would like to do, & cannot, viz. get the support of Oxonians. Burrows is the sort of man who would ruin anything he takes up**.

[44]

After writing a long letter home: I dined with Hutton at S. John's. A large party including among the strangers Hobhouse, Firth,[64] and Cooper (Keble).[65]

The League came in for a good deal of criticism not exactly of a friendly kind. The Rits try to stigmatise it as Erastian: the Radicals as Tory: the Low Churchmen as Jesuitical: and yet it is nothing of these.

---

[62] *Ex hypothesi* (Latin): 'From or according to the hypothesis, as a result of the assumptions made, supposedly, hypothetically': James Morwood, *A dictionary of Latin words and phrases* (Oxford, 1998), p. 58.

[63] The Church Defence Institution was formed in 1859 to defend the church against the Liberation Society, as well as hostile acts of parliament; in 1895, it amalgamated with the Church Committee for Defence and Instruction founded by the archbishop of Canterbury, Edward Benson, in the previous year.

[64] Charles Harding Firth (1857–1936; *ODNB*), Balliol Coll., Oxford; independent researcher at Oxford, 1883–1905; regius professor of modern history at Oxford, 1905–25; historian of Cromwell and the Cromwellians.

[65] Thomas Cooper (b. 1863), Keble Coll., Oxford; ord. 1889.

[45]

Monday, May 17th, 1886.

[George] Prothero returned proof sheets, with a letter containing an offer to go to Cambridge to help start the League: but making no mention of the Isle of Wight.

R.E. Walker[66] (Ch. Ch.) joined the League.

P. Lyttelton Gell[67] (Balliol) joined the League. He wrote a long letter on the necessity of Church Reform. At first I was in doubt what to do: for the Rits. have been casting in my teeth the probable accession of P.L.G. as a [*sic*] conclusive evidence of our Erastianism. And now here is the man. Ought to write back a letter emphasizing the non-Erastianism of the League so as to justify us. I even went **[46]** so far as to write such a letter. But then it came to my mind that it w^d be *pessimi exempli* [worst example] to go behind a man's accession to the League, & acceptance of its declared opinions. Therefore I tore up my diplomatic epistle, & simply returned a formal note accepting his subscription & entering his name. I shall hear more of this from Gore & Hutton.

The one chance of preserving the League from overthrow seems to me the bold stroke of forcing it into view, in order to commit those who join hopelessly to the project.

I dined with W.O. Burrows at Ch. Ch.: and met Ottley,[68] whom I had often wanted to meet. He is very beautiful to look at, but somewhat spoiled perhaps by the Canons.

[47]

Yarde-Buller brought a hesitating friend – Bardsley[69] – into Burrows's room to see me. He seemed a good fellow enough, and I think he will join. Y.B. has been very vigourous [*sic*] in whipping up news-papers [*sic*]: he has quite a number of answers. I am not quite satisfied with this fierce zeal, which pours itself out in all directions. The same Editor will be harassed by many men, which won't look well.

J. G. Simpson[70] has consented to be Secretary for Trinity.

[48]

Tuesday, May 18th, 1886.

The General Committee met in my rooms. Warren[71] presided in the absence of the President.

---

[66] Reginald Edmund Walker (1866–1945), Christ Church, Oxford; ord. 1895; vicar, Ledsham, 1896–1901.
[67] Philip Lyttelton Gell (1852–1926), Balliol Coll., Oxford; JP; company director; first chairman of Toynbee Hall, 1884–96.
[68] Robert Lawrence Ottley (1856–1933; *WWW*), senior student, Christ Church, Oxford, 1878–86; ord. 1882; vice-principal, Cuddesdon Coll.; principal, Pusey House, Oxford, 1893.
[69] Ernest John Bardsley (1868–1948; *WWW*), Worcester Coll., Oxford; ord. 1892; son of Canon James Bardsley, vicar of Huddersfield, 1884–1901.
[70] James Gilliland Simpson (1865–1948; *WWW*), Trinity Coll., Oxford; ord. 1890; curate of Leeds, 1889; dean of Peterborough Cathedral, 1928–42.
[71] (Thomas) Herbert Warren (1853–1930; *ODNB*), classicist and president of Magdalen Coll., Oxford, 1885–1928.

In all things the Committee are too timid. I would that they were bolder. Audacity is the very indispensable condition of success for a League placed as this is. I was extremely pleased by Warren's conduct: he is business-like and sensible.

Duff gave me Arnold's life and Sermons by Stanley, 3 vols.[72]

The idea of writing a history of Ireland came to me.

[49]

Wednesday, May 19th, 1886.

I asked Maynard to dine with me on Saturday.

Raleigh[73] irritated me by arguing in favour of Disestablishment, etc.

I dined with the Warden.

The Irish project still holds: I have borrowed Prendergast's Cromwellian Settlement[74] from the Library. The history should really begin with Henry II: an Introduction of 3 parts w$^\text{d.}$ do for the rest.

[50]

Thursday, May 20th, 1886.

Breakfast at Wadham with the College Secretaries.

Letter from Garry proposing an Autumn Campaign: also from Prothero & Venables.[75]

Irish scheme so strong in my mind *that I went to Gee & bought Carte's Life of Ormonde (30/–)[76] and Burton's Cromwellian Diary (24/–).*[77]

The Guardian contains a very flattering notice of the League: and happily includes an invitation to laymen & parsons to communicate with me.[78]

Duff and I went to New College Chapel:

---

[72] A. P. Stanley, *Life and correspondence of Thomas Arnold* (3 vols., London, 1877).
[73] Hon. Thomas Raleigh (1850–1920; *WWW*), Kt 1911; fellow of All Souls Coll., Oxford, 1876–1920; Edinburgh, Tübingen, Oxford; barr., 1877; legal member of the Viceroy's Council in India, 1899–1904; Henson officiated at his funeral at All Souls; he wrote, 'I owed him much, consulted him often, and loved him' (*Retrospect*, I, 318–19).
[74] John P. Prendergast, *The history of the Cromwellian settlement of Ireland* (London, 1865).
[75] Not identified.
[76] Thomas Carte, *The life of James, duke of Ormonde* (1735–6; 3 vols., Oxford, 1851).
[77] John Towill Rutt (ed.), *Diary of Thomas Burton* (4 vols., London, 1828).
[78] 'University and Collegiate, Oxford', *Guardian*, 19 May 1886, 733.

[51]

Friday, May 21ˢᵗ, 1886.

No less than 6 men from Ch. Ch. sent in their names, & shillings. So did Chevallier.[79] 7/– was handed over to Hobhouse.

Letters came from T.H. Bindley,[80] F. Sturge,[81] and the Rev. V. H. Moyle[82] – all inspired by the Guardian. The number of members slowly increase,

Committees	19
College Secretaries	20
Names on my list	24
Fletcher, Godley,[83] Bussell,[84]	
Haines, Headlam,[85] Burrows,	
Turner, Cruickshank,[86] Tracey,	
Madan,[87] Dixey, Cooper,	
Heyes,[88] Abbott, Curzon,	
3 Bible-clerks	=18
	81

[52]

Saturday, May 22ⁿᵈ, 1886.

Turner lunched with me.

Prothero's pamphlet out at last.

Something is done now.

---

[79] John Chevallier (1862–1917), Trinity Coll., Cambridge; fellow of New Coll. Oxford, 1883–91; ord. 1887 (Oxford); rector, Gt Horwood, Buckinghamshire, 1889–1917; assistant master, Giggleswick, 1917.
[80] Thomas Herbert Bindley (1861–1931; *WWW*), Merton Coll., Oxford; ord., 1890; patristics scholar.
[81] Not identified.
[82] Vyvyan Henry Moyle (1834–1908; *CCD*), vicar, Ashampstead, Berkshire, 1885–95; ord. 1861; Pembroke Coll., Oxford.
[83] John Cornwallis Godley (1861–1946), Corpus Christi Coll., Oxford; 1st class Lit. Hum.; civil servant.
[84] Frederick William Bussell (1862–1944; *WWW*), Magdalen Coll., Oxford; 1st class Lit. Hum., Theology; ord. 1892; vice-principal, Brasenose Coll., Oxford, 1896–1913; scholar and teacher of the humanities.
[85] Arthur Cayley Headlam (1862–1947; *ODNB*), New Coll., Oxford; elected fellow of All Souls Coll., Oxford, 1885, the year after Henson, and Henson's 'oldest clerical friend' when he predeceased Henson by a few months (Henson to C. A. Alington, 18 Jan. 1947, *Letters of Herbert Hensley Henson*, ed. E. F. Braley (London, 1951), p. 193); ord. 1889; celebrated Holy Communion for the first time at St Margaret's Church, Barking, with Henson as his server: Journal, 29 Oct. 1889; regius professor of divinity, Oxford, 1918–22; bishop of Gloucester, 1922–45; shared Henson's political conservatism although not his opposition to Nazism.
[86] Alfred Cruickshank (1862–1927; *WWW*), New Coll., Oxford; assistant master, Winchester school, 1894–1910; canon and professor of Greek and classical literature, Univ. of Durham, 1910–27; close, though difficult, associate of Henson in Durham.
[87] Falconer Madan (1851–1935; *WWW*), Brasenose Coll., Oxford; sub-librarian, 1880–1912, and librarian, 1912–19, Bodleian Library, Oxford.
[88] Not identified.

I issued notices of the Trinity meeting to the College Secretaries.

Maynard dined with me. He seems more wrong-headed than ever on religion. (Raves about admiring Satan, defying God, &c.)

Wakeman, Oman, Wells, and Crawhall[89] received pamphlets.

[53]

4th Sunday after Easter, May 23rd, 1886.

I sent the pamphlet to Ingram, Yarde-Buller, Smith,[90] Brodrick (Merton),[91] Bowlby, Burrows, Strong (Ch. Ch.),[92] Gore, Hutton, Fletcher, the Warden, & a parson.

I walked (1.) with Turner, (2) **with Gore**.

A very large party dined including some interesting strangers, viz. Lord Tavistock,[93] Craufurd,[94] Andrew Lang,[95] and Dr Child.[96]

I went to the Evening Service at Ch. Ch. and heard the hymn "Fierce raged the tempest o'er the deep".[97] The effect was quite spoiled to me by the zealous squalling of a young woman near to me.

[54]

Monday, May 24th, 1886.

A great part of this day was wasted in packing up & sending away Pamphlets.

Blackall lunched with me.

Oman brought George [Curzon] & Haines to dinner.

A paper from India arrived: it contains the exploded legend about Davitt.[98]

---

[89] Edmund Isaac Laroche Crawhall (1864–1937), Wadham Coll. Oxford; ord. 1892; curate of Easington, Co. Durham, 1891–3.
[90] Not identified.
[91] George Charles Brodrick (1831–1903; *WWW*), barr.; Liberal Unionist since 1886; warden of Merton Coll., Oxford, 1881–1903.
[92] Thomas Strong (1861–1944; *ODNB*), prominent Oxford high churchman. Christ Church, Oxford; dean, Christ Church, Oxford, 1901–20; bishop of Ripon, 1920–5, and Oxford, 1925–37; publications include *Christian ethics* (London, 1896; Bampton lectures) and (with A. E. Zimmern and R. H. Tawney), *Oxford and working-class education* (Oxford, 1908).
[93] George William Francis Sackville Russell (1852–93), 10th marquess of Tavistock, 10th duke of Bedford (1891), Balliol Coll., Oxford; MP (L) Bedfordshire, 1875–85.
[94] Alexander Henry Craufurd (ord. 1869; *CCD*), Oriel Coll. Oxford; curate, Rothesay, Isle of Bute, 1872.
[95] Andrew Lang (1844–1912; *ODNB*), anthropologist, classicist, historian; Balliol Coll., Oxford.
[96] Gilbert William Child (1833–96), MD, Exeter Coll., Oxford.
[97] Hymn by Geoffrey Thring (1823–1903) after Christ's calming of the tempest while crossing the Sea of Galilee (Mark 4:36–41).
[98] Michael Davitt (1846–1906; *ODNB*), campaigner for Irish nationalism in focusing on 'landlordism', the revolutionary implications of which he failed to instil into the Land League before its demise in 1881 under Parnell's leadership; supporter of Indian nationalism.

Skipwith[99] called on me, urging the claims of the Shelley Society: vainly of course.

Duff followed hard on Skipwith, & so destroyed my reading for today.

[55]

Tuesday, May 25th, 1886.

I went to New College for the Evensong, and heard that beautiful anthem "Thou shalt keep him in perfect peace, whose mind is stayed on thee" (Smart.)[100]

Mitchell[101] the new Vicar of Barford St. Martin dined with the Warden. He seemed a pleasant man with some considerable common-sense. In the *Coffee-Room the conversation gradually assumed a more religious tone.* **The Bampton Lectures led up to a discussion of the Salvation Army**, *which in turn made way for Apostolic Poverty. Everybody was against me on that: &* **the Warden took occasion to taunt me with my inconsistency in lecturing to the Bethnal Green folk, and yet living in All Souls**. *It is all quite true. It is treasonable inconsistency* **[56]** *but I see not how to escape. It is not my will to remain in luxury: I long to throw aside all, and be an ascetic as was Francis: but I am not free to do what I would: I am not rich enough to be poor. And yet even for others this money-earning is loathsome: & because it is loathsome I fail of success. Ah, how beautiful it wd be if I were only free. My slavery ruins me: making me a hypocrite and self-condemned. It is this constant, gnawing regretful sense of impotence to do what I feel to be the right thing that consumes me. In some sense – I know not yet in what sense – Poverty is a Benediction. If so it be, then the Poverty of the masses may be only a part of the spiritual endowment of humanity. Does Christianity teach men to enjoy* **[57]** *life – the life of this world? I trow[102] not. "Except a man hate Father & Mother &c he is not worthy to be my disciple."[103] Jesus Christ talks of a Cross to be borne by his followers, & that must mean Suffering[;] he talks of a plough from which no backward glances must be directed, & that means labour: Conformity to Him is the Goal of the Christian's life: and there is no Enjoyment of life. It cannot be true that the sincere follower of the Crucified ought to enjoy life. "Blessed are they that mourn."[104]* **I am convinced that the easy-going, popular, life-enjoying Christianity is a bald and impudent falsehood, not even parodically resembling the Truth**. *Yet how to shake myself clear from it all is not clear. "Except a man hate etc." The words must mean something.*

---

[99] Grey Hubert Skipwith (1860–1917), Trinity Coll., Oxford; 3rd class Modern History, 1884; religious writer; son of Sir Thomas George Skipwith, Bt.

[100] Henry Thomas Smart (1813–79; *ODNB*), organist and prolific composer of church music. Though it is unclear whether this attribution is correct: the most famous version of *Thou wilt keep him in perfect peace*, based on Isaiah 26:3 and other scriptural texts is by Samuel Sebastian Wesley (1810–76).

[101] Josiah Mitchell (ord. 1858; *CCD*), fellow of All Souls Coll., Oxford, 1856; vicar of Alberbury, dio. of Hereford, 1866–86; rector of Barford St Martin, dio. of Sarum, 1886, patron, All Souls Coll., Oxford.

[102] Trow (1a) *OED*: 'to trust, have confidence in, believe (a person or thing)'; Old English.

[103] Luke 14:26.

[104] Matthew 5:4.

[58]

Stanley Leighton's article on "The Endowment of Nonconformity" is very striking.[105] If he could be persuaded to re-write it in pamphlet form as no. 2 of the "O.L.L. Series": it would be a good thing.

Argyle's speech last night on the Deceased Wife's Sister's Bill[106] was one of the most powerful speeches I have read. The Bps do wisely in letting themselves be seen as little as possible. The division was a big one for the Lords, 149 – 127: and in view of the fact that 3 years ago the 2nd reading was agreed to by a majority of 7: it is consoling to get an adverse majority of 22. The bps were not in force: only 17 bps or 8 voted last night, beside the abps.

[59]

Wednesday, May 26th, 1886.

Goldwyn Smith lectured on "The Political History of Canada" to a great concourse in the New Schools. *He said that the French in Canada were positively driving out the English, who had been already driven out of Quebec. They were simple, ignorant, illiterate, priest ridden, superstitious. Minute sub-division of holdings went on as in Ireland. There was no amalgamation between the races: and communications with the old Country had been re-opened. He drew rather a black picture of the government of the Dominion. Corruption and ability combine to give power to one man. The Confederation was only born of the dead-lock between French & English Canada.*

[60]

A paper-constitution, he regarded, as necessary to a democracy. Party government he denounced: & a 2nd chamber he ridiculed. The independence of Canada he waited for contentedly only anxious that the common citizenship of the inhabitants of England & Canada shd be maintained. The Caucus came in for a stern condemnation.

---

[105] Stanley Leighton, 'The establishment and endowment of nonconfomity', *National Review*, 7 (May 1886), 343–52. The article defended the principle of Establishment in relation to all the churches, the safeguard of which was the Church of England. Against the 'anti-Church–State Association' (forerunner of the Liberation Society), the church was 'the guardian, in revolutionary times, of the freedom of religion, of religious worship, and of religious teaching' (352). Stanley Leighton (1837–1901; *WWW*), MP (C) Oswestry, 1885–1901; Balliol Coll., Oxford.

[106] George Campbell, 8th duke of Argyll in the peerage of Scotland and first in the peerage of the United Kingdom (1823–1900; *ODNB*), and Liberal statesman was speaking on the second reading of a bill in the House of Lords to permit marriages with the sister of a deceased wife; prohibited since 1835, they had been the subject of a groundswell of support since the 1860s. In a long and measured speech, Argyll defended the prohibition on grounds of the importance of marriage bonds to the maintenance of society. Such marriages were finally legalized in the Deceased Wife's Sister Act of 1907, legislation which Henson supported against widespread opposition in the church: see his 'Of the deceased wife's sister marriage act, 1907: an open letter to his grace the archbishop of Canterbury', in H. H. Henson, *The national church: essays on its history and constitution and criticisms of its present administration* (London, 1908), pp. 134–69.

The conclusion of the lecture was very eloquent, & listened to with breathless attention. The effect was marred by the Vice-Chancellor [Benjamin Jowett] who insisted on making a very foolish and irrelevant speech; & then prevented Goldwyn Smith from replying by turning to go out without a moment's delay – conceited meddler – but it is his last year! hooray!

[61]

I walked round Mesopotamia with Hobhouse: and then went to Magdalen for the Evensong. On leaving the Chapel I ran into Fawssett,[107] whom I had not seen in the chapel.

He engaged to lunch with me tomorrow.

I gave Raleigh a pamphlet. Johnson told me of a man who wants 6 hours with me. –a dullard who w^d escape a dead plough. Nasty work, but beggars mustn't be choosers. It will pay for Sismondi.

[62]

Thursday, May 27th, 1886.

Fawssett lunched with me. He is very full of the letter in Keble's Gazette. I was rash enough to promise to answer it, if anything more appeared. I can see very clearly that Raven[108] is something of a bête-noir to the Rector.

After seeing Fawssett to the Randolf[109] I went to Evans and was measured for a dress suit: after which I made my way to the Cricket Match: whereat I gazed in great discomfort for the space of more than an hour: and then returned to College.

Dr Child came to see me, and had got so far as to intimate that his son[110] w^d be a member of my reading party when our conversation was broken into. I wonder whether that Party will come off.

[63]

I dined with Duff, who was entertaining some friends, a widow and 2 daughters, whom for my sins I had accompanied about the place for the space of an hour before lunch. There can be no question that all "parties" are odious to me: especially when they contain females.

Duff is an extremely agreeable man, when he chooses to be so.

---

[107] Humphry Sandwith Fawssett (1862–), ord. 1887; curate, Prestwich, Lancashire, 1886–8; Exeter Coll., Oxford.
[108] Not identified.
[109] Randolph Hotel, Oxford, opened in 1866.
[110] Nicholas Gilbert Louis Child (b. 1866), Exeter Coll., Oxford; matric. 1885; barr.

[64]

Friday, May 28th, 1886.

My heart is sad tonight.– that sort of cynical-sadness born of sin and discontent hangs over me like a night-mist. **Shall I never be free**? *how I do long to throw aside all this life and be sincere & a follower of Jesus Christ! Yes, that is what I long for before all things: yet that is just what I have no prospect of being able to be. Round about me I see the irreligious are happy: and the "pious" are so likewise. I cannot be altogether irreligious for my being worships Jesus Christ; pious I am not: and I alone am wretched. An ennui of the soul destroys me. Oman is contented with his life: he is energetic, & prosperous. Curzon* **[65]** *is full-filled with his hopes and ambitions. Doyle*[111] *accomplishes his destinies peacefully & happily. Duff is cynical & satisfied. Wakeman is calm and rich and likewise satisfied.* **I alone of them all am not satisfied, not calm, not happy. I am cynical, but my cynicism only adds to my misery: I devour my own heart in my musings and longings. Hateful is the past, intolerable is the present, dear is the future: yet why? was not past & present once future too**? *"Lead kindly light amid the encircling gloom".*[112] *I would give much to hear those words sung by the Magdalen choir, but there is little or no chance of my getting an order.*

[66]

This gay sight-seeing Society elbows me out of the holy place. **Sometimes it seems that the end of it all will be in Romanism**. *If it were not for the state of the family, I mean, the abject poverty which threatens them – I believe I should be a "pervert"*[113] *within 12 mo^s. Yet why? assuredly not because I believe in Roman Catholicism: perhaps, because my restlessness spurs me on to change: If only Jesus Christ would come to me, & could speak to me as He spoke to the Saints of History, I would go thro fire & water to do His bidding. But now there is noise of voices everywhere, but His voice I hear not therein: nor do I see His form.*

[67]

I have not a little bit of interest in anything: reading is intolerable to me: coaching I hate, my "vocation" seemed to be clear to me once, now it is all dark: & I could shed tears for very hopelessness.

I played tennis with Oman, Curzon, and Hutton.

I forgot my invitation to dine with Fletcher at Magdalen where I especially wished to dine: I went to the Magdalen Historical Society, and made myself an ass, I think: then returning wrote this.

---

[111] John Andrew Doyle (1840–1907; *WWW*), Balliol Coll., Oxford; fellow of All Souls Coll., Oxford, 1870–1907; much respected by Henson: see Journal, 5 Aug. 1907.
[112] John Henry Newman, 'The pillar of the cloud' (1833).
[113] Pervert (noun) (1) *OED*: 'a person who has been perverted: *spec* a person who has forsaken a doctrine regarded as true for one thought false; an apostate'.

[68]

Saturday, May 29th, 1886.

Tamplin of University[114] *came to see me at 10. Poor wretch, there is a pathos in the utter self-abnegation with which he relates his academic history.* "**I'm not made for honours, he said, my brain's just a sieve: not a mere sieve, you know, but a sieve with glue in it, which holds the water till the water dissolves the glue.**" *Yet Tamplin has a great big forehead which ought to connote brains. The more I see of men the more I am dissatisfied with the forehead-test.*[115]

Yarde-Buller came and received 20 pamphlets for his men.

A long walk with Duff over soaking meadows, thro' dirty lanes **[69]** during a succession of rain-showers, filled up the afternoon. At Water-Eaton we looked at the little perpendicular chapel and the old Elizabethan House.

Yarde-Buller dined with me, and I think, he enjoyed himself. He is a dear little fellow, and awfully keen on the League: I shall cultivate his acquaintance. He and Bowlby are the two men whom I feel most drawn to out of the whole Staff of the League.

[70]

Tuesday, June 1st, 1886.

I accompanied the Architectural Society on a visit to **Salisbury**.

S. Thomas' (of Canterbury) Church is a fine big building.

The Cathedral is beyond description grand: yet terribly wanting in stained glass. The view of the building from the Bishop's garden is one of the finest I have ever seen.

Stonehenge disappointed me: not so "Old Sarum" which is indeed a most wonderful natural fortress.

3 circumstances marred the Expedition

1. The presence of ladies.
2. The speeches of Parker.[116]
3. The bad carriage arrangements between Salisbury & Stonehenge.

[71]

Wednesday, June 2nd, 1886.

Child came to see me: I like his appearance: he wants to read Foreign 18th century, which I must get up. I hope this "Reading party" will come off all right.

---

[114] John Mainwaring Tamplin (b. 1864), University Coll., Oxford; 3rd class Modern History, 1886; ord. 1889.
[115] The phrenology movement of the nineteenth century linked psychological traits with the shape of the skull, with a high forehead indicating superior intelligence.
[116] Not identified.

[72]

Thursday, June 3rd, 1886.

Adderley wrote to me asking me to join the "League of the True Vine" which he and Vidal are starting: and I have written my consent. Perchance the Vox Christi speaks to me thro' Vidal and Adderley: *they are the only men whom I have both loved & respected, I mean, the only young men.* How shall the hour's [sic] study come in?

9 – 1	"Pups"	4 hours
5 – 6	"Pups & League"	1 "
6 – 7	"Guild"	1 "
9 – 12	"Reading"	3 "
		9 hours.

That allows 4 hours for lunch & recreation, and 2 hours for dinner: surely enough!!

[73]

In the afternoon I spectated the distribution of prizes to the boys of the High School by the Dean of Ch. Ch. Speeches were made and much fulsome talk proceeded out of the mouths of the mayor & ex-mayor. It is rather interesting to see the Vice-Chancellor and Mayor sitting side by side in amiable inter-complimentation. It must be confessed that the Mayor's "poker" much exceeded the Vice's in size and magnificence.[117]

I dined with Dixey at Wadham and afterwards went to the Merton Concert which I, in a sense, enjoyed. The gardens were beautifully illuminated.

[74]

Whitsunday, June 13th, 1886.

Stuckey Coles[118] preached the sermon in Chapel. There was a good attendance of Fellows. **Duff received the Sacrament. There is something** *almost revolting in the thought of his communion: and yet – inasmuch as he came entirely of his own will, with no possible reason to bias him – no one is justified in condemning him.*

I do not give very much weight to irreligious talk: for that rarely expresses a man's real opinions. I should not like to be judged by my words: for I know they are often quite unrepresentative of my mind. Most of us have a natural tendency towards hypocrisy: "All men are liars."[119]

[Pages 75 and 76 are missing; the pages have been carefully cut out.]

---

[117] The Oxford city mace (1651) carried by the mayor's sergeant is the largest civic mace in Britain.
[118] Vincent Stuckey Stratton Coles (1845–1929; *ODNB*), Eton Coll.; Balliol Coll., Oxford; anglo-catholic minister and hymn writer; principal of Pusey House, Oxford, 1897–1909; warden of Community of the Epiphany, Truro, 1910–20.
[119] 'I said in my haste, all men are liars': Ps. 116.

[77]

The cessation of the falling process is a relief: the only possible motion is upward. The terrible question is always relative to the position itself, is it the worst? Have I struck the floor of the abyss? Or am I only detained for a brief moment on a ledge of rock projecting from its sides?

I cannot spend the Long at home: it would drive me mad: and it is almost as expensive as elsewhere. The Oxford House will take up something, perhaps a month: perhaps as much in two several portions will be spent at home: a month will be expended in some remote place: and the rest spent in Oxford. Not less than £35. will be absorbed by the Vacation.

[78] D̲ᵇ [debit]

	£	s	d
Slatter & Rose	2.	10.	
Gee	11.	3.	6
Thornton	5	–	–
J. H.	5	–	–
Subscriptions to Camden Soc. and Oxford Hist. Soc.	2	"	"
Blackwell	10	"	"
Midland Hotel	10	"	"
Harwood	5	"	"
Gee	10	"	"
Thornton	5 "	10	"
Redman	5 "		
Self	5 "		
J. H.	15 "		
Redman	4 "	10"	
Weddle	3"	"	
Self	5"	"	
G.A.H.	10		
J. H.	20		
Self	2.	10.	
	136.	5.	6.

[79] C̲ᵗ [credit]

	£	s	d
Balance	39"	13"	8.
By Cheque Fuller	10"	"	
" " Blackall	5"	"	
" " Waters	10"	"	
" " the Bursar	50"	"	
" " Ckk (G.A.H)	25"	11"	10"
" " Welby	10"	"	
	£150.	5.	6.

	£136.	5.	6.
Balance	£ 14.	"	"

H. Hensley Henson
Sept. 11th 1886

[80]

Other sums received and not put to my Banking Account:–

		£	s	d
From	Tamplin	2.	10.	.
"	Wilkinson	2.	10.	.
"	G.A.H.	2.	10.	.
P.O.O.		5.	.	.

[81]

Sunday, June 20th, 1886.

The meeting at Wadham was a great success so far as the attendance went. The Hall was even crowded. The Warden and Warren disappointed me: but [Rowland] Prothero made an admirable speech, and drew the meeting together again. **My speech was a failure.**[120]

[82]

Saturday, June 26th, 1886.

Vidal has left me.

Murray dined with me: he is a very great person; of whom I will see more if it may be. The world contains many precious things, but none so precious as these elect souls who shine out here & there from the old buildings of Oxford. Vidal & Murray are no ordinary men: both have looked at the mystery of mysteries, human life. *Jesus Christ is wonderfully attractive to both, but how differently. Vidal worships the God; where Murray admires the hero-martyr. Socrates, Jesus Christ, & Marcus Aurelius are to Murray three sublime heroes.*

To him as to Vidal and even to me there had come that self-contempt, which may inspire or degrade.

[83]

Nothing is more wonderful than the wide existence of that self-contempt. It will result in a great outburst of asceticism, only comparable with that which in the 4th century peopled the deserts of Libya with hermits & communities. The 4th century like the 19th

---

[120] Anxious to build on the success of what would appear to have been the League's inaugural meeting, Henson requested Anson to use his influence with the editor of *The Times* to ensure publication of a letter or article by Henson on its work: All Souls Coll., Oxford, Anson MSS, Henson to Anson, 22 June 1886. However, the letter did not appear until 13 August: see Introduction, p. ix, n. 6.

was an age of ennuied luxury, the sick-querulous old age of a very guilty & corrupt civilization. Both then and now the Noble Souls are revolted, horrified by the world. They w^d fly away anywhere to escape. Not that asceticism will ever again be as intensive as it once was. It will be eminently militant & practical. The asceticism of S. Basil is the asceticism of the X^ian Warfare: and that will be the asceticism of this age, when the resurrection from self-contempt into militancy comes.

[84]

Sunday, June 27th, 1886.

The Bishop of Ripon (Boyd Carpenter)[121] preached the morning sermon to a vast audience. He is very frothy.

I dined with Bowlby at the Golden Cross: Lang and Vidal were also there: we formed a very pleasant party. *Lang and I had a long argument as to Asceticism.*

Then we went to the Balliol Concert: & I was much vexed at everything. A programme mainly secular, concluded by a hypocritical hymn, by way of propitiating the Deity, I suppose: the Bp. of Ripon side by side with Henry Irving[122] in the audience – all revolted my religious sense.

[85]

Tuesday, June 29th, 1886.

I lunched with Gore, after which we talked for an hour or more, lying on cushions in the Garden of the Puseyum. He urged on me the duty of taking Orders, and not abandoning my Vocation. *At 4 I played lawn-tennis – and at 5.30 had strawberries & cream with the Sub-Warden & the Misses Anson: but all the while I ceased not to think of Gore's words. After dinner* **Hardinge came to my rooms, and talked earnestly with me, trying to dissuade me from going in for the B.C.L.:[123] he said I ought to take Orders,** *& give up hesitating, in fact, burn my ships. Hardinge knew not that he was confirming Gore. The coincidence gave victory to the argument.*

[86]

At once I left Hardinge and went to the Puseyum, and told Gore that I would burn my ships at last, and take Orders. Then I returned to my rooms and wrote to the Bishop.

I have burnt my ships.

See below p. 180 [Henson's later interjection]

---

[121] William Boyd Carpenter (1841–1918; *ODNB*), bishop of Ripon, 1884–1911; St Catharine's Coll., Cambridge; canon and sub-dean, Westminster, 1911–18; prolific writer of works that ranged from religious teaching to popular fiction; supported Henson in the controversy concerning his appointment as bishop of Hereford and attended his consecration: *Retrospect*, I, 247, 257.

[122] Henry Irving [né Brodribb] (1838–1905; *ODNB*), actor and manager of the Lyceum theatre, 1878–1905; first actor to be knighted (1895).

[123] Bachelor of Civil Law.

[87]

Wednesday, June 30th, 1886.

The warden caught hold of me and gave me 3 "pieces of advice" **about my public speaking. (1) Stand still (2) Stand up (3) Keep your hands out of your pockets**. *A fearfully critical trinity!!!*

I went home by the 12 o'clock train, and found Gillie[124] there: nobody expected me.

[88]

Wednesday, July 7th, 1886.

Gid & I rushed off on our wildgoose chase for a cheap, retired, interesting country place, wherein to spend a little time in reading. We were to be economical, very: but the beginning was not hopeful on that score. Our first day saw the end of more than £4. We were really shockingly gay.

The Colonial Exhibition did not satisfy our thirst for pleasures. The idea came to me **why not see Faust**? It was an inspiration (of uncertain origin!). Having loads of time we walked from King's X to the Theatre, asking our way of policemen. We reached the Lyceum about 7.10 & already a crowd were collected about the entrance to the Pit. A **[89]** horrid crush preceded entrance, & a tiresome waiting for ¾ of an hour followed it. But **the Play made ample amends for both**. Miss Ellen Terry[125] was not acting, but a very respectable substitute was provided in a young lady whose name I know not. The Church scene pleased me most. The Organ sounded so tremendously religious & the Church was so holy. The bells also were delightful. The scene on the Brocken I admire of course. The whole thing is a miracle: but **what does it mean**? Is the Devil lifting the veil & showing the now hopelessly ruined Faust how elaborate is the machinery of hell whereby the life of man is **[90]** on all sides surrounded.

Rushed off in great haste from our hotel & just caught the 9 o'clock train. I took tickets for Leeds without any obvious reason: except that it was in Yorkshire.

At Peterboro a very interesting old fellow got in & went as far as Grantham. He was an old-fashioned Liberal, very sound on economic questions with an inveterate distrust of Gladstone [,] an antique veneration for the landed aristocracy, a dissenter, but opposed to disestablishment.

[91]

Friday, July 9th, 1886.

We went to the castle and looked over it under the guidance of the porch-keeper. Skipton Castle is in splendid preservation: all the windows of the old castle opened on to the courtyard, in the centre of which grows a fine old yew-tree, credited with a

---

[124] His brother, Gilbert ('Gid').
[125] Ellen Alice Terry (1847–1928; *ODNB*), acclaimed actress, particularly noted for her Shakespearian roles.

respectable antiquity of from 500 to 700 years. The walls are 10 and 12 feet thick, and even in the top storey which was added by the famous Lady Anne Clifford, they are not less than 5 or 6. The hall is a noble room, where twice a year at the audit the tenants of the Estate are entertained at dinner. The Estate is 10 miles long, & the numerous tenants fill the hall twice over. The kitchen is splendid: with an enormous fire-place: the most gruesome place in the castle is the Dungeon, deep **[92]** underground, with no windows at all. The prisoners were taken to & from this hell-hole blind-folded. Escape would be quite impossible: an iron door was secured by a heavy bar of oak let into the stone: a number of huge bolts running into the stone, & a cumbrous lock.

Among the other noticeable points are General Lambert's chair, and Queen Mary's chair, the latter a most antique thing, in the round room where the wretched Queen was resident for a brief time.

No room is on the same floor with another: & every room has 2 doors: so that a very detailed resistance could be made to an Enemy. The porch-keeper seemed a splendid specimen of the feudal retainer.

[93]

Skipton Church is a large perpendicular building; abominably spoiled by a gallery inserted during the last century: withal containing some fine tombs of the Cliffords: and a very fine roof. The reredos is a good piece of modern work, and the old wooden screen is effective.

The guide was an ignorant, drinking, disreputable beast, who stolidly gave the date 1100 for the church, & everything in it, except the gallery which he unaccountably omitted.

After leaving the Castle we made our way to the top of a big moor: from which the most wonderful view of the country was obtained: after which we struck across the moor to Embsay.

[94]

Saturday, July 10th, 1886.

We walked from Embsay to Bolton Abbey. The road lay through a most beautiful valley. The abbey is wondrously situated: high enough to be free from all danger of floods but yet low enough to gain all the seclusion and shelter of the hills.

At the foot of the Abbey runs the river Wharfe, shallow, rapid, pebbly – crossed by a long row of big stones. *Words cannot express the beauty of this spot: and it is so sad too – those noble ruins of what once was so grand & greatly hopeful. Asceticism cried to the world "Trust me. I can save you: Enable me to exist"; and the World consented: & dowered ascetics richly indeed. The homes of anchorites were as the gates of Paradise for beauty.* **[95]** *and lo: here is the end of it all – asceticism in ruins, and the world unsaved. And why?* **Asceticism was hopeful even to the last. The bolt of destruction fell when a great work was just begun. Ere the tower rose more than 1/3rd of its intended height, Bolton was a ruin. Why? Is asceticism also a deceiver**?

We walked on through the grand woods until we reached the Stridd.

> The striding-place is called the "Strid"
> A name which it took of yore;
> A thousand years hath it borne that name,
> And it shall a thousand more![126]

The water was abnormally low. And it was a weird & terrible sight. A rushing stream 3 or 4 feet wide, between unmitigated rocks, & 30 feet deep!

[96]

3rd Sunday after Trinity, July 11th, 1886.

We went to morning service at Embsay Church. Terribly low: choir of both sexes: creditable as to singing but in appearance painful. Vicar a healthy secular quasi-farmer preacher – smug, canting, Evangelical.

A horde of Swedenborgians in Embsay.

In the evening we attended service at the old Church of Skipton. The service was very well conducted, though the choir was ludicrously small, but the sermon by a deacon with an Oxford Bachelor's hood was sad indeed: an average essay for a college tutor. The church was not half full: but it is a big building.

[97]

Dissent seems terribly strong up here. "Pubs & Schism-shanties" stare me in the face everywhere: while the Salvation Army blasphemes in the Streets after its kind.

[98]

Monday, July 12th, 1886.

The post brought from the Bishop *of Oxford a paper of questions, which I answered and returned. Thus proceeds this matter. Fawssett, Molony,[127] and Brennan[128] were the 3 parsons I mentioned to the Bishop: and to whom I forthwith wrote letters of apology for not first obtaining their permission. The League will be electrified by the news that I am taking Orders: and I admit they will have some reason: and I have no defence of myself: for my motives cannot be made public.*

[Rowland] **Prothero wrote an almost angry letter respecting the League**.

Wakeman returned my Essay[129] with suggestions.

---

[126] William Wordsworth, 'The force of prayer; or, the founding of Bolton Abbey' (1807).
[127] Henry Molony (1858–1918), non-coll., Oxford; bible clerk, All Souls Coll., Oxford, 1880–2; ord. 1883; curate, St Saviour, Hoxton, 1885–91; as vicar of Great Ilford parish church, 1892–1912, his paths crossed with Henson again when Henson became chaplain of St Mary's Hospital Chapel, Ilford, 1895–1900.
[128] Samuel Brennan (ord. 1870), chaplain, Mile End Infirmary, 1882–94; curate, St Benet, Stepney, 1886.
[129] Henson, 'The early English constitution', in *Essays introductory to the study of English constitutional history*, ed. Henry Offley Wakeman and Arthur Hassell (London, 1887), pp. 1–44.

[99]

Tuesday, July 13th, 1886.

The post brought a letter from Burbidge[130] making enquiries about the best college for Webster: to which I made answer at once, suggesting S. John's and Hertford, and dissuading from Pembroke.

Morrison the Liberal Unionist[131] was returned by a small majority over the sitting member Sir Matthew Wilson.[132] Skipton was in a great state of excitement, and many of the electors were drunk.

[100]

Wednesday, July 14th, 1886.

We walked to Barden, saw the Tower and Gil Beck Waterfall, (which was nearly empty) and then walked through the woods to the Strid, and thence to Bolton Priory. At a cottage near thereto we got some very excellent tea, and then walked to Skipton by East Halton. Having bought a newspaper we returned to Embsay.

[101]

Thursday, July 15th, 1886.

We walked to Ilkley through Draughton, and Addingham: and there procured some very nasty & dirty "tea": after which we walked through a very beautiful country to **Bolton Priory**, through the hamlets of Neston and Beamsley. The hedge-rows on either side of the road were delightful with honey-suckle and roses. Once more we surveyed with sad wonder the ruins of the Priory, and then returned to Embsay by East Halton.

[102]

Friday, July 16th, 1886.

We strolled into Skipton, and bought a paper: then made our way back to Embsay by a detour.

I sent off letters to Wakeman, Adderley, Hobhouse, & Brennan.

Mrs Tempest tells me that fresh butter from the farm is 10½ a pound, and eggs are 14 a shilling. Agricultural labourer's wages are 20/– a week.

The rent of this cottage (5 rooms and offices) is 4/– a week.

---

[130] Not identified.
[131] Walter Morrison (1836–1921; *ODNB*), businessman, politician, benefactor; MP (LU) Skipton, 1886–92; 1895–1900; Balliol Coll., Oxford.
[132] Matthew Wilson (1802–91), 1st Bt., MP (L) Skipton, 1885–6.

Some of the grass-land about Embsay yields a rent of £4 the acre: & one field near to Skipton fetches as much as £6.

The farmers enjoy the privilege of turning sheep on to the moors.

[103]

Ritual it seems to me should be regulated by two principles viz the principle of Decency, and that of Instruction: if it sins against either it needs reform. The intention of crossing oneself is I conceive, to declare devotion to Jesus Christ. The action per se is valueless: symbolically it is important. But if instead of conveying the idea of devotion to Christ it appears simply ludicrous, that is to say, if it fails to fulfil its symbolic function (which is its raison d'etre) then I think it should rightly be dispensed with.

Both Decency & Instruction are rather negative than positive. Ritual must not be indecent, & it must not convey false impressions. It were straining the function of Ritual to regard it as the vehicle of instruction <u>intentionally</u>. It is necessarily so.

[104]

In fine <u>Decency</u> is the first law of Ritual: <u>Instruction</u> is the condition – one of the conditions – of decency.

Decency being essentially external, it follows that ritual is decent or the contrary from the point of view of the congregation: for there is no such thing as <u>essential</u> decency; just as there is no such thing as essential scandal. And as the point of view of a congregation varies often, being changed by all the circumstances that affect the personnel, education, social position, opinions of the individual members, it follows that there is no absolutely decent ritual, no ritual that is permanently decent. Therefore to prove the antiquity of any ritual observance is not to prove its decency: & is therefore no **[105]** argument at all for introducing it today.

The permanent element in Ritual is contained in the permanent condition of Decency viz Instruction. One thing is Eternal & unchanging & that is the Faith once delivered to the saints. However various ritual may be it must not convey false impressions of that Faith. When it does that it ceases to be decent.

The principle of Instruction in Ritual may be transgressed in two ways. Either by inadequacy: or by Excess. Truth may be perilously ignored: or perilously wrapped up in Symbols. To maintain the via-media, which is Decency, is the object and reason of <u>Rubric</u>: but for obvious reasons Rubric fails to accomplish its object.

[106]

If the rule of decency varies from time to time, &, though putting forward an unchanging teaching, yet necessarily changing in order to do so: how is it at all reasonable to construct in one age a Rubric of Ritual to bind the subsequent ages. The excesses of individuals undeniably require the yoke of law: that is the raison d'être of Rubric. The eternal variation of human opinion which fixes decency: that is the raison d'être of Elasticity in Rubrical law: or rather it is the necessity on which is based a rubric-making power. **Rubric can only be at once efficient & elastic by being constantly changed with opinion. The misfortune of the Church is a lack of rubrical machinery**.

[107]

Saturday, July 17th, 1886.

We spent the day at Ingleton, visiting the waterfalls. Weathercote Cave is a most wonderful sight: we had to walk more than 4 miles to reach it. The road lay along the side of Raven Scar, a sort of outpost of Ingleborough, which is in truth a noble hill.

The spray makes the rocks wet and slippery: and the descent into the Cave is not without difficulty: but it is indeed worth going far to see. A magnificent stream of water rushes out of a large cavity in the rock, and falls more than 70 feet into the bottom of the cave, where it disappears down a subterranean passage to re-appear again about a mile further down.

[108]

Sunday, July 18th, 1886.

We walked to Bolton Abbey for morning Prayer, & arrived as the congregation were finishing the Confession. All the seats in the Church are quite free, so we had no difficulty in getting a good seat. Mr Howes[133] the present Rector is a pale, thoughtful young man & wears the hood of a Cambridge Master. The choir are vested in surplices, & sing very well, were it not for a grave drawback in the want of boys. There were only 4 choir-boys to 10 men. The service was short, the sermon good, and both were followed by a Celebration, to which we stayed. The organ is very excellent in tone, & appears to be well played.

[109]

It is a very debasing thing to be hypocritical: a ritual should not be too ecstatic lest it breed hypocrisy: it should not be too simple lest it fail to evoke the highest worship from the congregation, which is its function. Moderation should be the key-note of ritual: and, inasmuch as a congregation is very various in composition – ritual should be very intelligible. **Moderation in tone, simplicity in form, those are the conditions of Efficient Ritual from the point of view of the individual**. It is really astonishing how hypocritical even a simple ritual renders ordinary people: and although semi-unconscious hypocrisy cannot be placed quite on a level with deliberate hypocrisy yet there is a great amount of sin in it: & it does debase character.

[110]

We attended the evening Service at Skipton old Church. The curate happily did not preach: but a stranger gave a very good sermon – well delivered – best type of

---

[133] Arthur Plumptre Howes (ord. 1877; *CCD*), Pembroke Coll., Cambridge; rector, Bolton Abbey, 1882, patron, duke of Devonshire.

Evangelical. The service is very well conducted, although I doubt whether the Rector makes himself heard over the church.

The most vexatious thing about the place is the congregation; not filling the church by a long way, & containing such a very few men. The men of Skipton prefer to stand talking together in groups in the High Street. It is a foolish fashion with them & proves to my mind little against the Church. The choir numbered 11 boys and 9 men.

[111]

Monday, July 19th, 1886.

Received buttery-bill &c. for last term £31.10.: at least 30/– ought to be re-paid me by the League: but it will not be. The Hilary Term's bill was over £37. Together this makes about £69: and I have had an advance of £50. I must keep my next tennis expenses under £30: so as to ensure myself £50 in Feb.

I finished **Buckle's History of Civilization**.[134]

[112]

Tuesday, July 20th, 1886.

The post brought a letter from Freeman refusing to be on the Council. I am so sorry. Also one from Sir John Conroy[135] accepting the offer. He is the first man on the Council.

I also received a letter from Blackall dated from Belgium.

We spent most of the afternoon on the "crag" next to Embsay to the North. A dear little "beck" babbles down the side thereof: in which we "paddled" with much delight. It is much easier to get up these heath-covered hills with bare feet than with boots on.

[113]

Wednesday, July 21st, 1886.

We went on an expedition to Malham. A kindly old farmer gave us a lift down to the station: from which – by the 9 o'clock train – we made our way to Bell Busk: the nearest station for Malham. A walk of about 4 miles brought us to Kirkby Malham, where there is a fine perpendicular church dedicated to S. James. The columns are nearly all ornamented with vacant niches – a most unusual thing.

The pews, all of oak, & square are quaintly carved with the owners names *1619, 1637, 1667 & so forth, were the dates. Oliver Cromwell's signature is shown among the parish registers: and the Lambert family have sundry relics e.g. a bell given by Josias Lambert in 1602: & monuments to the memory of* **[114]** the son and grandson of Major-General Lambert.

---

[134] Henry Thomas Buckle, *History of civilisation in England* (2 vols., London, 1857–61).
[135] John Conroy (1845–1900; WWW), 3rd Bt (1869), fellow and lecturer, Balliol Coll., Oxford.

About 1½ miles from Kirkby Malham and ½ a mile distant therefrom is <u>Malham Cove</u>, a sort of amphitheatre of lime-stone rocks about 286 feet high, at the base of which the "river" Aire starts into existence – a tiny stream.

Returning to Malham we had lunch at the "Buck", and then made our way to <u>Gordale Scar</u> rather more than a mile away. This is a very narrow Gorge between lofty, overhanging cliffs of Limestone. A small stream falls in pretty cascades down the Gorge. We climbed the scar, by means of rough steps worn in its surface: and from the top gained a wonderful **[115]** view of the whole length of the Gorge. The appearance of the land at the top is extremely wonderful. Limestone rocks, all similar in appearance, ranged in long rows of detached pieces cover the ground for a great distance, giving the impression of an enormous hay field after the grass has been cut– all petrified.[136] After rambling about for some time we reached the shore of <u>Malham Tarn</u> said to be the longest piece of water in Yorkshire, but very unimposing. On its banks is the residence of Mr Morrison, the successful Unionist Candidate for the Skipton division. He would appear to be a good churchman: we were shown evidences of his pious zeal in the Kirkby Malham Church.

We returned to Malham and got tea in a cottage. While we were **[116]** there a violent thunderstorm came on accompanied by a deluge of rain. We did not leave our shelter until the rain had ceased: and eventually the evening became comparatively fine. Finding that we had some time to wait for our train: we walked back to Embsay: a long way but through a most delightful road. Near Gargrave we were pleased with the appearance of Eshton Hall the seat of Sir Matthew Wilson, the defeated Gladstonian candidate for the Skipton Division. The house is reported to contain a fine library of 15000 volumes.

Gargrave is a very pretty village: we reached Embsay about 8.30 p.m. very tired indeed having walked nearly 25 miles.

[117]

<u>Expenses of this Visit</u>

		£	s	d
Railway fare from Broadstairs to Skipton		2	10	4
Cab fares (α) To Kings X.	3/–			
(β) from Lyceum	2/–			
(γ) to Embsay	2/6			
(δ) to Skipton	2/6		10	
The Colonial Exhibition				
(α) Fees	5/–			
(β) Dinner	4/–			
(γ) Washing	–/6^d			
(δ) Programme	–/3^d			
(ε) Strawberries	3/–		10	

---

[136] Petrified (adj.) (1a) *OED*: 'that has been petrified; subjected to petrification; converted into stone or a stony substance'.

The Lyceum (α) Fees	6/–			
(β) Faust	–/6		6	6
Hotel (1) King's Cross		1	4	6
(2) Midland Hotel	19/–	2	3	6
Lodgings			4	5
Trip to Ingleton	16/–			
" " Malham	9/8	1	5	8
Sundries – teas, tips			5	
		11	16	

Besides fares home.

[118]

Tuesday, August 3rd, 1886. [All Souls College.]

Since I have been here all my old wickedness has returned. I am as cynical and reckless and blasphemous as ever: and I had hoped that if I steadily contemplated Orders at Christmas I should have found some immunity from all: but I was wrong: for the one & evident spring of all is radical and unchanging. So long as I do not believe in anything: it's no use trying to deceive myself into believing that I do, by repeating my belief with reiterated assurance. The process is not only unsuccessful: it is vicious for it depraves: & degradation is the test & measure of vice. And yet I am at a loss to know what to do. A fate seems to bear me **[119]** *on towards Orders in spite of myself: nay, not fate but some blessed Spirit who would save me from endless ruin: for thereto leads also all that is best in me: though only in yearning, not in conviction. How will that hallowed & weighty because hallowed yoke of Orders rest on this stubborn neck? Will it give the victory to my higher self: or will it indeed drive me the faster into the abyss of hatred of Good – so near & so possible. I know not: my will is nerveless: and* **I drift along: only wondering at the fact of my having written to the bishop at all**. *If it is purposed by the Eternal that I should do work, will his purpose fail? And if not purposed, what am I that I should fight against God?*

[120]

Wednesday, August 4th, 1886.

I walked over to Cuddesdon, to see Burrows. *Otley, Strong, Trollope,*[137] *Brockman,*[138] *& Batson*[139] *were all there. Everybody was most kind, and for Burrows I entertain sentiments of real respect, but I was not pleased with the place.* **A forced and therefore hypocritical spiritual hilarity seems to dominate everybody**. *"Inter-buttering" is the order of the day: and an entertaining mask of monasticism is kept up by a few rules*

---

[137] Mark Napier Trollope (1862–1930; *WWW*), New Coll., Oxford; Cuddesdon; bishop of Corea, 1911–30.
[138] Ralph Thomas Brockman (1861–1925), non-coll.; ord. 1887; curate, Cowley St John, Oxford, 1890–3.
[139] Vincent Lascelles Batson (1861–1920), non-coll.; ord. 1888; curate Carlton Colville, Lowestoft, 1887–9.

more childish than burdensome. I think that much real good might be done by <u>real</u> ascetic monasticism for 1 or 2 years as a training for Orders: but this elegant farce is useless.

[121]

[Rowland] <u>Prothero</u> *came up today. He has strengthened me by his mere presence.* "<u>You would have a great sphere of usefulness up here, after taking Orders,</u>" *he said. Is this so? If I turn the page the materials for a negative stare me in the face.*

[122]

Thursday, August 5<u>th</u>, 1886.

I walked alone by myself along the river-banks from Godstow: & – as the way was not burdened by people – sat down awhile [*sic*] to think. A sensation of despondent fatigue succeeds to the violent emotions of the last few days.

Massillon[140] soothes me while he makes me sad. <u>Nous ne sommes pas longtemps fidèles à Dieu, des que nous ne le sommes plus à nous-mêmes</u>[141] – there is an almost terrible frankness about this prelate: & he knows the heart of man[.] <u>Les premières larmes dans le pécheur qui va retomber, sont souvent plus vives et plus abondantes, que dans le pécheur qui persévère.</u>[142] How terrible is Massillon where he deters the sincere from presuming to act in the Sanctuary.

[123]

Eh! qui êtes-vous, pour vouloir être déjà un instrument des miséricordes du Seigneur sur les âmes? <u>Les seules fonctions d'un pécheure sont des larmes, le silence, la retraite, et la prière</u>. Attendez que Dieu vous envoie poure entreprendre son oeuvre: préparez, par de long exemples, l'efficace à vos discours: edifiez long-temps vos frères, avant que d'oser les exhorter: achetery, <u>par une longue fuite, le droit de les voir sans danger</u>; et souvenez-vous que les complices de nos passions, ne sauroient être d'abord que les éceuils de notre pénitence.[143]

---

[140] Jean-Baptiste Massillon (1663–1742), renowned preacher and bishop of Clermont, 1717–42; for the origins of Henson's interest in Massillon, see his letter to Charles Smyth, 27 Feb. 1940, in Letterbook 112, 345–6, the Henson Papers, Durham Cathedral Library.

[141] 'We do not long remain faithful to God, once we cease to be faithful to ourselves.' 'Sermon pour la jour de Paques [Sermon for Easter Day]', in *Oeuvres de Massillon, Évèque de Clermont* (2 vols., Paris, 1835), I, 533–44, at 540.

[142] 'The first tears of the sinner about to lapse once more are often sharper and more abundant than those of the unremitting sinner.' *Ibid.*, 537.

[143] 'Who are you, to want already to be an instrument of the Lord's mercy upon souls? A sinner has no occupation but tears, silence, seclusion, and prayer. Wait for God to send you forth to undertake his work. By your behaviour over a long time, nourish the effectiveness of your sermons. Build up your brothers, before you dare to hector them; by long exile earn the right to spend time with them without danger; and recall that our passions' first accomplices are the very reefs on which our penitence comes to grief.' *Ibid.*, 536.

[124]

Friday, August 6th, 1886.

A long talk with Headlam left me with a higher estimate of his character and a darker view of my prospects. It seems clear enough that my interests require me to stay up here: but how I can afford to do so does not appear. Gid is a terrible fact, and so is the Home. I can't do with less than £400 a year: and up here my income is not more than £300 at most.

[Pages 125, 126, 127, 128 have been cut out leaving approximately 1 cm of paper. Scraps of Henson's writing are visible at the edges of the pages.]

[129]

My lectures promised

1.	Sept. 19th	Bethnal Green		
2.	" 26th	"		
3.	Oct. 3rd	Bethnal Green		
4.	" 18th	Oxford		
5.	" 28th	Margate	?	
6.	" 29th	Broadstairs	?	
7.	Nov. 11th	Ilford		
8.	Sept. 21st	Poplar		
9.	Sept. 28th	"		
10.	Oct. 5th	"		

[130]

Dr [debit]

			£	s	d
By Cheque to Adderley			7		
"	"	" Hobhouse	4		
"	"	" Baker & Prior	20		
"	"	" Self	5		
"	"	" Gee	4	10	
"	"	" Adderley	10		
"	"	" Self	5		
"	"	" Mrs Parminter	7	4	3
"	"	" Self	1	5	
"	"	" J.H.	3	12	6
"	"	" Self	5		
			72	11	9

[131] C<u>r</u> [credit]

	£	s	d
Balance brought forward from p. 79.	14		
Oct. 19<u>th</u> Lamb[144] – cheque	5		
.. Lassetter ..	10		
.. Adderley ..	1		
.. 25<u>th</u> Rivington ..	1	1	
.. Blackall notes	10		
Dec. 6<u>th</u> Deudy chk.	2		
.. Sperling ..	10	10	
.. 9<u>th</u> Lord Valletort[145] ..	10	10	
Jan. 10<u>th</u> Soulsby[146] ..	10		
	£ 74	1	
	72	11	9
Balance	1	8	3

Jan. 17<u>th</u> 1887
   H. Hensley Henson

[132]

Saturday, September 11th, 1886.

I went to Oxford prior to beginning my sojourn in Bethnal Green. The College is empty everybody except Bertie being away. So I dined by myself in the coffee-room: and afterwards wrote letters of condolence to M<u>r</u> Rathbone, & Lyle, and Conybeare. The Grisly Monarch rages against the young and vigourous [*sic*]: both M<u>rs</u> Conybeare[147] and Edward Rathbone are quite young, and yet they have gone.

Gid troubles me much: he has no sense of responsibility. *"To enjoy life" seems his conception of duty: the scheme of his desires excludes duty to God and man. Assam has stamped out every spark of religion from his soul: and hardened his heart to an almost inconceivable degree. From what he says, Arthur is much the same.*

[133]

[B]oth cast aside Christianity at once and without effort as soon as they reached Assam. Yet both had gone far in the direction of profession here: and Arthur, at least, had given evident proofs of a sincere adherence to the cause of Christ. Why then did they

---

[144] Not identified.
[145] Piers Alexander Hamilton Edgcumbe, Viscount Valletort (1865–1944), Christ Church, Oxford; 5th earl of Mount Edgcumbe (1917).
[146] Basil Harrington Soulsby (1864–1933), Corpus Christi Coll., Oxford; BA History, 1887; assistant, Natural History Museum.
[147] See 3: **145** n. 167.

lose their religion with such fatal facility? Was it merely the influence of surroundings that created and destroyed it? Yet Arthur, at least, would seem to have persisted in his confirmation against very adverse circumstances. I can understand the gradual wearing out of faith in a man suddenly transplanted from a religious to an irreligious environment: but I cannot understand this sudden unreluctant abjuration on the spot. It gives the impression of **[134]** *men being suddenly set free from a yoke. There can be no doubt that the decadence of a man's faith proceeds very rapidly when once he abandons all means of keeping his religious faculty in wholesome activity. Especially when he is set in the midst of irreligious surroundings (such as those of Assam) this* laissez-faire *policy is fatal. The* genius loci *(i.e. impiety) has its normal and inevitable effect without encountering any opposition from a vigourous [sic] religious sense. Lax practice begets intellectual infidelity: the offspring of both is cynicism: that accursed blight of the soul, which is itself a sort of damnation.*

[135]

Sunday, September 12th, 1886.

I went to S. Barnabas for the choral celebration of the Eucharist, which grows on me the oftener I attend it. Yet I cannot shake off the suspicion that **my worship is more sensuous than spiritual***. I suppose it is possible to delude one's self in these matters in which case to attend ornate services is to court temptation: the barren spiritualism of Puritanism is the provision of a jealous conscience!* **On the other hand, what right has a man to quarrel with his own piety***? He should gratefully accept every means which can reduce him to worship. Ritualism is the creation of an ardent worship! Yet a man is born a Puritan or a Ritualist, & is not made so.*

[136]

I wrote a long letter to Arthur speaking very plainly about Gid, and religion generally. My letters must bore him to death: they are sermons: yet I cannot help myself: the defection of Gid fills me with fear, for Arthur, and for myself. Is my faith also so slightly attached to me as to vanish in a changed environment.

"Strait is the gate and narrow is the way, which leadeth unto life and few there be that find it."[148] Jesus Christ must mean what he says: yet we marvel at the defection of a single person.

Bertie, Fletcher, and I dined together. Fletcher has promised to take the 2nd lecture at Ilford.

[137]

1. Establishment of the Church.	C.W.C. Oman.
2. First Reformation.	C.R.L. Fletcher.
3. Second Reformation.	? R.E. Prothero.
4. The Laudian Revival.	J.A. Doyle.

---

[148] Matt. 7:14.

5. The Nonconformists   H.H. Henson.
6. The Modern Church.   H.O. Wakeman.

If the scheme is thus carried out; half the lectures will be on the old Foundation, and half on the New: very fairly representative of the college.

[138]

I have a lot of bad debts, e.g.

paid £10.10*	Sperling owes me	£15
paid*	Blackall " "	£10
	J.H. " "	£12
	G.A.H. " "	£16
		£53

* [added later]

Of which I scarcely expect to receive one penny: though it would pay half my debts!

Probable receipts:–

[symbol]	Lasseter[149]	£10
	Mich. Term.	£30
	Bursar	£45
	Hilary Term	£30
	Trinity Term	£30
	Total.	£145

My debts are at least £170: I shall have to draw on the Bursar again: which I did want to avoid.

[139]

Thursday, September 16th, 1886. [Oxford House.]

I have been here since Monday: and am on the whole very contented, except in the matter of work. I am far more useless than I expected. On Tuesday evening I took the night School in Mape Street. Four scavenger-scamps wrote & read for an hour. On Wednesday Lasseter came: (I am a most incompetent coach:) in the evening I spent 2 hours at a Committee of Recreative Evening Classes Society.

Buchanan,[150] a city man is here: a splendid fellow dear to my soul: & Lester,[151] who will come back to the League I hope: and Adderley who is Galahad.

---

[149] Leslie Beauchamp Lasseter (1865–1906), Magdalen Coll., Oxford; 3rd class Modern History, 1887; Roman Catholic priest.
[150] Patrick Buchanan, described by Henson as a Scottish merchant and a regular volunteer at Oxford House: *Retrospect*, I, 28, III, 366.
[151] Lester Vallis Lester (1860–1944; *WWW*), Magdalen Coll., Oxford; fellow of St John's Coll., Oxford, 1886–9.

[140]

Friday, September 17th, 1886.

I visited the London Hospital. Valentine[152] is a very pleasing person: tall, handsome, with a look of conscious earnestness. He shewed me round some of the wards. The children's wards are very light and cheerful. The patients look delightfully clean & refined: it is hard to identify them with the filthy objects of the streets: **V. says they are glad to return to their slums**. There is one endowed bed in the Hospital, "Willie's Bed". V. says that £2000 is required to endow a cot; which seems incredible.

A considerable number of the nurses are ladies.

[141]

Monday, September 27th, 1886.

The lecture on the Endowments of the Church went off well. There were 83 men there exclusive of the "aristocracy". Women were happily excluded. Last week the number of men was 69: so that there is a clear gain of 14. I should like to get into three figures. The old man who announced last Sunday his intention of "disproving my statements by dockyments" duly appeared with **Hallam's Middle Ages**[153] **tied up in a handkerchief**. The only decent point he raised was that about the 3-fold division of tithes: to which I made the answer that that division never existed in England. The old fellow rather pleased me: his admiration for Hallam was touching. He said that he was wont to visit [142] S. Paul's in order to look at Hallam's monument. The Secularist boy of course had his say: but made an exhibition of himself through his utter ignorance of the subject. Thus he expressed great wrath because the Churches were freed from rates, & the chapels not!! So that I had an easy task in scoring off him. M͏r Bates from the Mape Street Club came to me afterwards and asked about the tithe, & I was glad to be able to make it plain to him at last. Considering that there was a decided sprinkling of dissenters and secularists in the audience, the reception accorded to my remarks was admirable.

[143]

Today I went into the city to perform sundry commissions for Adderley. I saw again that offensive symbol – the three gilt balls & the still more offensive inscription "Subhoc Ligno floresco".[154] It seemed like the standard of Mammon contending in open day with the standard of Constantine and Christ. I love the gilt cross on S. Pauls: it is such a protest.

---

[152] Not identified.
[153] Henry Hallam, *View of the state of Europe in the middle ages: in two volumes* (London, 1818).
[154] 'Under this sign I shall prosper'. Henson is referring to a pawnbroking sign: what he found offensive was the punning reference to the Emperor Constantine's famous vision of the Cross before the Battle of the Milvian Bridge in 312: 'in hoc signo vinces' ('By this sign you will conquer').

[144]

Tuesday, September 28th, 1886.

My 2nd lecture at Poplar. "The Medieval Church". In my opinion a failure, but Adderley and Wagget[155] seemed to think otherwise. The audience was distinctly smaller than last Tuesday, which mortified me much. No doubt it is an useful rebuke to my foolish conceit. A host of little circumstances helped to put me out tonight – The loss of my notes, the hurry, the tram car, my hoarseness, the diminished audience &c. Yet I managed to say something about monasticism: which I believe in more than ever. Adderley builds hopes on the Duke of Newcastle:[156] which I hope may not prove vain.

[145]

Wednesday, September 29th, 1886.

I visited the London hospital and gave a book to a boy named Charles Nicholls. Valentine was just off for his holiday. At 9.30 p.m. I lectured at the University Club on "St Hugh, the Monk-Bishop". It went down very well, though the men can scarcely grip *what I mean: yet I love to dwell on the strangeness of the fact. A number of East End working men listening with interest to the story of a Saint's life. There is yet some hope for them.*

My criminal appeared, and succeeded in getting me to "lend" him 2/–; which made Adderley very angry. I am not yet convinced that he is hoaxing me.

[146]

Thursday, September 30th, 1886.

I spent the greater part of the day in "Retreat". As I had never been in "Retreat" before all seemed rather strange: the silence at meals was very funny: indeed I nearly shrieked with laughter. Trollope and Tracey "went off" too: & a catastrophe very nearly happened. On the whole I am favourably impressed by the Retreat: and think that they may be a real help to the sincere man. Sincerity is an enigma to me. I am constitutionally hypocritical. Now, to Reggie Adderley and the people here, I pose as an uncompromising Catholic: at Oxford I shall infallibly resume the position of a more or less scornful anti-ritualist. I am partially sincere in both attitudes: at first sight it would seem that a middle position wd suit me: but this is not so; whatever is uncertain **[147]** about me, one thing, I fear, is certain that a loose, undefined position (and every middle attitude must be so) will never commend itself to me.

---

[155] Philip Waggett (1862–1939; *ODNB*), Christ Church, Oxford; ord. 1886; member of the Anglican religious order, Society of St John the Evangelist (the Cowley Fathers), Cowley, Oxford, 1892.

[156] Henry Archibald Douglas Pelham-Clinton (1864–1928, *WWW*), 7th duke of Newcastle (1879), Magdalen Coll., Oxford; committed anglo-catholic; member of the London School Board, 1894–7.

Yet I am not exactly an Extremist. Politically I am a Trimmer like Lord Halifax:[157] **were it not for my insurmountable objection to Evangelicalism** I think I should be a Trimmer in religion too. As it is, **my aversion to Protestants renders me ultra-Catholic. Yet a Catholicism based on antipathy, and honeycombed by scepticism is not worth much**. I am more than ever convinced that real belief is modest and unassertive: while sham belief is arrogantly dogmatic and self-assertive. The true Cynic is the Sceptical Catholic: **the persecuting unbeliever is rather in my line**. All this comes of an arbitrary character and an unfortunate history.

[148]

Sunday, October 3rd, 1886.

About 65 men at my lecture: a bad falling off: to be ascribed, perhaps, either (1.) to the fine weather; or (2.) to the familiarity of both lecturer & subject. Yet it seemed to me that at least in two points there was improvement. (1.) The number of new faces seemed greater: the diminution was mainly owing to abstentions on the part of the Oxford House Club (2.) The interest was more deep and intelligent. At the close several people came to ask questions, & get books recommended. **The old man reappeared with his Hallam in a handkerchief: and made another onslaught: he went for me privately afterwards, but as he wouldn't let me say a word, the result was not great**. The secularist boy made a very foolish and violent [149] speech, which was very offensive for its blasphemies. He "put his foot" into it by charging the clergy with opposing the Temperance Movement: whereupon another person rose and scored-off him by mentioning that 13,500 clergy had presented a temperance petition. On the whole I think some effect has been produced by these lectures though the Secularist boy – far from being convinced – gets more violent.

After tea I made my way to S! Luke's, Victoria Docks: a most splendid new church, where Boyd[158] was wont to dwell: cost about £25,000: apsidal East End; fine organ; stained glass: delightful. My audience in the School room contained about 25 men: 40 females and a few boys. I was too tired & hoarse to do much.

[150]

Saturday, October 9th, 1886.

On Monday I gave the 3rd of my lectures on Political Terms to the Oxford House Club. It was on "Party Government": and I tried to show them that there was a dark side to party. It is possible to abuse the Caucus very effectually by treating it as an insult to the individual elector, and always coupling with it in anathema, the kindred but hostile Primrose League.[159] Next Monday I am to speak on the Empire: when I hope to show

---

[157] George Savile, 1st marquess of Halifax (1633–95; *ODNB*), leading restoration politician and writer; his 1685 pamphlet *The character of a trimmer* defended the policy of the *via media* in politics and some acceptance of protestant dissent within the church.

[158] Not identified.

[159] Organization created by Lord Randolph Churchill in 1883 to disseminate Conservative principles across Britain through inculcating loyalty to the movement; it proved hugely successful as a propagandist arm of the Conservative party, particularly in working-class communities, greatly overshadowing the work of the constituency associations.

that the House of Commons is quite unfit to govern the Empire. If Imperial Federation were practicable the Empire might be saved: but it is not practicable.

On Tuesday, I concluded my lectures on Church History to the Poplar folk. My subject was the modern church: and I tried to be [151] simple, but without success, I fear. How can you make clear to people who know nothing about the matter the difference between Anglican Independence of Rome, and Protestant Antipathy.

I emphasized the importance of reviving monasticism: *it is the one hope for the masses. I don't quite see the utility of the great number of services which the ritualists go in for. That seems to me rather unsuited to this age. Not that I would abolish all rudely.* ***I would have the 7 services daily in the House; but not, I think, Daily Celebrations***. *This is all detail. What I will stick out for is fixed hours of* study: *not mere edification & prayer:* that *the brothers must find in chapel & in their spare time: but real* reading: *and* **[152]** *this by no means technically religious. A division of labour according to natural powers. Political Economy, political Science, history, philosophy, even Science should be included in the work:* ***for the monastic system in its renaissance must again be what it was at the first viz. catholic in grasp: i.e. every side of thought and activity must be included within the monastic life***. *The 19ᵗʰ century must have a Roger Bacon, and a S. Bernard, an Aquinas, and a S. Francis, an Anselm and a Thomas. And so with the* practical *or outside work. Those only shall preach who are orators, & have something to say. Orations* shall not *any more be divorced from study: but shall* **[153]** *find therein its inspiration. One supreme object shall leaven all the work viz.* **the sanctification thereof by applying the incarnation**. *Is this clear to me! Scarcely yet, but I perceive dimly that it is* the *prime necessity.*

[154]

Tuesday, October 12ᵗʰ, 1886.

I went to the Eton Mission at Hackney Wick and lectured on "Establishment and Endowment". My voice was raven-hoarse; & I was generally not fit: moreover I was troubled by the mixed character of the audience. Yet the people of whom about 100 collected in spite of the rain, listened very attentively and several questions were forthcoming. Unequal distribution of endowment, lay tenure of tithe, the Roman Catholic claim, and Extraordinary tithe – all these points were raised, and either disposed of or evaded. On the whole I incline to think that, whether or no the folk remember what is said, it must be a good thing that they should **[155]** know that the Church has something to say for herself. I perceive that much may be done in the East End by emphasizing the religious inequality involved in voluntaryism.

Harold Boulton[160] arrived.

Shuttleworth[161] on Sunday was a failure, though more than 100 men turned up all very keen to hear him. **His unprincipled egotism revolts me**. In the evening Adderley and I each read a lesson: & I shocked everybody by bowing to the Altar as I went

---

[160] Harold Boulton (1859–1935; *ODNB*), songwriter and philanthropist; Balliol Coll., Oxford; one of the first residents of Oxford House and co-founder, with Jimmie Adderley, of the Federation of Working Men's Social Clubs; president of the Federation, 1895–1930; 2nd Bt (1918).

[161] Not identified.

to the lectern. On Monday evening I finished my 4 lectures on "Political Terms"; & announced the new course.

[156]

Engagements for Oct:–

Oct 3rd		"The Church & her Work" in Parish Hall, S. Andrews.
" 4th		"Party-Government" in Oxford House Club.
" 5th		"The Modern Church" at the Ch. Ch. Mission
" 8th		"S. Hugh of Lincoln" at the Mape St Club
" 11th		"The Empire" in the Oxford House Club.
" 12th		"Establishment & Endowment" at Eton Mission.
" 13th		"St Thomas of Canterbury" at Mape St Club.
" 18th		"Church Defence" in Oxford.

[157]

Wednesday, October 13th, 1886.

A very cold day and, with no fire, the House seemed wretched. I am unable or unwilling to be even a little too cold: **with what face can I talk about asceticism***. Tomorrow I return into the lap of luxury. Shall I be quite as I was therein? The broken pledges of past penitences declares yes. If only I were free from that financial burden I would come here & live altogether for a year. But, as it is, I cannot do so. In the Middle Age poverty was the sine qua non for sanctity, now it is property. I return to the 'Varsity very unwillingly: it will mean not only self-contemptuous relapse, but facing many awkward problems.*

[158]

Dalton[162] from the old Winchester Mission now All Hallows, East India Docks, came to dinner, and I showed him the clubs, with which he seemed much pleased.

I lectured on S. Thomas of Canterbury to the Mape Street Club. My audience was well over 30: rough, poor men yet very orderly and attentive. At the end Tracey and I were elected hon. members, and Auld Lang Syne was stumbled through with zeal.

This practically brings my work to an end. It has been little else than lecturing. The London Hospital has really been the only steady piece of work I have performed besides.

---

[162] Arthur Edison Dalton (1853–1958; *WWW*), Clare Coll., Cambridge; ord. 1881; curate, All Hallows, East India Docks, 1880–4; vicar, 1884–96; rector, 1896–1908.

[159]

The lectures have been as follows:–

1.	Sunday	Sept.	19th	Establishment
2.	Monday	"	21st	1. Political Terms
3.	Tuesday	"	23rd	Church History
4.	Sunday	"	26th	Endowments
5.	Monday	"	27th	2. Political Terms
6.	Tuesday	"	28th	Ch. Hist.
7.	Wednesday	"	29th	~~Monks~~ S. Hugh
8.	Friday	Oct.	1st	Anglo-French War
9.	Sunday	"	3rd	Church Work
10.	–	–	–	Est. & End.
11.	Monday	–	4th	3. Pol. Terms
12.	Tuesday	–	5th	Ch. Hist.
13.	Wednesday	–	6th	S. Hugh
14.	Friday	–	8th	~~Anglo-Fr. War~~ S. Hugh
15.	Monday	11th		4. Pol. Terms.
16.	Tuesday	12th		Est. & End.
17.	Wednesday	13th		S. Thomas

[The above lectures are struck through with a vertical line.]

[160]

Besides Bethnal Green I have lectured at the Christ Church Mission in Poplar, and the Eton Mission in Hackney Wick; also ~~for~~ at ~~the~~ S. Luke's, Victoria Docks. Altogether 18 lectures in about a month.

[161]

Monday, October 18th, 1886.

Lamb sent cheque for £5. Soulsby came to be coached. Lassetter sent cheque for £10 and Blackall promised a cheque on Saturday. If only Sperling would pay what he owes!

I lectured to the Church of England Young Men's Society[163] on "Church Defence". G. P. [George Prothero] and his wife were there to my astonishment: and the Hall[164] who presided was none other than he who was assistant-librarian at the Museum.

They tried to get me to make promises to come again: but I made none since I knew that the Low Church Party dominated.

---

[163] The Church of England Men's Society was created by Archbishop Frederick Temple in 1899 by a merger of earlier Church societies that sought in a Christian context to provide social and educational opportunities for young men. Cosmo Lang was an early national chairman of the Society, which had parish branches, diocesan unions and its own magazine.

[164] Not identified.

In the afternoon I went out a walk with the Warden: for the first **[162]** time in my life. We talked mostly about the Oxford House and Celibacy. He seems far more friendly to monasticism than heretofore.

[163]

Tuesday, October 19th, 1886.

To my great surprise no less than 7 men gave in their names for my lecture tomorrow: for which I had believed it to be unlikely that one man would turn up. On which basis I neglected to prepare my lecture, and, as a matter of fact, my first lecture is unprepared.

Soulsby, the jam-consumer, came to me. Big overgrown lout with a disgusting cod-fish mouth: and an air of impervious yet conceited stupidity. Like the rest of my men he will do me no credit. It looks very much as if this is all I shall have this term: I don't know how I can manage. My reckonings were ludicrously in excess of the fact. (see p. 138) [Henson's later interjection]

[164]

The question about my taking Orders will practically turn on the finance of this term. I must make every effort to raise the money for which I am pledged: and as coaching seems to fail me, and I get no chance of any college work, it remains that I must do that which I have long contemplated viz. take Orders and a curacy.

This afternoon I had a long walk with Maguire, and all the way we talked on the subject of X^{ity}. *When I am face to face with Maguire I seem to believe nothing at all: and that is the impression he has of me. And yet it is scarcely true. I do feel that the Personality of Jesus Christ commands my allegiance. If He were but to* **[165]** *come to this world, and call me to Him, and tell me to work for Him, I should haste to obey. Sometimes I dream of the Lord standing on the Altar-step, and saying "Herbert, follow me", and I seem to be kneeling at His feet, and He puts forth His hand and touches me, and says "I call thee, O Herbert, to sorrow, and service, suffering and an early death: wilt thou obey My call"; and I seem to answer "Lord Master, with Thee death is heaven: without Thee life is death: I will follow Thee to prison and to death." And the Lord blesses me and gives me a Mission to work for Him. It is, perhaps, with some such feeling that I look to Ordination.* **[166]** *It appears to me to be a real bowing my neck to receive the Yoke of Jesus. There are lots of reasons why I should not take Orders. I scarcely think my belief is adequate: but one thing I know well, and that is this, that if I do not take Orders I shall make shipwreck of my life.* **My two best-loved friends – Gore and Jim Adderley – see this, and urge me to take Orders**: *and when I wrote to the Bishop I believed that I had burnt my ships; yet all has become vacillation once more. The root of it all is my not going in for the Theology School, that was the first step in a long succession of treason to my higher self.*

[167]

I have been overcome by the perplexities of my position: and now I know not what to do, or where to turn. There is no one to whom I can betake myself: for to none am I free to relate my troubles.

While I have written this a thunderstorm has been going on: another loud clap!

[168]

Friday, October 22nd, 1886.

I gave my 2nd lecture. This time it was on Beda himself. The audience numbered 19, an increase of 2 on last time. They are not a very intellectual set to look at. Their locality points in the same direction.

6	from	S. Edmund Hall
3	–	Pembroke
4	–	Exeter
3	–	Queen's
1	–	University
1	–	Worcester
1	–	S? John's

One scarcely expects any good from any of these places. Yet they seem very industrious in taking notes.

[169]

Saturday, October 23rd, 1886.

Hassall sent me a pupil. **Lord Valletort, son of the Earl of Mount Edgecombe**. He looks a very pleasant fellow and I hope to do some good work with him. He and Soulsby will be, I suppose, the complete tale of this term. The guinea from Brightman for going through his notes on Bede will (supposing I get my money) yield £21 as the net result of the term. Then as Lamb's £5 was quite unexpected I may perhaps reckon it at £26. At this moment I have £19 in the Bank: £1 in hand: £10 owed by Blackall: and £20 to be anticipated from my pups. All = £50. And this to meet expenses & debts at least £120.

[170]

18th Sunday after Trinity, October 24th, 1886.

There was a Celebration in Chapel. The Warden, Gardiner, Headlam, one Bible-Clerk, the Chaplain and I formed the whole of those present.

The Bp. of Meath, Reichel's[165] father,[166] preached at S. Mary's. His text was "What think ye of X^t, whose Son is He?":[167] his sermon was mainly a strong statement of the argument of Liddon's 4th Bampton Lecture.

Headlam and I wrote invitations to the College Secretaries to breakfast on Thursday next at 8.45; and after lunch we walked round Kennington & Bagley.

[171]

A large party in Hall, including the Bp of Meath, "Father Grizel (?)", Sir John Conroy, Vidal, and Lang, who was my guest.

I spoke to Pember about work in the Oxford House: he is very promising: I am to ascertain particulars from Adderley on Tuesday.

[172]

Tuesday, October 26th, 1886.

My paper on Church Defence at the Tutors' Association was a dead failure. I think everybody was offended by it: and there was an unusually large attendance. **Gore spoke against me: and made himself rather foolish. Ince**[168] **spoke against Gore: and made me sigh for my supporters**.

Wakeman came to my rooms and nearly picked a quarrel with me. Watson made matters worse by flatly contradicting him more than once. Happily I remembered me in time, and poured oil on the waters: and Wakeman went away peaceably: but I am very ill at ease.

I don't think the cause of the League has been advanced tonight.

[173]

Friday, October 29th, 1886.

I went to Broadstairs. At Victoria I fell in with Wells,[169] the Secretary of the C.D.I.[170] (**a man who evoked my intensest antipathy**), and Starkey[171] the lecturer. Both were

[165] Harry Reichel (1872–1931; *ODNB*), first principal of the University Coll. of North Wales, Bangor, 1884–1927; Balliol Coll., Oxford; fellow of All Souls Coll., Oxford, 1880–94, and college examiner when Henson was elected to a prize fellowship; member, consultative committee, Board of Education, 1907–15; Anglican and 'staunch Conservative' *(ODNB)*.
[166] Charles Parsons Reichel (1816–94), professor of Latin at Queen's College Belfast, 1850–64, and bishop of Meath (1885–94).
[167] Matt. 22:42.
[168] William Ince (1825–1910; *ODNB*), theologian. Lincoln Coll., Oxford; ord. 1852; regius professor of divinity and canon of Christ Church Cathedral, Oxford, 1878–1910; his theological position described in *ODNB* as that of an 'old-fashioned high-churchman, but inclining, especially in his later days, to evangelical associations, and rejecting ritualism alike in form and doctrine'.
[169] Rev. Charles Arthur Wells (ord. 1872; *CCD*), Pembroke Coll., Oxford; curate of St Mary's, Windermere, 1876–85; secretary of the Church Defence Institution, 1885: *The official year-book of the Church of England, 1887* (London, 1887), p. 447.
[170] Church Defence Institution. See above, n. 63.
[171] J. H. Starkey, lecturer, Church Defence Institution: *The official year-book of the Church of England, 1887*, p. 447.

horribly complete – answer pat on every difficulty. Of course Theodore[172] "mapped out the whole land into parishes", and, no doubt, did so to spite the Liberation Society. The meeting went off fairly well. Mine was far the most moderately toned speech of the evening: whereat I was not displeased. **Whitehead[173] made himself very affable to me**. Burbidge[174] was as vulgar as usual. Raven & Palmer were absent from professional reasons.

[174]

Saturday, October 30th, 1886.

Very unpleasant journey up – young woman sick in the carriage, had to dodge about to keep dry: got sprinkled as it was – horrid. Strolled with Philip Moore[175] into the City: and had some tea. Made my way to the Wellington College Club, and got there half an hour too early. East Street, in which the Mission is situated, leads off Walworth Road. It was Saturday night, and the crowd was immense, buying and selling, with uproar. My hansom had to creep thro the people.

An audience of about 50 men and a few women. I spoke of Gordon with greater freedom than ever before, in a way that **[175]** subject was fresh again. The enthusiasm at the end was indescribable: I thought they w^d never have done clapping. That ridiculous process known as Kentish Fire[176] took the place of the usual vote of thanks. On the whole I think the lectures have had a good start.

[176]

19th Sunday after Trinity, October 31st, 1886.

Holy Communion at S. Andrews at 8. Mattins at 11. B.T.B. preached: horrid mercenary doctrine theory[.] Theory of Celestial Book-keeping i.e. tabular statement of profit & loss involved in X^{ity}. Most depressing in every way.

I had to get up from lunch and go off to Paddington. For I remembered me [*sic*] that Fuller dined with me this night.

I knelt for Adderley's benediction and he gave it in form which affected me. "May God bless thee, brother, & help thee to do thy duty in that state of life into which it hath pleased Him to call thee". I would I could make up my mind on the point.

---

[172] Not identified.
[173] Henry Whitehead (1853–1947; *ODNB*), Trinity Coll., Oxford; principal of Bishop's Coll., Calcutta, 1883–99; bishop of Madras, 1899–1922; brother of the philosopher and mathematician, Alfred North Whitehead; anglo-catholic who embraced ecumenicalism through his experience in India: see Journal, 7 Mar. 1920.
[174] Not identified.
[175] Not identified; see p. 233 below.
[176] Kentish fire *OED*: 'A prolonged and ordered salvo or volley of applause, or demonstration of impatience or dissent (said to have originated in reference to meetings held in Kent in 1828–9, in opposition to the Catholic Relief Bill: see *Notes & Queries* series 2, I. 182, 423; VIII. 278).'

[177]

All Souls Day, Tuesday, November 2nd, 1886.

Full attendance in chapel: but professors conspicuous by their absence. They were lecturing while the college prayed. This Scandal aroused natural indignation: and I don't think it will occur again. Large number of quondams[177] up for the gaudy.[178] There were altogether 42 people dining. I drank wine during dinner, but not in common room: whereat I secured my sobriety by a pitiable compromise. I ought to have abstained altogether. The songs and speeches in common room were unusually good. The Lord Mallard[179] excelled himself.

[178]

Thursday, November 4th, 1886.

I set out for a lonely walk, and on my way overtook Kettle[180] of S. John's with whom I walked round Godstow & Summertown. We talked about *Monasticism, and I developed my views at some length. He seemed much impressed.*

I dined with How[181] in Merton. Burrows also dined.

Carew Hunt[182] came in and talked about the League's prospects in Merton.

I arranged with Mildmay[183] for a meeting in New College on the 15th.

At present and for the last few days I have been afflicted with a strange gloom.

[179]

Friday, November 5th, 1886.

Twenty men came to my lecture on Bæda: one was absent. After my long absence I had feared to find many abstentions.

I went to the Puseyum and saw Gore: and had a talk with Stuckey about Disestablishment. On the basis of his parochial experience he advocates Disestablishment. The main charge he brings against the "Establishment" is the

---

[177] Quondams: former fellows of All Souls.
[178] Gaudy: a twice-yearly feast held at All Souls, one on the evening of the prize fellowship election in November, the other just before the State General Meeting in June. Only fellows and quondams may attend.
[179] A central figure at All Souls College on feast days and other important occasions. Elected by the fellows for excellence in singing, the Lord Mallard for most of Henson's life-time was Cosmo Lang: see www.hensonjournals.org/index.php/all-souls/.
[180] Rupert Edward Cooke Kettle (1854–1908; *WWW*), St John's Coll., Oxford; barr.; circuit judge, Oxford.
[181] Not identified.
[182] Robert Walter Carew Hunt (1865–1924), Merton Coll., Oxford; ord. 1891; curate of Littlemore, Oxford, 1890–3.
[183] (Aubrey) Neville St John Mildmay (1865–1955; *WWW*), 10th Bt (1949); New Coll., Oxford; ord. 1894; clerical and teaching career, mostly in Canada.

lack of discipline which it involves. **_Gore is in an absolute fix on the subject – pulled both ways, unable to make up his mind: waits the smash in indolent agony_**.

[180]

A notice about the Christmas examination came in: and this decided me. **I wrote to the bp postponing my ordination** until Trinity. I hope to regard that date as fixed.

[181]

Saturday, November 6th, 1886.

The Bishop wrote me a very kind letter in answer to mine. He recognizes the reasonableness of my delay, and hopes that I shall be duly ordained at Trinity. I hope so too, for I am tired of vacillation and change.

I am very much pressed for time this term yet I have only 2 pupils. It is the preparation of my lecture 3 times a week which bothers me. I can't see how I am to get that chapter on Early Oxford written. Rivington seems to have decided against the volume of Essays on Bæda: perhaps not unwisely: for Bright's Early English Church History[184] goes a long way to prevent its utility.

[182]

20th Sunday after Trinity, November 7th, 1886.

I went to the Early Celebration at S. Mary's; which was finished in ample time for morning Chapel at 8.45.

In the afternoon, I walked with Duff: most splendid sunset. Sun went down behind a deep violet bank of cloud, which was lined with a radiant rim of glory. Froude's metaphor about the Greenwich monks came to my mind.[185]

Tracey dined with me: after dinner we both made our way to B.N.C: where Lawley[186] and the Warden expatiated on the Oxford House to an audience of about 60 to 70 people. Great failure. **[183]** The Warden and I took Lawley to the top of our tower to see Oxford by moonlight.

---

[184] William Bright, *Chapters of early English church history* (Oxford, 1878). Bright (1824–1901; *ODNB*), regius professor of ecclesiastical history and canon of Christ Church, Oxford, 1868–1901.

[185] Froude was in fact referring to the execution of the monks of the London Charterhouse, ordered by Henry VIII in 1535–7. 'Courage and self-sacrifice are beautiful alike in an enemy and in a friend. And while we exult in that chivalry with which the Smithfield martyrs bought England's freedom with their blood, so we will not refuse our admiration to those other gallant men whose high forms, in the sunset of the old faith, stand transfigured on the horizon, tinged with the light of its dying glory.' J. A. Froude, *History of England, from the fall of Wolsey to the death of Elizabeth* (12 vols., London, 1856–70), II, 342–3.

[186] Algernon George Lawley (1857–1931; *WWW*), 5th Baron Wenlock (1918). Trinity Coll., Cambridge; Eton Missioner, Hackney Wick, 1881–6; vicar, St Andrew's, Bethnal Green, 1886–96; rector, St John at Hackney, 1897–1911.

[184]

Monday, November 8th, 1886.

I am 23 years old today. The canonical age for Ordination has been reached at last: and I feel far less pleased than I expected. On the whole a very melancholy birthday. No letters came at all, for the home letter came yesterday. My gloomy fit still hangs over me: and I feel utterly wretched. A walk with Turner and a Dinner at Keble were scarcely festive performances: and I write this in a fit of bad temper.

My 6th lecture on Beda was given this morning. 20 men came: Knightley[187] of Exeter has apparently decided [185] to give up attendance. He has not put in an appearance for the last 3 times.

Talbot[188] has promised to lecture at Hoxton on Dec. 9th. It is very pleasing to get him on to the active list with so little delay.

The cloud in the horizon is Wakeman's probable resignation which would give a severe blow to the credit of the League. He has been playing a double game for some time: and the relations between us are hardly amicable. Yet I should be loth [*sic*] to quarrel with any Socius.[189]

[186]

21st Sunday after Trinity, November 14th, 1886.

Last Thursday I made my way to **Wantage** in a pouring rain. The audience was extremely good considering the weather, & a counter attraction in the town-hall. I told the people about Buchanan and his work in the East End. Houblon[190] is a good fellow: his curate is terribly spoiled by mannerism. Why <u>must</u> curates drag out their words in such a heart-breaking drawl? Because Paget does so? **They are all apes**.

The next day I went to town. I had very interesting travelling companions. An old gentleman who had spent half his life in India: a parson who seemed to have been [187] all round the world: a young man whose manner was as offensive as his matter was worthless: but who served to amuse me. Our conversation began on the best means of utilizing sewerage: then branched into politics: Colonial Federation seemed to be scouted as chimerical. Finally it turned on travelling. Especially the wisdom or folly of taking friends with you. Both my travelled friend urged on me not to take friends with me but, pick them up en route. The net result of their experiences was agreed to be that "half the world was not nearly so good as it looks: & half not nearly so bad". An equation scarce as consoling as unobjectionable.

---

[187] Not identified.
[188] George John Talbot (1861–1938; *ODNB*), Christ Church Coll., Oxford.; fellow of All Souls Coll., Oxford, 1886; ecclesiastical lawyer and chancellor of six dioceses.
[189] *Socius* (Latin): fellow.
[190] Thomas Archer-Houblon (ord. 1874; *CCD*), vicar of Wantage, 1875, and rector of Peasemore, Berkshire, 1875–81.

[188]

I found that I had an hour and ½ to spare at Liverpool St. so I ran down to Oxford House and lighted on the Assembly at lunch. Winter[191] is obviously out of harmony with the rest: he must be removed.

I went down to Norwich by the 3.20 train from Liverpool St.: which got in about 6.35. The station at Norwich is a most magnificent erection. **Arrived at Tombland, whereto I was assigned**. I found myself in an old house (built by a Norwich Mayor in 1590): mine host – **Allen** – by name, was a doctor – big, serious, yet withal given to sudden bursts of laughter. He is President of the E.C.U.[192] and quite portentously learned **[189]** on all church subjects. He, unhappily, is in the habit of dining in the middle of the day: so that I had no dinner: and had to speak on an empty stomach.

The audience consisted of about 150 men, mostly respectable. A good many clergymen were scattered about the room:[193] and a small table for the reporters was placed in front of the platform. The chair was taken by Major Clayton,[194] who certainly was no orator. This ensured brevity. The Rector (Callis)[195] – a clear-nonconformist-brethren Evangelical – read a few collects; after which I was called upon to begin. **I spoke for an hour & 20 minutes & got over a good deal [190] of ground**. The audience were fairly attentive: & even enthusiastic at the end.

A parson named Hull (?)[196] came to breakfast – an old Pembroke man. He was very interesting. I went over the cathedral: even mounting the spire: which latter process is not easy: 10 ladders and no light form the last part of the process.

Hull met me and we went about the town. **I was cut to the heart to see a splendid Augustinian church used as a music room**. The choir was formerly in the hands of the Dutch colony; at the time of the Revolution 1689, it was granted to the Dutch chaplain **[191]** who turns up once a year to deliver a sermon in Dutch, for which he receives £50. Then the chancel was leased by the corporation to the Methodists from whom it has been received back, & is now used as a concert room.

There are 42 churches in Norwich: the population being about 90,000. Yet there are many Dissenters: indeed, Dissent is said to be baldly political here.

The Endowments of the churches are very small. One parish with a population of 1700 and an income of £50 is without incumbent. The Dean & Chapter can find nobody to fill it.

---

[191] Not identified.

[192] The English Church Union was founded in 1860 by Colin Lindsay to defend the catholic heritage of the Church of England. Its early history was dominated by Charles Wood, 2nd viscount Halifax, president from 1868–1919 and 1931–4; Dr Allen might have been president of the local branch.

[193] They included Archibald Ean Campbell (1856–1921; *WWW*), rector of Castle Rising, Norfolk, 1885–91; vicar of All Souls (Hook memorial church), Leeds, 1891–1901; provost of St Ninian's Cathedral, Perth, 1901–4; bishop of Glasgow and Galloway, 1904–21. Henson met Campbell again while on holiday in the Lake District: Journal, 2 July 1900.

[194] Not identified.

[195] John Callis (1838–1927), St Catharine's Coll., Cambridge; rector, Holy Trinity, Heigham, Norfolk, 1875–1909.

[196] William Ballyman Hull (1843–1901), Pembroke Coll., Oxford, rector of St Peter Hungate, Norwich, 1871–1901.

[192]

I dined this evening with Lester at S. John's. I find that Bosanquet[197] can talk sometimes. **He was positively excited in defence of Gosse.**[198] The President was very lively: he hates sub-committees: and is all for getting thro' business.

Lester and Ball had arranged a joint meeting of Oxford House and Toynbee Hall: they asked me to come, but of course I refused: and we went to Lester's rooms and talked over the matter. I am afraid I vexed Ball. But really joint meetings seem to involve a tacit repudiation of the original ground on which it was decided that a movement distinct from T. H. was necessary.

[193]

Tuesday, November 16th, 1886.

I dined with Burrows in his rooms at Ch. Ch. Hobhouse was there, and 4 undergraduates, of whom Yarde Buller was one. I spent a very pleasant evening.

Headlam asked me to spend part of the Vacation with him, but I refused, being pledged to Oxford House.

I accepted Rivington's proposal for a volume of Essays, more or less illustrative of Beda. 10 per cent on the published price (6/–) is the proposed remuneration.

[194]

Wednesday, November 17th, 1886. S. Hugh's day.

All my men turned up for Beda – 21 in all. I was a little better than usual.

Canon Bright called on me: and very kindly promised to give an Introductory Lecture on English Church History on Thursday, Dec 2nd. If possible the place will be All Souls Hall.

This must shut the mouths of the Puseyites on the subject of our Erastianism.

[195]

Thursday, November 18th, 1886.

I went to Reading by the 12.5 train and lunched with Garry. After lunch various clergy and lay people arrived to discuss the advisability of lectures & their arrangement. I explained to them the objects of the League: and, finally, it was decided to have 3

---

[197] Robert Holford MacDowall Bosanquet (1841–1912; *WWW*), fellow of St John's Coll., Oxford; scientist and musical theorist; FRS.

[198] Edmund William Gosse (1849–1928; *ODNB*), writer whose Lowell Lectures delivered in Boston, Massachusetts, in 1884 and published as *From Shakespeare to Pope* the following year, were the subject of a virulent attack by John Churton Collins for their inaccuracies. Gosse's reputation survived.

lectures in March. A committee of representative laymen was appointed to arrange lectures: and I, on my part, promised to send good speakers.

A paper from Norwich – the Norfolk Mail – arrived with my speech last Friday reported at length – 4 columns: and an article in the style of the Eatanswill Gazette.

[196]

Sunday next before Advent, November 21st, 1886.

I went to S. Mary's at 8: and college chapel at 8.45. After breakfast Pember came to my rooms: and remained with me until mid. day. At 12.30 a meeting of Upchurch Committee took place in Bertie's rooms. I stuck out for inviting more candidates. It seemed to me that (1.) we were bound to appoint the best man. (2.) that we were ipso facto bound to take every available means to find out who the best man was. Wakeman opposed me rather nastily: but the Warden declaring for postponement, my wish was gained.

I went to S. Mary's at 2. and heard Welldon[199] of Harrow preach. He is a young man, tall and stalwart, very ugly yet withal vigorous & manly.

[197]

He interpolated into the Bidding Prayer petitions for Eton & Harrow, which was bad taste. Then he assumed throughout that the mass of his audience were infidels: which – though probably true – was uncourteous, nay, arrogant. ***His style is simple, slow, and monotonous: his matter scarce ever original: platitudes put out with extraordinary appearance of sincerity.*** *It is even amazing to hear a man – a young man – set in so prominent position, boldly defying the intellect of the Universe, and, not content with accepting, positively glorying in the inevitable stupidity of X^{tty}!!* ***C'est magnifique mais ce n'est pas la guerre!***[200]

A long walk: and evening chapel: and a scandalously long menu completed the day.

[198]

Saturday, November 27th, 1886.

On Tuesday I went to town in a thick mist: and at 5.30 talked to an audience of pupil teachers on Constitutional History. They were mostly girls, and I was annoyed with them therefore.

---

[199] James Edward Cowell Welldon (1854–1937; *ODNB*), Aristotle scholar and headmaster of Harrow School, 1885–98; bishop of Calcutta, 1898–1902; canon of Westminster Abbey, 1902–6; Henson's successor as dean of Durham, 1918–33; relations with Henson never warmed, especially following Henson's return to Durham as bishop in 1920; differences of temperament, preaching style, and concerning social and political issues such as temperance kept them apart; educated at Eton Coll. and King's Coll., Cambridge.

[200] 'It is magnificent, but it is not war; it is folly [c'est de la folie]': the response of Pierre Bosquet, French army general, to the charge of the light brigade.

At 8, I went to the opening of the new Club in Brady Street. A fair number of them attended: I tried to be definitely Christian in what I said.

At 9.15 I took my Constitutional History Class in the Oxford House Club. Nobody expected me to come, so I had but an audience of about 12 men, which was partly my own fault, as I omitted to give notice.

[199]

On Wednesday afternoon I walked out with Adderley to look up people in the mission district. One man was making picture frames: his work consisted of cutting the prepared material into proper lengths, and glueing & nailing the pieces together. For this he received 2/6 a dozen and could do as much as 10 doz. in one day. At another house a woman was sewing babies' slippers: for this she could get 10$^{\underline{d}}$ a dozen, having to provide her own thread. By working 13 hours a day she could make as many as 1½ dozen i.e. 1/3. Her husband was a painter out of work. Though this couple looked quite young, they had had 9 **[200]** children of whom 6 were living.

Pember came down to the Oxford House in the evening and Adderley shewed him the Clubs. He seemed very much pleased.

I lectured on the Church to an audience of about 100 persons, who had come thro the fog to the Schools in Canal Road, Burdett R$^{\underline{d}}$, leading off Mile End Road. The vote of thanks to me was proposed by a man named White,[201] who declared himself to be an ex-Liberationist Secretary. Wallace[202] the vicar seems to me a madman: yet withal not uninteresting.

[201]

On Thursday I went back to Oxford: and spent the afternoon in sending out notices about the League to the graduates of the University.

On Friday evening I dined in Worcester with Bardsley; and met some freshmen in his rooms afterwards. They were rather an uninteresting set of people.

*On Saturday **I met Tom Hughes**[203] **at the Warden's**. He is an impressive looking man: and talks pleasantly.*

[202]

Advent Sunday, November 28th, 1886.

The Hall of Wadham was crowded: many people went away unable to get in. Tom Hughes received an ovation. He read his speech, which was fortunately short: and

---

[201] Not identified.
[202] Not identified.
[203] Thomas Hughes (1822–96; *ODNB*), social reformer and children's writer; author of *Tom Brown's schooldays* (London, 1857).

on the whole harmless.[204] Whitmore[205] was good, but went too much on the reform question. Hobhouse proposed a vote of thanks to the Warden and Fellows of Wadham for the use of their Hall: and I seconded, thinking it needful to say something about the League after Whitmore's speech. So I emphasized the necessity of opposing the organised calumnies of the Liberationists. Prothero said I spoke well. On the whole I think the meeting was a success.

[203]

Among those present were Prof. Legge,[206] Spooner,[207] Carlyle,[208] Miss Freeman,[209] Alexander,[210] Talbot the Burgess,[211] Pulling,[212] & many other graduates.

Foulkes and Armstrong[213] were also present.

[204]

Monday, November 29th, 1886.

Twenty men turned up to Beda. It was my 13th lecture: and I finished the second book.

Duff promised to give me £2. for distribution in Bethnal Green, on condition that I gave it myself, & not through any d—d Society.

In the afternoon Duff and I walked round Wytham. I wrote an account of the meeting in Wadham: and gave it to Maude,[214] who sent it to the Guardian.

I signed the agreement with Rivington.

---

[204] Thomas Hughes, *Church reform and defence: an address delivered at the invitation of the Laymen's League for church defence* (London, 1886).
[205] Algernon Whitmore (1851–1908; *WWW*), Eton Coll.; Balliol Coll., Oxford; fellow of All Souls Coll., Oxford; MP (C) Chelsea, 1886–1906.
[206] James Legge (1815–1897; *ODNB*), King's Coll., Aberdeen; missionary and first professor of Chinese, Univ. of Oxford, 1876–97.
[207] William Spooner (1844–1930; *ODNB*), New Coll., Oxford; fellow, lecturer and tutor of New Coll. from 1867; warden, 1903–24; associated with the verbal slip 'the Spoonerism'.
[208] Alexander James Carlyle (1861–1943; *ODNB*), historian and social reformer; Glasgow Univ. and Exeter Coll., Oxford; ord. 1888; curate, St Stephen's, Westminster, 1888–93.
[209] Possibly Florence Freeman (1855–1925), third daughter of the historian Edward Freeman, still living at the parental home in St Giles in 1891.
[210] William Alexander (1824–1911; *WWW*), Exeter and Brasenose Coll., Oxford; bishop of Derry and Raphoe, 1867; archbishop of Armagh and Primate of All Ireland, 1896–1911.
[211] John Gilbert Talbot (1835–1910; *WWW*), alderman and county councillor, Kent; MP (C) Oxford Univ., 1878–1910. Christ Church, Oxford; ecclesiastical commissioner.
[212] Edward Herbert Pulling (1859–1928; WWW), non-coll., Oxford; ord. 1885; curate, Melksham, Wiltshire, 1883–90; chaplain to the forces, 1890–3.
[213] Edward Armstrong (1846–1928; ODNB), historian and senior bursar, Queen's Coll., Oxford.
[214] Joseph Hopper Maude (ord. 1887, Oxford; *CCD*), fellow of Hertford Coll., Oxford, 1875–1900; rector of Pusey, 1915–25; Henson encountered him as a high churchman later in life and was unimpressed: see Journal, 10 Feb. 1917.

[205]

Tuesday, November 30th, 1886. St Andrew's day.

I lunched with the Warden of Keble[215] and met there his brother the Burgess [John Talbot], a mild mannered man, who pleased me. I promised to lecture for him on Gordon. One Talbot brother from Winchester was there: a nice pleasant English School boy.

I received from Tom Hughes a very pleasant and characteristic letter, in which he expressed his pleasure at his visit.

Ffoulkes was so impressed by the Wadham Meeting as to write to the Warden offering to Lecture on the "Reunion of Christendom" – queer old bird it is!

[206]

Wednesday, December 1st, 1886.

I dined with Conybeare in University. Faulkner[216] was there: and I got into conversation with him. He certainly is very mad. His remarks are mainly interjectional anathemas. Haines, Dendy,[217] and Hamilton[218] were there – a most melancholy company. The subject of conversation being religious, Dendy soon withdrew from any share in it, & slept peacefully. Conybeare's talk is sulky and scattered. Hamilton chatters apologetically but incessantly. Haines is silent and sensible.

The most comfortless common-room in Oxford, so far as my knowledge goes: worthily presided over by the stone image of an exploded fiction – King Alfred.[219]

[207]

Meeting Raleigh I sat down in the smoking room and talked. We were soon joined by [George] Talbot and Headlam.

They all think me utterly illogical and unreasonable on the Church: and, in truth, the impossibilities of my attitude become more apparent every day: and what the outcome of it all will be I cannot conceive. I wish I could really believe the Catholic position, for I loathe Protestantism.

The Ritualists grow more hateful to me every day of my life.

---

[215] Edward Stuart Talbot (1844–1934, *ODNB*), Christ Church, Oxford; first warden of Keble College, Oxford, 1870–88; vicar, Leeds, 1889–95; bishop of Rochester, 1895–1905, bishop of Southwark, 1905–11, and bishop of Winchester, 1911–23; prominent anglo-catholic and confidant of Randall Davidson, archbishop of canterbury, 1903–28.
[216] Not identified.
[217] Not identified.
[218] Not identified.
[219] The 'exploded fiction' being the apocryphal medieval legend that King Alfred the Great (*c.* 849–99) founded University Coll., Oxford in the year 872.

[208]

Thursday, December 2ⁿᵈ, 1886.

I went out a long walk with Tupper-Carey. He is a charming fellow in many ways. It would be a good thing to get up a Society for reading papers on the Church Question, to train men like him who are keen on the Church.

The lecture room was well filled with undergraduates for Bright's lecture. The Warden happily came in, and announced that we should continue these lectures next term.

[209]

Friday, December 3ʳᵈ, 1886.

I gave my last lecture this term on Beda. It makes 15 lectures in all. Only 17 men attended.

To my surprise I received from the Bursar of University £2 for Cobb[220] and Cockayne[221] the 2 men from that College.

A telegram from Adderley asking me to lecture on the 12ᵗʰ, & to wire subject. I wired "Martyrs", for subject: and asked him to be my chairman on the 13ᵗʰ.

Buchanan arrived safely: and we sat talking until past midnight. He is certainly a very good man.

[210]

Saturday, December 4ᵗʰ, 1886.

Running across the Quad through the rain to chapel I fell hastily: and though I jumped up quickly, and shewed Buchanan into chapel, I felt too faint to remain for the service.

I walked Buchanan about the place until lunch: and after lunch took him to see Campion at Keble: then we called at the Puseyum. I took Buchanan to the Cathedral, and, returning to my rooms read with Soulsby and Valletort until 7: then dressed for dinner at 7.30.

Burrows, How, Lester, Tracey, and Buchanan formed my dinner-party, which went off well.

[211]

2ⁿᵈ Sunday in Advent, December 5ᵗʰ, 1886.

Chapel at 8.45: scandalously small attendance. Buchanan and I then attended the Celebration at S. Barnabas. Stuckey Coles preached. Then we went to lunch with

---

[220] Charles Julius Cobb (1866–1890), University Coll., Oxford; 3rd class Theology, 1887.
[221] Henry Cockayne (1865–1940), University Coll., Oxford; Classical Mods., 1886; ord. 1891; curate, St Paul's, Chichester, 1889–92.

Lester: from whom we hurried off to the Varsity Sermon at 2. Aubrey Moore[222] preached and I slept. We walked with Burrows round the Ch. Ch. meadow: and at 5. the Warden and Wells came to my rooms for the Committee meeting. At 6. we went to Chapel.

E.H. Pember[223] and Bowlby dined with me.

Duff gave me some photographs of Elgin cathedral.

[212]

Monday, December 6th, 1886.

I took Buchanan to see Chandler.[224] With him we wasted more than an hour: then returned to All Souls. Buchanan went away by the 12.5 train, having paid me his £1 towards the X^mas Festivity Fund.

I bought Selborne's[225] book on Disestablishment[226] and read it most part of the afternoon. It is excellent beyond my expectation.

In Hall Oman paid me his £1 to the C.L.L. The other contributors are

1. Duff	£2. 10
2. Burrows	£1.
3. Tracey	£1.
4. Lester	£1.
5. How	£1.
6. Henson	£1.

Altogether it will make £9.10.

[213]

I went down to the Mission House in Marston Road, and spoke about Church Defence to an audience consisting of about 12 very elderly men. They spoke at huge length afterwards & bored me to death. What seemed to annoy them most was my diatribe against identifying the church with politics. Fathers Benson[227] and Wyon[228] made flaring Tory speeches.

---

[222] Aubrey Lackington Moore (1848–90), anglo-catholic priest and Christian Darwinian; tutor, Keble Coll., Oxford, 1881–90.

[223] Edward Henry Pember (1833–1911; *ODNB*), barr.; Christ Church. Coll., Oxford; leading draughtsman at the parliamentary bar, most notable for his guidance on the much-contested bill that created the Manchester Ship Canal in 1885; regular contributor to the press; father of Francis William Pember, Henson's close friend at All Souls.

[224] Arthur Chandler (1860–1939; *WWW*), ord. 1883; fellow of Brasenose Coll., Oxford, 1883–90; rector, Poplar East, 1891.

[225] Wiliam Waldegrave Palmer (1859–1942; *ODNB*), 2nd earl of Selborne (1895), politician and leading church layman.

[226] William Waldegrave Palmer, *A defence of the Church of England against disestablishment* (London, 1887).

[227] Richard Meux Benson (1824–1915; *ODNB*), Christ Church, Oxford; disciple of Pusey and founder of the Society of St John the Evangelist, 1866; vicar of Cowley St John, 1870.

[228] Walter James Wyon (ord. 1866; *CCD*), Mission House, St John the Evangelist, Cowley, Oxford, 1884.

N.B. I paid into the Bank Sperling's cheque for £10.10. and Dendy's for £2. = £12.10

[214]

Tuesday, December 7ᵗʰ, 1886.

I got up quite scandalously late, and breakfasted with Knox[229] who had risen at his usual hour.

All my spare time today i.e. about 6 hours has been given up to the preparation of my lecture on the Reformation for Ilford on Thursday. It is extraordinarily difficult to know what to emphasize out of so much: it being obviously impossible to retain much more than the leading facts, whatever they may be decided to be. Certainly what I want to make the Ilfordians understand is (1.) that the Reformation was the outcome of causes long previously working. (2.) that the process itself was very gradual, being spread over a period of at least 42 years.

[215]

(3.) that "the Reformers" were almost without exception scoundrels.
(4.) that the destruction of the Monasteries was [α] unjust. [β] impolitic [γ] unfortunate.
(5.) that the continuity of the Church was unbroken by the changes.
(6.) that the foreign influences were uniformly unhappy, whether (α) German, or (β) Swiss, or (γ) Spanish.

I want to eulogize Wolsey, *denounce* Cromwell, *defend* Gardiner[230] *and* Henry VIII, *estimate* Cranmer *and* Parker,[231] *and "go for" the Edward VI statesmen:*[232] *and all this to be included within the space of an hour. It is absurd. A course of lectures were all too little for the subject.*

[216]

Saturday, December 11ᵗʰ, 1886. [Oxford House]

I have been here since Thursday, being continuously reprobate until this present. **The lecture at Ilford went off all right, I suppose**, though the proportion of females in

---

[229] Edmund Vesey Knox (1865–1921; *WWW*), parliamentary barr.; Keble Coll., Oxford; fellow of All Souls Coll., Oxford, 1886–93; MP (N), West Cavan, 1890–5; Londonderry, 1895–8.

[230] Stephen Gardiner (*c.* 1495/8–1555; *ODNB*), bishop of Winchester, 1531–51, 1553–5; opponent of religious change during and following the reign of Edward VI.

[231] Matthew Parker (1504–75; *ODNB*), archbishop of Canterbury, 1559–75, and a leading figure in the Elizabethan church settlement and in reforms to eradicate Roman catholic practices.

[232] In his 'Historical sketch of the university', in *Oxford: its life and schools*, ed. A. M. M. Stedman (London, 1887), Henson referred to the reign of Edward VI as 'a period of calamity for the University'. 'The horde of pirates and fanatics which overran England, seizing the reins of government, and bringing the realm almost to destruction, were nowhere more disastrously active than at Oxford. Everywhere the destroyer was at work. Among the numerous acts of outrage, none was more reckless and lamentable than that which wrecked the reredos of All Souls College': pp. 1–26, at p. 21.

the audience was distressing. Barnes[233] wants me to give Gordon: but I doubt if I can find a day.

On Friday afternoon I went with Adderley & Moore to the Meeting in the Mansion House. I am less pleased with the Church House Scheme than ever.[234] The meeting was very unenthusiastic: & the speeches were mostly poor. Harvey Goodwin[235] & Lord Cranbrook[236] alone were good.

[217]

At 6.30 I had to take that horde of pupil teachers which goes sadly against my grain. A mixed class of about 20 boys & girls between the ages of 14 & 18, hateful! They are so horribly eager to learn: & take notes by the reams! This trial will be repeated on Tuesday.

Today, beyond issuing a number of invitations for the Abbot[237] I have been totally indolent. I have to give "Gordon" to the S. Bartholomew Club: for which I feel utterly indisposed. **Headlam is here for the "Spanish Armada" & I wanted to hear him**.

(10.30 p.m.) I have returned from S! Bartholomew's Club: and I know not with what feelings.

[218]

The men in that Club seem to me quite rivals to Mape in blackguardism[;] they are indeed to look at a very depraved, low, sunken set. But to be just. About 4 went to sleep: about as many went out: of the rest say 30 in number: about 6 were absorbed with interest: the rest were attentive & on the whole satisfied. As to the lecture itself, it varied very much from the previous "editions". I think it was better than ever before: but experience generally teaches that my thoughts do not coincide with those of my audience.

---

[233] Henry Broughton Barnes (ord. 1876; *CCD*), All Souls Coll., Oxford; vicar of Great Romford, Illford, Essex, 1881 (patron, All Souls Coll.).

[234] The Church House scheme was a proposal to build a central meeting place in which the church could conduct its business, marking the golden jubilee of Queen Victoria the following year. The inaugural meeting of the movement at the Mansion House was reported at length in *The Times*: 11 Dec. 1886, 7. Henson's dislike of the scheme may have been an early sign of his aversion to meetings of church bodies and even more, church bureaucracy and increased church expenditures that resulted: see, for example, his speech in the Church Assembly, 7 July 1925, supporting an amendment to reduce the proposed increase in expenditure for the Church Press Bureau: *Church Assembly: report of proceedings* (London, 1925), VI:2, 201–2.

[235] Key supporter of the Church House, Westminster construction project.

[236] Gathorne Gathorne-Hardy (1814–1906; *ODNB*), Viscount Cranbrook (1878), 1st earl Cranbrook (1892); lord president of the council, 1885, 1886–92.

[237] I.e. James Adderley; see 4: **5** n. 12.

[219]

Thursday, December 16th, 1886.

On Monday I went to the Hospital & found there a nice-looking boy, who gave me his name & address – Thomas Howls, 2, Wilson Street, Poplar. He has not been confirmed: & I urged upon him no longer to defer that ceremony. Whereat he returned self-defensive answers mentioning the unholy lives of many who have been confirmed. But this I would not admit as an argument. And I, forthwith, wrote to Dalton of All Hallows and informed him of this boy's condition. On Wednesday I sent him "Gordon", with the usual inscription: & I hope to see him next Monday. This morning I heard from Dalton, that the boy had been giving into doubtful ways recently. I am glad I found him.

[220]

On Monday evening I went to S. James Curtain R<u>d</u>. Parish of 5000 souls: 2 parsons, father & son A. Buss.[238] Audience consisted of about 14 women, 6 men, 4 girls, & about 8 boys. The vicar presided & I spoke for more than an hour: peace on my face, smiles on my lips, wrath in my heart. It is an absurd waste of energy to talk to such an audience.

On Tuesday I took my pupil teachers at 5.30 for an hour: and after a hasty dinner went off to S. James', Clapton, to speak on Church Defence. H.D. Pearson[239] the vicar presided: audience consisted of about 3 parsons, 4 gentlemen, 12 more-or-less bona-fide working men, 30 women: & 12 boys; all told under 70. Here again the waste of energy was painful in the extreme.

[221]

On Wednesday afternoon I went with the Abbot to visit the mission district. The people are in a very wretched condition; all draw the bitterest comparisons between past & present: & they do not confine themselves to vague expressions, which might mean anything or nothing. They state the weekly earnings then and now: the hours of labour: and the rent of houses: all are for the worse changed. One woman by working for the whole day could make 2 large shirts, almost overcoats, of "linen-duck" (whatever that means) such as draymen wear. She received for this coarse, hard, long work 7 a shirt i.e. ½ a day, or 7/– a week: & the rent of the house in which she **[222]** lived (& of which naturally she only occupied a part) was 10/6 weekly. Another woman we found nursing a measled baby: lamenting that she could not get to her trade i.e. cats-meat shop. One good point about her: she looked down upon the "Fish" trade, as even too smelly: & yet the smelling organ of a cats-meat seller cannot be delicate, & may be biassed.

These people bring vague charges against "America" & "the country" and "forring parts" as being the roots & origin of their woes.

---

[238] Alfred Joseph Buss (ord. 1855; *CCD*), King's Coll., London; vicar of St James, Curtain Road, London, 1884–1904; Charles Caron Buss (ord. 1883; *CCD*), Pembroke Coll., Oxford; curate of St James, Curtain Road, London, 1884–90.

[239] Henry Daniel Pearson (ord. 1847; *CCD*), Worcester Coll., Oxford; vicar of St James, Clapton.

Twice over the Abbot & I were reproached as "gentlemen". "Seems to me yon gen'elmen have the best of it. Needn't think what you'll have to eat every day of your lives", & the Abbot & I had **[223]** really nought to say.

In the evening I spoke to Mape about Gordon. There was nobody there: & so I had to act by & for myself: but the men were very good: & listened: 2 or 3 even were content to stand all through. I gave them ¾ of an hour: & succeeded in working in an exhortation to temperance at the end, which I carried down by addressing them as "Brother members of the Mape St. Club". Poor fellows, they are filthy, wretched, & debased: yet not without interest, & the more one knows them, the more one likes them. Lambert and Thame are very interesting specimens.

[224]

Friday, December 17th, 1886.

Yesterday I spent the afternoon with Lester and Baker exploring the docks. In the evening I made my way not without great difficulty to All Souls, Clapton Park, which I reached ¼ of an hour late. A seedy Rabbi, presumably the vicar presided[.][240] The audience, I suppose, numbered about 100 all told: perhaps a few more. About half were men: and none were children. Of the men about 4 were "working men": about 12 were clerks: 2 were parsons: 3 or 4 "gentlemen", & the rest, shopkeepers. I spoke for an hour and a half with a sore throat: and, though at first they seemed to me a little frigid, they soon thawed, and became enthusiastic: in fact, towards **[225]** the end, I could scarce finish my sentences for the cheering. At the end a man asked me whether I approved of the present system of patronage, to which I made a diplomatic answer viz. that it worked well, though bad in theory: & that I should be glad to see sale of livings prohibited.

This evening I spent in loafing about the clubs: rather aimlessly.

[226]

Saturday, December 18th, 1886.

In the afternoon I wandered aimlessly in the City with Lester & in the evening I made my way to the Garrick, and dined with Duff. Remembering the Abbot & the frost I was very temperate, & indeed drank less than ever before on a similar occasion. I returned to the House about 11.15 p.m.

[227]

Christmas Day, Saturday, December 25th, 1886.

The tenour [*sic*] of my story runs its way as usual. In spite of my firm declarations I ran home for the Nativity: yet with great reluctance: but there was obviously nothing to do in B.G. [Bethnal Green]: the Warden most kindly asked me to his place, but I,

---

[240] Not identified.

having already declined Duff, felt bound to decline him likewise, none the less his kindness touches me.

On Wednesday, the 22ⁿᵈ, I made my way to **Falconhurst**, *the home of* [John] *Talbot, and gave "Gordon" to a country audience of about 40 men and women. They were very attentive, though, of course, in a tiny room I could not be "eloquent".*

I found the Warden of Keble & Mʳˢ Talbot, as also the children, assembled at Falconhurst. I had a long chat **[228]** *with him about the Oxford House. Especially doing my best to show a strong case against the discussions on Sunday afternoons: to which I have always objected but since last Sunday have felt more strongly than ever their impolicy. For consider, Llewelyn Davies*[241] *is no doubt a very able man: a very much less able man could have shut up Robertson:*[242] *yet Ll.D. remained silent: he believed, forsooth, that "no good resulted from discussions". Yes, abundantly true in the abstract: but here in the concrete, nothing less than abject confession of defeat: and as such applauded by the Secularists. And it was so irritating for Robertson cut his own throat most thoroughly: in his 2nd five minutes, which we gave him. The argument for these perilous discussions is simply & solely this: that thus & thus alone will men be* **[229]** *attracted to the lectures. It must be made an understood thing that lectures* shall answer *objections. At worst, one unproved assertion is as good as another: and most of the Secularist logic consists of unproved assertions.* **As matters are, the Oxford House furnishes a platform for Bradlaugh.**[243]

The country about Edenbridge is hilly and well-wooded. Falconhurst is 4 or 5 miles from the nearest railway station: &, in itself, delightful. As I was being driven to the Station: ***I noticed 2 men beating out corn with flails: a startlingly primitive performance***.

On Thursday [23 December] I returned to the House, and in the evening the Abbot & I went for a short time to the Abbey St. P.T. Entertainment. Pearson was there & shook hands warmly.

[230]

After leaving the pupil teachers we escorted 2 parsons – (Jay,[244] of the Magdalene Mission for one) – over the clubs: and took them to the Whittington Club: which appears to be an elaborate organisation, containing a large number of beds, (rather too closely packed, it seemed to me) let at 1/6 and (a little more isolated) 2/– per week. I was astonished to learn that the members only numbered 150.

---

[241] John Llewelyn Davies (1826–1916; *WWW*), Trinity Coll., Cambridge; vicar, Christ Church, Marylebone, 1856–89; leading evangelical clergyman and almost the last surviving friend of F. D. Maurice.

[242] Possibly John Mackinnon Robertson (1856–1933; *ODNB*), freethinker, radical, anti-imperialist, journalist and prolific author on many subjects, including atheism, literature, economics and politics; MP (L) Newcastle, 1906–18, and prominent in the Asquithian Liberal organization.

[243] Charles Bradlaugh (1833–91; *ODNB*), joint founder with Annie Besant of the National Secular Society, 1866; MP (L) Northampton, 1880–91; at the fourth attempt in 1888, succeeded in changing the law on the parliamentary oath of allegiance, permitting affirmations instead.

[244] Arthur Osborne Montgomery Jay (1858–1945), St Catharine's Coll., Cambridge; chaplain, St Martin's Mission, Stepney, 1883–6.

Then leaving the parsons, the Abbot & I joined Boulton and Bethune[245] (a philanthropic masher[246] who inspects slums in a hansom!!!): *we all made our way to Billing, the vicar of Spitalfields.*[247] *I had heard about him from Raleigh, who declared him honest, honourable, and prudent. I formed my impression of him, & a right favourable impression. He seems eminently <u>effective</u>: going straight to the point.*

[231]

Billing took us to the casual ward. A very careful system is in operation. The men & women have to tub before turning in: the arrangements for this process seem admirable. The men tub without difficulty: the women are more troublesome. Whenever any person more respectable than usual puts in an appearance: if it seem incompatible that he should go into a casual ward: he is sent to Billing. There is power of forcible detention. The wretches are employed usefully e.g. they make their own bread, grinding the corn &c. We went into the ward: **& I nearly fell to the earth overpowered by the stench**. Yet these had all been seriously tubbed before turning in. They looked horrible lying on the ground, in hammocks of sacking, & covered with a blanket [232] and grumbling at the cold; in truth they must suffer terribly these frosty nights.

Then we, in like manner, followed Billing over the Infirmary: after which the Abbot & I returned home: the mashers continued their journey of inspection.

On Friday [24 December] *I started for home: & I missed the 11 o'clock train at Victoria by 4 minutes: whereupon I put my bags in the Cloak room, and strolled through the rain to Westminster Abbey. There entering I sat me down on a seat in the very west extreme of the Nave: and looked at the long wonder of the vaulted roof, the clustered columns & the wealth of windows, and I meditated sadly enough of many things. "Yes, my heart cried, it is beautiful,* **but is it true**?*["] All that creation of* [233] *Christian faith could vanish before a few pounds of infidel dynamite. Today it is sacred, tomorrow it may be a music Hall. Secularization! What is it but asserting the Supremacy of the Denial? Christianity has covered the land with temples, worthy of God's dwelling: but has it touched men's hearts? Are they juster, less grinding, fairer? "Alas for the rarity, of X*[ian] *charity, under the sun."*[248] *Confound the 15 per cent dividend of Bryant & May's shareholders!*[249] *Ay, &, no doubt, those shareholders are, in their day, "founders & benefactors" of churches! This great church itself, what does it really represent? Is it Faith in X*[st]*: piety & love? or is it the vainglory, vulgar vanity, the pride of power, and its magnificent abuse! At least in pity, cover up the monuments!!*

---

[245] Not identified.
[246] Masher (noun) (2) *OED*: 'A fashionable young man of the late Victorian and Edwardian era, esp. one fond of women; a dandy.'
[247] Robert Claudius Billing (ord. 1857; d. 1898; *WWW*), Worcester Coll., Oxford; rector of Spitalfields, 1878–87.
[248] Thomas Hood, 'The bridge of sighs' (1844).
[249] Already notorious for sweating its domestic out-workers, and for deducting fines from the wages of its employees – mostly women and girls – Bryant and May became a public company in 1884, paying generous dividends to its shareholders.

[234]

I reached Broadstairs about 4.30.

On Christmas day Podge and I went to the Celebration at 8. Choral.

[235]

Thursday, December 30th, 1886. [Bethnal Green.]

Yesterday Tracey and I visited the Hospital. ***To my great surprise I found there, Miss [Eleanor] Rathbone in the garb of a nurse***. She is there for 3 mos. It is really enough to put one to shame altogether to see her working there. I feel more completely an imposter every day – a conscious imposter! There were some very interesting people in the Hospital. One old man pleased me very much. He was an Irishman, and naturally eager for Home Rule. I won his heart by professing devotion to that cause. **This was not quite honest, perhaps: yet why not**? If there are such things as rights then, I think, Ireland ought to **[236]** have home rule if she wants it. I don't much think Home Rule will benefit Ireland: the real causes of Irish misery are far too deep: the conduct of the nationalists I regard as infamous, if any conduct can be regarded as infamous which is well adapted to secure an object, in itself excellent. On that point I feel increasing doubt.

On the whole, perhaps, my attitude towards Home Rule is this. While I believe in its justice, I do not believe in its utility: & therefore, while I recognize my obligation to take up the cause of justice, I do not feel bound to lift my little finger in the interest of this righteous chimera. As to my hospital **[237]** patriot; I did him good (by making him chirpy) in expressing devotion to Home Rule: and that must be my justification in the eyes of those who would charge me with dishonesty.

A Roman Catholic has just come in with a broken knee-cap, his attitude towards the Disestablishment question was honourable: & I thanked him for it.

Another man, also with a broken kneecap, was usually employed in sawing up mahogany. For this he received 23/– a week. He said that before the wood was soft enough for the saw, it had to be placed in boxed [*sic*] and steamed. This process took **[238]** a whole day. I suppose he referred to the thin slabs of wood used for purposes of veneer.

Today I have squandered all my time recklessly, I mean so far as any useful work is concerned. Oakly, the Mape man, whom I employed to stick up bills is an useless crock: and has stuck up none save a few outside S. John's church. I expect next Sunday afternoon an audience of about 25 people.

[239]

Saturday, January 1st, 1887.

The supper **last night** went off well beyond expectation. About 65 men turned up: rather fewer than we had expected: which was, on the whole, a good thing, as their appetites were unspeakably great. **89 lbs. of beef & mutton was almost entirely devoured by**

65 men: besides huge quantities of pudding, pies, & tarts. Mr G. Spottiswoode[250] & his son[251] and Wilson (Buchanan's partner & an excellent fellow to boot) and Vaillant[252] came to help us. The speeches were kept within reasonable limits. I and Tracey spoke. We both "improved the occasion" with a vengeance. Then we cleared **[240]** them out for a few minutes for obvious reasons: after which they came back for "cigars" and coffee. For nearly two hours they amused themselves by the most astonishing performances. Dancing (which they performed wonderfully) and singing (which in matter & style was execrable went on inexhaustibly. The Abbot accompanied on the piano. Then a few minutes before 11 the Pope[253] came in, & "said a few words", asking them to come to church: **& I seized the moment to call them all to follow me to the watch-night service:**[254] **and they all did: not a man failed**. They filled up the narrow aisle on the south of the church: and behaved **[241]** admirably. We (i.e. G. Spottiswoode, Tracey, Wilson & I) found places, and generally watched over them. They joined in the singing with zeal. It is more than ever my belief **that these men want leading**. They were splendid while I was giving the word at every turn: "Stand up": "Sit down"[:] "Kneel" (they did kneel these "publicans" while the protestant pharisees in the pews near by sat). Then we shook hands with every chappy as he went out, & wished a happy New Year. It was quite splendid. The service was capital: & though some slumbered (which remembering the beef was not to be wondered at) **[242]** yet the more part listened.

The Pope had set a clock somewhere nigh at hand to the Holiest place: & timed himself to the minute: so that in the few moments of silence which followed the address: the hour of midnight sounded melodiously & melancholy in the church. Some of the men asked me what it meant afterwards. I told them. It was the best evening I have spent in Bethnal Green.

This morning with much effort, I got to the Celebration. Even the long follies of a whole dead year have not altogether choked the aspiration to better things. **[243]** Far less hopeful of success, indeed I must be and am, for the long failures of so many years, but I should perish by my own hand, if I despaired of rising out of this slough.

"Tomorrow, tomorrow": perhaps it will never come. "O God, put back Thy universe & give me yesterday." Yet here again I commence the months of my latest shame with resolutions which will certainly be futile, but which are not (I know they are not) quite hypocritical in inception.

---

[250] George Andrew Spottiswoode (1827–99), partner in the family printing firm since 1854.
[251] John Spottiswoode (1874–1914), military career, 1894–1901; joined family printing firm, 1901; killed in first battle of Ypres.
[252] Wilfred Bernard Vaillant (1864–1947), Christ Church, Oxford; ord. 1894; curate, St Frideswides, East India Docks, 1891.
[253] Algernon Lawley: see n. 186 above.
[254] As Sarah C. Williams's study of Southwark has shown, 'watch-night' services on New Year's eve were integral to popular religion in London at the turn of the twentieth century, fusing folk-religion and Christian symbolism: *Religious belief and popular culture in Southwark, c. 1880–1939* (Oxford, 1999), ch. 4.

[244]

2nd Sunday after Xmas, January 2nd, 1887.

Bob Sharp[255] preached the sermon in the morning. Smith came to lunch, and went off early to hear Scott Holland[256] preach at St Pauls. A very dense fog came over Bethnal Green, and it was very cold. At 4.15 I lectured on St Paul in St Andrews's Hall to an audience of about 50 men (not so bad considering the weather – they were nearly all from University & Mape Street.) The Secularist boy made a speech in opposition to me, but I sat on him easily enough. In spite of my vicious intentions, he proposed a vote of thanks, which was seconded by the Secularist from **[245]** St Bartholomew's, and the audience broke up very amicably. I gave away all the copies of "Gordon" which I possessed in the room: among others to the Secularist boy.

The slavery question was harped on once more: I must get the Oxford House Committee to permit me to write a tract thereon. It is my pet point.

For once, I think, the discussion did some good.

Lawley, Nash,[257] Sharp, and Adderley were present at the lecture: the fog made it very difficult to speak, throat and eyes alike resent it.

[246]

I preached to 13 or 14 men in the Mission room in Brady Street.

The Abbot was too lazy to do it himself. Of necessity I took S. Matt. II. 28–30[258] for my text. Though they suspected it not, I was really telling them about myself, when I made mention of a *man to whom those words of Christ had been "the palladium of his X^{ity}, and the anchor of his belief". In speaking to men I feel very much the unhappy meaninglessness of the cant phrases. I want something tangible, something for them to do.*

I talked with the Abbot until 12.30.

[247]

Monday, January 3rd, 1887.

I spent an hour & a half in the Hospital. The Wards are unusually empty: yet there are some interesting people. A Wesleyan of very sombre appearance *rather struck me. To a casual remark of mine that there had been skating yesterday, he replied*

---

[255] Robert Farquharson Sharp (1864–1945, *WWW*), New Coll., Oxford; writer and curator, British Museum.

[256] Henry Scott Holland (1847–1918; ODNB), theologian and social reformer; canon, St Paul's Cathedral, 1884–1910; regius professor of divinity, Univ. of Oxford, 1910–18; co-founder, Christian Social Union.

[257] Not identified.

[258] 'Come unto me, all that labour and are heavy laden, and I will give you rest. Take my yoke upon you, and learn of me; for I am meek and lowly in heart: and ye shall find rest unto your souls. For my yoke is easy, and my burden is light.'

lugubriously "On the Sabbath, too, can you wonder, Sir (& he rolled his eyes round the nearly vacant ward) that there are many accidents." He dwelt in model dwellings in S. George's in the East: he was enthusiastic about his residence. For 6/6 a week he had 2 bed-rooms, a large kitchen, scullery, & pantry. Every week the landlord (Major –) presented the tenants with "a quarter" of coal: & good presents at X^{mas}[.] **[248]** His faith in Wesleyanism was unbounded. The Mission in S. George's had, to be said, "converted" numbers of loose women. Especially they succeeded in getting hold of the children: by the bribe of teas &c. With a secret shudder at the perilous prosperity of the schism I smoothly replied with hollow compliments on the excellence of the Wesleyan system &c. Honour (not honesty) made me tell him I was a Churchman, & hoped that the Wesleyans would unite with the Church.

The old Irish Papist & Home Ruler was still in the Ward. He asserted strongly that if the landlords would reside on their estates the tension would be relaxed. In his wrath against the middle-men I would sincerely sympathise: & won his heart by expressing my sympathy.

[249]

The little boy whose back was burnt was awake, & I had a talk with him. He was 14 years old: & worked in Bryant & May's match factory. Hours 6 in the morning to 6.30 in the evening. His employment as far as I could make out consisted of carrying matches from the dippers to the packers. ½ hour for breakfast, and 1 hour for dinner were allowed. Thus 11 hours work: pay 6/6 per week: i.e. 1/1 a day or rather less than 1¼^d per hour. He dwelt in Bow. His father was a labourer long out of work. He had a little brother. I asked him whether his father's want of work made home uncomfortable: how did they manage? He said there was no change: he supposed the money came from somewhere. The family lived in 2 rooms: one was the bedroom of the parents, **[250]** in the other the family dwell by day and the 2 boys slept by night. He had met with his accident undressing before the fire: his shirt ignited & burnt him badly.

I inquired next as to church. He went to church when at home. Was he confirmed? No. Was he going to be? He thought so. With sundry admonitions by way of strengthening his purpose in that direction, I left him.

The Roman Catholic, whose letters I posted last time, was very friendly: having received answers: whereby mine honesty (previously suspected apparently!!) was proven. He is employed in the Central News office.

The boy from Poplar was to go out the same evening.

[251]

I made a few calls in the Mission district in company with the Abbot and then betook myself to St Matthias, Stoke Newington. G. A. Spottiswoode, my chairman, was with me, and his son. The audience numbered about 80: and to some extent made up for the smallness of its numbers by the heartiness of its enthusiasm. I got back to the House about 11: and went to bed about 1 a.m.

[252]

Tuesday, January 4th, 1887.

Snow during the night, very cold. In the afternoon Denham came to see me: and I put him on to the lecture at S. James the Less.

I made my way to All Hallows and lectured to about 100 people, men, women, & boys on the Establishment of the Church. Unusually passive audience, though they were very attentive.

[253]

Wednesday, January 5th, 1887.

In the afternoon I visited the Hospital: and had long chats with my match-making boy, and the Methodist. **Miss [Eleanor] Rathbone was there**.

In the evening I made my way to Ilford and arrived late for dinner. The attendance was small the weather being bad, and an admission charge being made. Perhaps there were 90 people. I got back to the House about 11 o'clock.

[254]

Thursday, January 6th 1887.

I went to Lenham, putting out my luggage at Harrietsham, where **I was joined by mine host, Nutt**.[259] At Lenham we dined with the vicar, Nepean,[260] an old bat, and a good fellow enough. My chairman, General Akers[261] also dined at the Vicarage: he pleased me very much.

The audience was very unsatisfactory, numbering about 40 men and 1 woman: but it was a bad night for a meeting, the roads being as glass.

Nutt & I walked home about 2 miles: through a fairy scene of trees, & distant hills, & crisp snow, & "the long glories of the winter moon".[262]

---

[259] John William Nutt (ord. 1868; *CCD*), fellow of All Souls Coll., Oxford, 1858–75; rector of Harrietsham, Kent, 1879–88.

[260] Charles Edward Burroughs Nepean (ord. 1875; *CCD*), University Coll., Oxford; vicar of Lenham, dio. of Canterbury; 1876.

[261] Possibly Charles Style Akers (1828–1887), Royal Engineers; major-general; painter of Tasmanian landscapes from his posting there, 1854–55.

[262] Alfred Lord Tennyson, 'Morte d'Arthur' (1842).

[255]

Friday, January 7th, 1887.

I spent the morning in the vicarage reading & writing: an invitation to stay a few days came from R.S. Oldham,[263] Vicar of Little Chart, Kent, and a Secretary to the Anglo-continental Society.[264] I wrote to decline but promising a call on the morrow.

Nutt and I then made our way to Staplehurst with much delay. At Maidstone we had an hour to wait, and were met in the Church Institute by Moore,[265] a local vicar who writes much on the church question. He was once an Independent Minister – a little man with grey moustachios & whiskers, prominent eyes, and an **[256]** important manner. We had to wait an hour at Tunbridge. We arrived about 5.30 at the Vicarage. D̲ͬ Rainer[266] the vicar was an old Cambridge don, who waited long for this living. He married a young woman 30 years or more his junior: they have one son, Basil: and D̲ͬ Raieyner is very deaf. M̲ͬˢ Rainer is obviously discontented with her lot. The living is nominally a wealthy one – £1150 from tithe. Last year about £400 only came in to the rector: while his outgoings amounted to over £700. It is a pity that this fact is not more widely known.

The audience was again small: perhaps 80 of both **[257]** sexes. The chair was taken by the squire, a very pleasant fellow named Hoare.[267] I spoke for nearly an hour & a half: but these small audiences kill me: I degenerate into a piffling, conversational style quite unworthy of me and of my subject.

[258]

Saturday, January 8th, 1887.

The next morning Nutt and I after breakfast made our way into the noble Church: which has been well restored. It consists of a nave, chancel, and south aisle, a fine tower, and a remarkable door on the south side of the church. The antiquity of this door is indisputably very great: though not exactly ascertained. The ironwork is very bold. The curves and fishes &c. are very striking. The great want of the church is a choir screen.

We made our way to the station, & thence on to Maidstone, on our way back to Harrietsham.

---

[263] Richard Samuel Oldham (ord. 1847; *CCD*), Wadham Coll., Oxford; rector of Little Chart, Kent, 1881.

[264] The Anglo-Continental Society was founded in 1853 to promote understanding of the Church of England and the internal reformation of national churches, and to prevent infidelity. It became the Anglican and Foreign Church Society in 1904.

[265] Thomas Moore (ord. 1863; *CCD*), vicar, Holy Trinity, Maidstone, dio. of Canterbury, 1873–87); hon. MA, Univ. of Durham, 1886; author whose works included *The Englishman's brief on behalf of his national church* (London, 1879), revised several times and still in print in 1906 (British Library catalogue).

[266] George Raynor (ord. 1850; *CCD*), Clare Coll., Cambridge; rector of Hazeleigh, dio. of St Albans, 1869–89.

[267] The Hoare family of London bankers had a country house at Staplehurst Place. The Hoare mentioned may well be Henry Hoare (1838–98).

[259]

The parish church of Maidstone, dedicated to All Saints[,] is a noble building, with sittings for 2000 people, and in splendid preservation. The carved choir seats: and a very fine tomb in the south aisle-chapel, & a fine modern pulpit all struck me much.

Near to the church is an old palace of the archbishops of Canterbury, apparently in ruinous condition, and now "to let". Yet withal a noble structure, exactly adapted for a monastery.

From Maidstone we made our way to Harrietsham where Nutt got out, and I went to Charing, and then **[260]** was driven about 2 miles across country to Little Chart to pay my promised visit to the rector Oldham. Where I was received as an "angel of God" by the rector, his wife, and his 5 daughters **/who doubtless compensated by their beauties of character for their deficiencies in personal attractions./** The zealous little old man bored me terribly: and at length persuaded me to promise to call on the Warden of Keble about these Old Catholics.

I returned to Harrietsham with all the speed possible.

At 7.30 the Church Defence meeting took place. General Akers again in the **[261]** chair. About 70 people: for it was Saturday night and the roads were as slippery as glass.

On Staplehurst platform we fell in with the Abp. and Mrs Benson:[268] Nutt introduced me to the primate. He is astonishingly like Vidal.

[262]

1st Sunday after Epiphany, January 9th, 1887. [Harrietsham.]

I went to the Celebration at 8: and to Church at 10.45. The church is dedicated to St John Baptist, and is a very wonderful building. Nave and aisles, tower at the West End, and a beautiful choir screen crowned with a noble cross: also, a good peal of bells: sedilia, and aumbry in South Wall: also 3 aumbries in the East Wall by a very unusual arrangement. One of these was immediately behind the altar: and can scarcely by called an aumbry, since the Abp of Canterbury would seem to be right in his supposition that it was the **[263]** place where the priest secreted and locked up the Host at night.

After service I walked to Lenham and lunched with Nepean and John Riddell.[269] The latter accompanied me to service at Harrietsham.

In the evening, at 6.30 there was a "Mission Service" in the Chapel: after which I spoke to the people for about ¾ of an hour on "Church work in East London". About 100 attended.

---

[268] Edward White Benson (1829–96; *ODNB*), archbishop of Canterbury, 1883–96; m. (1859), Mary Benson, née Sidgwick (1841–1918; *ODNB* entry for 'Benson, Edward White'), sister of the philosopher Henry Sidgwick.

[269] John Riddle (ord. 1877; *CCD*), Jesus Coll., Oxford; chaplain, English Church, Cronstadt.

[264]

Monday, January 10th, 1887.

I returned to Bethnal Green by the mid-day train: & found a number of letters awaiting me including one from G. Spottiswoode asking me to speak at a big meeting on February 8th in Westminster Town Hall: **& one from the Provost of Oriel**[270] **asking me to take the History men at Oriel for 2 terms**.

In the evening I spoke on Church Endowments in some Board Schools in Shoreditch. Septimus Buss[271] presided. The audience was disappointingly small: but some compensation was made by the rare occurrence of a conversion. I spoke for 1 hour and ¾.

[265]

Wednesday, January 12th, 1887.

Adderley and I went to a meeting of the E.C.U in Uxbridge Rd, assembled to discuss the orthodoxy of the Church Army. John Riddell presided, and, espying me, called on me by name to speak. Whereat I was not a little wrathful because I had no wish to be observed in an assembly of the E.C.U. However I said a few things against the Army. **In fact, Carlile**[272] **the Secretary impressed me badly**.

[266]

Thursday, January 13th, 1887.

I went to St Peter's, London Docks and lectured on the Endowments. Small audience. On the whole I was favourably impressed with the place.

[267]

Friday, January 14th, 1887.

Tracey and I went up to Oxford, having to leave the major portion of our luggage behind for the unwillingness of the cabby to carry it. To our surprise the Varsity is surrounded by a frozen sea: & skating is the order of the day.

---

[270] David Binning Monro (1836–1905; *ODNB*), classicist and provost of Oriel Coll., Oxford, 1882–1905.
[271] Septimus Buss (1836–1914), temperance and municipal reformer; vicar of St Leonards, Shoreditch, 1881–99; fellow of the Royal Astronomical Society, 1912.
[272] Wilson Carlile (1847–1942; *ODNB*), rector, St Mary-at-Hill, City of London, 1891–1926; founded the Church Army in 1882, to undertake evangelization among the urban poor, in similar style to the Salvation Army.

[268]

			£.	s.	d.
March	2nd	J.H.	5	–	–
		Headlam (Rome)	30	–	–
		Headlam (Rome)	16	12	–
April	26th	Evans	25	–	–
April	28th	Saunders	11	16	–
May	4th	Baker & Prior	25	–	–
	9th	Self	2	10	–
	21st	Woodward & Richmond	5	–	–
		Wakeman	3	3	–
June	20th	Harwood & Son	5	–	–
	22nd	Foster	5	5	–
		Gee	11	17	–
		Goundry	2	16	6
		Hills & Saunders	3	3	–
To balance			80	10	7
			£232	**13**	**1**

[269]

			£.	s.	Cr. d.
Balance from p. 131			1	8	3
Jan.	25th	Farrer Cheque	10	10	–
Feb.	26th	Bursar	41	4	10
March	12th	Dendy	2	–	–
	14th	Valletort	10	10	–
April	26th	Fuller	10	10	–
	26th	Oriel College	33	–	–
May	4th	Soulsby	10	–	–
	12th	Farrer	7	10	–
June	9th	Dendy	2	–	–
	12th	West	5	–	–
	20th	Bursar	50	–	–
	21st	Oriel College	49	–	–
			£232	**13**	**1**

[270]

Saturday, January 15th, 1887.

I came down at the shamefully late hour of 10.30: and breakfasted with Raleigh in the Common Room. **After breakfast I called on the Provost of Oriel**. In the afternoon Headlam & I walked out: on my return I read Politics in Welldon's translation.[273]

---

[273] *The Politics of Aristotle*, transl. J. E. C. Welldon (London, 1883).

[271]

2<u>nd</u> Sunday after Epiphany, January 16<u>th</u>, 1887.

For the first time since my election I came into chapel after service had commenced. I went to *the Celebration at S<u>t</u> Barnabas. Stuckey Coles preached, and* **the usual assembly of flat-heads put in their appearance**. To my very intense annoyance I forgot the meeting of the Upchurch Committee. The afternoon I spent partly in writing letters, partly in reading Prothero's article in the Guardian on the Poverty of the Clergy,[274] and Dilke's article in the Fortnightly on the State of Europe.[275]

For the first time since my election I came into hall after dinner had commenced. Judge Manisty[276] dined: a chirpy old boy.

[272]

4<u>th</u> Sunday after Epiphany, January 30<u>th</u>, 1887.

I finished that troublesome little essay on Oxford University,[277] and sent it off to Stedman.[278]

Then Vidal came and talked to me for the space of more than an hour. He and I differ on two points (1.) as to <u>celibacy</u>. **I regard it as the first condition of independence itself[,] the first condition of the best work**. Vidal has come to believe in a quasi-Platonic union, which shall minister aid to rather than constitute a barrier to the highest work. He instances Kingsley.[279] (2.) As to <u>locality</u>. He believes that Oxford must be the scene of the effort. I believe that residence at Oxford would be to court failure. We should be a 9 days wonder: **[273]** furnish material for epigrams in common rooms: and attract a multitude of Ritualist flat-heads, and – as a result – perish in contempt – a merited overthrow.

In effect, what do I design? Briefly this. **I want to create a community which shall be bound together by the ties of common faith, common purpose, and common obedience. The great** evil under which Religion now suffers is <u>unelasticity</u>, an uncatholic inability to conform to new conditions: this is the result of the ignorance of the clergy. The fact is that the moral revival among the clergy[280] has its dark side.

---

[274] [From our special correspondent], 'Agricultural depression and the sufferings of the clergy', III, *Guardian*, 12 Jan. 1887, 47–8.

[275] [Anon., *Wellesley* attribution. Sir Charles Wentworth Dilke, 1843–1911], 'The present position of European politics', *Fortnightly Review*, 41:241 (Jan. 1887), 1–31.

[276] Sir Henry Manisty (1808–90; *ODNB*), QC, 1857; judge 1876; Kt 1876.

[277] Henson, 'Historical sketch of the university', in Stedman (ed.), *Oxford: its life and schools*, ed. Stedman.

[278] Algernon Methuen Marshall Stedman, né Stedman (1856–1924; *WWW*), 4th Bt, classicist and publisher; founder and head of Methuen & Co., publisher.

[279] Charles Kingsley (1819–75; *ODNB*), novelist, Church of England clergyman, and Christian socialist. Kingsley's love for Frances Eliza Grenfell whom he married in 1844 helped him to resolve his religious doubts, setting him on a path to ordination and moving his wife away from the celibate life in an Anglican sisterhood that she had contemplated; after his marriage he became a vocal opponent of celibacy in religious life.

[280] Both the evangelical and Tractarian movements saw themselves as remedying the moral and doctrinal shortcomings of a lax, lazy eighteenth-century Church of England. As myth, and for a robust and

In concentrating their attention on **morality** they have forgotten **intellect**. **[274]** This is the peril which I perceive to hang over the efforts now being made to supplement the deficiencies of the parochial clergy by diocesan missioners &c. &c. I think the function of monasticism today is identical with that of monasticism of the past viz. to protest against the evils of the existing system, and to remedy them. Therefore I think this community must before all things devote itself to study and preaching. These two – so long divorced – are to be re-united in the person of the monk.

The basis of union must be belief in Christianity as a living fact capable of universal application. If Christ be God: there is X^{ity} eternal: if so, this **[275]** modern talk about X^{ity} having done its work is all treason. There is no problem – social, political, moral – to which a solution cannot be supplied by X^{ity}. However bad the condition of the nation may be: (& God knows it is beyond expression bad) X^{ity} can set it right. X^{ity} still possesses that divine gift of adaptability which in the times past has enabled it to regenerate the most various societies. That must be our faith. Obviously the first necessity is to declare what is this X^{ity}? **I would base it on one dogma – the dogma of the Deity of Christ**. For practical purposes I should require every member to be of the Church of England.

[276]

Wednesday, February 2nd, 1887.

18 men were at my lecture on Beda.

Valletort lunched with me.

I called on Gore and charged him with hostility to the League which he denied.

Bright's lecture last night was attended by at least 100 men.

[277]

Saturday, February 19th, 1887.

I cannot any longer pretend to believe in "the Catholic Church". That "Exegesis of history" which brought me to love & perhaps trust in the "divinely ordered church", now bids me cast it aside as a mistake. Christianity is wider than the Church. Uniformity is not unity. Order is not "Heaven's first law". Sincerity will conquer at last.

Yet this is very painful to me: for I hate disorder: and the conception of the Church is dear. But it involves too much shutting one's heart against goodness: and I positively long to be able to welcome & cheer on every bit of goodness in the world.

---

influential debunking of it, see *The Church of England, c. 1689–c. 1833: from toleration to Tractarianism*, ed. John Walsh, Colin Haydon and Stephen Taylor (Cambridge, 1993), 1–64. Yet for all the social concern of nineteenth-century churchmen of all stamps, Henson clearly believed that critical reflection and study had come to be neglected.

[278]

How much have I given up? The "priest-hood" absolutely. I don't believe in the "Vicar of God-theory". **Henceforward no priests, but ministers, presbyters, servants, drawing their authority from the congregation of the "Saints"**. What about the Sacraments? The "consecration-prayer-theory["] I resign as unphilosophical, mechanical, and even magical.

"Ye shall know them by their fruits".[281] Apply this to the Ritualist theory of the Sacrament.

The Eucharist is par excellence the means of grace. He who frequently partakes therefore receives extraordinary grace. Necessarily he shows the fact in an extraordinary excellence of conduct. Non- **[279]** Catholics have no Sacraments &, therefore, no special grace. They must then be morally inferior to Catholics.

But this is obviously not so. Therefore either the Sacraments are not means of grace in any incommunicable manner or they are, and non-Catholics have them equally with Catholics.

The latter must be accepted, for that Sacraments are means of grace is patent: then it is obvious that the Catholic priesthood is no necessary fact to a church.

Why sh^d we learn from history for 4 centuries: and then abandon our teacher. History today has also her lessons.

[280]

Wednesday, March 2nd, 1887.

The History Tutors dined here. Wakeman stood host. Among the rest I appeared for the first time in that capacity. Yorke-Powell [*sic*] strikes me as a very genuine fellow: and Armstrong also is a good chap. Poole[282] and Ashley[283] bore me terribly. I like Firth: and Hassal, but emphatically not Lodge,[284] Marriott,[285] or Medley.[286]

Apparently I am to go to Italy after all. This may be well, for Heaven only knows when I shall have the chance again: and it is quite a very long time since I felt fresh.

---

[281] Matt. 7:16.
[282] Reginald Lane Poole (1857–1939; *ODNB*), Balliol Coll., Oxford; lecturer in history, Jesus Coll., Oxford; research fellow, 1898–1933; editor, *English Historical Review*, 1901–20.
[283] William James Ashley (1860–1927; ODNB), Balliol Coll., Oxford; pioneer of economic history; professor of commerce, Univ. of Birmingham, 1902–23; Kt 1917.
[284] Richard Lodge (1855–1936; *ODNB*), Balliol Coll., Oxford; fellow and lecturer of Brasenose Coll., 1878–94; professor of history, Univ. of Glasgow, 1894–9; professor of modern history, Univ. of Edinburgh, 1899–1925; Kt 1917; one of Henson's History examiners in 1884 – see Journal, 4 July 1931.
[285] John Marriott (1859–1945; *ODNB*), New Coll., Oxford; lecturer in modern history, New Coll., Oxford, 1883, and Oxford University extension delegacy, 1886–1920; secretary to the delegacy, 1895–1920; MP (C) Oxford City, 1917–22; member, Bryce committee on second chamber reform, 1917–18; Kt 1924.
[286] Dudley Julius Medley (1861–1953, *ODNB*), Keble Coll., Oxford; lecturer, 1884, and tutor, 1887, Keble Coll., Oxford; Professor of History, Univ. of Glasgow, 1899–31.

[281]

Tuesday, March 8<u>th</u>, 1887.

Knox held forth on Home Rule in the British School, Cowley. York Powell in the chair. **I spoke in support of Knox: and was received as the** *"prodigal son" by an elderly schismatic present; indeed he worked out the application of the parable with much minuteness.*

It vexed me to observe how enthusiastically they received Gladstone's name: and even Parnell's.[287]

[282]

Wednesday, March 9<u>th</u>, 1887.

I walked over to Cuddesdon, and spoke to the men about "Secularism in the East End". I was fortified with a longish letter from the Abbot on the subject, and the article in the 19<u>th</u> century for Feb. on "Artisan Atheism".[288] I did my best to say the truth, and be sincere: but my moral and spiritual being has sunk so low, that I only moved laughter, not – as I once could – touched hearts.

Ottley is a very good fellow: and made much atonement for ***the puerile ecclesiastic atmosphere of the place***. Of course I assumed the usual conception of the church.

[283]

Saturday, April 23<u>rd</u>, 1887.

I have been to Rome and returned <u>unspeakably</u> impressed. The total cost of the expedition was just about £<u>50</u> for 4 weeks and 5 days. We (i.e. Headlam & I) stayed 1 day at Milan: 18 days in Rome: 2 days at Perugia: 5 days in Florence: & 1 in Pisa. i.e. 27 days: 6 days were spent in travelling.

[284]

2<u>nd</u> Sunday after Easter, April 24<u>th</u>, 1887.

Chapel delightfully <u>intelligible</u>, genius of Mumbo-Jumbo finally exorcised. And decently attended too – warden and 6 fellows.

---

[287] Charles Stewart Parnell (1846–91; ODNB), anglo-protestant Irish landlord, elected MP in 1875 as a land reformer; leader of the Home Rule League and then founder of the Irish Parliamentary Party; notorious for acting as a disruptive force in the House of Commons and for his marriage to Katherine O'Shea (née Wood), following her divorce from her husband, a fellow nationalist, whom Parnell cuckolded. This split the nationalist cause into Parnellites and anti-Parnellites.

[288] William Rossiter, 'Artisan atheism', *Nineteenth Century*, 120 (Feb. 1887), 262–72.

Bampton Lecture No 4.[289] Great crush of people. A very eloquent sermon: too long: crushed into the hour at a heavy cost: the controversies of the Church slurred over painfully by consequence.

I walked with Gore after lunch: and told him of my hasty resolution to be ordained at Trinity. He approved of the idea*. It now remains for me to get through the Exam., of which as yet I don't know so much as the nominal subjects. It begins on May 4th and I have an interval of about 6 days for preparation.*

[285]

Wednesday, April 27th, 1887.

I walked with Burrows, and talked about religious subjects. He has been *informed of my intention but has engaged himself to conceal it.*

I added up my debts, and find them to be still not less than £100[.] [M]y balance in the bank (including earnings of last term not yet received) is £42. So I start with a deficit of £60. At the end of this term I hope to be nearly straight.

[286]

3rd Sunday after Easter, May 1st, 1887.

I went to the early celebration in chapel. It is not unfitting to communicate before taking a plunge into Orders. I read Hooker[290] for nearly 2 hours, & then strolled about the place.

Burrows dined with me: and we had a long chat together about the subject. I have pledged him to silence as to my intentions.

Gore has practically withdrawn his approval of my taking Orders at Trinity: but the impression deepens that I ought to do so*: of course I may come a great howler in the Exam.*

[287]

Tuesday, May 3rd, 1887.

The eve of the Battle! Troops in perfect stupefaction of terror: arms flung aside.

—In come two pupils. I here place on record that I have been subject to an unusual number of interruptions since I began to read for this Exam. Last night, for example, I had scarcely settled down to read, before de Quetteville[291] appeared, having taken that time to accept my kind (and sincere!) invitation "to come and see me sometimes".

---

[289] William Boyd Carpenter, *The permanent elements of religion* (London, 1889). Lecture 4, 'The relation of the three universal religions to the essential elements of religion'.

[290] Richard Hooker (1554–1600; *ODNB*), theologian and philosopher, much admired by Henson for his conception of a latitudinarian national church; author of *Of the laws of ecclesiastical polity: eight books* (1593–7).

[291] William Frederick Ludlow Quetteville (1865–1925); Oriel Coll., Oxford; BA 1888.

This evening Doyle engaged me in conversation until 11 p.m: then scarcely had I begun to read before Cholmondeley made his appearance, and talked until I was too sleepy to do anything. And so I prepare for an examination!!

[288]

Wednesday, May 4th, 1887.

The dies fatalis [fatal day] has come at last: and if gloomy skies, a dark atmosphere, and a dejected temper are forebodings of woe they are all here.

The first paper was on the Old Testament. I wrote 20 foolscap pages: not always very accurately: still I don't think I ought to be ploughed on that paper.

The 2nd paper was on Church History: on this I wrote 17 pages. It was not a fortunate paper for me, as there was positively not one question on that part of the work which I know best: but once more, I don't think I ought to be ploughed on that paper.

My secret is practically "out": as there were quite a shoal of **[289]** them who knew me present, including the melancholy but excellent Chevallier. Also, Aubrey Moore presided during the afternoon: and he will talk about the candidates certainly.

Max Müller[292] brought to **dinner Karl Haag, the artist**[293] **and his son, who has just entered at the military college**. *I entered into talk with him, & found much entertainment. He spent most of his life in Germany & France, and has very slight acquaintance with English ways: but he is shrewd and plain-spoken. I asked him (sincerely) to come & see me: and he seemed grateful.*

[290]

Thursday, May 5th, 1887.

I was so fagged last night that I went to bed soon after 11: and thus had a full 8½ hours night. The sun tries to shine this morning: & under the effort I go to the 2nd day's trial.

The paper this morning was on the New Test. About most of the questions I could say something: but of accurate knowledge I felt myself sadly deficient: and no wonder, seeing I have scarcely looked at the New Test. for 4 years, i.e. since I passed the Rudiments Exam. On the whole, though I certainly did a very indifferent paper, I don't think the Bishop will plough me on it.

In the afternoon we were examined on Hooker & Pearson:[294] **[291]** and I did a very bad paper. Hooker I had scampered through at a breakneck space during the last few

---

[292] Friedrich Max Müller (1823–1900; *ODNB*), fellow of All Souls Coll., Oxford, 1858; professor of comparative philology, Univ. of Oxford, 1867–75.
[293] Carl Haag (1820–1915; *ODNB*), Bavarian born artist who settled in England in 1847, becoming a full member of the Royal Society of Painters in Water Colours in 1853.
[294] John Pearson (1613–86; *ODNB*). Anglican theologian and scholar; master of Jesus and Trinity Colleges, Cambridge, successively; Lady Margaret professor of divinity, Cambridge; bishop of Chester. His *Exposition of the creed* (1659) was considered the authoritative Anglican work on the Apostles' Creed.

days. Of Pearson, I had read nothing. Therefore there was no reason why I should do a creditable paper. I should think I got perilously near being ploughed on my work this afternoon.

As far as I can see, no one in College yet suspects my intention. It is of course certain that Moore, Gore, or the Cuddesdon folk will reveal the fact to Wakeman in the course of the next day or two. If I only knew that I wasn't going to be ploughed, I wouldn't so much care about people knowing. Anyhow I myself will make no sign.

[292]

Friday, May 6th, 1887.

The last day of my trial breaks windy and wet: and I never hope to advance to any exam with a more miserably complete sense of unpreparedness.

The paper was on the Prayer Book, the 39 articles, and "Parochialia" whatever that may mean. There was *one question about the causes of Dissent, which I answered at great length, and with "brutal frankness", which may not improbably get me into hot water with the bishop. I answered lengthily a question on the Royal Supremacy, & 3 other questions I answered briefly. I should think I ought not to be ploughed on that paper.*

[293]

In the afternoon we had a short piece of Augustine to translate which I finished in a quarter of an hour. Thus came to an end the most singular examination I have ever been engaged in. It only remains now for me to await the result.

Bell Cox is in prison at last.[295] *And a good thing, too, if only this white livered sentiment which has grown over clergy and laity, would allow people to see the case in the true light. The ritualist contention would overturn all government in the church. It is simply anarchic. And to think that these law-breakers are revered as martyrs, is enough to make one mad with rage.*

[294]

Saturday, May 7th, 1887.

I cut chapel for the first time this term, &, not content with doing so, did not come down until past 9: when I found de Quetteville awaiting me.

The Privilege Debate has been brought to an end at last. Government in a majority of 84. Goschen made a trenchant attack on Gladstone.[296]

---

[295] For background, see 2: **106** n. 87. Bell Cox had been convicted in 1885 of offences under the Public Worship and Regulation Act (1874), and was suspended from duties for six months. He was re-arrested in 1887 for disregarding the suspension; he was released from his prison sentence after seventeen days on a technicality.

[296] In the adjourned debate, fourth night, on the Liberal leader's motion to establish a select committee of the House to inquire into cases of parliamentary privilege, Goschen – chancellor of the exchequer

In the afternoon I went out to Cowley and called at the Military College to see if I could find my brave young German. He was not in: & I left my card with a youth who volunteered to deliver it to Haag.

A large party in hall including Chevallier, whom I greeted with studied "insouciance": he was Headlam's guest, to whom he will probably reveal my secret.

[295]

I received a notice from the arch-deacon that I had "passed" in the "Bishop's Exam". As to the next step I am quite in the dark.

My finance is still in a very bad state. I hope to receive this term as follows:–

		£.
Oriel College	13 men	39.
	lecture	10.
3 pupils		22.10
Stedman &c		3.10
		£75

I do not reckon my debts at less than £100 at this moment.

My account for the 1st quarter of this year was £35.5.11½ including however £5 borrowed from Strudwick[297] on the eve of my departure from Rome.

[296]

Sunday, May 8th, 1887.

A splendid day. I got up an hour sooner than I intended: and thus had time to stroll into the Christ Church ground. Everything was perfectly delightful. There is nothing more beautiful than the grey of the old Oxford buildings.

The Bampton Lecture was attended by an immense crowd. I thought it distinctly inferior to the other lectures, but I am in a minority of 1. Max Müller seems vastly pleased with the Bishop [William Boyd Carpenter]. Of course it is always pleasing to non-Christians to be told that they are real miracles of virtue, self-sacrifice, and intellectual vigour. How few people recognize the unselfishness of loyalty.

– had excoriated Gladstone for 'throwing discredit upon the tribunals of the country'; the proper tribunal for disputed claims, he maintained, was a court of law. The suspicion was that Gladstone wanted to shield his allies – the Irish nationalists – and his own party in turn from adverse judgment resulting from the robust response of *The Times* to possibly slanderous statements made in the House by one Irish MP, at the expense of freedom of the press: 'Privilege (Mr Dillon and "The Times newspaper")' – Resolution, 6 May 1887, House of Commons debates, 314, c. 1207.

[297] Not identified.

[297]

Tracey dined with me. He seems very comfortable at Keble. Duff brought his odious friend Round[298] to dinner. How I loathe his goggle eyes, swash-buckler expression, & hyena laugh.

[298]

Monday, May 9th, 1887.

My lecture this morning could scarcely fill ¾ of an hour. 13 men came. The fellows who are in the Schools this term are, I think, rather disgusted at so much Prolegomena. It is curious how the plan of these lectures is being formed as I go on. So far 3 have been given viz.

1. Plan of course indicated: & books recommended.
2. Features in the English Church attributable to the circumstances of the Conversion.
3. Monasticism.

And I have announced as № 4 "Wycliffe". If possible, I hope to give 12 lectures altogether this term.

[299]

I went to New College for the Evensong. The singing & music are incomparably finer than anything one heard in that over-rated South.

Headlam came into my rooms and asked me whether I would take Orders this Trinity, to which when I replied vaguely: he pointed out that I had not passed the Exam. *Wherefore seeing that he knew not that I had got through the same, I returned into vague generalities. A most invincible objection to honesty in this matter rules my mind. One reason is, that I feel so hopelessly out of sympathy with the clerics here.*

[300]

Wednesday, May 11th, 1887.

A splendid day. Cokayne[299] lunched with me yesterday. I like him though he is most recklessly idle.

My lecture on Beda was quite scandalous. It had been prepared for about an hour & a half before delivery: and it terminated well within the ¾ of an hour. I notice that the 2 Univ. men continue to attend. I devoutly hope they will bring me in the usual £2.

---

[298] John Horace Round (1854–1928; *ODNB*), Balliol Coll., Oxford; historian of medieval England and genealogist with strong Tory attachments, most remembered for his criticism of E. A. Freeman for reading democratic ideals back into early English history.

[299] Morton Willoughby Cokayne (1866–94), Oriel Coll., Oxford; one of Henson's pupils; ord. 1891; curate, Carshalton, Rochdale, 1890–4; accompanied Henson on walking holiday: Journal, 11 Aug. 1889. Henson read with sadness of his early death in *The Times*: Journal, 14 Nov. 1894.

I met Ashley in the High & was induced by him to attend Freeman's lecture on Architecture. It was a very interesting performance: though, of course, everything he said has appeared in his books before. **His enthusiastic praise of Durham moves me much to see the place.**[300]

[301]

I wrote to the Warden asking him to give me a testimonial for the Bishop: and adding a request for silence.

I went to Dicey's lecture this morning: Hopkins[301] and Litton[302] were there.

[302]

Friday, May 13th, 1887.

My lecture on the Reformation seems fixed at 14. This morning I confined my attention to Wycliffe.

For next week I announced my intention of dealing with the Royal Supremacy.

[303]

Saturday, May 14th, 1887.

Prothero's letter appeared in the Reading papers. It is very able and to the point. I think it will provoke an answer: though it seems to be substantially unanswerable.

Bailward is staying with Prothero. I am most deeply grieved to hear that **Lady Norton is dead.**[303] *Poor Jim Adderley how sorry he will be! I make no question that bereavement will immensely confirm his belief in those parts of Christianity which seem to me untenable.*

My German did not put in an appearance at dinner, so I must believe the authorities refused him the necessary permission.

[304]

Sunday, May 15th, 1887.

Though I went 25 minutes before the time *I could not find a vacant seat in St Mary's: therefore I strolled to St Barnabas, and heard the Mass.*

I lunched with Dicey: Miss Smith, the sister of the Professor [Goldwyn Smith], was there: she is a very intelligent and interesting woman.

---

[300] On visiting Durham in 1898 (see p. 189, n. 211 above), Henson mentioned that he had first seen Durham Cathedral ten years earlier, accompanied by Arthur Headlam: Journal, 27 Jan. 1898.

[301] Not identified.

[302] Not identified.

[303] Julia Anne Eliza, Lady Norton (1820–87), m. (1842) Charles Bower Adderley, 2nd Lord Norton; mother of James Adderley.

I dined with Madan in B.N.C: the Principal is exceedingly good company, so very well-read and amusing. It is half the battle to enjoy one's own jokes: it at least creates a presumption in favour of what's coming if the speaker looks quite painfully full of suppressed enjoyment. This presumption Toby Watson[304] *always succeeds in creating. He is also not a bit laboured.*

[305]

After dinner we adjourned to Madan's house. M[rs] Madan[305] is rather nice: not a bit Oxfordy yet: & talks the rankest cockney heresy about our long holidays.

Then we went to Wadham to hear Boulton and Lord Selborne speak for the Oxford House. The hall was quite full: and on the whole the meeting was a success.

How had learnt from Gore that I was going to be ordained: and Turner also was possessed of the same knowledge, ostensibly from the same source: so that my secret has evaporated. What an ass I was to entrust it to Gore!

[306]

Tuesday, May 17th, 1887.

Walked round Bagley wood with Headlam.

I dined with Wells, and afterwards heard Gore hold forth in Dixey's rooms on the Bell-Cox case. He spoke very cleverly, and very sophistically. **I spoke briefly in opposition**. *These people are all sorely scandalized at me: indeed I am hopelessly in disagreement with them.*

I gave nearly all my secular clothes to William,[306] *who is going to sea* in a few days.

[307]

Wednesday, May 18th, 1887.

I went to New College to hear some music: *on the way I* **fell in with the Warden, who at once began to talk about my approaching Ordination as "compromising" the League**. *He seemed to speak with a certain reproachfulness which grieved me: so that after returning to my rooms I wrote him a letter asserting my determination to continue loyal to the cause of the League.*[307] *Also I walked about the garden at New College with Turner, and tried to make him comprehend my position.*

---

[304] Albert Watson (1828–1904), classicist; principal of Brasenose Coll., Oxford, 1886–9.
[305] Frances Jane Madan (née Hayter) (1862–1938); daughter of the leading railway and civil engineer, Harrison Hayter; m. (1885), Falconer Madan; three sons, one of whom was killed in action at Ypres, and two daughters.
[306] See **[321]** below.
[307] All Souls Coll., Oxford, Anson MSS, Henson to Anson, 18 May 1887, stating that he had always intended, and made known his intention, to serve the League for one year, and then take orders; as such, he was far from 'frivolously abandoning' the work he had commenced with the League. He wrote, too, of his desire to be made chaplain of the League, and of his belief that the organization would be strengthened by the appointment of a new secretary.

"Alcestis"[308] began in the Theatre.

[308]

Thursday, May 19th, 1887. Ascension Day.

Wet, wild, windy weather, and the first day of the Eights: in which New College went head, displacing Magdalen.

I ordered two suits of clericals at Evans: another step towards my object.

Also I went to New College for the singing, which was very beautiful.

Herkomer[309] brought *the Editor of Punch*[310] *to dinner, who was very ordinary, & said nothing worth remembering. Max Müller and Herkomer sat together in Hall: it was very strange & suggestive to see two born foreigners there.*

I wrote to Wills, Tracey, and How about my taking Orders.

[309]

Friday, May 20th, 1887.

Bitterly cold day: wind high: storms of hail and rain at intervals.

My lecture on the Reformation has sunk to 9: and no wonder! The Warden entertained at church a party of Colonials: but I did not accept his invitation.

The Church House Meeting in the Sheldonian was a failure: ladies & parsons formed almost the whole of the scanty audience.

I went to New College Chapel and heard a very fine anthem. Then with Northcote[311] I went to view the Eights. New College retained the headship with difficulty.

I dined at Oriel. Bussell was there.

[310]

Saturday, May 21st, 1887.

Rainy day. Bell-Cox released on a happy quibble. Will he remain free? or will the fanatic Hakes[312] *trade on the obstinacy of a rival fanaticism yet a second time.*

---

[308] Alcestis was a princess in Greek mythology who died in place of her condemned husband and was brought back from the underworld by Hercules; her devotion was popularized by Euripides in his tragedy *Alcestis*.

[309] Hubert von Herkomer (1849–1914; *ODNB*), Slade Professor of Fine Arts, Oxford, 1885–94; hon. fellow, All Souls Coll., Oxford; Kt 1907.

[310] Francis Cowley Burnand (1836–1917; *ODNB*), Trinity Coll., Cambridge; writer of comedies and burlesques; editor of *Punch*, 1862–1906; Kt 1907.

[311] Not identified.

[312] Dr James Hakes, surgeon and chairman of the Liverpool branch of the ultra-protestant Church Association, who conducted a legal vendetta against Bell Cox that continued into the 1890s. See 2: **106** n. 86.

We went to the Theatre, in all 9 from the college. The play is on the whole unsatisfactory. The music, however, is excellent: & the singing of the Chorus is also good. The Greek is generally well pronounced. But Pheses (Marriott) is too violent: and Apollo (Mackinnon) is too common-place: and Death (Bourchier) is an obvious old lady in muslin: while Alcestis is unbearable.

[311]

Sunday after Ascension, May 22<u>nd</u>, 1887.

<u>**Welldon of Harrow preached in S. Mary's**</u> *(the Bp of Ripon being at S. Margarets' Westminster, for the Jubilee House of Commons service).* **It was a good sermon but marred by his characteristic mannerisms**. *The argument was sufficiently simple viz: the Holy Spirit works continuously in the Church: the sphere of His action in the conscience:* <u>ergo</u>, *in conscientious objections to current dogmas e.g. eternity of punishment, inspiration of Scripture, doctrine of the church – we may recognise His teaching rather than bewail lack of faith. I gather that the sermon vexed some.* <u>Girdlestone's</u>[313] *grim visage grew longer as Welldon proceeded: &* <u>Dearmer</u>[314] *looked positively wrathful: & finally slipped out of the church.* **For myself, I rather liked the sermon**.

[312]

A large party dined in Hall including a very gross looking creature, Lord Herschell,[315] Burdon-Sanderson,[316] and my guest Murray, who carried his arm in a sling.

After Murray had departed, I prepared my lecture for Monday until after midnight.

I have entered on the last fortnight of my life as a layman: as the time for the great change draws on, I seem to grow increasingly unconscious of its approach. **Talking to Raleigh – with whom I seem more in sympathy than with anybody else on this great subject of religion** – *I acknowledged my own disbelief in eternal punishment, nay, in all purely penal punishment after death.* <u>Purgatorial</u> *punishment I can at least comprehend:* <u>deterrent</u> *punishment seems reasonable: but of the latter there will be no need in the world to come: of the former the church scarce tolerates the mention.*

[313]

What then do I mean by "hell"? That there is such a state as <u>destruction</u>, <u>perdition</u>, and <u>ruin</u> seems highly probable. There may be something to say for the theory of "conditional immortality". On all these matters I am completely in the dark. I only know

---

[313] Arthur Gilbert Girdlestone (ord. 1868, Oxford; *CCD*), Magdalen Coll., Oxford; vicar of All Souls, Clapham Park, dio. of Rochester, 1877.

[314] Percy Dearmer (1867–1936; *ODNB*), clergyman who sought to revive English forms of ceremonial and liturgy in the church; works include *The parson's handbook* (London, 1899); secretary, London branch of Christian Social Union, 1891–1912.

[315] Farrer Herschell (1837–99; *ODNB*), 1st Baron Herschell (1886), barr., politician, and lord chancellor, 1886 and 1892–5.

[316] John Burdon-Sanderson (1828–1905; *ODNB*), first Waynflete professor of physiology at Oxford, 1882–95, and regius professor of medicine, 1895–1903.

(1.) that the Almighty is most certainly just. (2.) that He is just according to human conception, for He himself deigns to appeal thereto. (3.) that the current conception of Hell is unjust according to the human idea of justice. **Yet it seems certain that the belief in Hell has been the motive-force of the great missions**: History bears witness to this: contemporary facts look in the same direction. Then has the church come to this, that she must undertake her work without her proved weapon? I think so: but how is this? Is it not because perfect love casteth over fear?[317]

[314]

Monday, May 23rd, 1887.

Dicey postponed his lecture for the 3rd time in succession: so I spent the hour in the barber's shop.

Wakeman and I walked round Bagley wood together: and on our return, I went to New College Chapel and heard some rather indifferent singing.

I received a letter from young Haag at the Military College containing some miss-spellings & very wonderful constructions.

My lecture on the Reformation numbered 10. It was on the relations between England & the Papacy during the Middle Ages.

[315]

Tuesday, May 24th, 1887.

Haag and a friend made their appearance about lunch time: it being the Queen's birthday the cadets had a holiday. I had a long talk with the boys: from which I gather that there is a good deal of bullying in progress at the Military College. **Haag has a great aversion to parsons, and frankly declares it to a quasi-parson. They are "unnatural", "effeminate", "cowards"**. This unreasonable feeling partly arises from his German prejudice in favour of the Military profession: partly, I fear, from a deep dislike to Christianity itself. He avers his disbelief in Jesus Christ, and gave utterance to many very sad doctrines. "You'll hate me, when you know me", he said. Not so, my friend, but I would to God that I could help you. It is passing strange that [316] I seem specially attracted towards young unbelievers. **Maynard, and Murray, and now Haag all alike in open revolt against the Faith. And all alike far too noble for the service of Satan. What is it that drives them from Christianity**? Of course it is true that much of such violent scepticism is begotten of ignorance & the headlong logic of youth, still I cannot but believe there is something more respectable deep down at the bottom. Revolt against official Christianity does a good deal: insensibility to the profounder sides of life does much. **But there is the fact – these bright, brave boys turning away from Jesus Christ, just when their fresh enthusiasm ought to be demanding the Crusading Cross**. It makes me more genuinely sad than anything

---

[317] 1 John 4:18 – 'There is no fear in love; but perfect love casteth out fear: because fear hath torment. He that feareth is not made perfect in love.'

else. I am so anxious to help them: & so utterly helpless. From the bottom of my heart I do sympathise with them.

[317]

Haag is a Lutheran, and has been confirmed in that church. I told him a Lutheran was just as good as an Anglican: and I do not regret saying so. A strong desire to be sincere comes over me when I speak to a boy like Haag.

It being the Queen's Birthday I suggested champagne, which was heartily agreed to by Max Müller, Duff, and Oman, who formed the rest of the party.

[318]

Thursday, May 26th, 1887.

I went out a stroll with Lester: we sat on a gate & talked. He impresses me very much as being manly and honest. Accordingly he is dead against the High Church theory. Particularly objectionable appears the now fashionable practice of private worship. Everywhere "oratories" and "chapels", & "shrines".

I told Lester that if ever I took Orders I should not conceive myself to be thereby taking pledge to believe a number of doctrinal statements: but simply **by Orders I understand a solemn taking the Side of Truth as against Falsehood, pledging oneself to honestly seek for the truth: and not to say things one doesn't believe**. What baptism is to the convert: or confirmation to the sincere churchman: that only in [319] much higher degree is Orders to me. **I do not suppose myself to be receiving any mystical powers: an increase of opportunities arising from the possession of an official public position, that is all**. I do regard myself as publicly declaring my belief in goodness, & light, & truth against vice, darkness, & falsehood. I am consciously saying to cynicism and dishonesty, "I have done with you, get you hence": whether or not convictions, intentions, professing will endure, I cannot say, but here is my position in respect of Orders. **Jesus Christ embodies the love, & truth, the light & honesty to which I give in my open allegiance. Therefore Orders means taking the sign of His service: following Him**.

[320]

I dined with Lock and the Theology lecturers: a most exceeding dull dinner, and severely business like. Even the sprightly Bussell seemed awed. I promised to lecture on Period III for the next 2 terms:

Hardinge made his appearance last night: and sat in my rooms until long past midnight, thus preventing me from preparing my lecture for tomorrow: which accordingly is only partially ready.

1.	~~Friday~~	~~Lecture~~
2.	~~Saturday~~	~~Sports at Military College.~~
3.	~~Whitsunday~~	~~Gaudy.~~
4.	~~Monday~~	~~Bethnal Green Men to lunch.~~
5.	~~Thursday~~	~~College Meeting~~
6.	~~Wednesday~~	~~Lecture~~
7.	~~Thursday~~	~~Go to Cuddesdon~~
8.	~~Friday~~	
9.	~~Saturday~~	
10.	~~Trinity Sunday~~	~~Ordination.~~

[321]

Saturday, May 28th, 1887.

I went up to the Military College and looked on at the sports. My friend Haag was there: and his brother, & one Bowton (?) Lee (?), apparently a great friend of both, (and also himself a good fellow). The sports interested me fully as much, perhaps rather more than I expected. My love for Emil Haag was deepened by watching him for half a day. He gains by contrast with his brother, a poor stick from Jesus College, Cambridge.

The scouts boy, William came to bid me good-bye. I gave him a pound and Palgrave's "Golden Treasury"[318] which I yesterday bought for myself, and so sent him on his way.

[322]

There was a large party in Hall tonight, for many people have already come up for the Whitsuntide meeting. Knox has returned from Fuller's home in Wiltshire. I was noisily companionable, but in truth most miserable: and so now. In *common room I* [had] *cause to speak about the college Communion to Knox. I urged him to attend. It does not mean, so I sincerely said, that you accept any doctrinal statements:* **it means that you believe that Jesus X**st **was the Truth, & that you mean to be loyal to the truth in the future. Jesus Christ is the incarnation of the Truth: the personified totality of the true decision in all the multitudinous issues of public and private life. Every act of honest [323] adhesion to, of deliberate selection of the truth is precisely an act of devotion, of service, of loyalty to Him, who declared that He was "the Truth"**. *I asked Knox whether he would be scandalized at my taking Orders: & he said No, with emphasis. I think the knowledge that one individual would be scandalized by it, would make me even now hold back from the irrevocable Step.* **But of a truth I am tired of wavering to and fro: I long for some finality: the "Kingdom of Heaven" must "suffer violence"**.[319] *These things I write one week before taking Orders!*

---

[318] *The golden treasury of the best songs and lyrical poems in the English language*, ed. Francis Turner Palgrave (London, 1861).

[319] Matt. 11–12: 'And from the days of John the Baptist until now the kingdom of heaven suffereth violence, and the violent take it by force.'

[324]

Whitsunday, May 29th, 1887.

Chapman woke me soon after 7, and as breakfast was not until 9, I made him bring me Arnold's Sermons,[320] and I read them until 8.30. The introduction in which he "goes for" Newman & C⁰ seems powerful and conclusive: *but I am conscious that the tide of reaction against the pseudo-Catholic theory of the Church is running too strongly in my mind to allow of my being fair to the Puseyites.*

The sermon was preached by Woods,[321] *the new President of Trinity, a strongly built man with florrid complexion, red hair & beard, and a pleasant voice.* It was a commonplace performance enough: quite unworthy of the occasion. Bertie was in chapel and I was pleased to see Knox communicate with the rest.

[325]

"Baby" Haag, and Lee made their appearance, and I gave them lunch: & afterwards walked them up to the College.

The gaudy tonight went off much as usual. I had beforehand resolved to be temperate: &, indeed, felt intolerably bored with the whole proceeding. I could not help contrasting the morning occupation of the College, with its evening festivity. The "table of the Lord" stood in glaring antithesis to the "table of devils". It was quite positively painful to see the preacher of the morning heart & soul engaged in toiling through that unchristian menu. So a great sadness held me, and as soon as possible, I escaped to my own room: & there read in peace until my usual hour for retirement arrived.

[326]

And so I end my last lay Sunday in utter sadness. And with full reason: there is cause enough for me to be sad: for I stride towards a crisis with the most melancholy forebodings. **Without definite belief, with a code of morals far too low, with a bad personal record, involved in complications, from which escape seems impossible without loss of honour, I advance towards my Ordination**. There is no hopefulness in it: on the contrary I fear the worst results. How glad I would be to have one true human friend, to whom I might tell my sorrows & weep over them without shame. But this is impossible. Friend I have none: & cannot hope to have. It is another witness to my frailty that I cannot kill out the longing.

---

[320] Thomas Arnold, *Sermons* (London, 1845).
[321] Henry George Woods (1842–1915; *WWW*), Corpus Christi Coll., Oxford; fellow, tutor, bursar and president of Trinity Coll., 1887–97; master of the Temple, 1904–15; chairman, advisory committee for the allocation of grants to University Colleges, 1906–10.

[327]

Whit-Monday, May 30th, 1887.

I had 7 Bethnal-Green people to lunch, among whom Tame[322] and Wilson.[323] **Reichel**, Hardinge, Duff, and Cokayne were good enough to lunch with us. I showed the whole party of 48, over the chapel, hall, & library, and the Hall of Oriel: and then went **on a stroll with Hardinge**. On my return I found the Abbot in my rooms: and in the very short interview I gave him I fear he had cause for being grievously shocked. *I am very sorry to vex him: but whensoever I come into contact with anybody like the Abbot, whom I deeply love, I feel bound to be misunderstood.*

West dined with me.

[328]

Whit-Tuesday, May 31st, 1887.

The college meeting lasted from 10 to 2.15: much shorter than I expected. A good many votes were taken: in every case I was in a minority: and in two matters I believe that I was really on the right side. viz. (1) in the matter of receiving the Warden's very generous but very ill-advised offer: and (2.) in the matter of electing two fellows or none.

The College in deciding to elect one Fellow only placed itself under the necessity of allotting the fellowship to one subject: thus establishing a most evil precedent.

Hardinge displayed the most reckless want of tact, & an unscrupulousness which ruined my legitimate ambitions and his illegitimate ones.

[329]

Cholmondeley came to my rooms to talk to me about Ordination. He is, of course, almost staggered at its suddenness: but otherwise he is not displeased. And he certainly approves of my anti-pseudo Catholicism. *I shall feel very thankful when the end of all this uncertainty has been attained: if only I could know for certain that I should be ordained next Sunday, it would perhaps be different: but, as it is, I feel hopelessly fogged. Indeed I do want to be true in this matter: and I do feel how very unworthy I am to take upon me this office: but I cannot but think that if I drew back now I should be "turning back"*[324] *from the plough of Christ. In His service I aspire to live my life: the time past is enough for the devil.*

---

[322] Not identified.
[323] Not identified.
[324] Luke 9:62: 'And Jesus said unto him, No man, having put his hand to the plough, and looking back, is fit for the kingdom of God.'

[330]

Wednesday, June 1st, 1887.

I walked with Raleigh round Bagley wood: and then went with him and Cholmondeley to New College Chapel, where we heard that beautiful anthem "As pants the heart": and also a very beautiful "voluntary".

After dinner I spent my time partly in talking to Pember & Talbot, partly in reading the "Golden Treasury". *Wordsworth's Ode to Duty is a most beautiful piece: & suits me down to the ground. I can adopt the words –*

> *Me this uncharter'd freedom tires;*
> *I feel the weight of chance desires;*
> *My hopes no more must change their name;*
> *I long for a repose which ever is the same*

And from the deeps of my heart I can echo the prayer of the last stanza which I here set down.

[331]

> *"To humbler functions, awful Power!*
> *I call thee: I myself commend*
> *Unto thy guidance from this hour:*
> *O let my weakness have an end!*
> *Give unto me, made lowly-wise,*
> *The spirit of self-sacrifice;*
> *The confidence of reason give:*
> *And in the light of Truth thy bondman let me live".*

[332]

Thursday, June 2nd, 1887.

I drove over to Cuddesdon in a hansom: and found that I was expected.

The afternoon was spent in writing a sermon on S. Luke 14.33 "So likewise, whosoever he be of you that forsaketh not all that he hath, he cannot be my disciple".

I wrote something about sacrifice as being integral to X^{ity}: worked in a few sneers against modern missionaries: & a few compliments to S. Francis & S. Boniface: & concluded with a few remarks about Christ's command over men being the real proof of his Deity. Then drew the practical references of self-examination & self-contempt. I did not do so good a piece of work as I had hoped.

After dinner the Bishop[325] addressed us in the Palace chapel, laying especial [333] emphasis on the duty of studying the Scriptures with discrimination. The apostolic precept to be "apt to teach" involved the other "apt to learn".

---

[325] John Fielder Mackarness (1820–89; *ODNB*), bishop of Oxford, 1870–88. On his death, Henson wrote in his Journal, 'The "Times" announces the death of Bishop Mackarness from whom I received

The Bishop pointed out that the clergy were the ministers of God's word and Sacraments: & that the importance attached to the study of the Greek Testament was the peculiar glory of the Church of England.

[334]

Friday, June 3rd, 1887.

I received the Holy Communion in the Palace Chapel at 8: the Bishop celebrated. At 10 Matins, and an address from Aubrey Moore, all about the work of the Holy Spirit in convincing of sin. During the morning I had an interview with the archdeacon,[326] who pointed out two mistakes I had made in my papers: which, however, were, he said, generally good, except the Pearson paper: considering that I had not read Pearson at all I was not unprepared for the news. At 3 there was Litany, and an address from the Vicar of Aylesbury, who is the bishop's eldest son.[327] It was all about "aptness to teach", which had been better handled by the bishop on the previous night.

[335]

After Evensong I had an interview with the Bishop. It lasted for more than an hour. He read my sermon through & criticized it, very kindly and wisely. It was far above country folks: and some phrases were in themselves objectionable. "It is very interesting, said his lordship, when he had finished reading, and in some places powerful, but it would be unintelligible to a country audience". The bishop reproved me for some sentences in which I had spoken contemptuously of modern missions. He asked me whether I was **a student of the French preachers**: and on my replying that that was so, he warned me against imitating them too closely. On the whole he seemed to prefer Bourdaloue[328] to Massillon which surprised me.

[336]

The bishop was pleased to say that I showed signs of being a good preacher presently: and gave me much useful advice as to method. Throughout he was most courteous: and quite won my heart by his kindness.

The vicar of ~~Watlington~~ Slough[329] gave the address at 9: his subject was that word of S. Paul "There stood by me this night the angel of God, whose I am":[330] and he dwelt much on the dedication of all our powers to God's service.

Ordination to the Diaconate & to the Priesthood. He was a good man & I honoured him': Journal, 18 Sept. 1889.

[326] Edwin Palmer (ord. 1868; *CCD*), Balliol Coll., Oxford; archdeacon of Oxford and canon of Christ Church, Oxford, 1878.

[327] Charles Coleridge Mackarness (1850–1918; *WWW*), Exeter Coll., Oxford; vicar of Aylesbury, 1887–9.

[328] Louis Bourdaloue (1632–1704), French Jesuit priest and theologian, renowned for his preaching, including at Versailles.

[329] Henry Savill Young (ord. 1871; *CCD*), Brasenose Coll., Oxford; rector of Upton, Slough, 1886.

[330] Acts 27:23: 'For there stood by me this night the angel of God, whose I am, and whom I serve.'

[337]

Saturday, June 4th, 1887.

The last day of my lay life was graced by a bright sun. The Bishop celebrated the Eucharist in the chapel at 8: & after breakfast, Matins were read & another address delivered by the vicar of Slough, in continuance of his discourse of last night.

Those who had already seen the bishop were then free for the morning. ***I wrote a letter to Raleigh thanking him for the help he had given me by his example & counsel to shake off the chains of the pseudo-Catholic theory****: also I finished the letter to the Abbot, which I have put together at intervals during the last few days, stating as far as I could my "attitude" on burning questions. Then I walked into the meadows beyond the church, &* **[338]** *sat on a style to meditate.* ***And as I thought the desire came to me to pledge myself to God there & then: which I forthwith did, bare-headed under the open heaven promising to be loyal to the Truth, wherever I found it, wheresoever it should call me to seek for it.***

After dinner the registrar, Davenport,[331] made his appearance: we all paid our fees (£2.7.) and then assented to the 39 Articles & the Book of Common prayer, and took the oath of allegiance: repeating the formulae after Davenport and after then signing our names to the same.

This ceremony took but a short time, and the afternoon was for the most part unappropriated. Meeting Archdeacon Palmer in the Palace grounds, I walked & talked with him most of the afternoon. **He told me that I was to read the Gospel tomorrow***. It gave me great* **[339]** *pleasure to find that he is in exact agreement with me on the Bell Cox case; and the whole ritual question. He calls himself an "old fashioned high churchman".*

After Evensong in church, and Tea, we retired to our rooms for an hour; and I read through the Pastoral Epistles, & tried to realize the crisis of tomorrow.

At 9 we went into the Chapel, & the Bishop delivered a "charge". He spoke on the words of Christ "Be ye witnesses *of me":*[332] *and urged on us the importance of evidential theology: & above all, the supreme necessity of leading holy lives. And so ends the last day of my life as a layman, which I abandon willingly, for it has been neither happy, nor honourable, nor useful.*

[Henson misnumbered the pages, omitting 340–59.]

---

[331] Thomas Marriott Davenport (1841–1913), Pembroke Coll., Oxford; solicitor; under-sheriff of Oxfordshire; registrar of the diocese of Oxford.

[332] Acts 1:8: 'But ye shall receive power, after that the Holy Ghost is come upon you: and ye shall be witnesses unto me both in Jerusalem, and in all Judaea, and in Samaria, and unto the uttermost part of the earth.'

[360]

Trinity Sunday, June 5ᵗʰ, 1887.

The service went off well. The bishop did his duty admirably. The only hitch was mine. I added "Here endeth the Gospel" which was de trop. ***Raleigh, Harding, & Headlam walked over to witness the ceremony***. I never knew until my return to the college that they had done so. It was very kind of them. I drove into Oxford as far as Father Benson's Church, where I got down sending on my luggage, & walked in. On Magdalen Bridge I fell in with Duff & Talbot, with whom I went round the Parks. Everybody in college is most kind: I never realized how good the fellows were before.

Bond[333] dined with me.

[361]

Monday, June 6ᵗʰ, 1887.

Eyton of Chelsea[334] dined here with Wakeman. He is a great heavy lout, with fat stupid features, coarse hands, & a protruding belly: a hoarse, internal laugh, full of intense inward delight: & a half-humorous, half-cunning twinkle of the eye. His conversation is amusing rather than brilliant: he impresses rather by occasional crude & forcible side-remarks than by wit or hard logic.

[362]

Friday, June 10ᵗʰ, 1887.

I read prayers in chapel for Johnson. At 10 I gave my last lecture for the term at Oriel: and a paper of questions. There were only 4 men present: I had an excuse from one: and several are in the Schools.

Nutt made his appearance. He came to my rooms & we discussed Bell Cox: he is rather disappointed in my attitude.

Hamilton of University came in, & bored me for some time.

[363]

Saturday, June 11ᵗʰ, 1887.

I have spent a wholly idle day. I began by spending the first hour from 9 to 10 in Christ Church grounds, where I picked up Leigh[335] of Corpus, and walked with him. He is a good fellow.

---

[333] Not identified.
[334] Robert Eyton (1846–1908), Christ Church, Oxford; rector of Upper Chelsea, 1884–95; canon of Westminster and rector of St Margaret's, 1895–9.
[335] Possibly John Highfield Leigh (1859–1934, *AO*), matric. Corpus Christi Coll., Oxford, 1878; barr., 1886; later theatre manager and owner of the Royal Court Theatre: 'Mr. J. H. Leigh', *Times*, 3 Mar. 1934, 14.

Then on my return to my rooms de Quetteville came with his schools papers. He expects a second. I think he will get a third. Then Cokayne for an hour: unless that boy works he will come utterly to grief. The other night he ingenuously confessed his indolence. He had been worried about money matters to the extent apparently of £30. I asked him to read Wordsworth's Ode to Duty, & showed him some apposite lines. He has certainly succeeded in monopolizing a very good place in my heart.

[364]

Raleigh and I walked out but the sun was very hot: & we rested often. I wish we were more agreed on the Disestablishment question: Raleigh, however, will not exert himself to bring it on.

Nutt and I went to New College and heard the anthem "Blest are the departed" (Spohr),[336] a very beautiful piece.

Wells dined with me.

[365]

1st Sunday after Trinity, June 12th, 1887.

I attended at the High Celebration at St Barnabas. The inevitable Stuckey Coles preached.

Then lunched with Headlam, & met Sunday undergraduates from New College.

Bowlby dined with me.

*In the committee meeting of the League I **was elected chaplain with zeal on the governing body, and no vote**. Tracey was elected secretary.*

Tonight I am most utterly wicked: quite as if I had never received the "grace of Orders". May God forgive me.

[366]

Wednesday, June 15th, 1887.

I read prayers for Johnson both morning & evening: and spent the most part of my time trying to think of something to say next Sunday.

Nutt & I strolled about in the gardens of New College & Magdalen, discussing various questions of history, architecture, ritual, and theology.

I wrote to Campion consenting to go on the Committee of the Oxford House.

---

[336] Louis Spohr (1784–1859), German composer whose rise and fall in popularity coincided with the early Romantic movement; the anthem 'Blest are the departed' is from his oratorio *The last judgment* (1826).

Vidal dined with me. *At 10.15 P.M. I read prayers in University College for Brightman.*[337] *There were two undergraduates present, & none else save myself. The college chapel system seems certainly near its final end.*

[367]

Thursday, June 16th, 1887.

Collections[338] began at Oriel. I spent the afternoon in lunching with How [Walter Wybergh How] at Merton (where Cooper made his appearance), and going to a garden party at Burrow's, where I had a long talk with Cheyne. I dined with Farrer & some New College undergrads, & afterwards spectated a performance of a Burlesque of Alcestis written by a New College undergraduate. It was very clever.

[368]

Friday, June 17th, 1887.

Collections continued at Oriel.

I dined with Arthur Butler[339] in the Parks: and afterwards wrote a report to the Provost [David Binning Monro], & letters to the Abbot & others.

[369]

Saturday, June 18th, 1887.

I sported my oak[340] and wrote my sermon for tomorrow.

In the afternoon I sat in Carew Hunt's rooms & talked with him: then fell in with Lester and discussed the O[xford].H[ouse].

I went to New College: and heard the anthem "O taste and see".

I dined at the Canning[341] with Tracey. Stanhope,[342] Lord Harris,[343] Whitmore, & Col. Saunderson[344] were the chief speakers: they all stay[ed] in College.

---

[337] Frank Brightman (1856–1932; *ODNB*), liturgical scholar; University Coll., Oxford; one of the original librarians of Pusey House, 1884–1902; influential teacher, and critic of the revised Book of Common Prayer, 1927; FBA, 1926.

[338] I.e. examinations.

[339] Arthur Gray Butler (1831–1909; *WWW*), University Coll., Oxford; ord. 1862; tutor, Oriel, 1875–95.

[340] Sported (14b) *OED*: 'Originally or chiefly British University slang: 'To shut or close (a door), *esp.* to shut (the door of one's room) as a sign that one does not wish to be disturbed.' One's 'oak' is the second, outer, door of one's college room.

[341] The Oxford Canning Club was founded in 1861 in order to advance Tory principles.

[342] Arthur Philip Stanhope (1838–1905; *WWW*), 6th earl (1875); Conservative politician; first Church Estates Commissioner, 1878.

[343] George Robert Harris (1851–1932; *ODNB*), Christ Church Coll., Oxford; cricketer and colonial administrator; 4th Baron Harris (1872).

[344] Edward James Saunderson (1837–1906; *WWW*), military and political career; MP (C) Co. Armagh, North, 1885–1906.

[370]

2nd Sunday after Trinity, June 19th, 1887.

Johnson celebrated at 8: and I helped him. It was the first time that I ministered the Chalice.

I preached at St Paul's for Duggan.[345] ***My text was Acts 22.11. "I could not see for the glory of that light[.]"*** **Oman, Vidal, and Mrs Talbot were among the congregation. *This was my first sermon*.**

Tracey and Carew Hunt dined with me.

I had a conversation with Colⁿ Saunderson after dinner, in the quadrangle. He believes that he has a mission to expose the Parnellites. Other object in political life he has none. He is a Protestant: the Bible is to him the Word of God in the most literal sense. He told me sundry stories **[371]** *about himself from which I gathered that he is one of those, whose convictions are strong enough to compel to action. His hatred of priest craft is almost comical in its intensity, but I unfeignedly admired the deep sense of duty which dwelt in him, and coloured all his language. When he was 29 years old he was "saved". In the very unreasonableness of his theories he finds the proof of their truth.* Credit quia absurdum.[346]

[372]

Dr.

			£.	s.	d.
June	22nd	Self	5	"	"
	25th	J.H.	50	"	"
July	1st	Spooner (Church House)	2	2	"
		Self	5	"	"
	13th	Blackwell	5	"	"
	26th	Parker & Co	5	10	"
August	16th	Self	6	"	"
September	19th	Self	6	"	"
October	25th	Seawell	4	13	6
	26th	Campion	4	"	"
December	12th	Blackwell	8	10	"
		Standen	9	16	"
		Self	5	"	"
December	26th	Balance in Bank	44	2	10
		£	160	14	4

---

[345] William Bottomley Duggan (ord. 1871; *CCD*), Lincoln Coll., Oxford; vicar of St Paul's, Oxford, 1871.
[346] A Latin phrase misattributed to Tertullian in his *De carne Christi*. Henson may have meant simply 'He believes because it is absurd.'

[373]

Cr.

		£.	s.	d.
Balance from p.269		80	10	7
Sept. 7th	Stedman	5	"	"
Oct. 25th	Valletort	10	10	"
Dec. 10th	Oriel College	49	"	"
12th	"Const. Essays"	1	13	9
13th	Univ. College	14	"	"
	£	160	14	4

[374]

Wednesday, June 22nd, 1887.

The lunch after the Encænia[347] went off very well. All my guests appeared. Miss Gedge,[348] Bowlby's love, is, certainly, a sweet girl: if I were not bound to the opposite cause, I could love her: she will make a capital wife for Bowlby.

"Baby" was rather nervous but he looked so nice, that everybody was pleased with him. Mrs Pember[349] is a strange little woman: I can't say she impressed me well: she is * quite unworthy of being the mother of the Pembers. (* I withdrew this. Bowlby admires her: and her influence over her sons is so excellent that she must be good. July 11th, 1887).

The Warden of Keble told me that **Philip Moor[e] was dead**. On Whit-Monday he was up here with the men from Bethnal Green: I had not even heard of his illness – gastric fever. The thought of death as a real fact possible if not probable to one's own self scarcely ever enters one's life. Yet how terrible it would be to die now, when **[375]** the record of one's life is only a sequence of selfishness. How one clings to the idea of redeeming the past by the future: ah there's the folly, if it were by the present, it were perhaps worth something, but this love for the future but too often serves as an apology for present indolence and self-indulgence. I am heartily ashamed of my life: it is utterly unworthy of a Christian man: to say nothing of a Christian minister.

I wonder whether I have any influence for good over "Baby": He says his prayers every night: which is good: not in itself so much, for such prayers are brief and hurried beyond belief, but involving much viz: *that veneration for prayer* as such; that adhesion to early training: that recognition of God in daily life, which must form a basis for subsequent advance: or at least which always render such advance possible.

---

[347] The Oxford Encænia is the ceremony in which honorary degrees are awarded. It takes place in the ninth week of Trinity term. In its present form, it dates back to 1760. The Greek word Encænia means 'festival of renewal'.

[348] Annie Margaret Bowlby (née Gedge) (1863–1949); m. (1889), Henry Thomas Bowlby.

[349] Fanny Pember (née Richardson), daughter of William Richardson of Sydney, New South Wales; m. (1861) Edward Henry Pember.

[376]

3rd Sunday after Trinity, June 26th, 1887.

I preached in the Church here (Broadstairs) at the morning sermon. I repeated mutatis mutandis my dedication sermon. The congregation consisted of about 300 souls: of whom certainly not more than 40 were grown males, even including the choir men, perhaps nearly 100 were children, and the rest were females. There must be something radically wrong in ***especial aim in my ministrations to gain men for Jesus X'***.

[377]

Monday, July 11th, 1887.

I stop here for a moment in my wild rush through my life to record the changes of the last few days.

On Thursday, the 7th the Committee of Oxford House met in the House itself. There were present –

1. The Warden of All Souls
2. Rev. W. Spooner
3. Rev. W.O. Burrows
4. Rev. W.J.H. Campion
5. Rev. H.H. Henson
6. H.O. Wakeman
7. W.W. How[350]
8. Rev. A. Chandler
9. R.W. Carew Hunt
10. [William] Murray
11. Hon. J.G. Adderley

The Committee had several important matters to arrange, and on the whole [378] got though its work well.

1. Buchanan's offer to take Forrest's[351] house with option of purchase, and to reside there himself with his wife and child was accepted. It was decided that O.H. should build him a Hall: & raise the money by a special appeal.

2. It was resolved to recommend to the Committee of the Webb Memorial the purchase of the present premises of the University Club, to be converted into a Boys' Club and Institute.

3. ***The question of the Headship was raised, and I was elected to enter on office at Christmas***.

4. A vote of thanks to Adderley was unanimously passed for his services to the House during the last 2 years.

---

[350] William Walsham How (1823–97; *WWW*), Wadham Coll., Oxford; bishop suffragan of Bedford, 1879–88; bishop of Wakefield, 1888–97.
[351] Not identified.

[379]

I spent the afternoon on the top of buses: in my excitement feeling drawn towards that sort of employment. Then returning to the House I found letters from Bowlby announcing that he was coming to All Souls, according to my former invitation. Whereupon having telegraphed to Chapman and Bowlby, **I went up to Oxford by the last train**. Bowlby was more delightful than ever. He has got a mastership in Eton before his class is known, a great & most richly deserved compliment. On Friday afternoon we went to Wytham and fed on the inevitable strawberries: and, on the way, meeting with Vidal, nailed him for dinner that evening. No less than 10 people dined, half of them strangers, [380] and after dinner we talked on the lawn for a long time. **Then carrying two candles across into the chapel Bowlby, Vidal, and I joined in Evening prayer. I read the service and Vidal the lessons**. *A most beautiful and touching function in a chapel, rarely mysterious for the night-silence, & the feeble light of two candles. It was delightful.*

On Saturday morning Bowlby departed: and after lunching with Vidal, I returned to Oxford House in time for dinner.

In the evening Chandler and I visited the People's Palace, and the various clubs. Freddie Seawell[352] turned up about 1 A.M. after everybody had gone to bed.

[381]

Sunday was a busy day for me. I received the Holy Communion at 8: and at the 11 o'clock service I preached a special sermon to the members of the Clubs connected with Oxford House. Out of about 800 members, there were present 67: I meditate printing the sermon: and issuing it to every member.[353]

At 3.30 I lectured in Victoria Park on "Jesus Christ, the same, yesterday, to-day, and for ever".[354] An old man who by his accent & manner of pronunciation appeared to be a German, denied that our Lord was an historical personage. A strong prejudice against him was no doubt caused by the suspicion of his foreign blood, but this was changed into a lawful [382] contempt by his wonderful obtuseness. His one point seemed to be that because X^t was not mentioned by sundry of his contemporaries (where names delivered in his strange jargon seemed quite strange to my ears) therefore he never existed. He admitted the historical reality of S. Paul: he allowed (with Baur)[355] the genuineness of at least 4 of the Pauline Epistles: he admitted that in those epistles the apostle spoke of Christ in a manner which presupposed the Gospel narrative: and

---

[352] Not identified.

[353] Henson, *Christian clubs: a special sermon preached before the members of the Oxford House, University, Mape Street and St Bartholomew Clubs, at their club-service, in St Andrew Church, Bethnal Green* (Oxford, 1887).

[354] Hebrews 13:8; one of Henson's favourite biblical passages, much quoted in his Journal and forming the text of many of his sermons, including his first episcopal sermon, preached – as he commented – 'not unfitly', in his first parish, Barking, following his appointment as bishop of Hereford: Journal, 9 Feb. 1918. He also invoked it in the sermon he delivered in Durham Cathedral, Trinity Sunday, 1937, marking the fiftieth anniversary of his ordination: *Ad clerum* (London, 1937), 48.

[355] Ferdinand Christian Baur (1792–1860), German theologian and biblical critic who, with the exception of four of St Paul's Epistles, dated key New Testament texts a century and more after the death of Christ.

being thus forced to acknowledge that in the 1st century Christ was believed to have existed: he asserted that S. Paul constructed the whole history out of "idle rumours" which he had picked up. I pointed out that prima facie[356] rumours about a person were evidence of that person's existence. I was very interested to observe how **[383]** keen the people were to listen on these points: and they seemed to follow my argument. After lecture we distributed a large number of Sunday's tracts.

It seems to me that these Sunday lectures (if conducted wisely) are capable of doing much good. It is not that many persons are actually convinced by them: **but it is far more important that the mass of people, who are wobbling between opinions, should understand that there are two sides of the question: that the Church has something to say for her Lord: and that the parsons are not afraid to come out of their uncompetitive pulpits and challenge opposition in the open air**. This last point is very important. Last Sunday a **[384]** man was overheard remarking about me, **that for once a parson didn't mind coming out of church to speak**. Selby Bigge of Univ.[357] was present to see how matters went: designing himself to lecture on Patriotism: *but he was frightened at the questioning, and refused to come.*

At 8.15 I preached from the open-air pulpit outside St Bartholomew's Church. My text was Eph. 6. 11:[358] and my sermon was practically a continuation of my last Sunday's address on St James 4.14.[359] The audiences seemed very attentive. I think an open air pulpit ought to be an invaluable adjunct to every East End Church. The great nuisance is the number of children, whose uproar disturbs the service.

[385]

This morning we held a chapter of the House: at which the work for the coming week was decided: and Buchanan reported the conclusion of his arrangements with Forrest. I came up to Oxford by the 4.45 train: and dined alone. Raleigh sent me a bundle of cast-off clothes for the East End.

Thus have I arrived at *another great Epoch in my life. The responsibilities of Oxford House are very great: and I am scarcely equal to a tithe of them: yet I think God intends me to go there: and I rely on His grace to guide and support me in all I do.*

[386]

Bowlby announced to me his engagement with Miss Gedge: I met the young lady at the luncheon at Commem. and was favourably impressed. Bowlby will be happy. The History Class. List scarcely surprised me. Bond and de Quetteville both got first seconds: Eagle-Bolt was ploughed: so was Valletort: Farrer got a 2nd: West and Fuller, thirds. McGregor, Edwards and Richardson got firsts.

---

[356] *Prima facie* (Latin): at first sight.
[357] Sir Lewis Amherst Selby-Bigge (1860–1951; *ODNB*), 1st baronet (1919), civil servant and author; fellow of University Coll., Oxford, 1883, and tutor in philosophy; permanent secretary, Board of Education, 1911–25; editor of David Hume, *A treatise of human nature* (Oxford, 1888).
[358] 'Put on the whole armour of God, that ye may be able to stand against the wiles of the devil.'
[359] 'But let patience have her perfect work, that you may be perfect and entire, wanting nothing.' Henson invoked this injunction sarcastically against the anglo-catholics in the 1930s, intent upon ridding the church of its national responsibilities, including the custodianship of historic churches: Journal, 30 July 1931.

Select bibliography

This list is of secondary works on Henson only and is confined to contemporary sketches or historical works about Henson, organized chronologically. Numerous further historical studies contain some references to Henson as part of wider discussions about the Church of England or English religion during the early twentieth century. For bibliographies of Henson's own writings, see the lists under 'Henson and his works' at www.hensonjournals.org.

'A gentleman with a duster' [Harold Begbie], 'Bishop Hensley Henson', in *idem*, *Painted windows: a study in religious personality* (London, 1922), 86–99

Marshall Freeman, 'A bishop and disestablishment', *English Review* (Feb. 1929), 198–203

Cyril Alington, *A dean's apology: a semi-religious autobiography* (London, 1952), chs. 6–8

Charles J. Stranks, 'Introduction', in Herbert Hensley Henson, *Theology and life* (London, 1957), pp. 7–10

Alwyn Winton [A. T. P. Williams], 'Henson, Herbert Hensley, 1863–1947', in *Dictionary of national biography, 1941–50*, ed. L. G. Wickham Legg and E. T. Williams (London, 1959), pp. 378–9

Horton Davies, *Varieties of English preaching, 1900–1960* (London, 1963), pp. 64–79

Michael Ramsey, 'Herbert Hensley Henson: a sermon preached in the chapel of All Souls College, Oxford, 16 June 1963', in *idem*, *Canterbury essays and addresses* (London, 1964), pp. 116–26

John S. Peart-Binns, 'Herbert Hensley Henson: some biographical reflections', *Historical Magazine of the Protestant Episcopal Church*, 43 (1974), 169–87

Owen Chadwick, 'The idea of a national church: Gladstone and Henson', in *Aspects de l'Anglicanisme*, ed. Marcel Simon *et al.* (Paris, 1974), pp. 183–205

Owen Chadwick, *Hensley Henson: a study in the friction between church and state* (Oxford, 1983)

Owen Chadwick, *Hensley Henson and the Durham miners* (Durham, 1983)

Keith W. Clements, 'From miracles to Christology: Hensley Henson and the "modern churchmen"', in *idem*, *Lovers of discord: twentieth century theological controversies in England* (London, 1988), ch. 4

A. L. Rowse, 'Hensley Henson: controversial bishop', in *idem*, *Friends and contemporaries* (London, 1989), 131–55

Matthew Grimley, 'Henson, Herbert Hensley', in *Oxford dictionary of national biography* (2004–)

Keith Robbins, 'Content and context: the war sermons of Herbert Hensley Henson (1863–1947)', in *War sermons*, ed. Gilles Teulié and Lawrence Lux-Sterritt (Newcastle-upon-Tyne, 2009), pp. 188–206.

John S. Peart-Binns, 'Herbert Hensley Henson, prelate and pastor', *Parson and Parish*, 173 (2013), 16–28, 33–46

John S. Peart-Binns, *Herbert Hensley Henson: a biography* (Cambridge, 2013)

S. J. D. Green, 'Hensley Henson, the prayer book controversy and the conservative case for disestablishment', in *The Church of England and British politics since 1900*, ed. Tom Rodger, Philip Williamson and Matthew Grimley (Woodbridge, 2020), pp. 102–19

Julia Stapleton, 'Ecclesiastical conservatism: Hensley Henson and Lord Hugh Cecil on church, state and nation, c. 1900–40', in *The Church of England and British politics since 1900*, ed. Tom Rodger, Philip Williamson and Matthew Grimley (Woodbridge, 2020), pp. 80–101

Richard Davenport-Hines, 'The trimming of Herbert Hensley Henson', in *Conservative thinkers from All Souls College Oxford* (Woodbridge, 2022), pp. 79–105

Julia Stapleton, 'Herbert Hensley Henson, J. N. Figgis and the Archbishops' Committee on Church and State, 1913–1916: two competing visions of the Church of England', *Journal of Ecclesiastical History*, 73 (2022), 814–36

Philip Williamson, 'Hensley Henson and the appointment of bishops: state, church and nation in Britain, 1917–1920 and beyond', *Journal of Ecclesiastical History*, 74 (2023), 325–48

Index of names and subjects

N.B. entries concerning Henson's activities, associations, and beliefs can be found under relevant headings; for personal matters, see under his name.

Abbott, Robert Lamb   140, 141
Adderley, James ('the Abbot')   xxv, 131, 132, 154, 171, 173, 178, 181, 188, 191, 194, 206, 217, 234
Alcestis   219, 220, 231
Alford, Henry, *The Greek Testament*   30, 34, 69, 88
All Souls College, Oxford, Henson and   viii, x, xii–xiii, xx
   College meeting   225
   Gaudy   182, 224
   Upchurch committee   187
Anglo-Catholicism, Henson and   xxiv.
   See also Puseyites; Ritualists; Tractarianism
Anson, William   xii, xiii, xiv, xv, xxi, 114, 115, 121, 149, 156, 158, 178, 187, 196–7, 218
Apostolicae curae (1896), and Henson   xix
Arnold, Matthew   99, 118
Arnold, Thomas, *Sermons*   224
Aspinall, Ada Isabella (Bella)   30 n.56, 66, 81, 82–3
Aspinall, Alexander Raymond   85
Aspinall (later Aspinall-Oglander), Cecil Faber   60, 63, 77, 78
Aspinall, Clarke   xx, xxii, 33, 34, 61, 74–5, 76, 78, 96
   Henson visits home of   33, 51, 86–7, 101
Aspinall, Edmund (Noel)   60, 63, 77, 78, 87
Aspinall, Frederick   75
Aspinall, Henry Kelsall   xviii, 34, 39, 53, 54, 61, 77, 96
   family of, Henson plays tennis with   53, 54, 60, 64, 66, 72, 76, 84, 91, 95, 105
   home of, Henson visits   55, 66, 75, 76, 77, 86, 94, 104, 110, 113
Aspinall, John Bridge   78–9, 94 n.40
Aspinall, Noel Lake   65
Aspinall, Sophia Maude   30 n.56, 55, 81, 83, 97
Aspinall, William Christian   85
Athanasius of Alexandria   19

Ball, Sidney   xiv, 29, 110, 186
Baur, Ferdinand Christian   235
Beard, Charles   112
Bell Cox, James   73 n.87, 214, 218, 219, 228, 229
Benedict XII   43
Benson, Arthur Christopher   x
Benson, Edward White   205
Benson, Richard Meux   192, 229
Bertie, Henry William   114, 115, 170, 187, 224
'Bethshanites', Henson and   40–6, 53
Bigg, Charles   137
Biggs, Arthur Worthington   26, 48
Birkenhead
   Anglican churches in and near, and Henson   6 n.3
   Holy Trinity   viii, xx, 6, 7
      Bible class   55, 60, 98, 108
      Mission   xviii–xix, 18, 19, 23, 48, 52, 57, 67, 74, 82, 90, 95, 101–2, 107–8, 114
      Sunday School   25, 37, 54, 60, 65
   Priory   6 n.3
   St Anne's, Rock Ferry   xx, 85
   St Barnabas, Tranmere   76, 78, 86–7, 96
   churches and sects in   xvii–xviii, 6
   Conservatism in   61
   Docks   xvi, 18, 19–20, 22, 25, 29, 34, 35, 51, 65–6, 67
   Hamilton Square   xvi
   housing in   7, 9, 93
   park   xvii, 102
   people of, and Henson   19
   unemployment in (1885)   xvii, 10, 74, 76, 83, 93, 96
   Woodside ferry   108, 110
   See also Salvation Army
Bluntschli, Johannes Kaspar   138
Booth, Charles, *Life and labour of the people in London*, Henson's review of   xxvi
Booth, William   15

INDEX OF NAMES AND SUBJECTS

Bosanquet, Robert Holford MacDowall 186
Boulton, Harold   175, 198, 218
Bourdaloue, Louis   227
Bowlby, Henry Thomas   136, 138, 143, 144, 153, 233, 235, 236
Boyd Carpenter, William   157, 212 n.289, 215, 220
Bradlaugh, Charles   197
Bradley, Andrew Cecil   111
Brassey, Albert   66
Bright, William   138 n.36, 183, 186, 191, 209
British and Foreign Bible Society   65
Broglie, Jacques Victor Albert, duc de, *L'église et l'empire Roman au IVe siècle*   37, 59, 62, 66, 69, 84, 86, 87, 91, 92
Bryce, James   122–3
Buchanan, Patrick   171, 184, 191–2, 200, 234, 236
Buckle, Henry Thomas   164
Bulwer-Lytton, Edward   96–7, 127
Burdon-Sanderson, John   220
Burnand, Francis Cowley   219
Burrows, Winfrid Oldfield   90, 92, 126, 144, 166, 192, 212
Buss, Alfred Joseph   195
Buss, Charles Caron   195 n.238
Buss, Septimus   206

Campbell, George, 8th duke of Argyll   150
Campion, William James Heathcote   125, 230
Carlile, Wilson   206
Cavendish, Spencer, 8th marquess of Hartington   140
Cecil [Gascoyne-Cecil], Robert, 3rd marquess of Salisbury   ix
Cecil [Gascoyne-Cecil], Rupert (William), 'Fish'   ix
Chamberlain, Joseph   xii, xxiii, 57, 97–8, 103, 137
Charity Organisation Society   xxii, 22, 63–4, 76, 83
Chester, Henson visits   24–5
Cheyne, Thomas Kelly   231
   Book of Isaiah   91, 92, 97, 98, 101, 102, 105
Cholera   49, 51, 53–4, 56, 57, 59, 60, 61, 62, 63, 64, 66, 67, 86
Cholmondeley, Francis Grenville   116, 143, 225

Christadelphians
   Christendom astray, Birmingham R. Roberts   33, 46–7, 57, 82
   Henson visits in Birkenhead   28, 31–3, 84, 86
Christian socialism, Henson and   xxv–xxvi
Christianity and history, Henson and   xxvii–xxviii, xxix
church, the, Henson's conception of   8–9
   authority of   xxviii, 9
Church Defence Institution   xxiii, 144, 180
Church of England, Henson and creeds of   xxvii, 8
   parochial system of   28, 83
   patronage in   196
   politics and   192
   Protestantism and   11, 86, 190
   subscription in   143–4, 222
Church of England Young Men's Society   177
Church House proposal   194, 219
Churchill, Lord Randolph   120
Coates, Allan   137, 140
Cokayne, Morton Willoughby   216, 225, 230
Coker Adams   59
Conroy, Sir John   164
Conybeare, Frederick Cornwallis   123, 125, 169, 190
Cronshaw, Herbert Priestley   142
Cross, Richard Assheton, Viscount Cross   59
Cross, William   58–9
Curzon, George Nathaniel   132, 152
cynicism, Henson and   xv, 68, 152, 170, 222
Cyprian   52
Cyril of Alexandria   103, 127

Dalton, Arthur Edison   176, 195
Davenport, Thomas Marriott   228
Dearmer, Percy   220
Deceased Wife's Sister Bill   150
Denham, Thomas   xii, 49, 68, 76, 132, 203
Derby, Edward Henry, 15th earl of Derby   111
Dicey, Albert Venn   xii, xiii, 125, 138, 217, 221
Diggle, John William   71, 73, 93
Disestablishment   xxix, 18, 143, 146, 182–3, 192, 199, 230
Dissent. *See* Nonconformity
Döllinger, Ignaz von   119
Doyle, James Borbridge   113

INDEX OF NAMES AND SUBJECTS

Doyle, John Andrew 152
Duff, Harry 114, 116, 120, 121, 127, 140, 151, 152, 153, 154, 183, 189, 216, 222, 225

Egremont 23
English Church Union 185, 206
Eusebius Pamphili 19
Eyton, Robert 229

Feilden, William Leyland 111, 112
Ffoulkes, Edmund Salisbury 119, 190
Finlay, George, *History of Greece* 97, 100, 101, 102
Firth, Charles Harding 144, 210
Fletcher, Charles Robert Leslie 84, 114, 147, 152, 170
Flowers, John French 121
Flowers, Richmond 121 n.156
Forcade, Monsignor Théodore-Augustin 93
Freeman, Edward Augustus 123, 124, 164, 217
Freeman, Florence 189
Froude, James Anthony 48, 118, 183

Gathorne-Hardy, Gathorne, Viscount Cranbrook 194
Gell, Philip Lyttelton 145
Giffen, Robert 74
Girdlestone, Arthur Gilbert 220
Gladstone, William Ewart 23, 137, 211, 214
    Establishment, changed views on 119
    Government of Ireland Bill (1886) 140
    Midlothian speech 97
Goodwin, Harvey 86 n.21, n.22
Gordon, Charles George xx–xxii, 25, 30, 33, 49, 53, 55, 63, 82, 83, 87, 88, 89, 91, 92, 111
    Francis William Pember, dislike of 63
    Henson, as inspiration for 26, 29, 35, 110, 127
    Henson's lecture on 90, 92, 121, 122, 124, 143, 181, 190, 194, 196, 197
    Gordon: a lecture 195, 201
    Thomas Sheriff, dislike of 33
Gore, Charles xxiii, xxiv, xxv, 73, 125, 140, 141, 148, 157, 178, 180, 209, 212, 218
    Disestablishment, views on 182–3
Goschen, George Joachim 98, 123, 214
Gosse, Edmund William xi n.13, 186

Gray, Andrew Edward Phillimore 10 n.11, 55 n.25
Gray, Robert Henry 10 n.11

Haag, Carl xiii, 213
Haag, Emile xiii, 213, 221–2, 223
Hakes, James 219
Hardinge, Arthur Henry 118, 119, 157, 222
Haselden, Ewan (Noel) 78, 81
Haselden, Joseph 81–2, 94, 99–100, 105
Hassall, Arthur 129, 130, 131, 132, 138, 179
Headlam, Arthur Cayley 147, 168, 179, 180, 186, 190, 194, 207, 211, 215, 216, 217, 229
Heath, Charles 66, 109, 111
'hell', meaning of for Henson 220–1
Henson, Arthur Edward 25, 126, 169–70
Henson, Emma Ann ('Jennie') 26, 36, 37, 51, 56, 59, 62, 68, 72, 83, 91, 94, 103, 104, 106, 109, 114, 116, 121
Henson (née), Emma Hensley Long 91, 94
Henson, Emma Theodora Parker ('mater') 26, 36, 37, 51, 56, 121
Henson, Gilbert Aubrey ('Gid') xii, xxiv, xxvii, 25, 94, 106, 117, 124, 158–65, 168, 169–70
Henson, Herbert Hensley
    early life ix–xii
    financial difficulties xxiv, 129–30, 140, 149, 168, 176, 178, 212
    Journal x
    non-collegiate status xii, xx, xxiv, 142. *See also* Oxford, University of
    ordination, approach of 124, 178, 183, 184, 212, 218, 220, 222, 223, 224, 225, 226–9
    vow to God xxii, 115–16, 124, 126
Henson, Marion Edith ('Podge') 26, 37, 106
Henson, Thomas x–xi, 37
'heresy hunting', and Henson.
    See 'Bethshanites'; Christadelphians; Pythagoreans; Salvation Army
Herkomer, Hubert von 219
Herschell, Farrer, 1st Baron Herschell 220
Hind, Henry Norman 141, 142, 143
Hobhouse, Walter 139, 144, 147, 151, 189
Holmes, Richard Ellis 132
Home Rule (Ireland) 199, 202, 211
Hooker, Richard xxviii, 212, 213
Horsfall, George Henry 50
How, Walter Wybergh 133, 231

How, William Walsham   234
Hubback, John Henry   10
Hugh of Lincoln, St   105
Hughes, Thomas   188–9, 190
Hugo, Victor   101, 102
Hunter, Leslie   xxv
Hutton, Gerard Mottram   124, 133, 136, 152
Hutton, William Holden   95, 117, 123, 124, 136, 141, 143, 144, 145

Ince, William   180

Jackson, William Walrond   117, 120, 123, 133
Johnson, Arthur Henry   116, 131, 141, 151, 229, 230, 232
Jowett, Benjamin   117, 151

Kennedy, Sir William Rann   61
King, Edward   86 n.22, 131
Kingsley, Charles   89 n.28, 208
Kitchener, Horatio Herbert   111
Kitchin, George William   141
Knox, Andrew (Jnr)   54
Knox, Andrew (Snr)   54
Knox, Edmund Vesey   193, 211, 223, 224

Laird, John (Snr)   7 n.4
Laird, John (Jnr)   xxii, 7 n.4, 61, 83
Laird, William (Snr)   xvi
Laird, William (Jnr)   7 n.4, 61
Laird's shipyard   10, 61, 96, 103, 106, 108
Lang, Andrew   148
Lang, Cosmo Gordon   123, 138, 157, 177 n.163, 180, 182 n.179
Lawley, Algernon George   183, 200
Leighton, Stanley   150
Lester, Lester Vallis   171, 186, 191, 196, 222, 231
Lewis, David   16–17
Liddon, Henry Parry   36, 37, 48, 78
Lightfoot, Joseph Barber   34
Liverpool, and Henson
  Alexandra Theatre   73
  art gallery (Walker)   xv, 62, 81, 88, 102
  Athenaeum   xv, 34, 51, 56, 57, 72, 76, 79
  Cathedral   17
  churches
    St Agnes, Toxteth   xx, 13, 71, 93, 103
    St Matthew and St James, Mossley Hill   71, 93, 104
  Cross's menagerie, Henson visits   58–9

Docks   106
Mersey tunnel   xxii, 61, 108
Museum (William Brown)   62 n.53, 87, 88
Picton Reading Room   17, 51, 57
Police court (magistrates' court)   74–5
Reform Club   79
Royal Court Theatre   59
St George's Hall   78
schism centre, as   142–3
Society for the Prevention of Cruelty to Children   27 n.48
wild-beast shops   58
Llewelyn Davies, John   56, 197
Lock, Walter   120, 141, 222
London, East End, and Henson   187–8, 193–6, 198, 199–203, 206
  lectures on church in   172, 174, 206
  lectures on secularism in   211

Macdona, John Cumming   87–8
Mackarness, Charles Coleridge   227
Mackarness, John Fielder (Bishop of Oxford)   160, 226–7, 228, 229
Mackay, Henry Falconer   9, 13, 14, 16–17, 23, 92, 143
Madan, Falconer   147, 218
Madan, Frances Jane   218
'Magistrate' (Arthur Pinero), Henson attends performance of   91
Maguire, James Rochfort   114, 115, 116, 126, 178
Makin, William   xviii, xxii, 22, 26–8, 30, 48, 49, 54, 63–4, 76, 83, 84
Manning, Henry Edward (Cardinal)   xx, 85–6
Marcellinus, Ammianus   84
Massillon   167, 227
Maynard, Herbert (John)   117, 124, 136, 148
Menageries, Henson's visits to   58–9, 66, 81
Meyer, Kuno   xxi–ii, 12–13, 14–15
Migne, Jacques Paul   14
'Mikado', Henson attends performance of   56, 59
Miller, Hugh   76, 84
Mills, Francis James   133, 135
monasticism, Henson and   xxix, 166–7, 175, 178, 182, 208–9
Montefiore, Sir Moses   59
Moore, Aubrey Lackington   192, 213, 214, 227
Morrison, Walter   161

Müller, Friedrich (Max)   213, 215, 219, 222
Murray, William   140, 156, 220, 221, 234

Napier, Arthur Sampson   120
Napier, William, *History of the war in the peninsula and in the south of France*   29, 69
Neander, August   xiii
Nestorius   103
Newman, John Henry   xxvii, xxviii n.89, 86, 116, 118, 152 n.112, 224
Noel, Baptist Wriothesley   x
Nonconformity, and Henson   xxviii, xxix, 5, 46, 54, 92, 143, 150, 160, 185, 214
Nutt, John William   203, 204, 205, 229, 230

Olshausen, Hermann, *Biblical commentary on the New Testament*   34
Oman, Charles William Chadwick   xii, 114, 121, 138, 142, 152, 222
Ottley, Robert Lawrence   145, 211
Oxford Canning Club   231
Oxford House, and Henson   xxv–xxvi, 171–7, 186, 188, 197–203, 225, 230, 234–6
Oxford Laymen's League, and Henson   ix, xxiii, xxiv, 132–3, 136, 138, 139, 141, 142–3, 144, 145, 146, 156 n.120, 160, 164, 180, 184, 186–7, 188–9, 218, 230
  Norwich, Henson lectures at for the   185
  Wantage, Henson lectures at for the   184
Oxford movement, and Henson   xxiii
Oxford, University of, non-collegiate students and Henson   90, 141–2

Paget, Francis   131, 141, 142, 184
Palgrave, Francis   17
Palgrave, Francis Turner   223
Pall Mall Gazette, and Henson   37, 38, 56
Palmer, Edwin   227, 228
Palmer, William Waldegrave, 2nd earl of Selborne   192, 218
Parnell, Charles Stewart   211
Patriotism, Henson's   xxi–xxii, xxiii
Payne, Joseph   59
Pearson, Henry Daniel   195, 197
Pearson, John   213, 214, 227
Pember, Edward Henry   192
Pember, Fanny   233

Pember, Francis William   52, 63, 118, 119, 180, 188
Pepys, Samuel   37
Phelps, Lancelot Ridley   133
Picton, James Allanson   59
the poor, and Henson   xxii–xxiii, xxvi, 9, 10, 17. *See also* London, East End; Oxford House; unemployment
Porter, Billinie   33, 65, 77, 84
Poulton, Edward Bagnall   117
preaching, Henson and   99, 227, 235, 236
Prothero, George   132, 139, 145, 146, 147, 177
Prothero, Rowland Edmund   114, 116, 119, 120–1, 156, 160, 167, 170, 189, 208, 217
Puseyites   131, 143, 186, 224. *See also* Anglo-Catholicism; Ritualists; Tractarians
Pythagoreans   50

Raleigh, Thomas   xxiv, 146, 190, 198, 220, 226, 228, 229, 230, 236
Randell, Thomas   120, 134
Raper, Robert   xiv, 110
Rashdall, Hastings   xxv
Rathbone, Acheson (Lyle)   xiv, 12, 15, 23, 25, 29, 35, 36, 37, 48, 49, 53, 54, 56, 57, 58, 59, 62, 66, 68, 69, 70, 72, 73, 87, 90, 91, 92, 94, 100, 102, 103, 104, 105, 110, 111, 112, 113, 114, 115, 169
  cynicism of, Henson rebukes   68
  Henson's dislike of   70, 96, 105, 107
Rathbone, Edward Lucretius   84, 103, 169
Rathbone, Eleanor   xiv, 71, 92, 103, 104, 113, 199, 203
Rathbone, Elizabeth Lucretia ('Elsie')   xiv, 112
Rathbone, Francis Warre   73
Rathbone, Henry (Harry) Gair   36, 48, 49, 51, 73, 79
Rathbone, Herbert   53
Rathbone, Philip Henry   54
Rathbone, Samuel Greg   111
Rathbone, Theodore William   49
Rathbone, Thomas (Ashton)   71, 72, 73, 74, 93, 103, 104
Rathbone VI, William   xiv, xxiii, 53, 75, 94, 110, 111, 112, 113
  Greenbank, home of, Henson visits   70, 72, 92, 103, 111, 112, 113
  Water Street, office of, Henson visits   113

Reformation, Henson and   xx, 23, 77, 86 n.19, 87, 214
  lectures on   193, 217, 219, 221
Reichel, Charles   xii, 180
Reichel, Henry (Harry)   xii, 180, 225
Retrospect of an Unimportant Life, Herbert Hensley Henson   ix, x, xii, xx, xxiii
Riddell, John   205, 206
Ritual   162–3
Ritualism   xxiv, xxix, 170, 210
Ritualists ('Rits')   143, 144, 190
Rolls series   14
Roman Catholicism, and Henson   xi, xiii, xix–xx, xxiv, xxvii, 11, 104, 118, 152, 173, 190, 209–10
Round, John Horace   216
Rubáiyát ['Quatrains'] *of Omar Khayyam*   24
Ryle, John Charles   17, 51

St Augustine's Roman Catholic church, Ramsgate   xi
Salisbury, Henson visits   153
Salisbury, Lord. *See* Cecil [Gascoyne-Cecil], Robert
Salvation Army, and Henson in Birkenhead   15–16, 37–9, 40, 56
Sanday, William   120
Sankey, Ira D. and Moody, Dwight L.   35
Scots, Henson's encounter with   23
secularisation, and Henson   198
secularists, and Henson   197
Selborne, Lord. *See* Palmer, William Waldegrave
Selby-Bigge, Lewis Amherst   236
Sheriff, Thomas   xix, 3, 9, 24, 33, 37, 47, 48, 49, 54, 55, 57, 58, 59, 61, 62, 63, 65, 67, 78, 82, 87, 98, 100, 104, 107, 108, 109
  Church of England and   18, 39–40, 52
  Disestablishment and   18
Shorthouse, Joseph Henry   xxiii
Simpson, James Gilliland   145
Sismondi, Jean-Charles de   133
Skipton, Henson visits   158–66
Smith, Goldwin   138–9, 150–1
Smith, William Saumarez   94 n.41
Snowdon Smith, Edward   94
Socrates of Constantinople   36, 58, 62, 66, 84, 86, 87, 95, 97, 100, 101, 102
Spottiswoode, George Andrew   200, 202, 206
Spottiswoode, John   200

Starkey, J. H.   180
Stead, William Thomas   37 n.76
Stephen, Leslie   14
Stevedores, and Henson   8, 17
Stubbs, William   10, 28 n.49, 34, 55, 97, 118, 129 n.1, 130
  Stubbs Society   vi, xix, 2
Stuckey Coles, Vincent   154, 191, 208, 230
  Disestablishment and   182–3

Talbot, Edward Stuart   190, 197
Talbot, George John   184, 190, 226, 229
Talbot, John Gilbert   189, 190, 197
Temple, William   xxvi
Thompson, Charles   xviii, 3, 27, 30, 34, 35, 39, 48, 52, 53, 61, 65, 100
Thornton, Joseph   36, 57, 84, 105
Thurstaston, Henson visits   69, 70
Toynbee Hall   xxv, 186
Tracey, John   132, 176, 183, 191, 199, 200, 206, 216, 219, 230, 231, 232
Tractarianism, and Henson   xxiii, xxiv, xxix. *See also* Anglo-Catholicism; Puseyites; Ritualists
Trimmer, Henson as   174
Tupper-Carey, Albert Darell   141, 191
Turner, Cuthbert Hamilton   138, 139, 218

unemployment, and Henson   34, 74. *See also* the poor; *and under* Birkenhead
Unitarianism, and Henson   62, 68, 112

Vidal, George Studley Sealy   125, 131, 132, 137, 154, 156, 180, 208, 231, 232

Wakeman, Henry Offley   xxiii, 115, 116, 139, 152, 160, 180, 184, 187, 214, 221, 229
Walkington, John   67, 74, 90, 101, 107, 114
Wallasey   10, 19, 23
Warr, Augustus Frederick   50
Watson, Edward William   xix, xx, 6, 8, 11, 17, 18–19, 22, 26, 28, 30, 34, 37, 48, 49, 52, 67, 71, 74, 75, 83, 84, 86, 90, 93, 94, 95, 101, 107, 113, 117, 124, 132, 180
  house visiting, Henson accompanies   9, 30–1
  as preacher   xix, 39, 73, 77, 78, 96, 99
  walks with Henson   16, 18, 19, 29, 33, 34, 35, 36, 51, 65, 68, 74, 82, 83, 92, 99, 100, 102, 105, 109, 111

Watson, Miles Walker   69–70, 75, 76, 77, 78, 81, 82
Welldon, James Edward Cowell   187, 220
  Politics of Aristotle (transl.)   207
Wells, Charles Arthur   180
Wells, Joseph   117, 133, 134, 138, 139
Wethered, Francis Owen   138
Whitehead, Henry   181
Whitmore, Algernon   189
Wombell's menagerie, Henson visits   81
Wood, Edward James   100

Woods, Henry George   224
Wordsworth, William   99, 160, 226, 230
Worrall, Samuel   54
Wyon, Walter James   192

Yarde-Buller, John   133, 138, 141, 145, 153
York Powell, Frederick   117, 210, 211
Young, Henry Savill   227

Zosimus   84

Church of England Record Society
COUNCIL AND OFFICERS FOR THE YEAR 2024–2025

Patron
Professor D. N. J. MACCULLOCH, Kt., M.A., Ph.D., D.D., F.B.A., F.S.A., F.R.Hist.S.

President
Professor ALEC RYRIE, M.A., M.Litt, D.Phil., F.B.A, F.R.Hist.S.

Vice-President
Canon Professor MICHAEL SNAPE, M.A., Ph.D.

Honorary Vice-Presidents
Professor FELICITY HEAL, M.A., Ph.D., F.B.A., F.R.Hist.S
Professor STEPHEN TAYLOR, M.A., Ph.D.
Professor ALEXANDRA WALSHAM, M.A., Ph.D., F.B.A., F.R.Hist.S., F.A.H.A.
DAVID WYKES, B.Sc., Ph.D.

Honorary Secretary
MATTHEW GRIMLEY, M.A., D.Phil., Merton College, Oxford, OX1 4JD

Honorary Treasurer
JOSHUA BENNETT, M.A., M.St., D.Phil.,
Lady Margaret Hall, Norham Gardens, Oxford, OX2 6QA

Honorary General Editor
GARETH ATKINS, B.A., M.Phil., Ph.D., F.R.Hist.S.,
Queens' College, Cambridge, CB3 9ET

Other Members of Council
MARK BYFORD, M.A., Ph.D.,
Professor HILARY CAREY, B.A., D.Phil.
DAVID CRANKSHAW, M.A., Ph.D.
Very Rev DAVID HOYLE, K.C.V.O., M.B.E., F.S.A.
HARRIET LYON, M.A., M.Phil., Ph.D.
JACQUELINE ROSE, M.A., M.Phil., Ph.D.
ANNE STOTT, B.A., Ph.D.
REBECCA WARREN, M.A, Ph.D.

Membership Secretary
Professor HILARY CAREY, B.A., D.Phil.

'The object of the Society shall be to advance knowledge of the history of the Church in England, and in particular of the Church of England, from the sixteenth century onwards, by the publication of editions or calendars of primary sources of information.'

PUBLICATIONS

1. VISITATION ARTICLES AND INJUNCTIONS OF THE EARLY STUART CHURCH. VOLUME I. Ed. Kenneth Fincham (1994)

2. THE SPECULUM OF ARCHBISHOP THOMAS SECKER: THE DIOCESE OF CANTERBURY 1758–1768. Ed. Jeremy Gregory (1995)

3. THE EARLY LETTERS OF BISHOP RICHARD HURD, 1739–1762. Ed. Sarah Brewer (1995)

4. BRETHREN IN ADVERSITY: BISHOP GEORGE BELL, THE CHURCH OF ENGLAND AND THE CRISIS OF GERMAN PROTESTANTISM, 1933–1939. Ed. Andrew Chandler (1997)

5. VISITATION ARTICLES AND INJUNCTIONS OF THE EARLY STUART CHURCH. VOLUME II. Ed. Kenneth Fincham (1998)

6. THE ANGLICAN CANONS, 1529–1947. Ed. Gerald Bray (1998)

7. FROM CRANMER TO DAVIDSON. A CHURCH OF ENGLAND MISCELLANY. Ed. Stephen Taylor (1999)

8. TUDOR CHURCH REFORM. THE HENRICIAN CANONS OF 1534 AND THE *REFORMATIO LEGUM ECCLESIASTICARUM*. Ed. Gerald Bray (2000)

9. ALL SAINTS SISTERS OF THE POOR. AN ANGLICAN SISTERHOOD IN THE NINETEENTH CENTURY. Ed. Susan Mumm (2001)

10. CONFERENCES AND COMBINATION LECTURES IN THE ELIZABETHAN CHURCH: DEDHAM AND BURY ST EDMUNDS, 1582–1590. Ed. Patrick Collinson, John Craig and Brett Usher (2003)

11. THE DIARY OF SAMUEL ROGERS, 1634–1638. Ed. Tom Webster and Kenneth Shipps (2004)

12. EVANGELICALISM IN THE CHURCH OF ENGLAND C.1790–C.1890. Ed. Mark Smith and Stephen Taylor (2004)

13. THE BRITISH DELEGATION AND THE SYNOD OF DORT (1618–1619). Ed. Anthony Milton (2005)

14. THE BEGINNINGS OF WOMEN'S MINISTRY. THE REVIVAL OF THE DEACONESS IN THE NINETEENTH-CENTURY CHURCH OF ENGLAND. Ed. Henrietta Blackmore (2007)

15. THE LETTERS OF THEOPHILUS LINDSEY. VOLUME I. Ed. G. M. Ditchfield (2007)

16. THE BACK PARTS OF WAR: THE YMCA MEMOIRS AND LETTERS OF BARCLAY BARON, 1915–1919. Ed. Michael Snape (2009)

17. THE DIARY OF THOMAS LARKHAM, 1647–1669. Ed. Susan Hardman Moore (2011)

18. FROM THE REFORMATION TO THE PERMISSIVE SOCIETY. A MISCELLANY IN CELEBRATION OF THE 400TH ANNIVERSARY OF LAMBETH PALACE LIBRARY. Ed. Melanie Barber and Stephen Taylor with Gabriel Sewell (2010)

19. THE LETTERS OF THEOPHILUS LINDSEY. VOLUME II. Ed. G. M. Ditchfield (2012)

20. NATIONAL PRAYERS: SPECIAL WORSHIP SINCE THE REFORMATION. VOLUME 1: SPECIAL PRAYERS, FASTS AND THANKSGIVINGS IN THE BRITISH ISLES, 1533–1688. Ed. Natalie Mears, Alasdair Raffe, Stephen Taylor, Philip Williamson and Lucy Bates (2013)

21. THE JOURNAL OF BISHOP DANIEL WILSON OF CALCUTTA, 1845–1857. Ed. Andrew Atherstone (2015)

22. NATIONAL PRAYERS: SPECIAL WORSHIP SINCE THE REFORMATION. VOLUME 2: GENERAL FASTS, THANKSGIVINGS AND SPECIAL PRAYERS IN THE BRITISH ISLES, 1689–1870. Ed. Philip Williamson, Alasdair Raffe, Stephen Taylor and Natalie Mears (2017)

23. THE FURTHER CORRESPONDENCE OF ARCHBISHOP LAUD. Ed. Kenneth Fincham (2017)

24. THE HOUSEHOLD ACCOUNTS OF WILLIAM LAUD, ARCHBISHOP OF CANTERBURY, 1635–1642. Ed. Leonie James (2019)

25. THE FIRST WORLD WAR DIARIES OF THE RT. REV. LLEWELLYN GWYNNE, JULY 1915–JULY 1916. Ed. Peter Howson (2019)

26. NATIONAL PRAYERS: SPECIAL WORSHIP SINCE THE REFORMATION. VOLUME 3: WORSHIP FOR NATIONAL AND ROYAL OCCASIONS IN THE UNITED KINGDOM, 1871–2016. Ed. Philip Williamson, Stephen Taylor, Alasdair Raffe and Natalie Mears (2020)

27. THE RESTORATION OF THE CHURCH OF ENGLAND: CANTERBURY DIOCESE AND THE ARCHBISHOP'S PECULIARS. Ed. Tom Reid (2022)

28. NATIONAL PRAYERS: SPECIAL WORSHIP SINCE THE REFORMATION. VOLUME 4: ANNIVERSARY COMMEMORATIONS, ADDITIONAL MATERIAL, 1533–2023, AND GENERAL INDEX. Ed. Philip Williamson, Natalie Mears, Stephen Taylor and Alasdair Raffe

29. BIRKENHEAD, ALL SOULS, AND THE MAKING OF HERBERT HENSLEY HENSON: THE EARLY JOURNALS, 1885–1887. Ed. Julia Stapleton and Frank Field

Forthcoming Publications

THE VISITATIONS OF HORACE SALUSBURY COTTON, ORDINARY OF NEWGATE: A PRISON CHAPLAIN'S JOURNAL, 1828–1838. Ed. Simon Devereaux

THE CORRESPONDENCE OF FRANCIS BLACKBURNE (1705–1787). Ed. G. M. Ditchfield

THE PAPERS OF THE ELLAND SOCIETY 1769–1818. Ed. John Walsh and Stephen Taylor

THE CORRESPONDENCE OF WILLIAM SANCROFT. Ed. Grant Tapsell

THE SERMONS OF JOHN SHARP. Ed. Françoise Deconinck-Brossard

THE CORRESPONDENCE AND PAPERS OF ARCHBISHOP RICHARD NEILE, 1598–1640. Ed. Andrew Foster

SHAPING THE JACOBEAN RELIGIOUS SETTLEMENT: THE HAMPTON COURT CONFERENCE, 1604. Ed. Mark Byford and Kenneth Fincham

THE 1669 RETURN OF NONCONFORMIST CONVENTICLES. Ed. David Wykes

The Letters and Papers of William Paley. Ed. Neil Hitchin

Charles Simeon's Letters: A New Collection. Ed. Andrew Atherstone

The Diary of an Oxford Parson: The Reverend John Hill, Vice-Principal of St Edmund Hall, Oxford, 1805–1808, 1820–1855. Ed. Grayson Carter

Suggestions for publications should be addressed to Dr Gareth Atkins, General Editor, Church of England Record Society, Queens' College, Cambridge CB3 9ET, or at ga240@cam.ac.uk.

Membership of the Church of England Record Society is open to all who are interested in the history of the Church of England. Enquiries should be addressed to the Membership Secretary, Professor Hilary Carey, coersmembers@gmail.com.